Guide to Life after 50 FOR DUMMIES®

by the authors and editors
at Dummies Press

WILEY

Wiley Publishing, Inc.

Guide to Life after 50 For Dummies®

Published by
Wiley Publishing, Inc.
111 River St.
Hoboken, NJ 07030-5774
www.wiley.com

WILEY

About the Authors

Lesley Abravanel, contributing author to *Florida For Dummies,* is a freelance journalist and a graduate of the University of Miami School of Communication.

Pam Allen, author of *Knitting For Dummies,* has published her knitwear designs in *Family Circle, Woman's Day, Vogue Knitting, Interweave Knits, Knitters,* and *McCall's,* among others.

Michelle Arnot, author of *Crossword Puzzles For Dummies,* is widely recognized for her book *What's Gnu: The History of the Crossword Puzzle* (Vintage Books, 1981).

Roy Barnhart, author of *Carpentry For Dummies,* enjoyed eight years as Senior Building and Remodeling Editor for two national home improvement magazines. For the last nine years, he has worked as a freelance writer, editor, and consultant.

Carol Baroudi, co-author of *The Internet For Dummies,* first began playing with computers in 1971 at Colgate University, where two things were new: the PDP-10 and women. Now she's an industry analyst.

Susan Brittain, co-author of *Crocheting For Dummies,* held the position of Assistant Editor for *Crochet Fantasy* magazine for a little more than two years, contributing as a designer as well. After moving west with her family, she continues to be a contributing editor and designer.

Dr. Joy Browne, author of *Dating For Dummies,* is a licensed clinical psychologist who has called the airwaves her practice for more than a decade and is now heard on over 300 stations by more than eight million listeners.

Gene Busnar, contributing author of *Making Marriage Work For Dummies,* is a respected author and collaborative writer.

Kathleen Cantillon, author of *Chicago For Dummies,* grew up in the Chicago area, where she attended Northwestern University. Kathleen works in public affairs and lives in the Lincoln Square neighborhood of Chicago.

Marsha Collier, author of *eBay For Dummies,* is a columnist, author of three bestselling books on eBay, and guest lecturer at eBay University. Thousands of eBay fans also read her monthly newsletter, *Cool eBay Tools,* to keep up with the changes on the site.

James Dillard, M.D., D.C., C.Ac., author of *Alternative Medicine For Dummies,* is the medical director for Oxford Health Plan's Alternative Medicine program and chairman of the Oxford Chiropractic Advisory Board.

Cheryl Fall, author of *Family Reunion Kit For Dummies* and *Quilting For Dummies.* Cheryl has authored nine books and more than 1,500 magazine articles published in publications such as *Woman's Day, Family Circle, Country Living,* and *Traditional Quilter.* She has also designed more than 1,000 quilting projects for publication. She's a regular contributor to many popular quilting, women's, and craft magazines.

Georg Feuerstein, Ph.D., author of *Yoga For Dummies,* is internationally respected for his contribution to yoga research and the history of consciousness and has been featured in many magazines in the U. S. and abroad. He has authored more than 30 books about yoga.

Barry Fox, Ph.D., author of *Arthritis For Dummies,* is the author, coauthor, or ghost-writer of numerous books, including the *New York Times* number one bestselling book *The Arthritis Cure* (St. Martin's, 1997).

Manny Fuentes, co-author of *T'ai Chi For Dummies,* is a clinical exercise physiologist in the cardiopulmonary rehabilitation department of Lafayette General Medical Center in Lafayette, Louisiana.

Fran Wenograd Golden, author of *Cruise Vacations For Dummies,* is travel editor of the *Boston Herald.* She is also the author of several travel books.

Dan Gookin, author of *Buying a Computer For Dummies* and *PCs For Dummies,* came to IDG Books Worldwide (now Wiley Publishing, Inc.) with a book proposal for a computer book "for the rest of us" — *DOS For Dummies.* The book blossomed into an international bestseller with hundreds of thousands of copies in print and in many translations.

In 1984, **Ron Guth,** author of *Coin Collecting For Dummies,* won the American Numismatic Association's Wayte and Olga Raymond and Heath Literary awards. He has written many coin-related articles and is listed as a contributor to several books.

Gene and Katie Hamilton are the husband-and-wife author team of the newspaper column "Do It Yourself . . . or Not?," *Home Improvement For Dummies,* and more than a dozen bestselling books on home improvement, including *Carpentry For Dummies.*

Maddy Hargrove, author of *Aquariums For Dummies,* is a contributing writer and columnist for *Tropical Fish Hobbyist* and *Marine Fish Monthly.* She is currently working on her master's degree in marine biology.

Mic Hargrove, author of *Aquariums For Dummies,* is a contributing writer for several tropical fish magazines. He is an expert advisor in the areas of aquarium equipment and water chemistry.

Russell Hart, author of *Photography For Dummies,* is executive editor at *American Photo* magazine. He has written for most other major photo magazines and is the author of a number of books on photographic subjects.

April Leigh Helm is the President of FamilyToolbox.net, Inc., and the editor and maintainer of the *Journal of Online Genealogy.* April has lectured on genealogy and other topics for various conventions, conferences, and groups.

Matthew L. Helm, author of *Genealogy Online,* is the Executive Vice President and Chief Technology Officer for FamilyToolbox.net, Inc. He is also the publisher of the *Journal of Online Genealogy.*

Mary Herczog lives in Los Angeles and works for the film industry when she's not writing *Las Vegas For Dummies, Los Angeles & Disneyland For Dummies, Frommer's New Orleans,* and one-half of *California For Dummies.*

Ellie Herman, M.S., Lac, author of *Pilates For Dummies,* runs two thriving Pilates studios, one in San Francisco and one in Oakland. The Ellie Herman Studios offer annual teacher training intensives in Northern California.

Michael Hodgson, author of *Camping For Dummies,* works as a content editor for Planet Outdoors and is a founding partner in GearTrends LLC — www.GearTrends.com.

Greg Holden, author of *Internet Auctions For Dummies,* is founder and president of a small business called Stylus Media, a group of editorial, design, and computer professionals who produce both print and electronic publications. He has authored several books.

Therese Iknoian, co-author of *T'ai Chi For Dummies,* has been a nationally ranked race walker and is an internationally published freelance health and fitness writer whose work has appeared in dozens of national publications.

Charles B. Inlander, co-author of *Family Health For Dummies* and President of the People's Medical Society, is a highly acclaimed health commentator on public radio's *Marketplace.*

Edie Jarolim, author of *Arizona For Dummies,* has written about the Southwest and Mexico for a variety of national publications. In addition to *Arizona For Dummies,* she authored *Frommer's San Antonio and Austin* and the *Complete Idiot's Travel Guide to Mexico's Beach Resorts.*

Eddie Kantar, author of *Bridge For Dummies,* has more than 20 bridge books in print and is a regular contributor to the *Bulletin, The Bridge World, Bridge Today,* and many other bridge publications. He was inducted into the Bridge Hall of Fame in 1996.

Mary Kenan, Ph.D., co-author of *Alzheimer's For Dummies,* is a faculty member with the Department of Neurology at Baylor College of Medicine and is a licensed clinical psychologist.

Kathi Keville, author of *Aromatherapy For Dummies,* is a nationally known herbalist, aromatherapist, and masseuse with more than 30 years experience. She is director of the American Herb Association and editor of the *AHA Quarterly Newsletter.*

Angela Harley Kirkpatrick, R.D., co-author of *The Healthy Heart Cookbook,* is a registered dietitian who is currently self-employed as a nutrition consultant to a variety of companies and fitness clubs in the Greater Boston area.

Mark Edwin Kunik, MD, MPH, co-author of *Alzheimer's For Dummies,* is a leading expert on dementia. He is a practicing geropsychiatrist who has conducted extensive clinical and health services research on dementia.

Michael Lasky, JD, co-author of *Online Dating For Dummies,* is a world-recognized speaker and sort-of playwright, having written, among other things, *Nightmare on Namestreet,* a parody (licensed by Warner Bros.) about the dire consequences of choosing the wrong brand name for your product.

Cheryl Farr Leas, author of *California For Dummies,* writes the Frommer's New York City travel guides, is author of *Hawaii For Dummies,* and contributes to such publications as Continental Airlines' in-flight magazine, Daily Variety, and Frommer's USA. She may live on the mainland, but she's a Hawaii girl at heart. Cheryl served as senior editor at Macmillan Travel (now Wiley), where she edited the *Frommer's Hawaii* travel guides for the better part of the 90s.

Pierre A. Lehu, co-author of *Rekindling Romance For Dummies,* has been Dr. Ruth Westheimer's "Minister of Communications" for 20 years. He is the co-author of several of Dr. Ruth's books.

John R. Levine, co-author of *The Internet For Dummies,* first became an official system administrator of a networked computer at Yale in 1975. Although John used to spend most of his time writing software, now he mostly writes books.

Leslie Linsley, author of *Crafting For Dummies,* is the author of more than 50 books on crafts, decorating, and home style. Her work appears regularly in national magazines, and she writes a weekly newspaper column that appears throughout the country.

Joseph Lowery, author of *Buying Online For Dummies,* is Webmaster for the MCP Office 97 Resource Center as well as other sites for a variety of clients, including a managed health care organization, an international public relations school, and a bar.

Michael MacCaskey, co-author of *Gardening For Dummies,* has a Bachelor of Science degree in ornamental horticulture from California State Polytechnic University, San Luis Obispo. His magazine writing has been honored by both the Western Magazine Publishers Association and the Garden Writers of America.

Karen Manthey, co-author of *Crocheting For Dummies,* illustrated and edited the magazine *Crochet Fantasy.* Karen also designs her own patterns and has had many of her creations published in *Crochet Fantasy* magazine.

Pamela Maraldo, Ph.D., R.N., author of *Women's Health For Dummies,* is chairperson of the board of the People's Medical Society and is one of the nation's foremost women's health advocates.

Bill Marken, co-author of *Gardening For Dummies,* is the editor of *Rebecca's Garden Magazine,* a new publication from Hearst Magazines Enterprises based on the popular television show.

Gary McCord, author of *Golf For Dummies,* is a 25-year Tour veteran. After retirement, he pursued a career in broadcasting with CBS. In addition to *Golf For Dummies,* he authored a collection of essays and stories about his life on the Tour, *Just a Range Ball in a Box of Titleists.*

Betsy Nagelsen McCormack, author of *Fit Over 40 For Dummies,* earned 35 victories in singles and doubles tournaments around the world before retiring in 1996 after 23 years in professional tennis.

Bryan Miller, co-author of *Cooking For Dummies,* has written nine other books and collaborated for 13 years with Pierre Franey on the syndicated "60-Minute Gourmet" column, which appeared weekly in *The New York Times.*

Karla Morales, co-author of *Family Health For Dummies,* Vice President of Editorial Services and Communications for the People's Medical Society, has co-authored several bestselling health-related books.

Kevin Forest Moreau, author of *New Orleans For Dummies,* is a longtime freelance writer and editor. He has recently moved from New Orleans, his hometown of 34 years, to Atlanta, where the gumbo isn't as good.

Marie Morris, author of *Boston For Dummies,* has lived in the Boston area for most of the past two decades. Since 1997, she has written the *Frommer's Boston* travel guide and contributed to *Frommer's New England.*

Bruce Murphy, author of *New York For Dummies,* was born in New York City, where he now works as a freelance writer. **Alessandra de Rosa** is a world traveler and professional tourist who has worked for the United Nations. Among their other books is *Italy For Dummies,* also published by Wiley.

Katherine Murray volunteers her research and writing skills to help selected nonprofit organizations with missions close to her heart. She has completed a certification in Fundraising Management from the IU Center on Philanthropy and become a kind of "fundraising coach" for small and struggling nonprofits.

John Mutz, author of *Fundraising For Dummies,* is a fundraising expert and speaker who has an extensive array of fundraising credits, including serving as President of the Lilly Endowment, one of the nation's five largest private foundations, which supports the causes of religion, education, and community development.

Amy Myrdal, M.S., R.D., co-author of *The Healthy Heart Cookbook,* is a registered dietitian with a Master of Science degree in Nutrition Communication. Amy is the Director of Marketing and Communication for the Rippe Lifestyle Institute.

The National Gardening Association is the largest member-based, nonprofit organization of home gardeners in the United States.

Blake Neely, author of *Piano For Dummies,* is an award-winning composer and author. Blake has worked as a composer, orchestrator, arranger, copyist, engraver, musicologist, and consultant for such prominent figures as Disney, Hal Leonard Corporation, and the Cincinnati Pops Orchestra.

Liz Neporent, co-author of *Fitness For Dummies,* is a certified trainer and president of Plus One Health Management, a fitness consulting company in New York City. She is co-author of several books, including *Weight Training For Dummies* and *Fitness Walking For Dummies.*

Lynn O'Shaughnessy, author of *The Retirement Bible,* has been writing about personal finance for nearly a decade. She has contributed countless articles to *Mutual Funds Magazine, Bloomberg Personal Finance Magazine, The Wall Street Journal, Forbes Magazine's* Web site, and a variety of other magazines and online ventures.

Larry Payne, Ph.D., author of *Yoga For Dummies,* is an internationally prominent Yoga teacher and workshop leader.

The People's Medical Society, author of *Women's Health For Dummies,* is the nation's largest nonprofit consumer health organization. Its mission is to provide consumers with up-to-date health information from health care professionals and the latest medical research.

Tom Price, author of *Washington D.C. For Dummies,* has lived in and written about Washington for more than two decades. His work has appeared in books, magazines, and newspapers, and on Internet sites.

Marie Rama, co-author of *Cooking For Dummies,* is an independent food, beverage, and media consultant, who also wrote *Grilling For Dummies* (with John Mariani), published by Wiley.

In 1992, **Andy Rathbone,** author of *Windows XP For Dummies,* teamed up with Dan Gookin to write *PCs For Dummies.* Andy subsequently wrote the award-winning *Windows For Dummies* series, *Upgrading & Fixing PCs For Dummies, MP3 For Dummies,* and many other *For Dummies* books.

Kurt Repanshek, author of *America's National Parks For Dummies,* is the author of *Hidden Utah* and *Hidden Salt Lake City & Beyond* (both from Ulysses Press), and his work has appeared in *Audubon, Sunset, National Geographic Traveler,* and *Hemispheres,* among other publications.

Barry Rigal, author of *Card Games For Dummies,* writes about card games for newspapers and magazines. In addition, he has written six books on Bridge. He is now a full time writer and his particular interest is in deceiving his opponents.

Carol Ann Rinzler, author of *Controlling Cholesterol For Dummies,* is also the author of *Nutrition For Dummies,* one of Amazon.com's ten-best health books of 1999, and *Weight Loss Kit For Dummies.* Carol writes a weekly nutrition column for the *New York Daily News* and is the author of more than 20 books on food and health.

James M. Rippe, M.D., author of *Heart Disease For Dummies,* is a board-certified cardiologist who serves on the faculty as an Associate Professor of Medicine (Cardiology) at Tufts University School of Medicine. He is the Founder and Director of the Rippe Lifestyle Institute and Founder and Director of the Rippe Health Assessment at Celebration Health.

Alan L. Rubin, MD, author of *Diabetes For Dummies,* is one of the nation's foremost experts on diabetes. He is a professional member of the American Diabetes Association and the Endocrine Society and has been in private practice specializing in diabetes and thyroid disease for over 28 years.

Jan Saunders, author of *Sewing For Dummies,* is a nationally known sewing and serging journalist and home economist. She has served as Education Director of one of the largest sewing machine companies in the country, and the Director of Consumer Education for the largest fabric chain in the country.

Suzanne Schlosberg, co-author of *Fitness For Dummies,* is a contributing editor to *Shape* and *Health* magazines and coauthor of *Weight Training For Dummies* and Kathy Smith's *Fitness Makeover.*

Deborah Shouse, co-author of *Antiquing For Dummies,* is a writer, speaker, facilitator, and creativity coach. She is a PEN winner and a Pushcart nominee. She has published several books and has been included in several anthologies.

Judith Silverstein, MD, co-author of *Online Dating For Dummies,* is as a Board certified dermatologist in private practice. In explaining the relationship between dermatology and online dating, she has been often quoted as saying, "you can get burned on a date, even if you are wearing sunscreen."

Steven Simring, MD, MPH, author of *Making Marriage Work For Dummies,* is Associate Professor and Vice Chair of the Department of Psychiatry at New Jersey Medical School. He is the recipient of numerous awards for outstanding teaching.

Sue Klavans Simring, DSW, author of *Making Marriage Work For Dummies,* is a practicing psychotherapist who specializes in working with couples and families. She is a lecturer at the Columbia University School of Social Work.

Dick Sine, author of *Stamp Collecting For Dummies,* has been known in stamp collecting for more than a quarter-century of writing and editing. He developed and produced the first electronic magazine for stamp collecting, *NetSTAMPS.*

Molly Siple, author of *Healing Foods For Dummies,* has a Master of Science in Nutritional Science and is also a registered dietitian. Her other books include two on female health, co-authored with Lissa DeAngelis.

Shirley Slater and **Harry Basch,** authors of *RV Vacations For Dummies,* are a husband-and-wife travel-writing team whose books, articles, and photographs have been published internationally over the past 25 years.

Julian Smith, co-author of *Travel Planning Online For Dummies,* has been writing since he could read and traveling since he could walk (and even before). He is the author of *On Your Own in El Salvador* as well as Moon Publications *Ecuador Handbook* and *Virginia Handbook.*

Patricia Burkhart Smith, author of *Alzheimer's For Dummies,* is an award-winning health and medical writer. Ms. Smith serves as a medical reporter for Houston Northwest Medical Center, which for the past two years has been the only hospital in Houston named to the prestigious annual list of 100 Top Hospitals in America.

Gina Spadafori is an award-winning author with two top-selling pet care books to her credit: *Dogs For Dummies* and *Cats For Dummies* (the latter co-authored with Paul D. Pion, DVM, Dipl. ACVIM). She also wrote *Birds For Dummies.*

Brian L. Speer, DVM, Dipl. ABVP (Avian Practice), ECAMS, author of *Birds For Dummies,* is one of only a handful of veterinarians certified as an avian specialist in both the United States and in Europe.

Nancy Stevenson, author of *Distance Learning For Dummies,* is an instructional designer and consultant who has written over two dozen books on topics ranging from motivating employees to online search techniques and a variety of software applications.

Nadine Taylor, M.S., R.D., author of *Arthitis For Dummies,* is a registered dietitian. She penned *Green Tea* (Kensington Press, 1998), *If You Think You Have An Eating Disorder* (Dell, 1998), and *Diana and Dodi: A Love Story* (Tallfellow, 1999).

Paula Tevis, author of *San Francisco For Dummies* and co-author of *California For Dummies,* has contributed articles and essays to *Family Fun* magazine, the *San Francisco Chronicle, Citysearch.com,* and *Variety.*

Bill Thompson, III, author of *Bird Watching For Dummies*, is the editor of *Bird Watcher's Digest,* the popular bimonthly magazine that has been published by his family since 1978.

Laura Tiebert, author of *Chicago For Dummies,* is a freelance writer whose travels have taken her from the frozen tundra of Dawson City in the Yukon Territory to the wide beaches of Muscat, Oman.

Cynthia Tunstall, author of *Florida For Dummies,* is a freelance writer and photographer whose work has appeared in *Better Homes & Gardens, Elegant Bride,* and the *Atlanta Journal-Constitution,* among others. **Jim Tunstall** has been an editor and writer for *The Tampa Tribune* since 1978.

Noah Vadnai, co-author of *Travel Planning Online For Dummies,* is currently the creative director of a new Web portal for the transportation industry. He has worked on numerous high profile Web sites and was the producer of NetGuide's Travel Channel.

Mary Abbott Waite, Ph.D., author of *The Healthy Heart Cookbook,* is an Atlanta-based writer and editorial consultant with a Ph.D. in English from Duke University. She specializes in health, fitness, and consumer issues.

Wallace Wang, author of *Microsoft Office XP For Dummies,* has written and co-written several computer books, including *Visual Basic For Dummies, Beginning Programming For Dummies,* and the previous editions of *Microsoft Office For Dummies.*

Dr. Ruth K. Westheimer, author of *Rekindling Romance For Dummies,* is a psychosexual therapist who helped pioneer the field of media psychology with her radio program, Sexually Speaking, which first aired in New York in 1980.

Mike Yorkey is the author, co-author, or general editor of more than 20 books, including *Fit Over 40 For Dummies.* In addition, his magazine articles have been published in the Los Angeles Times travel section, Skiing, Tennis Week, World Tennis, City Sports, and Racquet.

Margaret Levine Young, co-author of *The Internet For Dummies,* has co-authored more than 25 computer books about the topics of the Internet, UNIX, WordPerfect, Microsoft Access, and (stab from the past) PC-File and Javelin.

Terra Ziporyn, Ph.D., author of *Alternative Medicine For Dummies,* is a writer and historian who specializes in making science and medicine accessible to the public. She has written extensively on a wide range of health and medical issues in both professional and popular publications.

Ron Zoglin, author of *Antiquing For Dummies,* is an Accredited Senior Member of the American Society of Appraisers, a Certified Member of the Appraisers Association of America, an Accredited Member of the International Society of Appraisers, and a member of the National Association of Dealers in Antiques.

Rachelle Zukerman, Ph.D., author of *Eldercare For Dummies,* is Professor Emeritus of Social Welfare at UCLA, a gerontologist, and a clinical social worker. She is also a Visiting Professor at the University of Hong Kong and a Fulbright Scholar.

Publisher's Acknowledgments

We're proud of this book; please send us your comments through our Dummies online registration form located at www.dummies.com/register/.

Some of the people who helped bring this book to market include the following:

Acquisitions, Editorial, and Media Development

Senior Project Editor: Zoë Wykes

Compilation Editor: Colleen Totz

Editorial Manager: Rev Mengle

Cartoons: Rich Tennant, www.the5thwave.com

Special Help
Gabriele McCann

Composition

Project Coordinator: Kristie Rees

Layout and Graphics: Andrea Dahl, Denny Hager, LeAndra Hosier, Michael Kruzil, Lynsey Osborn, Heather Ryan, Jacque Schneider

Proofreaders: Laura L. Bowman, Dwight Ramsey

Indexer: Johnna VanHoose

Publishing and Editorial for Consumer Dummies

Diane Graves Steele, Vice President and Publisher, Consumer Dummies

Joyce Pepple, Acquisitions Director, Consumer Dummies

Kristin A. Cocks, Product Development Director, Consumer Dummies

Michael Spring, Vice President and Publisher, Travel

Brice Gosnell, Associate Publisher, Travel

Kelly Regan, Editorial Director, Travel

Publishing for Technology Dummies

Andy Cummings, Vice President and Publisher, Dummies Technology/General User

Composition Services

Gerry Fahey, Vice President of Production Services

Debbie Stailey, Director of Composition Services

Contents at a Glance

Introduction

⦿⦿

*G*uide to Life after 50 For Dummies is your one-stop reference for life solu-
tions in your middle years and beyond. In this book, we provide quick
answers to your most pressing questions about your health, your relationships,
your finances, and your free time. We cover a lot of ground — everything from
eating the best healing foods to creating a budget for retirement — and while
we can't promise that we cover *everything* you need to know, we hope to at
least hit the highlights and then some.

About This Book

To create *Guide to Life after 50 For Dummies,* we culled hundreds of books from
the *For Dummies* series for the best, most relevant, most interesting bits of information about healthy living, midlife relationships, retirement planning, active
and leisure hobbies, and travel, and distilled them into one catchall book.

We also added new content on the fascinating world of *freebies.* In fact, we pep-
pered every chapter with information about places to go or available resources
where you can get all sorts of free (or *almost* free) products and professional
advice or guidance. We even give you a couple of chapters dedicated specifically to freebies. Hey, you'll just have to see 'em to believe 'em for yourself.

Our hope is that this book becomes your favorite companion, helps you make
the most of your middle years, and puts a smile on your face in the process.

How to Use This Book

Like all *For Dummies* books, this book is a reference book. This means that
you can turn to any section that interests you, whether it's in the front, back,
or middle of the book, and start reading without missing a beat. You don't
have to read Chapters 1 and 2 to understand Chapter 3.

You can use the Table of Contents in the beginning of the book and the Index
in the back of the book to help find exactly what you need when you need it,
or you can flip through the book until something of interest catches your
eye. Whatever you do, be sure to check out the gray text boxes that appear
throughout the book — these "sidebars" contain valuable nuggets of information that you won't want to miss!

You can also read this book from cover to cover. We've done it ourselves and had a great time! But how you use this book is totally up to you.

How This Book Is Organized

We organized this book into eight parts that cover the topics and areas of interest that matter the most to you. We cover everything from the building blocks of good health and strong relationships to vacation hot spots and leisure activities.

Part I: Extraordinary Health at 50 and Beyond

This part of the book imparts the secrets of achieving great health. You get the rundown on everything from the routine screenings every man and woman over the age of 50 should have, to living well with common conditions such as arthritis and diabetes.

We even devote an entire chapter to the healing foods that help promote health.

Part II: Great Fitness Strategies at 50 and Beyond

This part is all about feeling 20 years younger. Whether you decide to walk yourself fit or sign up for a yoga or Pilates class, the chapters in this part give you the introduction you need to get started. We also give you a chapter about eating for a healthy heart — all that hard work exercising is no good if you don't fuel the system properly!

Part III: Saying "I Love You"

Are you facing an empty nest? Are you and your spouse looking to strengthen your relationship? You've come to the right part of the book. We give you the five signs of a marriage that works so that you can see how your relationship measures up. Then we offer proven techniques for rekindling the romance in your relationship, creating a stronger bond and a marriage that lasts.

During middle age many people find themselves "sandwiched" between their elderly parents and their growing kids. To help bridge the generation gap, this part shows you how to provide great care for your aging parents, and gives some fun tips for getting the whole gang together at a family reunion.

And for those who are dating, we have a chapter that offers great ideas for a successful first — and second! — date. We even offer a chapter about adopting a pet for a companion, too.

Part IV: Money Matters for Folks over 50

The chapters in this part help you prepare for retirement. We show you how to calculate your current worth and set up a budget to increase your value. We also give you the rundown on your various investment options, including tax-deferred investments such as 401(k) accounts and IRAs. And we help you make sense of Social Security and all its restrictions and benefits.

For those who are closer to retirement or retired already, we provide tips for stretching your fixed income as far as it will go. For everyone, we offer advice on planning your estate, including setting up a trust and drawing up a will.

Part V: Fun, Fun, Fun: Hobbies

Did you know that crocheting can help offset the pain of arthritis? Or that you can find great carpentry tips on the Internet? Read all this and more in Part V, the "hobbies" part of the book. Whether you want to get up and get moving, or sit back and relax, this part has a hobby that's right for you.

Part VI: Here You Go Again: Travel

If you're looking to get away for a week, two weeks, or even just a weekend, pack your sunblock, because this part of the book is the part for you. We cover the sunniest of the sunny, from Arizona and Florida to California and Hawaii. We provide tips for choosing a cruise vacation that suits your mood, whether you're looking for a romantic getaway or a table for 12. If you're looking for a night on the town, check out our chapter about the liveliest cities in the United States and abroad.

And if nature is your thing, you won't want to miss our coverage of the best places to enjoy an RV or camping vacation. We cover the best, most scenic national parks in North America, too.

Part VII: Going High-Tech

In this part, you get up and running the quick and easy way with your new computer. Before long, you'll be navigating the Windows XP desktop and surfing the Internet with the best of them. What are all these eBay commercials you see everyone singing about? Chapter 23 gives you the full scoop.

For an added bit of interest, catch the latest craze: distance learning. Earn credit from a real university or certification for a new skill. The world is waiting!

Part VIII: The Part of Tens

We should have called this the "Part of Top Secret Stuff," because when you dig into all the goodies in these chapters, you won't believe your eyes. We list the ten best bargains for those over 50 and ten online freebies (or *almost* freebies). And so that you don't have to worry about being bored in retirement, we tell you the ten best things about being retired.

Icons Used in This Book

The little graphic symbols that you see sprinkled throughout the margins of this book are a staple of the *For Dummies* experience. These symbols — or *icons* — highlight the following points:

This icon covers tidbits of knowledge and advice that can make your life easier.

You won't want to forget what you read here.

This icon indicates important information that helps you avoid something unpleasant, uncomfortable, or just plain dangerous.

When we go into a little more depth on a topic, we indicate that you can skip the information by including this icon.

Where to Go from Here

Don't know where to start? Turn to the Table of Contents and see if something piques your interest. Or — our favorite way — flip through until something strikes your fancy, and hit the ground reading.

Part I

Extraordinary Health at 50 and Beyond

In this part . . .

What's the key to great health? The chapters in this part give you several possible answers to that magic question. Using the tools in this part of the book, you can slow the aging process, live well with common conditions, and possibly even live longer.

This part also explores the benefits of healing foods that should be part of every good diet.

Chapter 1

Taking Charge of Your Health

· ·

In This Chapter

▶ Achieving optimal health at any age

▶ Health screenings everyone over 50 needs

▶ Understanding the many facets of Medicare

▶ Dying with dignity

▶ Ensuring that the people in your life get what you want them to have

· ·

*I*n this chapter, you find out what optimal health really means and how much attitude matters in heading off illness at the pass. We also outline the key health screenings that every adult over age 50 should have and how often they should have them. These facts should give you the motivation you need to make prevention a priority in your life.

Later in the chapter, we give you the rundown on Medicare — the different programs and becoming eligible for them — and the easy, trouble-free way to plan ahead and ensure that when the time comes, you can give what you want to the people you want.

Three Keys to Great Health

Lose right now the thought that health is a state of being or is something that *happens* to you.

Instead, you need to take control of your health. Don't get us wrong — many factors, such as genetic makeup, environmental factors, and just plain chance, can adversely affect your body and your mind. It's all too true that bad things happen to good people. But you can do a great deal to boost your health. Probably more than you think!

The three keys to great health:

- ✔ Give your body the right type of fuel (in other words, eat well).

- ✔ Run your body regularly (or, get enough exercise).

- ✔ Have routine inspections to make sure that everything is in order (see your doctor for regular checkups).

Your body is a miracle machine. Like a miracle, your body is self-healing and adjusts to the performance demands you place on it. Like a machine, however, your body requires maintenance to keep the miracle alive.

Maintaining Your Miracle Machine

The key to maintaining health is heading off problems before they occur. How can you detect problems? By going to your doctor for regular checkups and keeping to a schedule of specific preventive tests, known as *health screenings*.

The recommended screenings vary among men, women, and seniors, so we break them up here according to those categories to make life easier. Keep in mind, though, that these recommendations aren't set in stone. Everyone has different needs, and your doctor should tailor a screening schedule to meet your needs. Plus, doctors, leading medical groups, and government agencies often disagree on which screenings are necessary and when.

Must-have screenings for everyone

Despite obvious differences between the male and female anatomies, a body is a body. So it's easy to understand that several routine tests are appropriate for both men and women.

Basic physical

Every year after the age of 50.

Here's what to expect:

- ✔ The doctor will ask a series of questions about your lifestyle, occupation, and current and past health problems. A thorough history is often the key to diagnosing risks and problems, so answer the questions carefully and honestly.

✔ The doctor will check your eyes, ears, and skin (including the appearance of any moles or other lesions), the lining of your mouth and throat, and your height and weight. He will also perform the familiar whack-on-the-knee reflex test.

✔ The doctor will run standard screening tests, such as

- **Urinalysis** (every year after 50)

- **Blood pressure** (at least once per year according to the American Heart Association, but most practitioners take your blood pressure at every visit)

- **Blood tests** (annually)

- **Tuberculosis test** (every five years)

Chest X-ray

Every year for smokers. (Note, though, that some experts do not believe this annual screening to be beneficial.)

If you smoke, you need to have an annual chest X-ray to look for lung damage and lung cancer. But you could save yourself the trouble — and simply save yourself — by quitting.

Colorectal cancer screening

Experts disagree on frequency of screening for colorectal (or colon and rectal) cancer, but generally recommend annual testing after age 50. Adults at risk of colon and rectal cancer, including people with strong family or personal history of colon and rectal disease, should be screened earlier and more often.

Screening for colorectal cancer includes two tests:

✔ **Fecal occult blood test:** You provide a stool sample for your doctor, who tests it for blood. Blood in the stool indicates that cancer may be present.

✔ **Sigmoidoscopy:** A flexible or inflexible scope is inserted into the rectum. Through the scope, your doctor can see whether cancer or other diseases are affecting the lower part of the colon.

Electrocardiogram (ECG or EKG)

Every three years after age 30 if your doctor thinks that you're at risk for heart disease; every three to four years after 50 if you're not at risk. Some doctors suggest that you get a baseline ECG test at age 40 to compare to later results.

An ECG involves electrodes pasted to your chest that, believe it or not, actually pick up your heart's electrical activity right through your skin. The heart is a big muscle, and the way your nerve impulses travel through it reveals a lot about how good a job it's doing. If you can step back from the situation, the electronics freak in you may find this test pretty cool.

Men, it's time to bite the bullet

When it comes to prevention, men are the worst offenders. And it's not just a stereotype: Medical research shows that men are more uncomfortable with physicians than women are, and that they're less likely to keep to a schedule for preventive health. In fact, many experts think that this phobia about doctors may explain why men don't live as long as women — an average 72 years for men versus 79 for women.

The following sections summarize the screenings that men should make an effort to get.

Digital rectal examination (DRE)

Every year after age 40, although many doctors perform the test on patients at an earlier age.

The doctor's going to do what? Yes, guys, get over it. In a DRE, the doctor dons a glove, lubricates it, and then inserts a finger into the lower part of the rectum. This exam picks up the following problems with your prostate gland:

- Prostate cancer
- Benign prostatic hyperplasia, or enlarged prostate

This test probably does more to keep squeamish men from getting physicals than any other, but realize that it causes minimal discomfort and is over in a minute or less.

Prostate-specific antigen test

Annually after age 50.

To check for signs of prostate cancer, your doctor may perform a simple blood test called the prostate-specific antigen (PSA) test. The test measures the amount of prostate-specific antigen in your blood. High levels of this substance may indicate cancer.

Not all doctors agree about the course of action to take with a positive result on the PSA because roughly a third of the time it either misses the disease or says that a person who doesn't have it has it. Talk with your physician about this test.

Testicular examination

Annually by a professional, along with monthly self-examinations, starting in adulthood.

Although it accounts for only 1 percent of all cancers in American men, testicular cancer is the most common cancer in men between the ages of 15 and 34. Many doctors perform the exam during an annual physical, and experts recommend self-examination monthly. Self-examination increases the chance that the disease is caught early, when it's most curable. Figure 1-1 shows the correct method for performing a testicular self-exam.

To perform a testicular self-exam, or TSE, do the following:

✔ Look for any swelling on the surface of the scrotum while standing before a mirror.

✔ Gently examine each testicle by placing your index and middle fingers underneath the testicle and your thumbs on top. Roll the testicle between your thumbs and fingers, feeling for any abnormal lumps. Do not confuse the epididymis (the cord within the testicle that transports sperm) with a lump.

✔ If you feel anything unusual, visit your doctor as soon as possible. Lumps occur for reasons other than cancer (for example, infection), but only a professional can make a diagnosis.

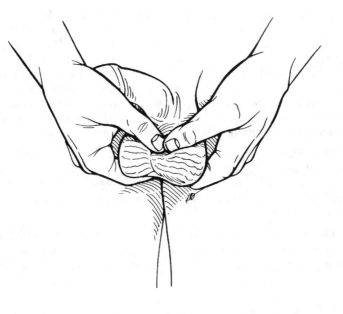

Figure 1-1:
Men should perform a testicular self-exam monthly to increase the chance of detecting cancer early.

Women, keep up the good work

When it comes to healthcare, women are generally in charge. From the teenage years, women begin to learn their way around the medical system, thanks to concerns about menstruation, birth control, and pregnancy. The education continues as women take the roles of partners, wives, and mothers.

Prevention, of course, matters very much to women, so make sure that you get what you need. Don't limit your contact with your doctor to a mere phone call when your birth control prescription runs out. The following sections cover a few of the basic screenings that you should get, and when you should get them.

Gynecological exam

Annually after age 18 and for women who are sexually active.

The gynecological exam usually includes a pelvic examination, a Pap test, and a breast examination:

- **Pelvic exam:** This exam allows the doctor to check for signs of infection and view the cervix, the opening of the uterus, or the womb. With a swab or brush, the doctor takes samples of the mucus covering the cervix to check for infection and also does a Pap test.

  After removing the *speculum* (used to spread apart the walls of the vagina), the practitioner inserts two gloved fingers into the vagina and places the other hand on the abdomen. The doctor then feels the uterus and ovaries, checking for any abnormalities. The doctor may also insert a finger into the rectum to check for problems.

- **Pap test:** A Pap test (sometimes called a Pap smear) is nothing more than a special way of sampling cells from the cervix for an early detection of changes that could turn into cancer. During the pelvic examination, the gynecologist uses a swab or small brush (the latter has been found to be more effective) to collect cells, which are then examined under a microscope. An abnormal result means that some cells may be showing changes that could lead to cancer or that cancerous cells are already present. But don't panic: Noncancerous conditions, such as vaginal infections, sometimes produce abnormal results as well.

  If your Pap test shows abnormal results, a colposcopy and a biopsy are sometimes performed as follow-ups. A *colposcopy* sounds a little scary, but it's actually just the use of a magnifying scope to view areas of the cervix up close. Through the scope, practitioners can see areas they'd like to sample.

  After an area is located, a biopsy is done. In a biopsy, a small amount of tissue is removed to be tested for abnormal cells. Through biopsy, practitioners can tell whether cancer is present and, if so, how advanced it is.

Some women who get a clean bill of health from a Pap test three times in a row may be able to get the test less frequently.

✔ **Breast exam:** For this test, you lie on your back and extend one arm above your head. The practitioner gently feels the breast and armpit for any abnormal lumps. Then you switch arms, and the practitioner examines the other breast.

Don't leave the breast exam up to your doctor — perform it yourself on a monthly basis. (See the following section.)

Examining your breasts at home

A breast exam is your first line of defense against breast cancer. In fact, about 80 percent of breast cancers are detected through women checking their breasts themselves. The value of breast self-examination can't be stressed enough. When caught early, breast cancer can be cured. When caught late, you can die.

Try to remember to do this exam at the same time every month because your breasts can change throughout your menstrual cycle. You can do this test in the shower, if you prefer — the water and soap make it easier for fingers to slide over the skin. To perform a breast self-exam, says the American Cancer Society, do the following. (Figure 1-2 illustrates the procedure.) See your doctor immediately if you notice anything unusual during the exam.

✔ Lie down, place a pillow under your right shoulder, and stretch your right arm over your head. Use the three middle fingers of your left hand to feel the right breast for any lumps or thickening. Press hard enough to know what the breast feels like. Repeat the process for the other breast.

A pattern helps make sure that you don't miss an area. You can move your fingers in straight rows across the breast, start at the center and spiral outward, or start from the center and radiate outward in a star pattern.

✔ After checking for lumps, examine the nipples for any changes and squeeze them gently. Tell your practitioner of any irregularities or discharge.

✔ Finally, stand in front of a mirror and look for any dimpling or swelling in the breasts. Check with your hands at your sides and then raise your arms above your head and check again.

Many women skip the self-exam because the idea of doing it makes them worry about breast cancer — not a welcome thought. Try to think of the exam as a way to stay healthy and catch any molehills before they turn into mountains.

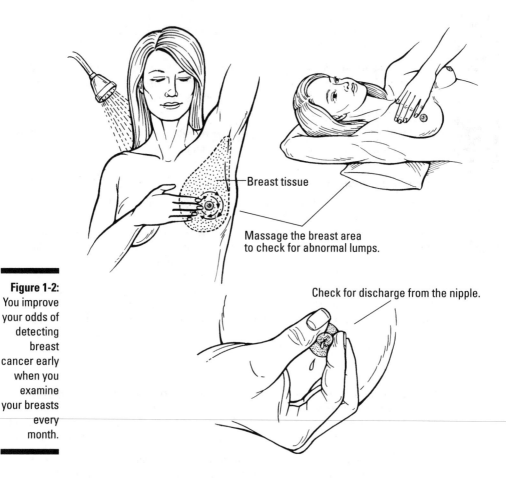

Breast tissue

Massage the breast area
to check for abnormal lumps.

Check for discharge from the nipple.

Figure 1-2:
You improve
your odds of
detecting
breast
cancer early
when you
examine
your breasts
every
month.

Mammogram

Annually for women over age 50 and for women at risk of breast cancer.

A mammogram uses X-rays of the breast to detect breast cancer. A technician places your breast between two flat plates, which are then gently squeezed together as the X-ray picture is taken. In terms of comfort, it may not be a barrel of laughs, but it's worth it if you value your health.

Here are some important points to keep in mind about mammograms:

✔ A *radiologist,* an expert in deciphering X-rays, interprets the results of a mammogram according to the appearance of the image. Images on X-rays are not always what they appear, however, and because the picture is judged by an individual, results are somewhat subjective. A mammogram is not a diagnosis of cancer.

✔ Diagnosis of cancer can be done only through a breast biopsy, a procedure that removes a small amount of tissue for lab tests. The biopsy can take the form of a small surgical operation or can be done with a hollow needle that samples a smaller amount of tissue.

✔ Experts are unable to agree on when women under age 50 who don't have a risk for breast cancer should begin to have regular mammograms. (Cancer is hard to detect in younger women because the breast tissue is denser. As a result, the younger you are, the greater the chance you will be misdiagnosed and have to undergo an unnecessary biopsy.) Regardless of your age, your decision on mammography should be based on your personal needs, so talk over the issue with your practitioner.

Seniors: Staying young at heart

We can't stress strongly enough that age does not equal disease. Granted, many people do face more health problems as they grow older, but that doesn't mean that they're inevitable or that you have to take them lying down. What's more, it doesn't mean that you should neglect prevention. Whatever the adage says, it's not all downhill from here.

Here are some rules to live by:

✔ Stick to your preventive schedule much as you have in the past, but be sure to speak with your doctor about exceptions and additions to your plan. For example, if you've had regular Pap tests throughout your life and have not experienced abnormalities, you may be able to forgo that test. If colon and rectal cancer run in your family, preventive screening may need to be stepped up a bit. Everyone is unique, and the older you become, the more your care will need to be individualized to suit your needs.

✔ Find a practitioner who specializes in *geriatrics* — treatment of the elderly. These doctors, who sometimes subspecialize in heart disease or cancer treatment, have additional training that puts them in tune with seniors' needs. Contact the American Geriatric Society at 212-308-1414 to find a geriatric specialist in your area.

That said, consider these additional preventive screenings that are recommended for older adults.

Vision and hearing tests

A doctor uses standard testing to test your eyes and ears. Unfortunately, the senses of hearing and sight often deteriorate with aging — but again, you don't have to accept it. Regular testing can help catch problems early, before they put you out of action.

Influenza and pneumonia vaccinations

As an older adult, you're more vulnerable to the flu and the complications that it can cause. To prevent problems, the Centers for Disease Control and Prevention recommends an annual flu vaccine and pneumonia vaccine for everyone over the age of 65.

Nutrition tests

Physicians should monitor nutrition as well. Surprisingly, some older adults have trouble getting enough vitamins and minerals. Some men and women find it hard to get out to buy food, and others have problems with their teeth and gums. Seniors with memory problems may simply forget meals.

Polypharmacy

No, *polypharmacy* is not the name of the latest drugstore chain. That's what experts call the problem of the complicated mix of over-the-counter and prescription drugs that many older people take. As a preventive measure, a doctor should sit down with you regularly and go over the medications that you're taking to ensure your good health.

Why is this step necessary for seniors? Because the kidneys and the liver become less effective at ridding your body of toxins with age, it's especially important that your doctor knows all the medicines you're taking. Some medicines can interact harmfully and may even cause a problem that would require a visit to the doctor.

Navigating the Medicare Maze

Medicare is, by definition, the federal insurance plan that covers individuals who are age 65 and older, who are permanently and totally disabled, or who have end-stage renal (kidney) disease.

The Social Security Administration (SSA) is responsible for processing applications for Medicare from their offices around the country. If you have any questions about Medicare — and chances are good that you will — address your questions to the SSA.

Understanding the two parts of Medicare

Medicare has two parts: Part A and Part B. The following sections explain the benefits included with each part.

Medicare, Part A: Hospital insurance

Part A of Medicare, which is free to applicants who meet the eligibility requirements, deals with hospital insurance and helps pay for hospital stays and care in a skilled nursing home or from a home health agency.

Medicare, Part B: Physician and outpatient fees

Part B of Medicare, which has a premium set by federal guidelines, covers

- ✔ Physician fees
- ✔ Outpatient hospital services
- ✔ Medical supplies and services

You have a copayment requirement after a deductible, plus any additional charge above the amount charged by the provider as approved by Medicare.

Medicare supplemental policies that cover the additional expenses and deductibles not paid by Medicare are available from private insurers.

Am I eligible for Medicare?

To be fully eligible for Medicare, you must meet the following requirements:

- ✔ You've worked a minimum of 40 quarters, or a total of 10 years, in jobs covered under the Social Security Act, or you're covered under the Railroad Retirement Act. Applicants who have not worked the full 40 quarters can apply for benefits but are required to pay a premium based on the number of quarters worked.
- ✔ You're a citizen of the United States, either by birth or by naturalization, or an alien admitted for permanent residence who has lived in the United States for at least five years.

A person who has not fulfilled the work requirement alone may be eligible for coverage on the record of someone else who is covered. Here are some examples:

- ✔ Spouses are eligible if they're 65 or older and if their spouse is insured.
- ✔ Widows and widowers are covered if they were married to their spouse for at least one year prior to the death of that spouse and are over 65.
- ✔ Divorced persons are eligible if they were married to the covered person for at least ten years and have not remarried.

- ✔ Mothers of covered children are eligible if they're over 65.

- ✔ Parents of children eligible for Social Security who were receiving at least half of their support from the child at the time of the child's death or disability are eligible when they reach age 65.

Sign me up!

Being 65 or older doesn't mean automatic enrollment in Medicare. If you're in doubt, submit an application when you turn 65. The worst that can happen is that you'll find out your application has already been taken care of.

A "window of opportunity" exists for Medicare enrollment. In order to have Medicare effective as of your 65th birthday, you can apply any time within three months of turning 65. If you apply more than three months after your 65th birthday, Medicare becomes effective on the date of application. This may leave you with a period of no coverage, because most private insurance plans stop on your 65th birthday.

A few different situations exist regarding enrollment:

- ✔ If you're already receiving benefits under Social Security or Railroad Retirement benefits, you are automatically enrolled for Parts A and B of Medicare when you reach age 65. You should receive your insurance card three to four months prior to your 65th birthday. However, the card is not effective until that birthday. If you receive no card and you're eligible for benefits, a hospital or other provider can bill under your Social Security number. You can obtain a Temporary Notice of Medicare Eligibility in these instances from the Social Security office.

- ✔ If you are 65 or older and are applying for Social Security benefits, you're automatically enrolled in Medicare as part of the process. The card is sent to you in the mail. If you are found eligible for Social Security, you are automatically eligible for Medicare.

- ✔ Individuals with end-stage renal (kidney) disease are automatically enrolled if they are receiving Social Security disability benefits. If not, they must apply for coverage under Medicare.

- ✔ If you have not applied for Social Security or Railroad Retirement benefits before age 65, you must file an application to enroll in Medicare. Notification that you are now eligible to receive these benefits, which was formerly sent automatically, has been dropped as a cost-cutting measure. If you have any doubts regarding your eligibility for Medicare or Social Security, contact your local Social Security office for clarification of your status.

Even though you can spell out your desired methods of treatment in a Durable Power of Attorney, having both a living will and a Durable Power of Attorney or a Durable Power of Attorney for Healthcare (a limited form of Durable Power of Attorney) is a good idea. The document must be signed, dated, and witnessed, and can be canceled (in writing) at any time.

The most critical issue is deciding who is the appropriate decision maker. Most experts recommend that you consider these factors:

✔ Whom do you trust with life-and-death decisions?

✔ Who knows you best — your attitudes and values?

✔ Who would respect your wishes?

Most people appoint spouses or close family members — good choices because they know you well — but if they are beneficiaries of your estate, they may have a conflict of interest.

Designating Who Gets What: Six Easy Steps

The top two reasons to plan your estate now are

✔ To protect it from the government to the greatest extent that you can

✔ To exercise as much control as possible over how your estate is divided up; in other words, to designate who in your life receives which portion of your assets

To that end, the best way to approach estate-planning is to treat it as a process. We recommend using the *critical path method* to planning your estate, which includes the following steps:

1. **Define your goals.** Before you begin, decide what you're trying to achieve. Are you trying to make sure that your spouse has enough income for some period of time if you were to die suddenly, for example.

   Write down your goals; don't just think about them. By writing down your goals, you get a better handle on how they relate to one another, and you make sure that you haven't forgotten anything.

2. **Determine which estate-planning professionals you want to work with.** Different professionals (attorneys, financial planners, insurance

agents, and accountants) provide different services. You need to determine which professionals can best help you meet your goals.

3. **Gather information.** Whether you work with professionals or not, the following questions help you assess where you are currently in your estate-planning process:

    1. Do you have a will right now, and if so, when did you prepare that will?

    2. What in your life has changed since you created that will?

    3. What insurance policies do you currently have?

    4. Have any insurance policies expired?

    5. What property is in your estate and what is the value of that property?

4. **Develop your action plan.** Get ready to work on your will, decide if trusts make sense for you, figure out what you need to do to protect your business, and so on.

5. **Actually conduct your plan.** Take the plans that you developed in Step 4 and actually do them. Don't procrastinate!

6. **Monitor your action plan.** Estate planning is an ongoing process. You periodically need to resynchronize your estate plan with any major changes in your life.

Ten great Web sites for free health information

Being uninformed about your health is no longer excusable! You can find out just about anything you'd need to know at one of these free health-information sites:

✔ www.webmd.com: Search for a symptom or a condition and WebMD gives you lists of causes, symptoms, when you should see a doctor, home remedies, medications, treatments, and risk factors. You also find message boards, newsletters, and live interactive broadcasts from doctors so that you can hear from others with your condition. You have to sign up, but it's free.

✔ www.mayoclinic.com: In addition to information on diseases and conditions, the Mayo Clinic site offers decision guides and self-assessments to help you weigh the pros and cons of treatments you may be considering. It has specific health centers for men, women, and seniors, with information on screening tests, intimacy and aging, maintaining independence, anti-aging hormones, and in-depth info on many common health concerns.

✔ Medlineplus.gov: From the U.S. National Library of Medicine and the National

Institutes of Health, MedlinePlus gives you information on health topics and drugs, links to clinical trials, doctor/dentist/hospital directories, and a medical dictionary. It also has friendly interactive tutorials that guide you through all aspects of over 150 different diseases, conditions, tests, and surgeries.

- ✔ ClinicalTrials.gov: This site provides regularly updated information about federally and privately supported clinical research in human volunteers. ClinicalTrials.gov gives you information about a trial's purpose, who may participate, locations, and phone numbers so that you can get more details.

- ✔ Nihseniorhealth.gov: You can tell that this site was developed by the National Institute on Aging. You can enlarge the text, make the site high contrast for easy reading, or click on information to have it read aloud to you. As for the information, it's about specific health issues, such as arthritis, balance problems, and Alzheimer's.

- ✔ www.healthfinder.gov: At Health-Finder, you can access health information based on gender, age, race, or ethnic origin. You can also find background information on healthcare providers, hospital and nursing home ratings, health insurance guides, and Medicaid. The site is also in Spanish.

- ✔ www.familydoctor.org: From the American Academy of Family Physicians, this site lets you search by symptom for

in-depth information on diseases and conditions, including treatment, risks, and living with the condition. It includes a section on senior healthcare with tips on managing medical care and preventing medical errors. You can read the site in Spanish.

- ✔ www.intelihealth.com: Although this site is sponsored by Aetna Insurance, it has a collection of valuable articles from the Harvard Medical School faculty on various health topics.

- ✔ www.ivanhoe.com: Check out Ivanhoe for the latest news on medical issues and links to specific health issue-related Web sites. In the cancer section, for example, you can search the latest cancer clinical trials, get a list of the ten best cancer hospitals in the United States, and link to other specific cancer-related sites. Sign up for free e-mail newsletters.

- ✔ http://nccam.nih.gov: If you're curious about alternative medicine but not quite sure whether you trust it, this site from the National Center for Complementary and Alternative Medicine provides valuable info on the safety, effectiveness, and possible drug interactions of herbal and dietary supplements (note that the site comes from a Western/conventional medical approach). It includes guidelines for selecting a complementary medical practitioner and has a great list of criteria for evaluating medical information on the Web — like who runs and pays for the site.

Chapter 2

Living Longer and Better

*H*ealth is something you may not fully appreciate until it's gone. We drink to each other's health; we teach children to be healthy, wealthy, and wise; and we all know that if you have health, you have everything. But what really is health? What are its components? How can we choose health over frailty, and what can we do today to ensure health for life?

This chapter unlocks the secrets you need to accomplish all these goals, slowing the aging process and living well in the meantime.

How Old is Old?

When is old? Two hundred years ago, anyone over 35 was old. Sixty years ago, 70-year-old grandparents were considered "very old." Now we know that "old" doesn't start until the start of the last third of life, at your 80th birthday, and that is "young old." "Old old" doesn't begin until you are 100.

The effects of risk factors, or life habits that negatively impact longevity, are important. When we eliminate all risk factors, we have the chance to die of aging.

Aim for 100-plus!

Bob Butler, first director of the National Institute on Aging, wrote "We have not found any biologic reason to prohibit us from living to 100."

The wisdom of Okinawa

The people of Okinawa, a small island off the coast of Japan, have fascinated researchers ever since it was discovered that they live longer than anyone else on the planet. And not only do they live longer, they are healthy well into their senior years.

After World War II, Okinawans who grew up with the traditional Okinawan diet, which is rich in low-calorie vegetables such as sweet potatoes, had the added benefit of the newly introduced Western medicine. This combination of factors saw the Okinawans thriving well into their 90s and past 100. What's more, the Okinawan people aged slowly with low occurrence of chronic diseases normally associated with aging, including heart disease, dementia, and cancer.

So how can you get in on the Okinawan secret? For starters, eat your vegetables. Look for vegetables such as those Okinawan sweet potatoes — filling but low in calories. And stay active! Okinawans may not have exercised at a health club, but with activities like fishing, farming, and walking, they sure stayed active.

The *centenarians* (people who have lived to be 100 years old or more), the most rapidly growing segment of the population, give evidence of this possibility and its defining features. Consider these examples:

- ✔ George Burns quipped that one of the reasons he looked forward to being 100 was that very few people over 100 die — because very few people live past the age of 100, of course! George Burns did live to see 100, and many more people are doing so as well.
- ✔ The longest life on record is that of Madame Jeanne Calment, a French woman who was born February 21, 1875, and died August 4, 1997 — that's 122 years, 225 days.
- ✔ Currently, the *Guinness Book of World Records* reports that Eva Morris of Staffordshire, England, is the world's oldest person, having been born on Dec. 18, 1885.

Life at 100

Centenarians are by definition "successful agers." What about them makes them seemingly invulnerable to things that kill off other people of the same age?

Centenarians do seem to share some characteristics:

- ✔ Stability
- ✔ A sense of equanimity and order
- ✔ Lack of anxiety

How Madame Jeanne Calment reached 122+

Physicians reported Madame Calment's health as being pretty robust for her whole life. She retained vigor and attractiveness until shortly before she died in 1997. She hailed from Arles in the south of France. During her long lifetime, she lived in only three homes, leaving the second (a second-floor walkup apartment with no elevator) for a rest home at age 110. She broke her hip at 100, the last year she still ran for exercise. In fact, Madame Calment credited her exercise program for her health. She exercised once or twice daily and rode her bike until the age of 115. Madame Calment occasionally smoked a cigarette or a cigarillo after meals, but she quit at age 117. She also gave up her Port, which was a long-time companion, but she never surrendered her chocolate, a dear love.

Why did Madame Calment live so long? Some scientists say it was genetics. The majority, however, agree that her record-breaking lifespan was mostly attributed to her lifestyle, which included exercise, a healthy diet, and a positive attitude.

✔ A capacity to get along with others

✔ Regular exercise

✔ Healthy diet

✔ Adequate rest

✔ Involvement with family, community, nation, and world

✔ Love of music

✔ Optimism; a "can do" attitude

✔ Understanding of the meaning in their lives

✔ A sense of control of their lives; change what should be changed and accept what must be accepted

✔ Understanding of their responsibility to be a resource to their community and nation — not a liability

✔ Acceptance of aging as a normal part of life

Three Great Strategies to Help You Live Longer

People are living longer because they know a lot more than they used to. The new knowledge base is increasingly available to all. The following list presents you with even more knowledge and delineates three strategies for living longer.

✔ **Believe that you will live a long life.** Aging truly is a self-fulfilling prophecy. How long you live is a direct result of your expectations. If you think you're going to be dead at 60, or 70, or 80, then that's likely to be the case. Or perhaps you think, "Well, maybe I won't be dead by then, but I'll probably be in a forlorn nursing home with a plastic tube in my nose, endlessly contemplating ceiling tiles." Again, we believe that if you say that you'll end your days in a nursing home, you probably will.

Each day you behave in such a way as to guarantee the accuracy of your own prediction. Now, pretend that you believe, "I'm going to live to be 100 because that's what I am programmed for." If you can stop pretending and truly believe that statement, then it's likely to come true. But, your behavior must support your prediction.

Believe in 100. Reaching 100 is your birthright, so not living to 100 is a discredit to your natural design.

✔ **Take control of your life.** To seize control of your destiny, you must first recognize that *you* are responsible for living a long life. You are in charge, not only of how long you will live, but, more importantly, of how well you will live. You can't delegate the task. In this more than anything, your destiny is what you make it. Of course, helpers exist along the way. No one is smart or strong enough to go it alone, but after all is said and done, you craft your own future.

✔ **Know that it's never too late.** No matter how old you are or what shape you're in, you can take steps to help reverse the process of aging that's already occurred and to slow your rate of aging in the future.

Lamenting, "If only I had started sooner," or "If only I had known about this," doesn't work. "If onlys" get you nowhere. The human organism's capacity to renew is vast, and the renewal capacity exists until the moment your toes curl up. Bones mend, and scrapes and scratches heal, even in centenarians. Using age as an excuse for being less than your best is just plain wrong.

Three Not-So-Secret Secrets to Superb Health

What advice do you think that the world's healthiest person would give you on how to stay as healthy as she is at that given moment?

Here's a hint: Her advice would cover three main areas —

- ✔ **Exercise:** Of the three components — exercise, diet, and rest — exercise is the single most important one.

- ✔ **Diet:** We all need fuel to live. The kind of fuel you put into your body can determine how well your body runs, and how long it lasts.

- ✔ **Rest:** Lack of sleep increases the speed of the aging process.

Within these three broad categories lie all the secrets of health. How can we validate this bold claim? Take away one of the three and see where you end up. For example, exercise and make sure to eat well, but get no rest. Or, get plenty of rest and exercise, but don't allow yourself to eat. Or eat and rest, but don't do any exercise. Any one of these three alternatives would lead to a profound loss of performance, and eventually poor health.

The sections that follow cover each of these categories in detail. Sure, these three basics aren't glamorous. In fact, you've heard them all before, and really, the topics are pretty boring. But that doesn't change the fact that they're the three best ways to achieve and maintain great health.

Don't count on doctors to fix years of poor maintenance on your part; prevention is key, even if it's not exciting or dramatic.

Viewing exercise as a must, not an option

Exercise cuts down mortality rates at any age, but the protection grows increasingly stronger the older you become. The lesson: Starting late is better than never starting at all!

Some people call exercise the universal therapy. They're right — exercise is good for just about everything. In fact, listing conditions in which you shouldn't exercise is much more difficult than nominating illnesses for which exercise is a healer. Consider the following important benefits of exercise:

- ✔ **Healing your heart:** The American Heart Association labels lack of exercise as one of the major causes of heart trouble. In fact, exercise is a mandated part of the post-attack treatment phase. Exercise promotes healing and enables arteries to become bigger and better, helping to prevent another attack.

- ✔ **Warding off cancer:** Harvard alumni who exercised 2,000 calories per week (approximately 3½ hours of jogging or 7 hours of moderately paced walking) had a 40 percent lower chance of developing prostate cancer.

Five ways to stay motivated

The key to any exercise program is staying motivated to follow through and attain your goals. Here are some tips to help you keep up your momentum.

- ✔ Build on success. Start with small goals that lead to larger ones.

- ✔ Be realistic. Set attainable goals. (See previous point.)

- ✔ Reward yourself when you achieve your goals.

- ✔ Create variety in your exercise routine to prevent boredom.

- ✔ Make exercise a part of who you are, not just something you do.

Exercise is an on-board experience. You can't import energy flow from the sports section of a newspaper or television, but taking a brisk walk, raking leaves, and riding your bike sure can give you an energy boost!

For information on creating an exercise program that's right for you, see Chapter 6.

Fueling your future with good food

The saying, "You are what you eat" is inescapably true. Your food makes up your anatomy. Although the image your mirror reflects today looks pretty similar to the one you saw last year, the truth is that you are almost entirely new — newly constituted from the raw material of the thousand meals that you ate over the last year.

Food is more than just your structure. Food is your energy source. Not only does your food provide your structure, it also supplies the fuel to run that structure, to do what you want and need to do. When you look at nutrition over your life span, you need to consider both the structure-building and energy-generating properties of food.

Understanding what is meant by "a balanced diet"

Over a 100-year lifetime, you eat around 75 million calories. That's enough food to feed the entire hungry crowd at the Super Bowl. Calories are divided into three parts:

- ✔ **Carbohydrate:** Short-term energy supplier. Carbs should make up 50 percent max of your daily calories. Complex carbohydrates, such as grains and vegetables, are considered to be the most nutritious. Simple sugars, such as table sugars, contain no vitamins, minerals, or fiber, and therefore are the least nutritious.

✔ **Fat:** Long-term energy source. Thirty percent max of daily calories should be derived from fat — and preferably, that fat should come from the plant or unsaturated fats, such as olive oil, peanuts, and fish.

If you are inactive or have high cholesterol, you should restrict your fat intake. This advice holds true for a 90-year-old or a 40-year-old.

✔ **Protein:** Structure, the "meat" of us. Protein constitutes 15 to 20 percent of a healthy diet.

Eating too much of any one of these three can make you fat, but eating fat will make you fat faster because it is so rich in calories compared with the other two.

The U.S. Department of Agriculture food pyramid, shown in Figure 2-1, emphasizes variety in the diet. The emphasis is on vegetables, fruits, and grains. For more information on these important components to your diet, refer to *Nutrition For Dummies,* by Carol Ann Rinzler (Wiley).

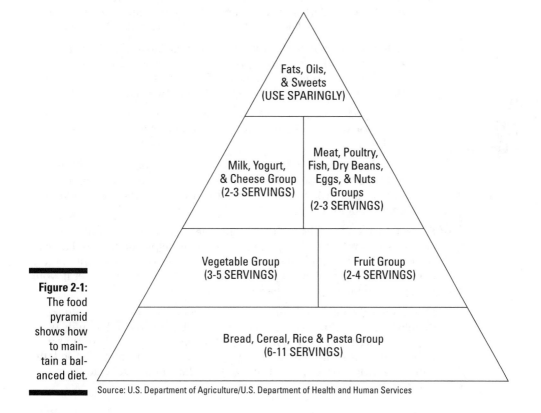

Figure 2-1: The food pyramid shows how to maintain a balanced diet.

Fats, Oils, & Sweets (USE SPARINGLY)

Milk, Yogurt, & Cheese Group (2-3 SERVINGS)

Meat, Poultry, Fish, Dry Beans, Eggs, & Nuts Groups (2-3 SERVINGS)

Vegetable Group (3-5 SERVINGS)

Fruit Group (2-4 SERVINGS)

Bread, Cereal, Rice & Pasta Group (6-11 SERVINGS)

Source: U.S. Department of Agriculture/U.S. Department of Health and Human Services

Supplementing your diet — the smart way

In addition to categories of calories, you should supplement your diet with the following catalysts. A *catalyst* is a facilitator, a helper, a promoter, that allows a chemical reaction.

- **Vitamins:** *Micronutrients* — vitamins and minerals — are as essential as *macronutrients* — protein, fat, and carbohydrate. Without micronutrients, a whole assortment of deficiency conditions may arise, from anemia to nerve problems. Supplementing your diet with a simple multivitamin with minerals each day helps mitigate problems.

  Vitamins are not a substitute for a good, balanced food program.

- **Minerals:** Salt, calcium, and iron are the most important minerals. Our needs for minerals don't change as we age.

  Salt: Throughout life, salt should be used moderately. Luckily, the kidney, that wonder organ, usually compensates for under- or over-salting of food. If we eat too little salt, the kidney dams up salt in its excretion, and if we take in too much, it simply gets rid of it. Some people, particularly overweight people, are sodium retainers, which puts a person at risk for the development of high blood pressure.

  Calcium: Calcium is the stuff of our bones. Most of us have heard about the epidemic of *osteoporosis* — the reduction of bone density. The recommended intake is 1.5 grams of calcium per day — that's the amount of calcium you'll find in two glasses of milk!

  Although low intake of calcium over a lifetime is a major cause of osteoporosis, insufficient exercise is a much bigger part of the problem.

  Iron: Iron is mostly important as part of our hemoglobin in the red blood cells. Generally a well-balanced diet provides enough iron for all purposes. Meats and green vegetables are excellent sources of iron.

- **Fiber:** Fiber is often lacking in older people's diets, and it is difficult to compensate for by taking a pill. Plenty of fiber helps you to avoid constipation and to control cholesterol levels. Fiber, of course, is found largely in grains and vegetables, but if you can't seem to get enough fiber in your diet, you can take it in a prepared, drugstore form.

- **Fluid:** A word about fluid and aging. A few reports suggest that older people lose their thirst sensitivity, so remembering to drink liquids is important, particularly in hot weather. Sometimes if you rely on thirst to be your indication that you need a glass of water, it's already too late, and you are dehydrated. Be sure that your daily fluid intake adds up to two quarts.

Making time for a little R&R

Society's casual attitude toward diminished sleep is wrong. Each of us, young, old, thin, chubby, rich, poor, and so forth, needs to make rest and relaxation a high priority. Not only does performance suffer without this dedication, but so too will length and quality of life. Plan on making rest as much a part of your health plan as diet and exercise!

Eight ways to cure insomnia

A great deal of self-treatment of insomnia is common sense, so if you're having trouble sleeping, try these tips:

- ✔ Have a routine before bedtime, so that your body can queue itself when the time comes to shut down. Going to bed at 8:30 p.m. one night, 1 a.m. the next, and 9 p.m. the next night messes up the body's signals.

- ✔ Tend to your pet's and your own toilet needs before retiring. A full bladder is an alarm clock.

- ✔ Environmental control is a basic and obvious helpmate for good sleep. Beds should be cozy, quiet, warm, and dark.

- ✔ Beds should be reserved for sleep time and making love, not for fretful ceiling staring. (Having a bedmate is associated with good sleep patterns.)

- ✔ Get rid of stimulants such as coffee, chocolate, tea, and nicotine. Your brain doesn't need chemical clamor as it winds down.

- ✔ Avoid heavy exercise before retiring. All the gears of the body and mind need to be in neutral for sleep to find a happy haven.

- ✔ Don't eat a big meal just before bedtime. A full belly means the body must attend to its needs and in so doing keeps the machinery going.

- ✔ Don't nap. A good night's sleep quota can be robbed by gratifying the rest need early in the day.

Don't take sleep aids!

Sleeping pills are dangerous. They're addictive, and, in general, do much more harm than good. Of the hundreds of products available, none has been shown to be ideal. Consider the following:

- ✔ Some pills are short acting, and some are long acting.

- ✔ Hangovers are common.

- ✔ Sleeping pills disrupt the normal five-stage anatomy of sleep.

- ✔ Sleeping pills contribute to or aggravate depression.

✔ Combining use with alcohol is particularly unwise.

✔ Regular sleeping pill users have a substantially higher mortality rate — in other words, sleeping pills shorten life.

Sleeping pills are foreign chemicals for which the body is not prepared. None of the sleeping pills are smart enough to confer good sleep without demanding an unacceptable payback price. Don't pay the ransom demanded by taking a sleeping pill.

The only legitimate use of sleeping pills is to help reset the sleep clock to a normal routine after some disruption. This should take only a few days. Hopefully, melatonin will emerge as a safer and more effective tool for this purpose as well.

The best advice about sleeping pills: Don't take them!

When a true problem exists

If a major issue with poor sleep exists, it's important to ask whether any illness could be involved, including the following possibilities:

✔ Some hormonal conditions, such as an overactive thyroid gland, can cause sleep distress.

✔ Menopause often unsettles the rest pattern.

✔ The aches of arthritis are major sleep disrupters. Numerous therapeutic approaches are available that, when the distress is lessened, permit a good night's sleep.

✔ Both depression and anxiety are notable for their disruption of sleep.

✔ Many medications have stimulatory effects and must be acknowledged.

Minimizing Your Risk of Disease

In the last century, doctors have matured in their understanding of disease. Physicians now identify disease for what it is — a condition often caused by an offending agent that, through its action, harms the patient. Such agents come in two principal varieties, infections and malignancies, both of which have changed over the course of centuries. Other varieties exist, as well; we focus on infection and malignancies, which are in most cases preventable and curable.

✔ **Infection:** Infections result from some invading bug taking up residence in a person's body where it is not welcome. These can be viruses, bacteria, fungi, or worms.

The current spectrum of infection differs completely from the spectrum of infection a few years ago. Medical science has done a brilliant job of limiting the force of infectious disease.

✔ **Malignancies:** Malignancies, or cancer, are caused by some agent (cigarette smoke, for example) upsetting the magnificently controlled genetic machinery responsible for cell growth and repair. Cancer occurs when the sequence of genes that monitor the orderly process of tissue regeneration becomes disorderly, and uncontrolled growth (cancer) results.

Malignancies, too, are yielding to medical science. The process is more difficult, but daily miracles occur in the cure of leukemia and lymphoma, which were uniformly fatal not long ago.

After you identify a disease as a real or potential problem, you can choose between two active strategies to change what you can change. The first strategy is cure, and the second is prevention. Most of the medical research in the past century has gone toward the effort to cure, and successes abound. However, prevention holds the true glory.

Health has three sturdy legs to stand on: good exercise, good nutrition, and adequate rest. All three are crucial, and all of them require regular and persistent personal involvement. The only good disease is the one that you prevent. Working with your doctor, you can develop this ideal health insurance policy.

Maximizing Your Brain Power

Staying in touch with family and friends, engaging your mind and body in challenging ways, and participating in a variety of activities are central strategies for successful aging. The richness of your personal involvement with other people is key to having a good quality of life. Being alone and out of touch just doesn't cut it. Maintaining contact with the outside world is a survival tool as necessary as eating and breathing.

Using your five senses to live an interactive life

Interaction is a fact of life. In fact, interaction *is* life. A mountain of evidence asserts that the more acutely you maintain your interactive capacities, the more your days will gratify you. Our senses — hearing, seeing, tasting, touch (balance), smelling — enable us to interact with others.

✔ **Eyesight:** Everyone over 60 years of age should schedule routine eye doctor visits. By adopting a routine exam program, your doctor can note any loss of vision. Sudden vision changes, pain in the eye, flashing lights, or double vision should prompt an immediate visit. Eyesight is so precious that procrastination and denial make no sense whatsoever!

✔ **Hearing:** Most experts now agree that people could avoid most hearing loss if they weren't exposed to loud noises. Noise-induced hearing loss is very common. Because excessive noise has such a large role in provoking deafness, you should change what you can by avoiding exposure to loud noise. Also, don't forget to keep your ears clear of wax. Unquestionably, many older persons are suffering the indignity of hearing loss merely because their ears are full of wax, which is easily and conveniently cleaned out.

Simple soapy water with a rubber syringe is usually all that is necessary to keep ears clean. If this doesn't work, there are a number of ear drops (Cerumenex or Debrox) that are stronger. If these fail, your doctor's nurse is probably an expert at ear wax removal.

✔ **Touch (balance):** Most of us take balance for granted. A fall often precipitates the first recognition of the problem. Certainly age plays a role in decreased balance. For example, our capacity to detect vibration goes down with aging. Still, much evidence indicates that you can improve your balance by using simple exercises.

Vertigo is the severe form of dizziness in which the room or you actually seem to be spinning. If you have vertigo or any other difficulties with your balance, consult your doctor for a referral to an otolaryngologist who specializes in balance disorders.

✔ **Smell and taste:** Both the intensity and the differentiating capacity to smell diminish with the years. The same holds true for taste; we may find certain foods too bitter at a young age and then be able to handle them as we age. This phenomenon leads many older people to seek more flavor in their food.

If your ability to smell and taste declines significantly, you may ultimately experience decreased pleasures of eating. If you believe your senses of taste and smell are diminished, have your doctor consider dental and medication issues. Sometimes dental fillings or gum infections may alter taste. A long list of drugs can provoke senses of bitterness or acid or metal.

Smoking is bad for taste and smelling capacity, as it is for everything else.

Don't take your senses for granted. Guard them, recognize if they are suffering in the least, and cherish them. Don't assume that any lessening of sight, hearing, balance, smell, taste, or adaptability to heat and cold is an inevitable part of growing old. Most of the changes, which have been attributed to aging, aren't due to aging, and are therefore subject to our active review and corrective effort.

Staying sharp — the creative way

Although not one of the five senses, creativity is an important way to keep your senses stimulated and engaged. A creative mind will keep your eyes and ears sharper. The process of creativity provides a focus for all your attention — you see more, hear more, feel more as you expand your experience by creating.

Here are some tips for staying creative until the day you breathe your last breath:

- Accept the ongoing responsibility to remain creative by constantly reviewing your skills and needs — reviewing the needs you want to gratify in filling out your life design and the skills you employ in getting the job done.

- Believe in your capacity to give something of value that may endure, nurture, teach, and comfort. For example, if you have a flair for gardening, volunteer at your local nursery and teach a class on growing your specialty.

- Model your effort on those people whom you respect.

- Test market your ideas for their potential effectiveness.

- Don't look for guarantees and don't look for what is a sure thing. Look for what *might* become a sure thing. Creativity leaves a rich legacy.

- Look to the political process. Public policy dictates what kind of world your descendents will live in. Work on it. Writing is a very creative form of expression. If you disagree with a certain political process or policy, write to your congressman.

- Allow yourself to be surprised.

Creativity with a capital "C" applies to those few whose gifts to humanity are widely hailed. But more important is the creativity with a small "c," which stands for all those innumerable acts of bringing new form and reality to the world that previously held a void or incompleteness. The small "c" creativities range from a garden, to a song, to learning a new language, to making you a more complete person. The process of aging allows time for the completeness of the person, realization of one's potentials, self-actualization.

Ten Essential Tips for Taking Medication Safely

Medications can be extremely helpful in preventing unwanted medical conditions, but only if they're taken properly. The ten tips in this section apply to all medications, from the simplest and safest to the most complex and hazardous.

✔ **Simplify, simplify, simplify!** Do you carry six, eight, ten vials in your purse or pockets? Some patients get to a point where they take some medications just to treat the side effects of another medication! Often, taking fewer medications instead of more is better. And don't forget, good diet, exercise, and rest are strong medicines too, and they are cheap, safe, and easily available.

✔ **Knowing when to stop taking a medicine:** Never take a pill just because so-and-so once prescribed it — maybe for reasons that are no longer present. Be aware of the expiration dates on your pill bottles — they are there for your protection. Finally, never, never take someone else's medicine.

✔ **Knowing when to continue taking a medicine:** Insulin, thyroid, and heart medications are good examples of medicines that require continued use. If you are tempted to stop taking a medication for some reason, check with your doctor first. Forgetfulness and cost are probably the main reasons why people fail to take their medicines, but minor side effects such as nausea or weakness might also prompt an interruption in dosage. Check with your doctor about changing the dose or even changing the medicine, because usually acceptable substitutes are available.

✔ **Taking the lowest dose possible:** People, especially older people, should always take the lowest possible dose of a medicine. Your physician should be aware of this, but is probably accustomed to prescribing a standard, higher dose for young people. Take responsibility by asking your doctor about a lower dosage.

✔ **Updating your prescriptions:** Check your prescriptions regularly to see whether the disease diagnosis for which a medication was originally prescribed is still appropriate. Medical conditions change regularly. When they change, your doctor should take a new look at your prescriptions.

✔ **Keeping your drug history current:** Always update your drug history. Note whether or not a medicine worked for some condition. Did the medicine cause a problem? An ongoing inventory of medication experience is important because the memory is a faulty device, so noting the facts when they occur is best.

✔ **Staying aware of possible drug interactions:** Although you might not have a problem with a medication when you take it alone, adding other medications to the mix can cause bad interactions. Whenever you start taking a new drug with a previous prescription, be extra cautious of unexpected side effects and contact your doctor immediately if they occur.

Medications are complicated enough when used singly, but combinations really increase the complexity. Keeping a personal drug diary is a good way of keeping track of unexpected and unpleasant interactions. Many pharmacies now have computer systems that will track your prescriptions and identify any possible interactions. Although these can be very helpful tools, they're certainly no substitute for strong communication between you, your doctor, and your pharmacist.

In addition, patients often display physical symptoms, such as:

- ✔ Tremors, rigidity, and slowness of movement. These kinds of physical symptoms may also indicate the development of another condition or a problem due to medications interacting.

- ✔ Restlessness or agitation.

Ten signs that it's time to seek help

So how do you decide whether you need to take your loved one to a doctor for assessment? *Any ongoing memory loss requires professional evaluation.* Remember that doctors are looking for memory loss *and* at least one other cognitive deficit or problem in day-to-day functioning in order to make a diagnosis of AD. AD *may* be the cause if memory loss is accompanied by

- ✔ Difficulty speaking or comprehending information

- ✔ Confusion

- ✔ Disorientation (for example, confusing the days of the week or problems estimating or telling time)

- ✔ Problems recognizing or identifying objects

- ✔ Problems with motor skills

- ✔ Personality changes (such as sudden irritability)

- ✔ Agitation (such as restlessness, pacing, unprovoked verbal or physical aggression)

- ✔ Problems recognizing similarities or differences between ideas and concepts

- ✔ Problems planning, reasoning, judging, and other higher-level thinking

- ✔ Any significant change in day-to-day functioning that contradicts your loved one's normal conduct

If you suspect AD, start keeping a record of any symptoms and behavioral changes that you notice in your loved one. Gathering this information gives your doctor a leg up as she starts the diagnostic process.

Treatment options

Only four drugs have been FDA approved for the treatment of Alzheimer's disease. The standard of treatment calls for the administration of one of the three drugs still in use, along with a recommended 2,000 IU of vitamin E daily. Depending on your loved one's condition, additional medications may be used to treat other behavioral symptoms of AD that can occur at any point in the course of the disease. Your doctor will work with you and your loved one to determine which medications and treatment options are best suited to your particular case.

Staying Ahead of Arthritis

Ouch! There it goes again! That grinding pain in your hip; those aching knees that make walking from the kitchen to the bedroom a chore; the stiff and swollen fingers that won't allow you to twist the lid off a sticky jar or even sew on a button. Arthritis seems to get to everybody sooner or later, slowing us down, forcing us to give up some of our favorite activities, and just generally being a pain in the neck (sometimes literally!). In more advanced cases, it can seriously compromise quality of life as sufferers surrender their independence, mobility, and sense of usefulness while being relentlessly worn down by pain.

The good news is that you can manage your arthritis, if not cure it, with a combination of medical care, simple lifestyle changes, and good old common sense.

The eight faces of arthritis

Here's a quick look at some various types of arthritis and arthritis-related diseases.

- ✔ **Ankylosing spondylitis:** A chronic inflammation of the spine, this disease can cause the vertebrae to grow together, making the spine rigid. Although the cause is unknown, heredity is a factor.

- ✔ **Gout:** This "regal" form of arthritis is caused by the build-up of a substance called uric acid, which forms sharp crystals that are deposited in the joint. These needlelike crystals cause severe pain and are most commonly found in the "bunion" joint of the big toe, the knees, and the wrists. Genetic factors, diet, or certain drugs may cause gout.

- ✔ **Infectious arthritis:** Bacteria, viruses, or fungi that enter the body can settle in the joints, causing fever, inflammation, and loss of joint function.

- ✔ **Juvenile arthritis:** This is a catchall term for the different kinds of arthritis that strike children under the age of 16, the most common of which is *juvenile rheumatoid arthritis (JRA)*. Pain or swelling in the shoulders, elbows, knees, ankles, or toes, chills, a reappearing fever, and sometimes a body rash are the typical symptoms of JRA. The cause is unknown.

✔ **Osteoarthritis:** In this, the most common type of arthritis, the cartilage breaks down, exposing bone ends and allowing them to rub together. The result can be pain, stiffness, loss of movement, and sometimes swelling. Osteoarthritis is most often found in the weight-bearing joints, such as the hips, knees, ankles, and spine, but it can also affect the fingers. It may be the result of trauma, metabolic conditions, obesity, heredity, or other factors.

✔ **Pseudogout:** Like gout, pseudogout is caused by the deposition of crystals into the joint, but instead of uric acid crystals, they're made from calcium. Pain, swelling, and sometimes the destruction of cartilage can result.

✔ **Psoriatic arthritis:** This form of arthritis occurs in people who have the inherited skin condition called *psoriasis,* which causes scaly, red, rough patches on the neck, elbows, and knees, as well as the pitting of the nails. Often settling in the joints of the fingers and toes, psoriatic arthritis can cause the digits to swell up like little sausages.

✔ **Rheumatoid arthritis:** In this, the second-most common form of arthritis, the immune system turns against the body, causing inflammation and swelling that begins in the joint lining and spreads to the cartilage and the bone. It often affects the same joint on both sides of the body (for example, both wrists).

Arthritis can also be present as part of another condition, such as Lyme disease, or as a companion to another condition, such as carpal tunnel syndrome or fibromyalgia.

Is it really arthritis? Signs and symptoms

With all the different kinds of arthritis, how do you know if you have one of them? Arthritis can strike anyone at any time, and many times it's difficult to tell whether the pain is serious enough to warrant medical attention. Typical warning signs of arthritis are

✔ Joint pain

✔ Stiffness or difficulty in moving a joint

✔ Swelling

The warning signs may come in *triplicate* (pain plus stiffness plus swelling), two together, or one all alone. Or there may be other early signs such as malaise or muscle pain. But if you experience *any* of these or other symptoms in or around a joint for longer than two weeks, you should see your doctor.

A therapeutic diet for arthritis sufferers

If you suffer from arthritis, you can help manage your pain by eating a therapeutic diet. For example, avoid foods that can aggravate inflamed joints. This means avoiding vegetables of the nightshade family (tomatoes and potatoes, for example), dairy, and red meat. Eat as many fruits and vegetables as you can, and incorporate oily fish and whole grain products into your diet. Also include lots of vitamin C—essential for maintaining cartilage.

You're not alone: Accepting your diagnosis

The good news is that arthritis can be managed in many cases. It may take some time and effort to find the right treatment(s) for your particular version of the disease, but there are answers. Although your doctor may recommend medication to help relieve the pain, you can do many things yourself to keep the pain at bay and, perhaps, prevent further damage and help your joints to heal.

The goal in chronic pain management is to block pain messages before they reach the brain. You can try several natural ways, apart from using drugs. For example:

- Exercise that's appropriate to your condition
- Hot or cold treatments
- Water therapy
- Massage
- Magnets
- Topical pain relievers
- Relaxation
- TENS (transcutaneous electrical nerve stimulation)

On the other hand, several "natural" things can make your pain even worse:

- Anxiety
- Depression
- Fatigue
- Focusing on your pain

✔ Physical overexertion

✔ Progression of the disease

✔ Stress

Understanding Cancer Basics

Cancer — an uncontrolled growth and spread of abnormal cells — is actually a general name for about 100 different diseases characterized by the following traits:

- ✔ **Abnormal cell division:** Unlike normal, healthy cells, which grow, divide, and replace themselves to keep the body healthy, cancer cells don't have the control mechanism that turns off growth; they divide without restraint. When cancer cells divide over and over, they can become an abnormal growth called a *tumor.* Cancerous, or *malignant,* tumors can push aside or invade healthy tissue and cause organs to stop functioning.

- ✔ **Invasiveness:** Cancer cells often crowd out their neighboring cells and affect the function and growth of normal cells by competing with them for available nutrients. The cancerous growth takes over the organs so that they can no longer perform their usual duties.

- ✔ **Metastasis:** Cancer cells can spread from their original site to other organs, often via the blood or lymph system, a process known as *metastasis.*

- ✔ **Recurrence:** Cancer has a tendency to come back. After a period of remission, in which symptoms decrease or disappear, it may strike again, in the same part of the body or elsewhere.

Cancer can affect any body organ or tissue. In fact, we often refer to cancer in terms of the organ in which it originated (breast cancer or lung cancer, for example). Left untreated, cancer is usually fatal; its tendency to invade healthy tissue causes organs to cease functioning until the patient dies. However, sometimes cancer can go into spontaneous remission, which means that the symptoms either decrease or disappear entirely.

There is no one cause of cancer, and no one knows exactly why cancer develops in some people but not in others, but both external and internal factors play a role in cancer development. People who are exposed to environmental *carcinogens* (cancer-causing agents) such as high doses of ultraviolet light, radiation, tobacco smoke, asbestos, and toxic industrial substances, for example, are likely to get cancer. Poor dietary habits can also increase the risk of certain cancers, as can infection. Internal factors, such as hormones, immune and metabolic conditions, and heredity also contribute to cancer.

If cancer is caught early on, before it destroys much surrounding tissue or spreads to other parts of the body, the chances of a cure are much greater.

Detecting and diagnosing cancer

Because early detection increases the rate of cure, *screening tests* — periodic tests to discover the most common forms of cancers — have become a standard part of health care. In addition to undergoing the recommended screening tests, you need to be self-aware and look for any unusual changes. The American Cancer Society recommends that you see your doctor immediately if you notice any of the following warning signs of cancer:

- ✔ A change in bowel or bladder habits (frequency, consistency, pain)
- ✔ A sore that does not heal
- ✔ Unusual bleeding or discharge
- ✔ Thickening or a lump in a breast or elsewhere
- ✔ Indigestion or difficulty swallowing
- ✔ An obvious change in a wart or mole
- ✔ A nagging cough or hoarseness

If your doctor suspects cancer, she will likely perform tests, including x-rays, blood tests, and a *biopsy,* a laboratory study of a tissue sample, to confirm the diagnosis. Diagnosis involves analyzing a sample of cells under a microscope. Because each type of cancer has its own rate of growth and spreading pattern, your doctor or *oncologist* (a doctor who specializes in treating cancer) will perform tests to identify the type and location of the cancer, as well as the extent to which it has progressed.

Treating cancer

Depending on the type of cancer and how far it's spread, cancer treatment may consist of a single treatment or a combination of treatments. The primary treatment (often surgery) is often followed by an *adjuvant,* or supplemental, therapy, such as chemotherapy. The three most common cancer therapies are

- ✔ Surgery
- ✔ Radiation therapy
- ✔ Chemotherapy

Risks You Can Reduce (continued)
High levels of low-density lipoproteins ("bad" cholesterol)
Low levels of high-density lipoproteins ("good" cholesterol)
High levels of triglycerides
High levels of homocysteine

Source: _National Cholesterol Education Project._

"Clustering" of risk factors occurs most frequently in overweight individuals who, in addition to excess weight, often have one or more other risk factors for heart disease. This condition makes them particularly susceptible to dying from heart disease. The reason for this probably relates to abnormalities caused by fat cells in general and abdominal fat cells in particular.

You don't have to be enormously overweight to experience a connection between your higher weight and a higher risk of heart disease. Being as little as 20 percent over your suggested healthy weight raises your total cholesterol and your "bad" LDLs while lowering your "good" HDLs. And if you are overweight, you should make it a point to discuss with your physician whether you have other risk factors for heart disease in addition to your obesity. The odds are that you do.

Types of heart disease

Following are some types of heart disease to be aware of:

- ✔ **Arteriosclerosis and atherosclerosis:** The origins of coronary heart disease often lie with arteriosclerosis and atherosclerosis. _Arteriosclerosis,_ or "hardening of the arteries," describes a number of conditions in which fatty deposits and minerals collect in your arteries, causing the vessels to become rigid and inflexible. In _atherosclerosis,_ the most common form of arteriosclerosis, the walls of your arteries become thick and irregular due to the accumulation of cholesterol, fats, and other substances, called _plaque._ Arteriosclerosis sets the stage for heart attack by narrowing your arteries and reducing blood flow to your heart. Also, your rigid blood vessels can't expand to allow greater blood flow when needed. Because you can't feel the buildup of plaque, the only signs of atherosclerosis may be angina pectoris or heart attack.

- ✔ **Angina pectoris:** Atherosclerosis leads to angina pectoris (often abbreviated as _angina_). During stress, exercise, or an emotional situation — even after a large meal — your heart beats faster and works harder, which means that your heart muscle must get more oxygen-rich blood to maintain the pace. But if you have arteriosclerosis, the arteries leading to your heart become rigid and narrow, and they don't allow enough oxygen-rich blood, filled with nutrients, to reach your heart muscle during these situations. The pain felt during this oxygen deficiency is angina. Nearly 3 million American men have angina.

✔ **Heart attack:** A heart attack, or myocardial infarction (MI), takes place when a blockage (clot) — perhaps caused by a buildup of plaque — occurs in your heart artery. As a result, blood containing oxygen is cut off from your heart and your oxygen-deprived heart muscle is damaged.

You have close to a 90 percent chance of survival after a heart attack if no complications arise. Alarmingly, 23 percent of previous heart attack victims will have another attack within six years of their first attack.

Here are some common signs associated with painful heart attacks:

- Crushing, breathtaking pain that starts in the chest and radiates into the left arm, back, or shoulder

- Cold, clammy sweat

- Vomiting

- Pain that lasts longer than 15 minutes or is not affected by nitroglycerin medication

What every woman must know about heart disease

Although heart disease is an equal opportunity killer, many people, both men and women, continue to think that heart disease is primarily a *man's* problem. Wrong!

✔ More women than men die of heart disease in the United States.

✔ While men do suffer heart attacks an average of 10 years earlier than women, after menopause women catch up. Within a year after a heart attack, 42 percent of women will die as compared to 24 percent of men.

✔ Women are less likely to know the warning signs for heart attack.

✔ Women smokers have a six times greater risk of heart attack than nonsmoking women.

Amazingly, some recent surveys have shown that women are more afraid of breast cancer than cardiovascular disease. While there's no question that breast cancer is a serious disease, only one woman in 27 dies from breast cancer, while one in two dies from heart disease. In the final analysis, heart disease is at least as dangerous for women as it is for men.

The good news is that we know so much about prevention today. Follow the tips in this chapter, and check out *The Healthy Heart Cookbook For Dummies* for great recipes to help ward off heart disease.

- Control diabetes.

- Monitor your cholesterol levels.

- Ask your doctor whether you have *atrial fibrillation,* a heart condition that encourages the formation of blood clots.

Dealing with Diabetes

Many different kinds of sugars exist in nature, but *glucose* (also known as blood sugar) is the sugar that has the starring role in the body, providing a source of instant energy so that muscles can move and important chemical reactions can take place. Sugar is a carbohydrate, one group of the three sources of energy in the body. The others are protein and fat.

After much debate and deliberation, the American Diabetes Association published the new standard for diagnosis for diabetes mellitus, which includes any one of the following three criteria:

- ✔ **Casual plasma glucose** concentration greater than or equal to 200 mg/dl along with symptoms of diabetes. Mg/dl stands for *milligrams per deciliter.*

- ✔ **Fasting plasma glucose (FPG)** of greater than or equal to 126 mg/dl or 7 mmol/L. *Fasting* means that the patient has consumed no food for eight hours prior to the test.

- ✔ **Blood glucose** of greater than or equal to 200 mg/dl (11.1 mmol/L), when tested two hours (2-h PG) after ingesting 75 grams of glucose by mouth. This test has long been known as the Oral Glucose Tolerance Test. Although this test is rarely done because it takes time and is cumbersome, it remains the gold standard for the diagnosis of diabetes.

If one of the preceding criteria is positive one time, that's not enough. Any one of the tests must be positive on another occasion to make a diagnosis of diabetes.

Four early symptoms of diabetes

The following list contains the most common early symptoms of diabetes. One or more of the following symptoms may be present when diabetes is diagnosed:

- ✔ Frequent urination and thirst

- ✔ Fatigue

    ✔ Weight loss

    ✔ Persistent vaginal infection among women

Note: Diabetes mellitus is not the only condition associated with thirst and frequent urination. Another condition in which fluids go in and out of the body like a siphon is called *diabetes insipidus*. Here, the urine is not sweet. Diabetes insipidus is an entirely different disease that you should not mistake for diabetes mellitus.

Discovering ways to treat diabetes

The pancreas produces a crucial substance, called *insulin,* that controls the glucose in the blood. Extracted and purified insulin is used as a treatment for diabetes and has saved many lives. Oral drugs to reduce blood glucose have become available only in the last 40 years.

Three basic treatments for diabetes include

    ✔ **Diet:** No matter how you slice it, your weight is determined by the number of calories you take in, minus the number of calories you use up by exercise or loss of calories in the urine or bowel movements. If you have an excess of calories coming in and have insulin with which to store them, you will gain weight. If you have fewer calories coming in than going out, you will lose weight. If you are overweight, you will benefit from even a small weight loss.

    Basically three foods contain calories: Carbohydrates, proteins, and fats. We recommend a diet of 40 percent carbohydrate, 30 percent protein, and 30 percent fats, with less than a third of that amount coming from saturated fats.

    To feel better and be healthier, drink a minimum of ten cups, or 2½ quarts, of water a day.

    Fear of the "danger" of sugar in the diet has led to a vast effort to produce a compound that could add the pleasurable sweetness without the liabilities of sugar. Interestingly enough, despite the availability of a number of excellent sweeteners, some containing no calories at all, the incidence of diabetes continues to rise. Still, if you can reduce your caloric intake or your glucose response by using a sweetener, you will have an advantage.

    ✔ **Exercise:** The major benefit of exercise for both types of diabetes is to prevent macrovascular disease, which affects the entire population of nondiabetics and people with diabetes alike but is particularly severe in people with diabetes.

    Prior to beginning a new exercise program, a person with diabetes who has not exercised previously should check with a doctor, especially if over the age of 35 or if diabetes has been present for ten years or longer.

Unless you have a physical abnormality, you have no limitation on what you can do. You need to select an activity that you enjoy and will continue to do.

✔ **Medication:** Most people don't care for shots. You may be an exception, but we doubt it. Fortunately, drugs that can be taken by mouth have been available for some time.

No drug should be taken as a convenient way of avoiding the basic diet and exercise that's the key to diabetic control.

If you're a person with Type 1 diabetes, insulin is your savior. If you have Type 2 diabetes, you may need insulin late in the course of your disease. Insulin is a great drug, but it must be taken through a needle at the present time and that's the rub (or the pain). Inventors have come up with many different ways to administer insulin, but most people still use the old technique of a syringe and a needle.

Diabetes and the elderly

The incidence of diabetes in the elderly is higher for many reasons, but the main culprit seems to be increasing insulin resistance with aging, even if the elderly person with diabetes is not particularly obese or sedentary. Doctors do not yet understand why insulin resistance increases. When they look at the pancreas, it seems to be able to make insulin at the usual rate. The fasting blood glucose actually rises very slowly as you get older. It's the glucose after meals that rises much quicker and leads to the diagnosis. Because the fasting blood glucose is usually normal, some doctors recommend using the hemoglobin A1c to help to make the diagnosis in the elderly population. A hemoglobin A1c that is 1½ percent higher than the upper limit of normal for that lab is considered diagnostic of diabetes. Because most labs have a normal of up to 5.4 percent, a value of 7 percent or greater is probably diabetes. Between normal and that value is a gray zone that is probably impaired glucose tolerance.

Elderly people with diabetes often don't complain of any symptoms. When they do, the symptoms may not be the ones usually associated with Type 2 diabetes or the symptoms may be confusing. Elderly people with diabetes may complain of loss of appetite or weakness, and they may have lost weight rather than become obese. They may have incontinence of urine, which is usually thought of as a prostate problem in elderly men or a urinary tract infection in older women. Elderly people with diabetes may not complain of thirst because their ability to feel thirst is altered.

Four special considerations for the elderly

Special considerations when managing an elderly person who has diabetes include

✔ **Intellectual functioning:** You need to evaluate the intellectual function of an elderly person with diabetes because management of the disease requires a fairly high level of mental functioning.

The patient can take *cognitive screening tests* to determine his or her level of function. Testing makes it easier to tell whether the patient can be self-sufficient or will need help. Many older people now living alone with no assistance really require an assisted-living situation or even a nursing home.

✔ **Proper diet:** In addition to the intellectual function required to understand and prepare a proper diabetic diet, the elderly have other problems when it comes to proper nutrition:

  • They may have poor vision and be unable to see to read or cook.

  • They may have low income and be unable to purchase the foods that they require.

  • Their taste and smell may be decreased, so they lose interest in food.

  • They often have a loss of appetite.

  • They may have arthritis or a tremor that prevents cooking.

  • They may have poor teeth or a dry mouth.

Any one of these problems may be enough to prevent proper eating by the elderly person with the result that the diabetes is poorly controlled.

✔ **Eye problems:** Elderly people with diabetes have the same eye problems that are brought on earlier by diabetes. They get cataracts, macular degeneration, and open angle glaucoma in addition to diabetic retinopathy, all of which can affect proper care.

✔ **Urinary and sexual problems:** Urinary and sexual problems are very common in elderly people with diabetes and greatly affect quality of life. Paralysis of the bladder muscle and overflow incontinence may result in frequent urinary tract infections, and sexual potency may be an issue (albeit a treatable one) for elderly men.

Considering treatment

The level of care may be basic or intensive.

✔ **Basic care** is meant to prevent the acute problems of diabetes like excessive urination and thirst. You can accomplish this goal by keeping the blood glucose under 200 mg/dl (11.1 mmol/l). Basic care is used for an elderly diabetic who isn't expected to live very long because of the diabetes or other illnesses.

✔ **Intensive care** is meant to prevent diabetic complications in an elderly person expected to live long enough to have them. The goal here is to keep the blood glucose under 140 mg/dl (7.7 mmol/l) and the hemoglobin A1c as close to normal as possible while avoiding frequent hypoglycemia.

Treatment always starts with diet and exercise, and then medication is added if necessary. Exercise may be limited in the elderly person with diabetes, however.

A patient who is transferred from self-care to institutional care may require a significant reduction in medication because he or she may not have been taking the medication properly.

Managing Menopause

Menopause refers to that point in a woman's life when your body stops menstruating. In addition to changes in your period, menopause produces changes that affect your entire body:

- ✔ Due to a lack of estrogen, estrogen-sensitive organs (such as your uterus, ovaries, and breasts) shrink, while other estrogen-sensitive tissues (such as the vaginal walls and the tissue of the urethra) become thinner and less elastic.
- ✔ Bone mass begins to decrease.
- ✔ Skin becomes thinner and less elastic.

These changes may not produce symptoms, but if they do, they're likely to take some time to appear. Other symptoms, such as hot flashes, may occur immediately after estrogen production goes down.

Seven proven ways to deal with hot flashes

You hear all sorts of remedies for those dreaded hot flashes. But which really work? Here are some practical ways to deal with hot flashes that have proven effective for most women:

- ✔ **Avoid spicy foods, hot drinks, caffeine, and alcohol:** All these can trigger hot flashes.
- ✔ **Change your blankets:** Use a light blanket and sheet at night.
- ✔ **Dress lightly:** Wear layers that you can take off when you get too hot.

- ✔ **Keep cool:** Turn room temperatures to a low setting.
- ✔ **Exercise:** Women who exercise regularly report fewer hot flashes.
- ✔ **Reduce stress:** Practice stress reduction techniques, such as meditation and yoga.
- ✔ **Keep a journal:** Track your flashes to see what your triggers are.

Hormone replacement therapy (HRT)

Hormone replacement therapy is just what its name implies — a therapy in which you take hormones to supplement or replace those you lose during menopause. Replenishing these hormones alleviates many of the effects of menopause. HRT is used to relieve menopausal symptoms, to treat and prevent osteoporosis, and to prevent heart disease. HRT comes in many forms.

- **Estrogen:** The main ingredient in HRT, not surprisingly, is estrogen. In fact, you may hear some people refer to HRT as estrogen replacement therapy, or ERT.

  Estrogen comes in several forms:

  - **Pills and patches:** Pills and patches provide estrogen systemically, which means that these forms are processed through your whole body and provide many of the health benefits we detail later in the chapter.

  - **Creams:** Estrogen cream is applied directly to, and affects only, the vagina and genital area. The cream is prescribed for women who have trouble with the drying and irritation of vaginal atrophy.

  - **Implants:** Still in development, the vaginal ring is inserted deep in the vagina where it continuously releases low amounts of estrogen. The vaginal ring is designed for women whose major complaints are vaginal atrophy and urinary problems.

- **Progesterone:** Estrogen isn't usually prescribed alone. Without progesterone to balance estrogen, your uterine lining (endometrium) builds up and thickens. Over the long term, this buildup can lead to an increased risk of abnormal cell growth or even endometrial cancer. However, if you've had your uterus removed, you may be prescribed estrogen alone, or *unopposed*. You may also receive estrogen alone in cream form. In most cases, estrogen is prescribed in combination with progesterone.

- **Male hormones:** In some cases, your doctor may recommend that you also take *androgens*. Before menopause, your ovaries not only produce estrogen, but they also produce male hormones. Once you reach menopause, both types of hormone production fall. At this point, experts don't know exactly how the loss of male hormones affects women, though it's thought that loss of sexual urge (libido), low energy, moodiness, nervousness, inability to sleep, and discontent may be due at least in some cases to a low level of male hormones. If estrogen replacement doesn't help offset these particular symptoms for you, your doctor may recommend the addition of male hormones.

The pros and cons of HRT

There's no question that taking hormone replacement therapy (HRT) relieves the symptoms of menopause, and for many women who take it, that's the issue. Over time, studies have been done on the long-term effects of taking HRT, and benefits and drawbacks have come to light. Consider the following:

- HRT relieves symptoms such as hot flashes and vaginal atrophy, helps cut your risk of developing heart disease, and prevents osteoporosis. Estrogen may also delay the onset and lower your risk of developing Alzheimer's disease, reduce tooth loss and macular degeneration (a leading cause of blindness among the elderly), and lower the risk of colon cancer.

- On the minus side, when estrogen is taken alone (without the counteraction of progesterone), it can cause your uterine lining to thicken and grow, which can ultimately lead to endometrial cancer. Taking progesterone along with estrogen reduces this risk.

- HRT may also increase gallbladder problems. Women on HRT are more likely to have their gallbladder removed than women who are not.

- The more controversial issue is HRT's impact on breast cancer. Although some studies have shown that HRT slightly increases the risk of breast cancer, others have shown no increase or even a reduced risk. The difficulty in establishing an HRT/breast cancer connection lies in the fact that no one yet knows what causes breast cancer and that some, but not all, forms of breast cancer depend on estrogen for growth. For this reason, women with breast cancer should not take HRT.

- HRT can pose problems for certain women, such as those with a history of blood clots, particularly if these clots occurred during pregnancy or during birth control use. Women with active liver disease and women with undiagnosed vaginal bleeding should also have a thorough workup before going on HRT.

Fighting vaginal dryness

Here are some ways to combat vaginal dryness.

- **Have more sex:** Frequent sex or masturbation helps maintain lubrication and vaginal elasticity.

- **Use lubrication:** Try water-based lubricants, such as K-Y Jelly.

- **Talk to your doc:** Your doctor can prescribe estrogen. Oral or patch forms of estrogen have benefits for your entire body, including the genital area, but estrogen creams inserted directly into the vagina will work faster to produce the desired local effect.

As scientists learn more about the specific effects of HRT on different parts of a woman's body, they will be able to develop therapy approaches that bypass the risks and still provide the benefits. This process has already begun. Products that are targeted specifically toward the prevention of osteoporosis and prevention of heart disease are already on the market.

Alternatives to HRT

If you can't take HRT or you decide against it, you can still do plenty of things to relieve menopausal symptoms and cut your health risks. A proper diet and exercise plan can help reduce your risk of both heart disease and osteoporosis. A healthy sex life can help reduce symptoms of vaginal atrophy. But that's only the beginning. Table 3-2 outlines some other non-HRT options for dealing with the risks and symptoms of menopause.

Table 3-2	Alternatives to HRT
Alternative	**Description**
Medications	If you opt against HRT, you can still opt for medical treatment. A large number of medications are available to treat heart disease. And in recent years, a number of medications have come on the market to prevent or slow the progression of osteoporosis. These medications are targeted primarily at postmenopausal women. Medications are also available to treat symptoms such as hot flashes and vaginal dryness.
	For hot flashes, your doctor may prescribe antihypertensives, or blood-pressure-lowering medications, which may provide relief to women with high blood pressure; and sedatives and tranquilizers, which relieve anxiety and have a calming effect.
	For vaginal dryness, your doctor may recommend vaginal lubricants.
Phytoestrogens	Some plant foods, such as soybeans, flax seed, and whole grains, contain chemicals that your body can convert to estrogen. These chemicals, known as phytoestrogens, or plant estrogens, offer only about $\frac{1}{400}$ the dose of a pharmaceutically prepared estrogen; however, in women who eat a diet high in the foods that contain them, they may reduce mild hot flashes. Bear in mind, though, that although phytoestrogens are natural, they are still a form of estrogen, and determining what dose you are getting is difficult. If you're considering phytoestrogens as an option, talk with your practitioner.

Alternative	Description
Herbs	Herbs have been used for years to treat a variety of conditions, including menopausal symptoms. Just because they are natural doesn't mean that they are always safe, however. Some can cause unexpected allergic or toxic reactions if they are taken in too large or too frequent a dose, and some can interact with other medications. You're wise to consult your doctor for recommendations of formulas and dosages. That said, the herbs sometimes used to relieve menopausal symptoms include the following: **Dong quai:** A phytoestrogen that is used to relieve hot flashes, breast tenderness, sore joints, insomnia, and anxiety. **Ginseng:** A phytoestrogen used to treat menopausal discomforts, stimulate the immune system, normalize blood pressure, and reduce cholesterol levels. **Black cohosh:** A phytoestrogenic herb whose root is used to relieve hot flashes, night sweats, vaginal dryness, incontinence, irritability, anxiety, headaches, and depression. **Licorice root:** This herb may relieve vaginal dryness and hot flashes, possibly by balancing the estrogen-progesterone ratio, although scientific data doesn't exist.
Biofeedback	This psychological therapy uses the conscious mind to control involuntary body functions, such as respiration, heartbeat, and body temperatures. After training in the therapy, some women are able to reduce the frequency and severity of their hot flashes.
Alternative therapies	Other alternative therapies are also used to treat menopausal symptoms. These include *homeopathy, naturopathy, acupuncture,* and *acupressure.*
Attitude	Finally, remember that your attitude has a lot to do with your menopausal experience. If you approach menopause as an exciting new phase in your life rather than as an end to your youth, you may find the adjustment easier to make, regardless of what, if any, treatments you choose.

Sticking together: Getting help from associations

Sometimes you just need to talk to others who are going through the same thing you are — either to find out practical information about your condition or to get help coping. The following associations help you make those connections, as well as provide you with the professional medical information you need to make the important decisions facing you:

✔ www.alz.org: The Alzheimer's Association supports research into the prevention, treatment, and eventual cure for Alzheimer's disease. Find a chapter in your area to tap into services that include 24/7 information and referral, safety services, and education and support groups. The association also has helpful articles on how to maintain your brain now.

✔ www.arthritis.org: The Arthritis Foundation site explains the over 100 different types of arthritis and shows you how to assess your risks and symptoms. A useful surgery guide helps you decide when surgery is appropriate and what to prepare for pre- and post-operation. Another guide goes through the many types of doctors who specialize in treating arthritis and provides directories to locate someone right for you. Also check out the arthritis drug guide and the chat rooms where you can talk to others who have your condition.

✔ www.cancer.org: The American Cancer Society. This site lets you access a wealth of information about the different types of cancer and cancer statistics, as well as information on prevention and early detection. Learn what types of treatments are available, their risks and benefits, the possible side effects, and how to manage them. You can read up on new clinical trials and connect with other patients and survivors on the message boards or by finding groups meeting in your area.

✔ www.americanheart.org: The American Heart Association. Research heart diseases and conditions and register for your free, confidential, personalized treatment options report. You also have access to medical journal articles and research studies written in an easy-to-understand format. Other helpful tools include the cardiovascular disease risk assessment tool, a family history tree, and a heart healthy tracker for monitoring your blood glucose levels and blood pressure.

✔ www.diabetes.org: The American Diabetes Association. Research the different types of diabetes, their risks, and their symptoms. This site also has a huge section of nutritional and delicious recipes. You can search by meal category or by a particular ingredient. You can even print out a shopping list for the recipes you select. Helpful tip sheets provide you with ideas on how to lose weight, stay motivated, and maintain weight loss.

Chapter 4

Delving into Healing Foods

· ·

In This Chapter

▶ Setting up your healing foods kitchen

▶ Shopping at great places to find the best healing foods

▶ Discovering nature's best healing foods

▶ Treating medical problems with super healing foods

· ·

The earth naturally produces all sorts of healing foods. Fruits, grains, vegetables, beans, nuts, seeds, as well as meats, fish, and poultry contain nutrients that help ensure good health. These ingredients as they are found in nature are called *whole foods,* because they have all their parts. The advantage of eating whole foods is that you're more likely to consume all the nutrients a food actually contains, and in the right proportions. A refined food will be missing some of these. For example, a whole grain that is unrefined retains its nutritious germ and fiber-rich bran. In contrast, a refined grain has had its germ and bran taken away. You only get to eat the starchy part that's left.

What about products that are fortified with nutrients that have been removed? Well, some compounds that occur naturally in foods haven't even yet been discovered, so there is no way a product will be enriched with these. Far better to go with the original food and benefit from nature's complete package.

Before we get into which foods are the best and why, we're going to offer some ideas for setting up your kitchen and some tips for preparing food healthfully.

Giving Yourself a Healthy Place to Cook

If you really want to make changes in how you prepare food, don't just cook with healthy foods. Make sure that your kitchen is a healing place as well. Working in a kitchen that doesn't suit you can be stressful, and stress is known to weaken the immune system. Fix up your kitchen so that it suits you.

Simplify storage. Give yourself good lighting and fresh air. Use nontoxic cleaning agents and avoid those that contain chemicals linked to various ailments. Bring a fresh clarity and cleanliness to your work space. Walking into your kitchen should be a pleasure, and an invitation to start cooking!

Your environment is an expression of where you are in your life. Making your kitchen as comfortable as possible can lessen stress and give you breathing room to cook daily meals. Once your kitchen is comfortable to work in, you may even eat more meals at home, which are probably healthier than the ones you eat out. Whether you happen to be building a new kitchen, remodeling an old one, or just wishing that you could fiddle with the kitchen you're stuck with, here are some pointers to keep in mind:

- ✔ **Decide whether you want an open kitchen where people can gather around an island and socialize as you cook, or a closed kitchen where you can close the door for privacy.**
- ✔ **Consider your height when you are planning counters.**
- ✔ **Design a spacious kitchen.**
- ✔ **Give yourself ample storage space.**
- ✔ **Reduce clutter.**
- ✔ **Make sure that your kitchen has proper lighting.**

A grotty kitchen is a downer, an uninviting room that drains your energy, not to mention that it's not sanitary and may harbor bacteria. Treat yourself to a sparkling-clean kitchen, a space that inspires healthy cooking. Wash the shelves, mop the floor, and get up your courage to look behind the refrigerator. Just make your best effort to ensure that the cleansers, degreasers, disinfectants, and polishes in your broom closet don't contain potentially harmful chemicals, including benzene, xylene, naphthalene, phenol, and carbon-based compounds (VOCs) that release from cleaning agents as gasses.

Cooking in Healthy Ways

As important as buying healthy ingredients is preparing your meals made from those ingredients in healthy ways. You can turn healing foods into less-than-healthy dishes just by the way you cook them. It pays to understand how different cooking techniques affect the nutritional value of various foods.

- ✔ **Steaming** is great for vegetables.
- ✔ **Boiling** vegetables results in nutrients escaping into the cooking liquid. Add this cooking liquid to soup, and you can still benefit from these nutrients.

How risky is grilling?

When you grill, the fat melts, drips down onto the charcoal or wood chips, sizzles as it heats to super-hot temperatures, and then begins to undergo chemical changes that produce a substance called benzopyrene. In animal studies, benzopyrene has proven to be carcinogenic. As smoke from the coals rises, the benzopyrene is carried with it and deposits on your chops!

How much of a risk is grilling food? Very slight, say some experts, if you eat grilled foods only occasionally. However, eating barbecued foods regularly coupled with the vast array of chemicals you are exposed to daily may change the odds. If you want to add a charred, smoky flavor to food, a healthier alternative is smoking meat, a process that generates fewer toxins.

✔ **Poaching** foods such as fish, poultry, vegetables, and fruit in a small amount of liquid collects nutrients into the relatively small amount of liquid used and also keeps the food moist. You can reduce this liquid to make a nutrient-rich sauce.

✔ **Stewing** foods such as meats and poultry over a period of time breaks down these foods so that you can easily digest their protein and absorb the nutrients. And all the juices become the broth.

✔ **Sautéing** at low temperatures in a small amount of butter or oil is a gentle way to cook chops, chicken parts, and seafood.

✔ **Stir-frying,** which uses only a small amount of fat, is a method of quick cooking that preserves nutrients. Use it for preparing meats, poultry, seafood, and vegetables.

✔ **Baking** requires no fat, and nutrients are retained.

✔ **Grilling** adds intense flavor to slimming foods such as vegetables, fish, and chicken breasts without requiring the addition of fat. But grilling is a mixed blessing. Cooking fatty foods over charcoal or wood chips can generate carcinogenic compounds that can end up in your food (see the sidebar "How risky is grilling?").

Shopping in Good Places

Your supermarket is a fine source for such natural and whole foods as fruits, vegetables, and fresh herbs; whole grains, such as brown rice; many kinds of dried beans, lentils, and peas; and bottles of filtered water. You may also find wild rice, raw nuts and seeds, 100 percent rye pumpernickel bread, soba buckwheat noodles, corn tortillas, fresh soybeans, and fresh-made fruit and vegetable juices. Even organic fruits and vegetables are beginning to sneak into produce sections of many supermarkets. And you may find naturally raised chicken.

Table 4-1 lists products we spotted in a tour of our neighborhood supermarkets. Some of the brands listed are free of additives, others are unrefined or organic and don't contain caffeine, hydrogenated oils, or added sugars.

Table 4-1	Healing Foods in Your Supermarket
If You're Shopping For . . .	*Check Out This (These) Brand(s) . . .*
Breakfast cereal (organic)	General Mills
Breakfast cereal (whole grain)	Quaker Oats, Weetabix, Familia, McCanns, Roman Meal
Brown rice	Carolina
Buckwheat	Wolff's
Dairy foods	Horizon, Alta Dena
Eggs	EggLand's Best, Naturally Nested, Saunders
Extra-virgin olive oil	Bertolli, Colavita
Fruit juice	R.W. Knudsen, Martinelli's, Sunsweet
Fruit spreads	Smucker's, Polanar, Dickinson's
Herbal and green teas	Lipton, Good Earth, Bigelow
Maple syrup	Maple Grove Farms
Pilaf packaged mixes	Near East
Raisins (preservative-free)	Sun-Maid, Dole
Raw nuts	Diamond, Flanagan Farms
Spaghetti sauce	Newman's Own, Five Brothers
Whole-wheat bread and bagels	Oroweat, the Baker, Matthews
Whole-wheat crackers	ak-mak Bakeries, Carr's

Three additives to avoid

Over 2,000 additives are approved for use in the manufacture of food products. Most are added to preserve the food, make it easier to prepare, or to enhance the appearance of the food to make it more appealing to a potential customer. Relatively little is known about the health hazards of most of these chemicals, especially their long-term effects.

Here are three such additives to avoid:

- ✔ **MSG:** A suspected neurotoxin is monosodium glutamate (MSG), a flavor enhancer, which is also present in such substances as hydrolyzed vegetable protein (HVP).

- ✔ **Aspartame:** Aspartic acid, found in aspartame marketed under the name NutraSweet, can also cause an MSG-type reaction.

- ✔ **Sulfites:** Some individuals are sensitive to sulfites, a common additive. Reactions can range from diarrhea and nausea to acute asthma attacks, loss of consciousness, and *anaphylactic shock,* an allergy-like reaction.

  The highest levels of sulfites exist on dried fruit, in fruit juices made from concentrates, dehydrated potatoes, molasses (unless otherwise specified), and possibly some canned foods served in restaurants.

Animal studies indicate that when several additives are present in the animal feed, as they are in the foods you eat, health is undermined more than when additives are ingested one at a time. Not enough is known about which additives may be carcinogenic or toxic to the nerves and brain. You can sidestep the issue by simply increasing the amount of natural, unprocessed foods in your diet.

Eight great natural-food stores

You probably have a natural-food store in your area. These food stores are popping up in many cities and towns as the demand for healthy food increases. You may have in your area a branch of one of the several new and innovative chains of natural-food stores. Look for these store names:

- ✔ Wild Oats
- ✔ Bread & Circus
- ✔ Fresh Fields
- ✔ Bread of Life
- ✔ Merchant of Vino
- ✔ Wellspring Grocery
- ✔ Whole Foods
- ✔ Trader Joe's

You'll find that the great majority of foods for sale at natural-food stores are natural, whole, organic, unadulterated with chemical additives, and minimally processed. Browsing the aisles, you're sure to find unusual soups, interesting packaged pilafs, whole-grain breakfast cereals galore, a wide selection of nuts and seeds, raw honey, naturally raised chicken and meats, and on and on.

Mother Nature's Best Foods

The following sections describe the healing benefits of the best foods nature has to offer.

Whole grains

The health benefits of whole grains are well documented. According to an article published in the American Journal of Clinical Nutrition in 1999, various studies show that eating whole grains reduces the risk of the following:

- ✔ Coronary heart disease
- ✔ Diabetes
- ✔ Hypertension
- ✔ Some types of cancer

For example, whole wheat is a great source of B vitamins, which are important for liver function and the health of the nervous system; vitamin E, a potent antioxidant that also promotes heart health; magnesium, which helps sustain a steady heartbeat; zinc, which provides energy; fiber, which facilitates healthy bowel function; essential fatty acids, which transport oxygen to the cells; and more than 16 other major and trace minerals that are involved in all sorts of activities throughout the body.

When flour is made from whole wheat, all these nutrients remain in the final product. The reason is that the entire kernel of wheat is milled, and all three of its primary parts — the germ, the bran, and the endosperm — are ground into flour.

- ✔ The **germ,** which is the portion of the grain that sprouts when the grain is planted, contains fat-soluble vitamins E and K, essential oils, a range of minerals, and some protein.
- ✔ The **bran,** which is the outer covering of the kernel, consists of fiber, plus some protein, B vitamins, and minerals, particularly iron.
- ✔ The **endosperm,** which makes up the bulk of each grain, is mostly starch.

But guess what happens when whole wheat is refined to make flour? The germ and bran are removed! (The wheat is also bleached to make the flour white.) This process eliminates the risk that the oils in the wheat will turn rancid, lengthening the shelf life of the flour and any baked goods made from it. This is just what a manufacturer wants, but the person eating such food is shortchanged. Flour that is missing the germ and the bran is also missing vitamins, minerals, and fiber.

Combating gluten sensitivity

Gluten is a protein in flour that gives dough its elastic quality. It's part of the reason bread rises. Wheat is high in gluten, but rye, oat, and barley also contain varied amounts.

Some individuals, especially as they age, develop a sensitivity to grains and baked goods that contain gluten. Enjoying a lovely croissant made with wheat flour can result in intestinal distress, fatigue, and brain fog.

If you are sensitive to gluten, we have great news for you: A whole host of helpful information is available on the Internet to help you manage your special diet needs.

One great site to check out is www.gluten free.com. The site lets you search for retailers who carry their Gluten-Free Pantry products, and the folks who put together the site even provide free recipes and support for gluten-sensitive readers. You can find many other Web sites for the gluten disinclined simply by typing "gluten sensitivity" into your favorite search engine.

When shopping for grains, including bread, flour, pasta, rice, and more, look for the word *whole,* which means that all three nutritious parts of the kernel are present in the product. Only a whole grain is a complex carbohydrate, the original with all its parts. A refined grain is just a carbohydrate, and it's less nutritious. You sometimes hear and see "complex carbohydrate" used loosely, referring to a food made from refined grain and flour. Now you know the difference!

Applauding legumes

Beans, peas, and lentils belong to a single class of foods termed *legumes* or *pulses.* Beans offer the following health benefits:

✔ Beans offer a nonmeat source of high-quality protein. If you're looking for the perfect diet food, beans are the answer!

✔ By eating beans, you also increase your intake of fiber: what your great-grandmother called "roughage" — that is, bulk.

✔ Beans supply B vitamins, such as thiamin for memory, calcium and boron for bones, iron for energy, potassium for reducing high blood pressure, and zinc for immunity. They are an excellent source of folic acid, which is essential for cell division and is required by women during pregnancy. Beans also contain protease inhibitors, which are known to prevent the development of cancerous cells. Unlike many vegetables, beans still retain most of their nutrients even after long cooking.

Standard, canned, barbecued beans are normally swimming in a sugary sauce that supplies plenty of calories. They have all the nutritional shortcomings of any sugar-coated food.

Getting bushels of health benefits from fruits and vegetables

Fruits and vegetables contain vitamins and minerals that are essential for health. Once inside your body, vitamins and minerals don't just sit around giving off good vibes. They go to work, participating in thousands of critical chemical reactions that generate energy, build tissue, and generally run the goings on in your body. Many scientific studies testify to the health-protective effects of fruits and vegetables.

For example, fruits and vegetables that are especially beneficial for your heart include

- Avocados
- Beet greens
- Broccoli
- Cabbage
- Cucumbers
- Figs
- Green peas
- Mushrooms
- Oranges
- Papayas
- Prunes

Meat's meat

How much protein from animal sources do you gobble up each day? Moderate portions are now the rule. The average person needs a total of about 65 g of protein a day. From animal sources, this is equivalent to one egg, one chicken leg, plus one hamburger patty the size of the palm of your hand. However, grains, beans, and other plant foods also supply protein, so if you're getting protein from plant foods, you need even less from animal sources.

Comparing various meats and poultry

You probably know that saturated fat is bad. You might point out that fat is a flavor carrier, so lean meat isn't as tasty as a fat-streaked center cut. But regardless, it's prudent to cut back on animal fats, which are saturated and solid at room temperature, because research shows that eating these fats can raise your cholesterol levels and clog your arteries, leading to heart disease.

Table 4-2 shows you how various meats and poultry compare in terms of calories, total fat, saturated fat, and cholesterol.

Table 4-2	Comparing Types of Meat and Poultry			
3-Ounce Portion	*Calories*	*Total Fat*	*Saturated Fat*	*Cholesterol*
Beef round	164	6.6 g	2.8 g	69 mg
Chicken dark meat	174	8.3 g	2.3 g	79 mg
Chicken light meat	147	3.8 g	1.1 g	72 mg
Lamb leg	162	6.6 g	2.4 g	76 mg
Pork loin chop	171	6.9 g	2.5 g	70 mg
Turkey dark meat	158	6.1 g	2.1 g	72 mg
Turkey light meat	133	2.7 g	.9 g	59 mg

Winning with game

Add variety to your diet by eating some game once in a while — quail, pheasant, wood pigeon or squab, rabbit, venison, buffalo, or ostrich. Upper-end supermarkets and some natural-food stores stock these foods, and they even show up at farmers markets. If you have a gourmet supermarket or butcher in your city, you may be able to special order elk, wild boar, and alligator. You can substitute rabbit for chicken in any recipe. You can also make a very acceptable curry dish by using buffalo.

Game is an excellent source of nutrients and lower in fat than most meats. Take a look at these comparisons:

✔ Most 3-ounce servings of cooked game contain 130 to 175 calories and only 2 to 5 g of fat, which is generally lower than in standard meats.

✔ Game contains about the same amount of cholesterol as other meats.

✔ Game contains a higher percentage of polyunsaturated fats, especially the omega-3 fatty acids, than most red meats because of the wild foods the animals eat. The omega-3s support the health of tissues throughout the body.

✔ Compared to other meats, game birds contain significantly more thiamin, vitamin B6, vitamin B12, calcium, phosphorous, potassium, and iron.

✔ The breast meat of one breed of duck, White Peking, is lower in fat than chicken breast if you don't eat the skin — but who can resist?

Commercially produced game may be given hormones and drugs just like herds of cattle and sheep are. Your butcher should be able to tell you how the game you're buying was raised.

Saving a place for seafood

Food from the sea is a more reliable source of minerals than food grown on the land because as farmland is overworked, minerals are depleted from the soil. The oceans, however, are still an abundant source of many major and trace minerals. Consider the following facts:

✔ Seafood such as cod, ocean perch, and lobster, to name just a few, supply calcium, copper, iodine, iron, magnesium, manganese, phosphorous, potassium, and zinc.

✔ Seafood contains a range of B vitamins, and the oilier fish, such as salmon and tuna, are good sources of the two fat-soluble vitamins, vitamin A and vitamin D. Herring and mackerel also contain vitamin E. When you choose to make a meal of seafood, your calories are well spent.

✔ Fish is not a fattening food, with many types of fish — such as turbot, bluefish, striped bass, pompano, and oysters — being relatively low in fat. In addition, fish is low in saturated fats, which are associated with heart disease, and high in the healthier polyunsaturated fats, such as the omega-3 essential fatty acids (more on omega-3s in a bit).

✔ Omega-3 fatty acids are found in abundance in the tissues of the brain, the nervous system, the eyes, and the sex and adrenal glands. They transport oxygen, remove cholesterol from arteries, prevent blood clots from forming, and lower blood pressure. And omega-3 fatty acids are anti-inflammatory. (Studies show that fish oils reduce the swelling and pain associated with joint diseases such as arthritis and rheumatoid arthritis.) The fattier a fish, the more omega-3 essential fatty acids it contains.

Caviar (fish eggs) is exceptionally high in omega-3s, but the following fish also deliver ample amounts: anchovies, herring, kippers (little smoked herrings), mackerel, salmon, sardines, and tuna.

As part of a healing foods diet, high-quality fish and shellfish belong on your menu two or three times a week.

Four extraordinary facts about eggs

Eggs are one of nature's finest products. What a shame that they've gotten such bad press recently! The worry is that cholesterol in the yolk promotes heart disease. But, in fact, the American Heart Association now okays eating up to four eggs a week as a general rule, even if you're watching your cholesterol. If you consume a predominantly vegetarian diet, you can eat even a few more.

If you have elevated cholesterol, you need to restrict the number of eggs you eat. For lunch, a tuna sandwich is a better choice than an egg salad sandwich.

The good news about eggs is pretty sensational:

- ✔ Eggs contain the highest quality protein of any known food. Eating egg protein in the morning can give you energy that lasts for hours.

- ✔ Eggs provide small to significant amounts of all needed vitamins, with the exception of vitamin C, and several minerals including iron, selenium, and zinc.

- ✔ One egg provides only 75 calories, and most of the fat in eggs is the healthier, unsaturated kind. In addition, the cholesterol that you consume when you eat an egg does not automatically increase the amount of cholesterol circulating in your blood.

The healthiest ways to cook eggs are poaching and soft-boiling. These methods minimize the effect that cooking has on an egg's cholesterol. (When cholesterol is exposed to heat and oxygen, it turns into a harmful substance.) Frying and scrambling eggs are the least healthy ways to prepare them.

Dairy products: A mixed blessing

Consider these pros and cons of dairy. Yogurt comes out on top, with the most health benefits, but milk and cheese can play a role in a healthy diet, as well.

- ✔ **Milk:** Most people who drink milk regularly do so for the calcium it contains. However, many people find that they are not able to drink milk comfortably because they are lactose intolerant or simply allergic to milk. Other reasons people avoid milk are because of the fat content or, if the fat has been removed, the issues with the remaining protein content. (When you remove the fat, you have first, altered the whole food product, and second, have a relatively concentrated source of protein. A high-protein diet can be a risk factor for osteoporosis.)

✔ **Cheese:** Like milk, cheese is a high-calcium food and a good source of vitamin A (important for immunity as well as eyesight). Cheese has a place in a generally healthful diet, enjoyed in small amounts as a condiment or to accent a meal. If you are sensitive to milk, you may also have problems with cheese. However, cheese that is higher in fat is less likely to trigger an allergic response. Fat slows the emptying time of the stomach, which is well-known clinically to reduce the allergic effect.

In addition, because the fat slows the absorption of food into your system, fatty cheese curtails how much insulin you produce and helps to keep blood sugar levels steady. Keeping control over insulin and blood sugar benefits the heart and helps you not gain weight. When you eat low- and nonfat cheese, your insulin output is more likely to increase and lead to medical problems. Better to eat regular cheese with all its fat, but only small amounts at a time.

✔ **Yogurt:** Yogurt — not the sugary-flavored, fruit-mixed-in, or fruit-on-the-bottom kind, but plain yogurt — belongs in your refrigerator as a staple. Yogurt is high in calcium, and if you're lactose intolerant, you may have less difficulty digesting this milk product.

Finding the finest fats and the best oils

Of all food categories, fats are undoubtedly the most talked about, written about, worried about, measured, manipulated, and misunderstood. Here's what you need to keep in mind:

✔ High-quality fats and oils are healthy, and your body needs them to function properly.

✔ Poor-quality fats and oils are unhealthy, and you should go out of your way to avoid them.

✔ You may need to cut back on the quantity of fatty foods you're eating, but quality is all-important.

Fats (such as butter, which is solid at room temperature, and cooking oils, which are liquid at room temperature) are fragile substances. Heat, oxygen, and especially light can attack and break down their structure. In fact, light can break down oils a thousand times faster than oxygen. Cooking fats at high temperatures, as in frying, converts a perfectly acceptable fat into a poisonous toxin. The way cooking oils are commonly processed and refined also produces a product that contains toxic compounds, and such oils are also stripped of nutrients.

The benefits of cholesterol-reducing margarine

The fact that margarine is not healthier than butter is old news. The fact that butter is not healthy is also old news. But gone are the days when you had to eat your bread dry. The newest spreads that claim to reduce cholesterol actually work. The first of these to hit the market was the highly beneficial Benecol. Many brands now flood the supermarket shelves and are worth checking out.

High-quality fats are a source of fat-soluble vitamins, minerals, lecithin, essential fatty acids, phytohormones, and natural antioxidants. The quality fats and oils described in the following list deserve a place on your table.

- **Unsalted butter:** The virtue of organic butter, besides its delectable flavor, is that it's relatively unprocessed and stable at high temperatures and does not form toxic compounds such as transfatty acids. Butter is also a source of vitamin A and some vitamin E, a natural antioxidant that helps prevent it from going rancid.

- **Extra-virgin olive oil:** Extra-virgin olive oil is the first pressing of the olives, made without heat or chemicals. Nutrients are retained, and the oil is not likely to contain transfatty acids. Olives are high in monounsaturated fats, which are associated with a lower incidence of heart disease, and they are the star ingredient of what has been identified by researchers as the healthful Mediterranean diet. Compared to polyunsaturated fats, such as those found in safflower oil, corn oil, and soybean oil, monounsaturated fats are less likely to oxidize — a process that may contribute to narrowing of the arteries.

Seeds and nuts: Concentrated nourishment

Birds and squirrels search about for seeds and nuts to sustain themselves and to store away for future meals. These creatures are after the array of nutrients that seeds and nuts contain. What a contrast with our own eating habits, with nuts demoted to cocktail snacks and seeds having the connotation of hippie health food. If the only nuts you eat are the peanuts handed out in little packets on airplanes, you have a whole category of food to discover!

Some nuts have exceptionally high amounts of certain nutrients. For example:

- **Pistachios** are high in folic acid, which is essential during pregnancy.

- **Almonds, hazelnuts,** and **Brazil nuts** are especially high in vitamin E, a fat-soluble vitamin that helps ease a woman's passage through menopause.

- **Almonds, pistachios, hazelnuts,** and **pumpkin seeds** provide calcium and magnesium, both of which are needed to maintain the structure of bones and prevent osteoporosis.

- **Sunflower seeds** and **pistachios** are high in iron, which makes the transport of oxygen in the blood possible.

- **Chestnuts** and **sunflower seeds** provide potassium, a mineral that helps regulate blood pressure.

- **Pumpkin seeds** and sesame seeds supply zinc, used by the prostate gland to produce fertile sperm.

- **Brazil nuts** are unique in that they are a superb source of selenium, a trace mineral that functions as an antioxidant and protects against heart disease.

Seeds and nuts also contain special compounds that ward off disease. Flax seeds have anti-tumor properties and are linked to a low incidence of colon and breast cancer. In addition, flax seeds contain phytoestrogens, which help balance hormone levels. The ellagic acid in walnuts has anti-cancer properties, as does oleic acid, found in almonds. Studies have linked a low intake of nuts and seeds, which provide vitamin E, with a greater risk of Parkinson's disease. Nuts also contain magnesium, an essential mineral for bone health.

Selecting the healthiest beverages

Hands down, water is your best beverage choice. But the following list explores your other options, as well.

- **Water:** Water is the ideal beverage. It replenishes fluids in the system, but because water doesn't need to be digested or metabolized by the body, it provides benefits with a minimum expenditure of energy. Water is a primary and fundamental nutrient, just like protein, fat, and carbohydrates. The reason for this is that water does much more than quench thirst. Water's crucial functions within the body include the following:

  - Transports vitamins and minerals

  - Takes part in water-dependent chemical reactions

  - Plays a role in energy production

  - Acts as an adhesive to bond cell structures

  - Provides lubrication around joints

  - Serves as a shock absorber inside the spinal cord and eyes

  - Acts as a solvent for substances, such as mineral salts, that maintain the vital balance between acidity and alkalinity in body tissues

✔ **Ginger:** Warms the body, increases circulation, promotes sweating and the release of toxins from the body for the treatment of colds and flu, aids digestion, eases arthritis pain, and helps lessen the risk of clogged arteries. Ginger has been found to relieve the nausea that comes with seasickness or as a side effect of anesthesia. Even the amount of ginger in gingersnaps or ginger ale may be adequate to relieve mild queasiness.

✔ **Mustard seed:** Stimulates appetite, aids digestion, relieves chronic constipation, and helps arrest the onset of a cold. Mustard is a relative of broccoli and cabbage, and its active constituents are mustard oils, which contain allyl-isothiocyanate. To benefit from mustard's healing properties, add one of the many varieties now available — French Dijon, whole-grain German mustard, English mustard powder, and American ballpark mustard — to salad dressings, roasted meats, vegetables, and sandwiches.

Mustard greens are considered a traditional tonic for the liver. Many groceries now carry this vegetable, a standard ingredient in Southern cooking.

✔ **Turmeric:** Reduces inflammation, making it useful in the treatment of such conditions as hay fever, muscle injury, and arthritis. Also treats itchiness and skin disease when applied externally, according to ayurvedic medical treatises dating back 3,000 years. The active component of brightly colored, yellow-orange turmeric is curcumin, which in studies has been shown to be as effective at reducing inflammation as common anti-inflammatory drugs, but without the side effects.

Three condiments that deliver more than flavor

Certain foods used as flavorings also have medicinal value. For example, onion and garlic have long been revered for their many healing properties. Condiments such as chili peppers, horseradish, licorice, and certain sweeteners also provide unique health benefits. Ancient peoples recognized the value of these foods, paying them ceremonial honor. King Tut was entombed with piles of licorice.

The following condiments have medicinal value that you want to be aware of:

✔ **Chili peppers:** Warm the body, promote good digestion, act as a mild diuretic to help remove toxins, and used to treat respiratory ailments.

Capsaicin, one of the compounds that give hot peppers their bite, has powerful medicinal properties. Capsaicin dampens pain and is administered as a cream to reduce the pain of shingles and arthritis. Capsaicin also stimulates the flow of digestive juices, thereby protecting the lining of the stomach from damage by acids and alcohol. Research also suggests that capsaicin lowers blood pressure and can even play a role in blocking the development of cancer.

✔ **Horseradish root:** Promotes urination and removal of toxins, stimulates circulation, strengthens immunity, fights bacterial infection in the lungs and urinary tract, and treats gout and rheumatism. The healing properties of hot-tasting horseradish root are due to the mustard oil it contains. To benefit from horseradish, you need to use the fresh root. Horseradish root is not recommended for persons who have low thyroid function or who are taking thyroxine.

✔ **Licorice root:** Lessens bronchial congestion, helps balance estrogen to curtail symptoms of PMS and menopause, and treats inflammation associated with asthma and allergies. It also helps heal ulcers, supports liver and kidney function, promotes cardiovascular health, acts as an antidote to toxins such as diphtheria and tetanus, and fights bacterial and viral infection, including hepatitis B. Licorice root is an excellent source of vitamin C and beta-carotene.

Five natural and nutritious sweeteners

You do have options if you have a sweet tooth. The following sweeteners also provide some vitamins and minerals, and some, like honey, even have a medicinal effect.

However, don't kid yourself. All these foods are sugars, and eating these sweeteners in quantity will have the same effect on your system. Sugars of all sorts cause insulin levels to rise. (Insulin is the hormone that manages blood sugar and allows you to store sugar in your cells for later use.) And abnormally high levels of insulin can lead to medical problems, including diabetes, hypertension, atherosclerosis, and coronary artery disease. If you do use sweeteners, use them in moderation.

✔ Maple syrup

✔ Date sugar

✔ Blackstrap molasses

✔ Honey

✔ Stevia (Stevia is an herb that grows primarily in South America, where it has been used as a sweetener for more than 600 years. Although stevia is noncaloric, it is 250 to 300 times sweeter than sugar. You can find stevia in natural-food stores.)

Treating Medical Problems with Super Healing Foods

Used properly, the following foods can help treat medical problems:

✔ **Waking-up strategies:**

- Refresh yourself with water.

- Eat foods that contain energizing nutrients, such as most whole foods. Fill your refrigerator and your dinner plate with an array of fresh fruits and vegetables. Go out of your way to eat whole grains. Select leaner cuts of meat, cut back on red meats, and eat more fish. Beans are an excellent low-fat, protein alternative. Nuts and seeds supply vitamins, minerals, and essential fatty acids and provide protein, too.

- Eat breakfast. Breakfast is a particularly important meal in terms of how much energy you have throughout the day, so don't short-change yourself. Eat a real meal. If you eat only something starchy, like toast or an English muffin, and wash it down with coffee, you'll have energy for a couple of hours at most. Instead, give yourself some protein and fat as well. Foods that supply protein and fat burn more slowly than carbohydrates and can keep your body, and your brain, going until lunch. If you're a slow starter in the morning, you particularly need to make the effort to feed yourself.

✔ **Improving your mood with food:**

- **Calming down:** Eating carbohydrates such as potatoes, cereals, and sweets can help you feel relaxed and give you a sense of general well-being. When you're all worked up, have a couple of hand-fuls of popcorn or one or two slices of whole-grain bread with all-fruit preserves.

- **Perking up:** If you're feeling lackluster and not up to speed, you may need protein foods. When you compose a protein meal to increase your alertness, limit your intake of fat and carbohydrates for maximum effect. For example, have some tuna or snack on a cup of plain yogurt.

- **Cheering up:** Feeling a little depressed can be linked to poor nutrition. Both sugar and caffeine give you an energy lift, but the up is always followed by a down. These foods have a depressant effect, as does alcohol.

- **Steadying blood sugar levels:** Low blood sugar, or hypoglycemia, can leave you low on energy, and it can also trigger emotions. Eat three meals a day and, if necessary, a mid-morning and mid-afternoon snack. In addition, at each meal, include protein, complex carbohydrates, and fats, and avoid all concentrated sweets, including refined white table sugar, honey, maple syrup, and fruit juice. Have whole fruit instead.

- **Balancing female hormones:** Phytohormones, which are hormone-like compounds found in foods, can help minimize the swings in hormone levels. Eating more plant-food-based meals adds phytohormones to your diet. Specific foods that are high in phytohormones include soybeans, currants, and buckwheat.

✔ **Eating for a healthy heart:** You probably know the standard advice about watching your intake of fat, cholesterol, and sodium. General recommendations are painted in broad strokes. But the details about what to eat are also important to know. For example, some fats are associated with a lower risk of heart disease; eating a lot of sugar is another risk factor; certain forms of cholesterol are more harmful than others; antioxidant vitamins are especially healthful; and high blood pressure is associated with several minerals, not just sodium.

✔ **Reducing your risk of cancer at every meal:** Research shows that the right sort of diet, when coupled with a healthy weight and regular exercise, can help prevent about 30 to 40 percent of cancer cases worldwide. In particular, eating fresh fruits and vegetables appears to protect you from most forms of cancer. General population studies show that people who eat five or more servings a day have half the cancer risk of people who eat just two servings a day.

Conversely, research shows that people with cancer have lower intakes of raw and fresh fruits and vegetables. In particular, they eat less citrus, leafy green vegetables, carrots, lettuce, and cruciferous vegetables such as broccoli and cabbage. Intake of fiber and whole grains may also help prevent some forms of cancer.

✔ **Fighting arthritis pain with foods and supplements:** Which fruits, vegetables, meat, or fish should you eat? There are no absolute rules, but the results of studies and case histories suggest that these foods may be helpful: anchovies, apples, cantaloupe, chili peppers, curry, fish, garlic, grapes, mango, nuts, papaya, water, and omega-3 fatty acids.

Antioxidants

Given that oxidized cholesterol appears to be the culprit in cardiovascular disease, researchers have turned their attention to the antioxidant vitamins beta-carotene, vitamin C, vitamin E, and selenium. Although the findings of this research have not been totally consistent, the results generally demonstrate that a diet high in antioxidants is associated with a significantly lower risk of heart disease, as well as a lower incidence of signs of heart disease such as chest pain or angina pectoris.

You may decide to take an antioxidant supplement, but eating a variety of foods that supply antioxidant nutrients is still necessary.

Creating your own meals from healing foods

So you know that you need to eat your blueberries and your broccoli. These free-recipe sites provide you with a way to do that:

✔ www.pccnaturalmarkets.com: This site is an online health food store (which you may find helpful), but click on the Recipes link to get to the free section. You can search recipes by the healing ingredient you want to use, by an allergen or condition (egg-free, wheat-free, or diabetic recipes), by the meal course (dessert or entrée), or by any combination of these.

✔ www.rwood.com: This site is a selection of free, healing food recipes from published author Rebecca Wood. You can also find FAQs about healing foods and kitchen remedies for minor conditions.

✔ www.allrecipes.com: You'll find some unhealthy recipes here, but skip them like a good kid and go quickly to the healthy food section, which has diabetic, heart healthy, and lo-cal recipes. You can also check out reader ratings and reviews for each of the recipes — a helpful feature when you're wondering whether that broccoli bake is really worth making.

✔ www.heart.kumu.org: Check out free recipes for healthy heart appetizers, entrees, and desserts. Recipes include helpful preparation hints and nutritional information. A nice feature is that the recipes are ready for printing on a single page — no superfluous tool bars or links cluttering up your recipe.

✔ www.wholehealthmd.com/hk: The Healing Kitchen at WholeHealthMD is a little different from the other sites in this list. It matches common ailments with the particular healing foods related to them and then gives you four to five recipes rich in those healing foods. Or you can browse recipes by course, special diet, or key ingredient. The site also tells you how to buy and store healing foods for the best nutrition.

Part II
Great Fitness Strategies at 50 and Beyond

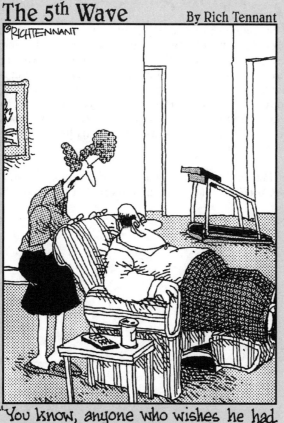

The 5th Wave   By Rich Tennant

"You know, anyone who wishes he had a remote control for his exercise equipment is missing the idea of exercise equipment."

In this part . . .

You may be 50 or even 60, but with the tips in this part you'll feel 20 years younger. The health benefits of regular exercise and a heart-healthy diet are well documented, but the surplus of information available can be intimidating. This part gives you the basics: Just what you need to know to get started, whether you're looking to take up a simple walking program, venture into the world of yoga or Pilates, or increase your heart health by eating a healthier diet.

The chapters in this part get you geared up and ready to move. You'll be off the couch and on your feet in no time!

Chapter 5

Feeling as Fit as a 20-Year-Old

. . . .

In This Chapter

▶ Understanding the benefits of regular exercise

▶ Incorporating the three types of exercise into your program

▶ Planning for success

. . . .

*W*e have some news for you: You can feel as fit as a fiddle — like you did 20 or 30 years ago. That's right. If you make the effort to trade your sedentary lifestyle for one that contains the crucial component — physical activity — there's no reason why you can't turn back the hands of your body clock.

We concede that aging is inevitable, and yes, we're all going to die some day. But those facts don't mean that you have to shuffle off into old age all shriveled up, walking with a cane and looking for the nearest park bench to sit down on.

If you're in your early forties, you can feel as fit as you did when you were in your mid-twenties; if you're in your late fifties, there's no reason why you can't match the physical fitness you enjoyed on the first anniversary of your 39th birthday. No, you won't ever measure up to the fitness peak you enjoyed during your late adolescence, but you can reclaim lost years if you start exercising today.

The Benefits Are Hardly Marginal

When you are physically fit, you

✔ Reduce your risk of dying prematurely (especially from heart disease).

✔ Reduce your risk of developing high blood pressure.

✔ Reduce your risk of developing colon cancer.

✔ Reduce your feelings of depression and anxiety.

✔ Help control your weight.

✔ Help build and maintain healthy bones, muscles, and joints.

✔ Become stronger and better able to perform tasks.

✔ Promote your psychological well-being.

Six ways exercise can reduce stress

Exercise is an excellent antidote to stress. Here are some examples of how exercise may help reduce your daily stresses:

✔ Huffing and puffing on the treadmill, for example, blows off steam like a teakettle.

✔ Walking in the quiet of the morning helps you prepare for your day by giving you time to think about your schedule — what you need to accomplish, whom you need to call, and what appointments you must keep.

✔ An energetic tennis game during the work day stimulates the mind and provides a mental break from reading reports and crunching numbers.

✔ A low-intensity sport like golf provides a welcome change of scenery from the home or office.

✔ Exercising after work — instead of sitting in frustrating rush-hour traffic — may be a two-for-one way to reduce stress: (1) You exercise, and (2) you drive when less traffic is on the road.

✔ Doing yard work or going on a spring cleaning binge may provide a quick-fix for your stress. You also feel some degree of accomplishment.

Four ways that being fit helps your sex life

Sex enriches your life in a unique way. Making love is a form of "sexercise" — an athletic activity that has physical release. The act of making love is good for the heart and muscles, reduces stress, and induces feelings of happiness and well-being. An active sex life may motivate couples to maintain their fitness levels — or lose those "love handles."

If the physical relationship is important to you, being physically fit enhances your experience as follows:

✔ Getting fit and losing weight can increase your sexual appetite.

✔ A fitness program tones your body, results in weight loss, boosts your energy level, and leaves you feeling healthy.

✔ For men, working out isn't going to cure impotence, but the strong heart that results from regular exercise increases blood flow and circulation in your reproductive area, and that increased blood flow helps you remain virile and effective under the bedsheets.

✔ For women, physical activity energizes you in your pre- and post-menopausal years, and even helps offset the symptoms of each.

The Big Three: Aerobic, Anaerobic, and Stretching Exercises

You always want to include these three forms of exercise in your regimen:

✔ **Aerobic:** The body is said to be working aerobically when it operates at a pace that allows the cardio-respiratory system (the lungs, heart, and bloodstream) to replenish energy as you exercise. Put another way, aerobic exercise causes the body to use oxygen to create energy. This is basically anything that gets the heart going, like walking on treadmills, cycling on stationary bikes, or stepping on stair-stepper machines.

✔ **Anaerobic:** Anaerobic exercise causes the body to make energy without oxygen because the demand for energy is so fast and huge that the body must create it from numerous natural body chemicals. Anaerobic exercise is any form of nonsustained physical activity that typically involves a limited number of specific muscles over a short time, such as strength training or lifting free weights.

✔ **Stretching:** Don't forget about this one. Stretching increases your range of motion and prevents muscle strain and injuries. Stretching helps your joints stay healthy, keeps circulation levels high, and allows you to recover more quickly from your workouts.

The heart of fitness: Aerobic exercise

The great thing about aerobic exercise is that you can mix 'n' match. You can embark on a Saturday afternoon hike in the mountains, golf on Sunday, walk on a treadmill on Tuesday, play tennis on Thursday, and use a stepper machine on Friday — and you'll be way ahead of the fitness curve.

Here's what you need to know about aerobic exercise:

✔ The American College of Sports Medicine recommends that aerobic activities be performed three to five times a week, for 20 to 60 minutes on each occasion.

✔ When performing aerobic exercise, you need to be aware of what the maximum heart rate and target heart rates are. For those of us over 40 years of age, our focal point should be reaching the "training zone" or target heart rate, which is the range between 60 percent and 80 percent of your maximum heart rate. Working within this zone gives you the maximum health and fat-burning benefits from your cardiovascular activity.

You can use Figure 5-1 to eyeball what your target heart rate should be. For a more precise method, go to healthchecksystems.com and calculate your minimum and maximum training heart rates based on whether you are a beginning, intermediate, or advanced exerciser.

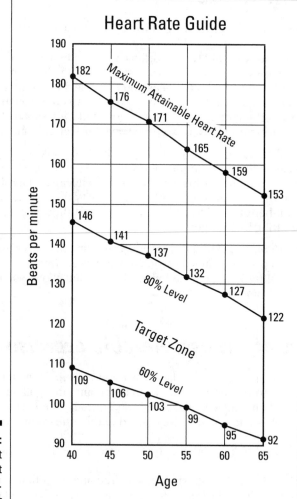

Figure 5-1: Figuring out your target heart rate.

✔ Most exercise machines (even those built for the home-equipment market) have a heart rate monitor in the electronic display. You grasp a metallic sensor, and the heart rate monitor immediately palpates your pulse. This allows you to monitor how fast your heart is beating without stopping on your treadmill, stair-stepper, or stationary bike.

✔ If you rely on walking through the neighborhood or thrice-weekly tennis games to raise your heart level, you should still monitor your heart rate to make sure that you're reaching the target zone. You can accomplish this in many ways, but we recommend using handheld pulse meters, which you hold in your hand, stick in your pocket, or affix to a piece of equipment. The heart rate monitor reads your pulse from your fingertip and displays the results digitally. Handheld pulse meters are cheap; many can be found for under $50.

Don't forget that your goal in all of this is to get inside your target heart rate range and stay there for at least 20 minutes. Do this three times a week, and you are well on the road to having a healthy heart.

The "no excuses" plan to an aerobic lifestyle

When you're working your heart at 60 to 80 percent of its maximum heart rate, you're engaging in *aerobic* exercise. But what if you don't have a clock handy to time your heart beats? Here's a simple way to gauge how hard you're working: If you're moving at a brisk pace, but you can still talk—that is, you're not breathless—then you are probably working aerobically.

Any ordinary activity can become aerobic. Take house cleaning, for example. Running a vacuum cleaner at a steady pace can get your heart rate up. So can cleaning windows or scrubbing the bathtub. And don't forget about yard work. Raking leaves, mowing the lawn, weeding your garden—all of these activities can be done in

such a way that they are aerobic. Just be sure to use large muscle groups and keep your pace of movement steady and—we'll say it again—brisk.

Here's some really great news: New research shows that you don't have to work 20 minutes consecutively to benefit from aerobic exercise; you can break it up into smaller chunks, and as long as the grand total for the day is 20 minutes, you benefit the same.

So forget your excuses—move briskly and get that heart rate up, and you'll feel 20 years younger in no time.

How you can benefit from strength training

Without adequate muscle exercise, most adults lose 20 to 40 percent of the muscle they had as young adults. With too much muscle loss, you have difficulties performing daily activities that allow you to live independently.

But with strength training, you can actually reverse the effects of aging on your muscles.

With better muscle condition, you have a better sense of balance, less risk of falls and fractures, and the ability to climb stairs or carry groceries. Strength training can even improve the strength of your bones and help you manage your weight well into your senior years.

The fitness heavyweight: Anaerobic exercise

Anaerobic exercise is usually accomplished through using strength-training machines such as Nautilus or Hoist or by lifting free weights — dumbbells and barbells raised without the guidance of a machine. But you don't have to lift weights to get some anaerobic exercise. Body weight exercises such as sit-ups, push-ups, or pull-ups can suffice.

Here are some of the benefits of strength training:

✔ Unless you incorporate some type of resistance strength training into your exercise schedule, you'll lose a half pound of muscle for every year past the age of 20. Even if you still weigh the same as you did 20 years ago, you've probably replaced 10 to 12 pounds of muscle with 10 to 12 pounds of fat. While aerobic exercise helps to burn excess fat, strength training is the only remedy to build muscle.

✔ Regarding bone mass, strength training cannot turn back the clock on osteoporosis after you have it, but recent research shows that regular strength training does maintain bone mass. It can even help those suffering from certain types of arthritis and chronic back pain.

✔ Anaerobic exercise in the form of lifting weights gives us the muscular strength to go through life with a minimum of discomfort and lower risk of injuries. Expending the effort today to build and maintain strength should give you the ability to live independently and function normally for years to come.

However you do it, just do it (sorry, Nike!). To lose weight and become fit when you're over 50, you must add anaerobic exercise to your fitness regimen.

The forgotten exercise: Stretching

You'll never go wrong by stretching before working out or playing a sport. You should even stretch before you start your day job because the improved circulation and greater range of motion will allow you to go about your daily tasks feeling better.

Stretching is easy to overlook because most individuals (present company included) perceive stretching to be tedious, boring exercise that's uncomfortable and downright painful. But stretching has many benefits. Here's what stretching can do for you:

- ✔ Increase your circulation and blood flow.

- ✔ Relax your body.

- ✔ Improve your coordination.

- ✔ Reduce your anxiety and stress; you feel mentally alert.

- ✔ Make your body less prone to injury (after you become more flexible), improve your range of motion, help you to recover from workouts more quickly; you just plain feel better.

Guys should know this about stretching: You need it more than women do. Men generally have less flexibility than women do because women have more of the muscle protein elastin, which promotes muscle flexibility.

Stretching is not a pleasant chore, but you're going to prevent a whole host of problems down the road if you do it regularly. Some exercise books and fitness gurus counsel stretching for 15 to 30 minutes, but this isn't realistic. Many of us cannot make the time commitment to stretch that long. But we can certainly stretch for several minutes before exercising or playing a sport.

Your Plan of Attack

You wouldn't start a business without a plan — a clear-cut idea of where you want to take your company and how you propose to get there. You assess your cash flow and expenses, choose a location for your office, decide on your hours of operation, and develop strategies to overcome obstacles.

The same is true of beginning an exercise program. You need to establish goals and have realistic expectations of what you can accomplish.

Setting your goals

When you start an exercise program, you need to set a few different types of goals. Look at the big picture while giving yourself stepping stones to get there. Having mini-goals makes your long-term goal seem more feasible. Here's a look at the different types of goals you should set.

✔ **Long-term goals:** Give yourself a realistic goal for the next three to six months. Some people get really creative with their long-term goals. Examples of long-term goals include:

- Complete a 50-mile bike ride that's four months away.
- Drop 3 percent body fat in 10 weeks.
- Do one full pull-up.
- Walk one mile in under 15 minutes.

✔ **Short-term goals:** Six months is a long time to wait for feelings of success. In order to stay motivated, you need to feel a sense of accomplishment along the way. Here are some examples:

- Take two step-aerobic classes a week for one month.
- Improve your one-mile walk time by 20 seconds.
- Use the stair-climber four times this week for 30 minutes each time.
- Bicycle 60 miles a week for the next four weeks.

✔ **Immediate goals:** Now we're talking about goals for each day or each workout. This way, when you walk into the gym, you won't waste time figuring out which exercises to do. Here are examples of immediate goals:

- Spend a full 10 minutes stretching at the end of a workout.
- Do upper-body weight exercises and 20 minutes on the stair-climber.
- Run two miles.
- Bicycle a hilly 20-mile course.

✔ **Back-up goals:** You always need a Plan B, in case something happens, and you're not able to reach your primary goal as soon as you want to. By setting back-up goals, you have a better chance of achieving something, and you won't feel like a failure if your long-term goal doesn't work out.

Let's say that your long-term goal is to lose 10 pounds by eating healthier and walking 3 miles a day. Your back-up goal could be increasing your stamina enough to walk 3 miles in less than an hour. Or say that you're training for a 10k run in the spring, but you sprain an ankle and have to stop running. If one of your back-up goals is to strengthen your upper body, you can still keep on track while your ankle heals.

You let your kids watch their favorite video when they bring home good grades. You give your golden retriever a doggy treat when he fetches the Frisbee. Be nice to yourself, too. Attach an appropriate reward to each of your goals. If you drop 3 percent body fat over the next two months, buy yourself a nifty sports watch. If you lift weights three days a week for a month, treat yourself to a massage. Sure, it's bribery, but it works.

Writing everything down

It's easy to set goals and rewards; it's even easier to forget what they are. You can keep yourself honest — and motivated — by tracking your goals and accomplishments on paper. One friend of ours tapes his goals to the inside of his gym locker. Some people program their computers to flash their goals on-screen twice a day.

Here's what you need to do:

- **Make a goal sheet.** Write down your goals on a piece of paper or index card and put it somewhere so that you can see it every day, like next to your desk or on your refrigerator. Next to every goal, write down the corresponding reward.

- **Keep a workout log.** Whatever your goals are, a training diary can help you get better results. You can look back at the end of each week and say, "I did that?" And you may be inspired to accomplish even more. Keeping a log shows you whether your goals are realistic and gives you insight into your exercise patterns.

  Here are some suggestions for filling in the blanks:

  - Date and day
  - Goals for the day
  - Cardiovascular training
  - Strength training
  - Stretching
  - Notes

Six ways to make exercise a habit

The following tips can help you get over the hump and boost the odds that you'll stick with your new program:

- Expect to feel uncomfortable at first.
- Pace yourself.

- ✔ Work out with friends or join a club.
- ✔ Keep it interesting by changing your workouts every couple of months, or even every time you exercise.
- ✔ Buy the right equipment.
- ✔ Be proud of yourself!

Chapter 6

Getting Your Mind and Body in Synch

*T*he mind-body exercise movement is in full force at health clubs and workout studios nationwide. yoga, Pilates, and meditation classes are now staples on most gym class schedules, right alongside step aerobics and body sculpting. You also can buy mind-body videos or hire personal trainers who specialize in these techniques.

We think everyone can benefit from adding a mind-body activity to their exercise repertoires. You can substitute these workouts for your regular program once or twice a week. For instance, instead of lifting weights, do a session of yoga or Pilates. Instead of your regular stretching routine, take a tai chi class. Some mind-body classes are intensely demanding, so make sure that you don't overload your workout schedule. In this chapter, we discuss the most popular forms of mind-body exercise.

Stretching like a Noodle with Yoga

In a nutshell: Developed in India more than 5,000 years ago, yoga consists of a series of poses (known as *asanas*) that you hold from a few seconds to several minutes. The moves — a blend of strength, flexibility, and body awareness exercises — are intended to promote the union of the mind, body, and spirit. yoga classes have a different feel than the usual Western workouts, often including a spiritual element such as chanting or burning candles or incense. (However, many classes these days dispense with the traditional Indian touches and just get right down to the business of kicking your butt.)

Whenever you're told yoga is *just* this or *just* that, your nonsense alert should kick into action. Yoga is too comprehensive to reduce to any one thing. Yoga is like a skyscraper with many floors and numerous rooms at each level. Here's what yoga is not:

- Yoga is not *just* gymnastics.
- Yoga is not *just* fitness training.
- Yoga is not *just* a way to control your weight.
- Yoga is not *just* a technique for stress reduction.
- Yoga is not *just* meditation.
- Yoga is not *just* the "huffing and puffing" of proper breath control.
- Yoga is not *just* a way to improve and maintain your health.
- Yoga is not *just* a spiritual tradition from India.

To put it simply, yoga is all these things — the catch is that it's also a great deal more. (You would expect as much from a tradition that's been around for 5,000 years.) Yoga includes physical exercises that look like gymnastics — some of which have even been incorporated into Western gymnastics. These exercises help you become or stay fit and trim, control your weight, and reduce your stress level. Yoga also offers a whole range of meditation practices, including breathing techniques that exercise your lungs and calm your nervous system or charge your brain and the rest of your body with delicious energy.

Moreover, you can use yoga as an efficient system of healthcare, one that has proven its usefulness both in restoring and maintaining health. Yoga continues to gain acceptance within the medical establishment. More and more physicians are recommending yoga to their patients not only for stress reduction but also as a safe and sane method of exercise, as well as physical therapy (notably, for the back and knees).

The eight main branches of yoga

When you take a bird's-eye view of the yoga tradition, you see a dozen major strands of development, each with its own subdivisions. Picture yoga as a giant tree with eight branches — each branch has its own unique character, but each branch is also part of the same tree. With so many different paths, you're sure to find one that's right for your personality, lifestyle, and goals.

Here are the eight principal branches of yoga, arranged alphabetically:

✔ **Bhakti yoga (pronounced *bhuk-tee*):** The yoga of devotion. Bhakti yoga practitioners believe that a supreme being transcends their lives, and they feel moved to connect or even completely merge with that supreme being through acts of devotion. Bhakti yoga includes such practices as making flower offerings, singing hymns of praise, and thinking about the divine being.

✔ **Guru yoga (pronounced *goo-roo*):** The yoga of dedication to a yoga master. In Guru yoga, one's teacher is the main focus of spiritual practice. Such a teacher is expected to be enlightened or at least be close to being enlightened. In Guru yoga, you're asked to honor and meditate on your guru until you merge with him or her. Because the guru is thought to be one with the ultimate reality, this merger is believed to duplicate his or her spiritual realization in you.

✔ **Hatha yoga (pronounced *haht-ha*):** The yoga of physical discipline. Hatha yoga practitioners believe that unless the body is properly purified and prepared, the higher stages of concentration, meditation, and ecstasy are virtually impossible to achieve — such an attempt would be like trying to climb Mt. Everest without the necessary gear.

✔ **Jnana yoga (pronounced *gyah-nah*):** The yoga of wisdom. Jnana yoga teaches the ideal of *nondualism* — that reality is singular and your perception of countless distinct phenomena is a basic misconception. What about the chair or sofa that you're sitting on? Isn't that real? What about the light that strikes your retina? Isn't that real? Jnana yoga masters answer these questions by saying that all these things are real at your present level of consciousness, but they aren't ultimately real as separate or distinct things. Upon enlightenment, everything melts into one, and you become one with the immortal spirit.

✔ **Karma yoga (pronounced *kahr-mah*):** The yoga of self-transcending action. Karma yoga seeks to influence destiny positively. This path's most important principle is to act unselfishly, without attachment, and with integrity. Karma yoga practitioners believe that all actions — whether bodily, vocal, or mental — have far-reaching consequences for which we must assume full responsibility.

✔ **Mantra yoga (pronounced *mahn-trah*):** The yoga of potent sound. Mantra yoga makes use of sound to harmonize the body and focus the mind. It works with *mantras*, which can be a syllable, word, or phrase. Traditionally, practitioners receive a *mantra* from their teacher in the context of a formal initiation. They are asked to repeat it as often as possible and to keep it secret. Many Western teachers feel that initiation is not necessary and that any sound will do. You can even pick a word from the dictionary — such as *love, peace,* or *happiness*.

- **Raja yoga (pronounced *rah-jah*):** The royal yoga, also known as *classical yoga*. When you mingle with yoga students long enough, you can expect to hear them refer to the *eightfold path,* as codified in the *yoga-Sutra* of Patanjali. This is the standard work of Raja yoga. Another name for this yogic tradition is *ashtanga-yoga* (pronounced *ahsh-tahng-gah*), the "eight-limbed yoga" — from *ashta* ("eight") and *anga* ("limb").

- **Tantra yoga (pronounced *tahn-trah*), including Kundalini yoga (pronounced *koon-dah-lee-nee*):** The yoga of continuity. Tantra yoga is the most complex and most widely misunderstood branch of yoga. In the West and in India, Tantra yoga is often confused with "spiritualized" sex. While sexual rituals are used in some schools of Tantra yoga, this isn't a regular practice in the majority of schools. Tantra yoga is actually a strict spiritual discipline involving fairly complex rituals and detailed visualizations of deities. These deities are either visions of the divine or the equivalent of Christianity's angels and are invoked to aid the yogic process of contemplation.

Five ways to empower yourself with yoga

Outside agents like physicians, therapists, or remedies can help us through major crises, but we ourselves are primarily responsible for our own health and happiness. Especially the source of lasting happiness that lies within us. Yoga reminds us of this truth and helps us mobilize the inner strength to live responsibly and wisely.

Yoga offers the following empowering benefits:

- **Maintaining health and happiness.** What is health? Most people answer this question by saying that health is the opposite of illness. But health is *more* than the absence of disease. It's a positive state of being. Health is wholeness. To be healthy means not only to possess a well-functioning body and a sane mind but also to vibrate with life, to be vitally connected with one's social and physical environment. To be healthy also means to be happy.

- **Finding out what being healthy really means.** Because life is constant movement, you shouldn't expect health to be static. Perfect health is a mirage. In the course of your life, you can expect inevitable fluctuations in your state of health — even cutting your finger with a knife temporarily upsets the balance. Your body reacts to the cut by mobilizing all the necessary biochemical forces to heal itself. Regular yoga practice can create optimal conditions for self-healing. You achieve a baseline of health, with an improved immune system that enables you to stay healthy longer and heal faster.

Yoga over 50

With its rejuvenating effects on the body and its calming effects on the mind, yoga truly is a personal "fountain of youth" for those who practice it. By practicing yoga, you increase your awareness of yourself physically, mentally, and spiritually.

Yoga is adaptable to any age or physical condition, and some say it's even more effective than training with weights for building strength and flexibility. Yoga helps build stamina and breath control, and it relaxes you, enabling you to manage your stress better. In fact, yoga has been clinically shown to lower blood pressure, increase circulation, build muscle tissue, increase flexibility, relieve stress and stress-related symptoms, and strengthen the respiratory system. No wonder seniors everywhere are jumping on the yoga bandwagon!

✔ **Healing rather than curing.** *Yoga is about healing rather than curing.* Like a really good physician, yoga takes deeper causes into account. These causes, more often than not, are to be found in the mind, in the way you live. That's why yoga masters recommend self-understanding.

✔ **Taking an active role in your own health.** Most people tend to be passive in health matters. They wait until something goes wrong, and then they rely on a pill or a physician to fix the problem. Yoga encourages you to take the initiative in preventing illness and restoring or maintaining your health. Taking control of your health has nothing to do with self-doctoring (which can be dangerous); it's simply a matter of taking responsibility for your health. A good physician will tell you that healing is greatly facilitated when the patient actively participates in the process. For example, you may take various kinds of medication to deal with a gastric ulcer, but unless you learn to eat well, sleep adequately, avoid stress, and take life more easy, you're bound to have a recurrence before long. You must change your lifestyle.

✔ **Following your bliss.** Yoga suggests that the best possible meaning you can find for yourself springs from the well of joy deep within you. Joy is like a 3-D lens that captures life's bright colors and motivates you to embrace life in all of its countless forms. Yoga points the way to happiness, health, and life-embracing meaning.

The Basics on Pilates

In a nutshell: First off, this form of exercise is *not* pronounced PIE-lates, but rather pih-LAH-teez. It's named after its inventor, Joseph Pilates, a former carpenter and gymnast who invented the technique for injured dancers. Many of the moves were inspired by yoga or patterned after the movements of animals such as swans, seals, and big cats.

You can practice Pilates two ways:

✔ You can take a group class that involves performing specialized calisthenics exercises on a mat.

✔ You can take private lessons on a series of low-tech machines with exotic names like the Cadillac and the Reformer. The Cadillac, with its array of springs, straps, poles, and bars, looks like a bed that the Marquis de Sade might enjoy. The Reformer looks like a weight bench souped up with assorted springs, straps, and pads.

Either way, Pilates moves are designed to work your powerhouse muscles — abs, lower back, thighs, and buttocks. Unlike gym machines, where you typically focus on one or two muscle groups at once, Pilates moves require you to engage virtually your entire body. At times you might try to strengthen one muscle while stretching another. Pilates moves take a lot of concentration; you can't simply go through the motions like you can on gym equipment.

The eight great principles of Pilates

Here are the core principles of Pilates:

✔ **Control.** One of the most fundamental rules when doing Pilates is to control your body's every movement. This rule applies not only to the exercises themselves but also to transitions between exercises, how you get on and off the equipment, and your overall attention to detail while working out.

✔ **Breath.** People often hold their breath when performing a new and difficult task. When you hold your breath, you tense muscles that can ultimately exacerbate improper posture and reinforce tension habits. That's why consistent breathing is essential to flowing movement and proper muscle balance. Every Pilates exercise has a specific breathing pattern assigned to it.

✔ **Flowing movement.** If you were to glance quickly at someone doing Pilates, you might think the person was doing yoga. But when doing yoga, you generally hold your position for at least a moment (if not for what seems like an eternity) before moving to the next posture. And although Pilates borrows some of its movements from yoga, rarely do you ever hold a position for a long time in Pilates. In this way, Pilates is more like dance, in that the flow of the body is essential. The essence of Pilates movements is to allow your body to move freely and, at the end of each movement, to finish with control and precision. This way of moving brings flexibility to the joints and muscles and teaches the body to elongate and move with even rhythm. Flowing movement integrates the nervous system, the muscles, and the joints and trains the body to move smoothly and evenly.

✔ **Precision.** Precision is a lot like control but has the added element of spatial awareness. When initiating any movement, you must know exactly where that movement starts and where it will end. All Pilates exercises have precise definitions of where the body should be at all times, such as what angle the legs are moving, what direction the elbows are held, the positioning of the head and neck, and even what the fingers are doing! The little things count in Pilates.

✔ **Centering.** Most Pilates exercises focus on developing abdominal strength either directly or indirectly. Never forget to pull the belly in or you'll be reprimanded by the Pilates gods!

✔ **Stability.** The focus on stability when performing the exercises is part of the beauty of Pilates and what makes it such a perfect rehabilitation system. In fact, many Pilates mat exercises are meant to focus primarily on torso stability. *Stability* is the ability to *not* move a part of the body while another part is challenging it. For instance, when raising your arm up as high as you can in front of you, try not to arch your back. In order to accomplish this, you must use your abdominal muscles so that the rib cage doesn't rise up as the arm rises above the shoulder level. Maintaining stillness in the spine as you move the arms and legs requires torso stability accomplished mainly by the abdominal muscles.

✔ **Range of motion.** Pilates exercises tend to require the body to move to its fullest length, thereby increasing the range of motion, or flexibility, of your limbs. People whose muscles are very tight will begin to notice an increase in flexibility after doing a few hours of Pilates exercises. If you're very tight, you may need to do some specific stretching exercises in addition to the Pilates exercises, or modify the poses until you gain the flexibility necessary to execute them in their classical forms.

✔ **Opposition.** You can lift your arms thinking only of lifting your arms. Or you can think "down to go up" as you lift your arms, first pulling the shoulders down the back and then raising the arms, focusing on lifting the arms from the back muscles instead. This is opposition in action. When lifting your arm from your back rather than from your arm, you're actually stabilizing the shoulder as you lift the arm.

What you need to get started

The good news is that you don't need much! Just the basics:

✔ **A firm mat.** The mat only needs to be as long as your spine and as wide as your body. This mat should be firm enough to support your back when rolling on the floor. You will hurt your vertebrae if you only use a towel or a yoga mat.

✔ **Comfy clothes.** Wear what you would wear to a yoga class, dance class, or stretch class. Nothing should bind you — no buttons or tight waistbands. Wearing something formfitting is nice because it lets you see if your belly is pooching out or not.

✔ **Bare feet.** Socks tend to slip on the floor, so we recommend bare feet.

In addition, a small ball is great, although it's not necessary. A small ball is a great cheap tool to have, especially when you're first starting out.

Easing your back pain with Pilates

Most back pain is due to faulty posture. Do you sit at a desk and stare straight ahead? Unfortunately, most people do, and they find it very difficult to sit up with proper posture for eight hours at a time. It becomes a vicious cycle: First you sit for long periods of time in a way that doesn't properly support the spine (generally, in a slightly hunched-over position). Then you lose strength in your postural muscles by not using them day after day, and then you can't sit up properly even if you want to because you've lost strength! What to do — besides quitting your day job and joining the circus? Well guess what? Pilates! Once again, Pilates can save the day.

Here's how:

✔ When trying a new exercise, see if the movement makes your back pain worse or better. Use this information to heal yourself. For instance, if you find that flexion (rounding the spine forward), like in Spine Stretch Forward, makes your back feel great, then you can proceed with all the flexion exercises with a fair bit of confidence. In that case, exercises that do the opposite movement, extension (arching the back), as in the Rising Swan, may make your back hurt. If this is so, avoid all exercises that extend the back. The act of twisting may be the source of the problem, or it could be twisting in just one direction. Take note of what hurts and apply this information to your workout.

✔ Most of the Pilates mat exercises strengthen the muscles necessary to properly support the spine and bring an awareness about what proper posture actually is. It's not enough just to do Pilates mat exercises; if you want to improve your posture and heal your back pain, you must incorporate Pilates into your daily life. If you can incorporate the deeper Pilates concepts into your daily life (yes, while sitting at your desk), you'll notice changes immediately — in your back pain, in your posture, and in your sense of well-being.

When you're in pain, you must be very mindful when trying out new exercises. We recommend seeing a doctor first to make sure you don't have any serious injury, and then going to a trained Pilates instructor if you're worried about hurting yourself.

Getting to Know Tai Chi

In a nutshell: This ancient Chinese form of exercise, stress management, and body awareness is considered a martial art but bears little resemblance to anything you're likely to see in a Jackie Chan action flick. Tai chi is characterized by soft, slow, flowing movements that emphasize precision and force rather than brute strength. Every morning along the banks of the East River in New York City, groups of older Chinese men and women gather for a tai chi session. From a distance, it almost looks as if they're moving underwater.

Here are some facts about tai chi:

- ✔ Tai chi has its roots in yoga and other martial arts forms. Literally translated from Chinese, *chi* means "energy" and is often referred to as a "meditation in motion." One of the purposes of the movements is to move your ball of "chi" to different places to improve your balance, flexibility, and strength. Tai chi enthusiasts also say these movements improve circulation, balance, and coordination while relaxing and strengthening the muscular and nervous systems.

- ✔ A study conducted at Johns Hopkins University in Baltimore found that tai chi lowered blood pressure in older adults almost as much as 30 minutes of daily brisk walking did. A growing body of research suggests that tai chi can improve the quality of life for seniors and reduce their risk of falling. Tai chi is now used in some cardiac rehabilitation programs and by people with conditions such as fibromyalgia, arthritis, and multiple sclerosis.

- ✔ The slow movements are beautiful to watch and calming to perform — a great break from hardcore workouts. Plus, there's virtually no chance of getting injured during a tai chi class. Once you learn a basic routine, you can do it anywhere and at any time. Tai chi generally won't develop as much strength as yoga or Pilates, but some stances do require a great deal of muscle power. For instance, the horse stance requires you to squat for several minutes as you perform movements with your upper body.

- ✔ A few cautions: Some people may feel self-conscious about moving so slowly through a series of unfamiliar positions. And for others, tai chi simply doesn't involve enough sweating. Tai chi requires a long-term commitment to gain a deep understanding of the skills and philosophies, so it's not for those who are impatient about seeing results.

- ✔ Where to try it: Most larger health clubs offer tai chi classes or another form of "soft" martial arts like Quikong (SHE-gong) or tai chi Chaung. (Both are similar in terms of philosophy and movement to tai chi.) tai chi classes also are offered at some martial arts and yoga studios. Learning tai chi from a book or video is tough, so we recommend group or private lessons.

Minding yourself

You can practice tai chi — as well as yoga or other mindful movement methods — in two ways:

- ✔ **Physically:** You basically crank out *forms* or movements to get a good workout, a nice stretch, or some pleasant exercise.
- ✔ **Physically *and* mindfully:** You use your body physically, but you also use your mind in a meditative and inwardly focused manner during all movements and forms.

To get the benefits that can reach far beyond the results of a nice workout, applying a meditative manner and an inward focus is the way to go.

Breathing through the forms

In tai chi, breathing fully and deeply makes or breaks the mind-body practice. Keep in mind the following points:

- ✔ **You breathe only when you have to.** Those breaths are prompted by your body's involuntary need to suck in oxygen to survive and no conscious effort on your part as a part of movements or otherwise.
- ✔ **You exhale and inhale fully as you do the movements.** When moving through the forms, breathing is as important as the movements. Instructors and books prompt you to breathe, especially in particular places, while moving through forms.

Muscling up to the movements

Meditation is mindful and can be a vital part of any practice. But if you just *sit* and meditate — which is certainly a beneficial practice — you miss a certain component — movement. Add some movement, which uses muscle and adds some intensity at even low levels, and you may realize other benefits. You can do some minor movements, which don't have to include high-intensity push-ups and maniacally jumping around. Just lightly use your muscles in some way.

Intensifying or not

Then there's the question of aerobic intensity. If you do any traditional exercise, such as walking or aerobics, you're familiar with the health and weight-loss benefits. And traditional exercises can be nice supplements to mind-body practices like tai chi because you can gain more benefits, such as combating osteoporosis or losing weight.

Tai chi may not be high-intensity, but that's okay. You can do tai chi at a very low level (which is perfect for seniors or someone new to exercise) or at a pretty high level (which is great for adding mindfulness to an athlete's training or for balancing the lifestyle of someone who does traditional exercise).

The intensity you achieve during the forms depends on the following factors:

✔ What style or school you choose

✔ How often you do the forms

✔ How many times you repeat the forms at one time

✔ How low you bend your knees or sink

Stretching your dollar while stretching your body

Many yoga and Pilates centers offer senior discounts and often specific classes for seniors. Your best bet is to just call up a few of those listed in your phone book and ask. Also check with your insurance — some providers offer discounts on healthy living activities — such as yoga and Pilates.

If you want to tackle yoga or Pilates at home, you can often get videos or DVDs at a used bookstore or on www.amazon.com. If you're willing to do a little work in order to save a buck, however, here are some sites with free yoga and Pilates poses that you can print out and try on your own:

✔ www.santosha.com: This site has some pretty good yoga postures that are catalogued in a helpful index and offer step-by-step instructions, animated illustrations, varying difficulty levels, and buttons to print out the posture. It also has several essays on meditation.

✔ www.yogajournal.com: The site for *Yoga Journal* magazine has a section on poses where you can search for dozens of poses by name, the part of the anatomy you want to focus on, or specific health problems. It also contains in-depth information on yoga history and philosophy, the latest medical research on how yoga affects health and healing, a food section complete with recipes, and a directory of yoga programs.

✔ www.yogasite.com: This useful site contains step-by-step yoga postures in a concise and easy-to-understand style, as well as articles about yoga and health and directories of teachers, organizations, and training.

✔ www.noboundaries.tv/pilates: This site provides tips and modified Pilates exercises for seniors who may have limited mobility. Register for the newsletter to get regular senior Pilates exercises.

✔ www.agelessfitness.com: Okay, so this site doesn't offer free poses, but it does have inexpensive Pilates videos created specifically for seniors.

Research suggests that a low to low-moderate intensity is best. Dump the heart rate calculations for a moment and just think about how you feel. If you rate how you feel on a scale of 0 to 10 (with 0 being so easy it's as if you're lying in bed and 10 being so hard that you may fall over exhausted), your feeling of effort during movement shouldn't exceed about 5.

Remember, though, that tai chi isn't really about heart rates and such stuff, but rather about feeling and focus. Don't forget that fact as you move forward along the Eastern path.

Chapter 7

Tackling Other Popular Exercise Activities

*T*his chapter is a catchall for the easiest ways to get the exercise you need to achieve a higher fitness level. We discuss the benefits of walking and swimming, which are the easiest exercises on your joints. We also cover exercise videos — how to choose one that's right for you and some ideas for places to get them — and using water to become fit.

Wondrous Walking

"It is better to walk than to run," says a Hindu proverb, and that's good fitness advice, too. Walking is probably the most perfect exercise you can do and is a surprisingly effective strategy for long-term health. Walking doesn't cost a cent (unless you walk on a treadmill), can be done at any time, is not injurious, and can be as intensive as you want it to be. This load-bearing exercise places a gentle strain on the hips and the rest of the body.

Top ten benefits of walking yourself fit

Allow us to rhapsodize in greater detail about this superb, all-around form of fitness:

- ✔ Walking gently exercises all parts of the body in a steady rhythm, gradually imposing mild stress on the heart. This mild stress makes the heart work harder, builds up heart muscle, and builds a fail-safe collateral circulation system that provides another way to bring blood to the heart if a clot or blockage occurs.

- ✔ Walking can be done at any time you want. You can get up and go during dawn patrol, forego the morning coffee break for a walk around the industrial park, walk on your lunch hour, jump on a treadmill after work, or watch the sun set in the west during an after-dinner stroll.

- ✔ You go at your own pace. You decide how much you want to put into this exercise.

- ✔ You can walk every day. Unlike strength training and hard jogging, where the muscles need 24 to 48 hours to recoup, walking is an exercise that can be done every day.

- ✔ You can walk after eating. No one feels like jogging, running around the tennis court, or playing in a senior basketball league on a full stomach. But you can walk after any meal.

- ✔ Walking is a great social exercise. Because you're not panting from exertion, you can carry along a civilized conversation with a friend or loved one as you stride down the sidewalk or through the picturesque countryside.

- ✔ You don't mess up your hair by getting all sweaty. When the temperature is cool or cold, you rarely perspire unless you're power walking. Not getting all sweaty is another reason why walking is a favored work-time exercise: You can walk during your break without having to shower and blow-dry your hair afterward.

- ✔ Walking can jump-start your day. If you feel stiff and lethargic upon waking up (and who doesn't these days?), taking a five-minute walk right away will wake up your nervous system. If you're fighting early morning lethargy, stick your feet in a bucket of ice water and then go on a walk, something that's sure to get you going.

- ✔ Walking can be done in the privacy of your home. Many people prefer to do their walking on a treadmill, which we heartily approve of because we use our treadmill for that purpose. If it's cold or rainy or dark outside — or if you don't feel safe walking in your neighborhood after hours — step on a treadmill.

✔ Walking gives you time to think. We're so rushed these days, who has time to think things through? Walking is a welcome respite from our 500-channel, ten-phone-messages, tons-of-e-mail existence that assaults our senses each day.

Getting started: A one-month walking plan

Walking is a form of exercise in which you choose the pace, but you'll greatly help your overall fitness if you follow a proven walking program. If you're ready to choose walking as your exercise, you need to be aware that the President's Council on Physical Fitness and Sports has designated three walking speeds:

✔ Slow, or 3 mph

✔ Brisk, or 4 mph

✔ Fast, or 4.5 mph

Table 7-1 indicates how fast it takes to walk a few specific distances at each of these speeds. After you know how far you are walking and the pace you want to keep, you can set a target time.

Table 7-1	Time (in Minutes) for Various Distances		
Distance	**Slow Walk (3 mph)**	**Brisk Walk (4 mph)**	**Fast Walk (4.5 mph)**
0.5 mile	10:00	7:30	6:40
1 mile	20:00	15:00	13:20
1.5 miles	30:00	22:30	20:00
2 miles	40:00	30:00	26:40
2.5 miles	50:00	37:30	33:20
3 miles	60:00	45:00	40:00
3.5 miles	70:00	52:30	46:40
4 miles	80:00	60:00	53:20
4.5 miles	90:00	67:30	60:00
5 miles	100:00	75:00	66:40

Note: Many people 50 and up cannot keep up a "fast" pace while walking, but it's a goal to shoot for.

Time yourself for a half-hour walk through your neighborhood and then drive the same route in your car to measure how far you walked. With that information, you'll get a good idea of how to pace yourself when following this walking plan:

First Week

Day 1	Walk 1 mile slowly (at 3 mph pace)
Day 2	Walk 1 mile slowly
Day 3	Walk 1.5 miles slowly
Day 4	Walk 1.5 miles slowly
Day 5	Walk 2 miles slowly
Day 6	Walk 2 miles slowly
Day 7	Rest

Second Week

Day 1	Walk 2.5 miles slowly
Day 2	Walk 2.5 miles slowly
Day 3	Walk 3 miles slowly
Day 4	Walk 3 miles slowly
Day 5	Walk 3.5 miles slowly
Day 6	Walk 3.5 miles slowly
Day 7	Rest

Third Week

Day 1	Walk 4 miles slowly
Day 2	Walk 2 miles briskly (at 4 mph pace)
Day 3	Walk 4 miles slowly
Day 4	Walk 2.5 miles briskly
Day 5	Walk 4 miles slowly
Day 6	Walk 3 miles briskly
Day 7	Rest

Fourth Week

Day 1	Walk 4.5 miles slowly
Day 2	Walk 3.5 miles briskly
Day 3	Walk 5 miles slowly
Day 4	Walk 4 miles briskly
Day 5	Walk 5 miles slowly
Day 6	Walk 4.5 miles briskly
Day 7	Rest

After two weeks of walking, your blood pressure begins to drop. In weeks three and four, cholesterol counts fall (unless you're eating puffed cheese snacks while you walk). With a couple of months under your belt, your heart and lungs become stronger and work more efficiently. Your resting pulse decreases, and your bones become stronger. You can even expect to lose a pound or two with each month of walking.

Running to fitness

Running or jogging can be hard on the body's muscles and joints, especially the knees and back. Most people over the age of 50, we believe, would rather walk away from running, and we understand the rationale. Running isn't easy and requires discipline. At our age, we're better off playing an enjoyable sport, walking, or using fitness machines to become fit, which is why we contend that running in the fifties and sixties is best left to lifelong adherents to this form of exercise. Now that we've dissed jogging, let us point out some of the positive aspects of this demanding physical activity:

✔ Like walking, you can jog anytime and anywhere. You don't need a buddy, and you don't need lots of equipment. Proper clothes and good running shoes are enough.

✔ Jogging delivers the same benefits as walking — only faster. Running improves muscle tone and strength, relieves stress, and combats osteoporosis, heart disease, and arthritis.

✔ Running burns plenty of calories, especially for intense road workouts. A half-hour jog burns around 750 calories, a lot for a short time. A jogging workout is a very efficient way to achieve cardiovascular fitness.

✔ Jogging is a great exercise for business travelers. Finding convenient fitness centers on the road can be difficult, and they're expensive. You can jog from your hotel when you have a break in your schedule.

✔ You experience a "runner's high." Something can be said for how good you feel after a good run when *endorphins* (neurotransmitters found in the brain that have pain-relieving properties similar to morphine) are released by the body into the bloodstream.

Stay safe!

We've all heard the all-too-familiar news reports of joggers and walkers being hit by cars or suddenly ambushed by strangers intent on doing harm. Even if you live in a safe neighborhood, please take the following precautions to stay out of harm's way while you're running (or walking):

✔ Invite a friend along. Two is always better than one.

✔ Lock your house and take a key with you. Someone may be casing your place.

✔ Stick to areas you know. When you're on a jog, this is not the time to go exploring.

✔ Avoid going out after dark, if possible. If not, stay on lighted streets.

✔ Consider running or walking indoors. Many cold-weather fitness clubs have elevated tracks that ring the inside perimeter of the building.

✔ Go against traffic. Assume that you don't have the right-of-way.

✔ Wear bright colors so drivers can see you. Even glow-in-the-dark shoes can help.

✔ Stay away from bushy areas where someone could hide.

✔ Carry a Mace-type or pepper spray with you.

✔ If followed, go to the nearest house or business and call 911.

✔ If someone looks like he's going to attack you, yell your head off.

You're going to find yourself in super shape after following a walking regimen. A rosy-apple glow will reappear in your cheeks, the fruit of a fresh sense of well-being. Your body will have a new foundation for fitness that you can call upon if you pursue other athletic endeavors, such as playing on a softball team, snow skiing in the Rockies, or joining a tennis league.

Swimming in Exercise

If you don't like getting sweaty while you exercise, want to take a load off your weight-bearing joints, and just love being in water, swimming could be your sport.

Here are the benefits of swimming for exercise:

✔ Water has an irresistible appeal. Its magical qualities are readily apparent from the moment you jump in; the upward force of water buoys you and diminishes the downward pull of gravity. This phenomenon results in less stress on load-bearing joints like the knees and hips and, therefore, fewer injuries. The only way you can get hurt would be swimming straight into the pool wall or jumping into water that's shallower than you are expecting.

✔ Water supports you, adds natural resistance that tones and strengthens the body's muscles, and works your muscles in the same way that light weights do. Water creates buoyancy that reduces the effects of gravity by 90 percent, allowing you to exercise with minimal impact on your joints. The pressure of water against your chest works your lungs and improves the body's respiratory system. And you don't have to be any good at it to benefit from its aerobic-inducing qualities — you can dog paddle up and down the swimming lanes and still receive a workout that leaves you panting.

✔ If you're monitoring your heart as a swimmer, realize that your target heart rate will be around 13 beats per minute slower than with any other exercises. This is because you are usually in the prone position while swimming, and your body is submerged in a cool environment. But you don't have to swim longer to get the same cardiovascular workout as you would in other sports.

✔ Swimming is great exercise for those rehabbing from a sports injury or minor surgery. Swimming can keep your fitness up until you're able to get back to your usual weight-bearing sport, such as walking or skiing.

✔ Because swimming is so easy on the joints, it's commonly recommended for those suffering from arthritis or those who are extremely overweight.

The drawbacks of swimming

Even avid swimmers have to admit there isn't much to look at while they train, unlike joggers and bicyclists, who can enjoy the outdoor scenery as they pump their legs.

Other drawbacks include:

✔ Swimming isn't a weight-bearing exercise, so swimming laps won't prevent osteoporosis.

✔ Unless you have your own pool, you're limited to swimming at certain hours in public facilities. Many neighborhoods have community pools these days, but they're drained during the winter months.

✔ Swimmers are guaranteed wet hair dripping with chlorine, which can dry and dull hair (which is why you don't see too many swimming aficionados with long hair these days).

Overexertion is common among swimming neophytes who dive into the pool and begin thrashing away, arms and legs churning like a Mississippi steamboat. If you haven't swum in years but think you can pick up where you left off when you won the peewee division at a summer swim meet, guess again. Take it easy! Warm up by stretching before you jump in the pool, and then swim two or three easy laps before taking stock of your fitness. You may want to call it a day right there, which is fine. Tomorrow, swim three more laps.

Six alternatives to swimming laps

You certainly don't have to swim laps to get a water workout. The following exercises can be done in the shallow end of the pool:

- ✔ **Toe raises:** Toe raises are a good exercise to start with. Stand next to the pool wall with your feet shoulder-width apart and hold the edge. Rise up on the balls of your feet and hold for a count of four. Relax for a few seconds, and then stand on your toes again for a count of four. Do a set of ten. This exercise makes your calf muscles stronger.

- ✔ **Leg curls:** Leg curls stretch your quadriceps and work your hip joints and lower back. To do leg curls, turn sideways to the pool wall and hold the edge with your left hand, feet shoulder-width apart. Bend your right leg as far as you can; then reach down with your right hand and bring your right foot to your right buttock. Stretch to a count of five. Do a set of six, and then turn and repeat the exercise with your left leg.

- ✔ **Lunges:** This exercise stretches your hamstrings and leg muscles while working the knees. Start the exercise by placing both hands on your hips in shallow water. Step forward with your right leg as far as you can, and then hold the step for a count of six. Straighten up to a standing position. Now step forward with your left leg as far as you can. Hold the step for a count of six. Repeat 12 times.

- ✔ **Arm circles:** The arm-circle exercise firms up your shoulders and upper arms. This exercise requires that you move to deeper water, about neck height. In the deeper water, stretch out both of your arms and make tiny circles in a clockwise direction. Count to 20; then rest. Repeat this step six times. Next make arm circles in a counterclockwise direction to a count of 20; rest. Repeat the counterclockwise step six times as well.

- ✔ **Pull-ups:** If your pool has a small diving board, you can do a water version of the pull-up. Jump up and grab the end of the diving board. Pull yourself up, much like chin-ups in the school yard. Repeat 12 times. Pull-ups strengthen your upper back and arms.

- ✔ **Running from side to side:** This is a great aerobic exercise that strengthens the legs. Start at one side of the pool in the shallow end and then run to the other side of the shallow end. Keep your legs churning. Rest. When you're ready to go again, take off for the other side. Do this ten times or until you're no longer capable.

Employing Exercise Videos

A popular exercise option these days is to pop a video into the VCR and perform stretches and aerobic exercises in tune with the chirpy leader on the screen. Some exercise videos are very good at what they do (giving you a complete workout), while others are campy efforts that have been around so long that they're ripe for parody.

Deciding whether videos are right for you

Although fitness videos can be exercises in cheesiness, and it's easy to poke fun at the cloying hosts and annoying antics, they do have their place in the pantheon of fitness. Exercise videos may work for you if you can answer *yes* to any of these questions:

- ✔ Do you live far from a health club? Many people live in rural areas or in city outskirts that are too far from a fitness facility.

- ✔ Are you housebound? Perhaps you are taking care of an aging parent or special needs child and can't leave the home.

- ✔ Do you live in a cold-weather climate that makes it difficult to leave the house during the winter?

- ✔ Do you have a limited budget? If you can't afford to purchase home fitness equipment, exercise videos are a stopgap measure.

- ✔ Is your space limited where home-exercise equipment is concerned? We don't all live in homes with extra room for a treadmill or exercise bike.

- ✔ Do you prefer the privacy of your home? Some folks don't want to exercise with others.

- ✔ Do you realize the limitations of exercise videos? You're alone with just an exercise mat and perhaps a couple of dumbbells and a kitchen "step" piece. You'll probably get a nice cardiovascular workout, but don't expect to do much strength training unless you use a video that includes dumbbells.

If you think that you and exercise videos would be a good match, ask friends for recommendations. Personal trainers can point you in the right direction. Research the Internet. You can always find someone new who's "hot."

Choosing the right tape

You can find hundreds of exercise videos out there, all vying for a place in your VCR. Videos based on yoga, martial arts, jumping rope, kickboxing, aerobics, step aerobics, and stretching are everywhere. Rent or borrow an exercise video that you would never purchase. Experiment!

Before buying, renting, or borrowing an exercise video, however, you need to know whom the intended audience is supposed to be. Are you on the fitness comeback trail and need a video filled with slow stretches and easy movements? Or would you prefer something more energetic? Of course, you want a video where proper form is demonstrated and explained so that you won't injure yourself when performing the exercises.

Read the verbiage on the video jacket.

- ✔ **Low impact** means that one foot is always in contact with the floor.

- ✔ **High impact** indicates that both feet leave the floor during jumping or hopping moves.

- ✔ **Mixed impact** refers to a combination of both low-impact and high-impact moves during the aerobic portion or the addition of jump moves during step aerobics.

What does the video jacket say about intensity of the workout? Search for clues that reveal how difficult the workout is in relation to exercise selection, sequence, and complexity. Look for the following words on the video jacket verbiage:

- ✔ Beginner means you haven't exercised for a half year or longer. Your aerobic capacity, strength, and flexibility are suspect. You aren't sure how to monitor your heart rate to determine how much you are exercising.

- ✔ Intermediate means you're back on track, exercising consistently at least twice a week. You are familiar with the importance of stretching and are versed in various types of aerobic activities.

- ✔ Advanced means that you are in excellent shape, exercise three to five times a week, and can follow more complex routines. You know all about dance aerobics, step aerobics, and other modes of body conditioning. You feel fit and trim and have good coordination around the exercise floor.

Wetting Your Whistle While You Work Out

For a healthy person, there's no such thing as drinking too much water. On a day-to-day basis, water plays an essential role in maintaining health by

- ✔ Regulating body temperature.
- ✔ Carrying nutrients and oxygen to cells.
- ✔ Cushioning joints.
- ✔ Protecting organs and tissues.
- ✔ Removing toxins.
- ✔ Maintaining strength and endurance.

Your fluid requirements depend on your body weight, lifestyle, age, sex, and the climate in which you live. Younger people need more fluids, as do those in hot climates — no surprise there.

You've probably heard that you should drink eight to ten glasses of water each day. That's a lot of water. Can you do it? The answer is yes, but you have to work at it.

If you suddenly increase your water intake, you may be wondering where the next toilet can be found. You don't have to drink water, however. Those recommended eight glasses can come from other fluids: sports drinks such as Gatorade, fruit juices, milk, and drinks such as Crystal Light. Anything non-caffeinated counts. You also receive significant water from eating fruits and vegetables and even potatoes, cottage cheese, and meat.

Can you drink water and lose weight?

Some people drink as little water as possible, thinking that water will bloat their bodies and keep them from losing weight. Nothing could be further from the truth. Christen Woodland, R.D., performed a study at the University of Utah revealing that participants who had lost three or four pounds through dehydration experienced a 3 percent decrease in how many calories they burned at rest. So the truth is when you don't drink enough fluids, you don't burn as many calories, which means it takes longer for you to lose weight.

The five best ways to stay hydrated

If you fail to drink enough fluids or lose too much fluid through sweating, your body goes into the tank, so to speak. Yet most people keep striding away on the treadmill, unaware that they should be sipping on a water bottle every ten minutes or so. The next time you work out, remember these tips regarding proper fluid replacement:

- ✔ The time to start drinking water is before your athletic activity, not afterward. Drink a glass or two of water in the hour or two leading up to your workout. This extra fluid will offset sweat losses; any excess will be excreted as urine before you work out. If you're an early morning walker and don't feel like drinking bland water at 6 a.m., drink a glass of orange juice before you walk out the front door. Then grab a water bottle and sip on it while you pace through the neighborhood.

- ✔ While exercising, quaff 8 to 16 ounces of water during every 30 minutes of intense exercise — more in hot and humid conditions.

- ✔ If you're working out at a health club, get into the habit of packing a water bottle. Many fitness emporiums are happy to sell you a liter of bottled water for $2. Save the money by bringing your own water, or you can fill up your bottle at the club's drinking fountain, which often dispenses refrigerated water.

- ✔ If, during your match or competition, you have a headache, flushed skin, light-headedness, and a cotton mouth, it's probably too late. Your body has lost too many liquids. You need to drink immediately to stave off the further effects of dehydration, which hamper your performance and can lead to serious health problems, such as heat illness.

✔ After finishing your exercise, drink a tall glass of water. Your body is primed to replenish vital fluids that were lost while working out. Slake that thirst right away — before you forget.

Motivating yourself for free

Sometimes you just can't motivate yourself to exercise, even when you know how good it is for you. The following Web sites offer you some ways to keep going, such as exercise logs so that you can see your progress or online programs that provide some accountability and structure:

✔ www.justmove.org: This site, created by the American Heart Association, helps you design a fitness program based on your current fitness or special needs. Then you track your progress towards your fitness goals with an online exercise diary. The site also includes articles and links about exercise and eating, exercise and health conditions — you get the picture.

✔ www.internetfitness.com: Although this site sells books and exercise equipment, it offers helpful guidelines for walking, running, and strength training. Some example guidelines are deciding between treadmill or outdoor walking, reaching thresholds, and proper exercise posture.

✔ www.strongwomen.com: The Strong Women site introduces three different strength-training programs for older women: "Strong Bones" for combating osteoporosis, "Stay Slim" for healthy weight loss, and "Vibrant Aging" to help those over 60 combat muscle weakening and balance issues. Although to complete the entire program you have to buy a book, the Web site gives an in-depth overview and gets you started on the first steps. The site also includes healthy recipes to complement your exercise program.

✔ http://nutrition.tufts.edu/research/growingstronger: Growing Stronger is interactive strength training for older adults that helps you increase the strength of your muscles, prevent your bones from weakening, and improve your balance, coordination, and mobility. The program includes an initial evaluation, an exercise program, and tips to keep you motivated.

✔ http://exercise.about.com/mpchat.htm: If you have a good exercise program, but just want someone to keep you on track or to ask questions of, then joining an exercise chat room may be all you need. Check out this site for a conversation you may want to join.

✔ www.coolrunning.com/log/: Track your personal running history with this free online running journal. You can record time, distance, heart rate, weight, weather, time of day, workout type, even the shoes you wear. It also automatically calculates the pace of each run and tallies your weekly, monthly, and annual mileage along with total time run and average pace.

✔ www.videofitness.com: Video Fitness is a great site for those of you who like exercise videos. Among the best features are detailed reviews of every type of exercise video imaginable, articles on setting up a video program, a list of buying sources, an index of exercise video instructors, and a guide to choosing the right activity and video for you. But best of all for the budget conscious is the video exchange — you can turn in the old videos you're tired of or that didn't work for you for new ones.

If you have a hard time modifying your eating habits, seek help from a support group such as Weight Watchers or Overeaters Anonymous. They can provide information and moral support.

Five Rules of the Game

Like riding a bicycle, playing tennis, or singing at the Met, successful weight loss takes practice. Sometimes a lot of practice. Nobody's born knowing exactly what to eat to lose weight, but learning the ropes makes it easier to pick a better way to go. In other words, to win at weight loss, you have to know the rules. Translation: You have to know when you're ready to lose weight, and once you've decided that, you have to know how to distinguish a healthful program from the merely okay or the truly awful.

The five rules listed here are a good guide:

- ✔ Rule #1: Be sure that you actually need to lose weight.
- ✔ Rule #2: Don't start a weight loss program until you're ready.
- ✔ Rule #3: Pick a diet that provides all the essential nutrients.
- ✔ Rule #4: Choose a diet with sensible goals.
- ✔ Rule #5: Pick a diet you can live with forever.

How to Recognize a Fad Diet

Of all the words written about weight loss, *fad diet* are the two that stir the greatest ire in a nutritionist's heart. Say the words slowly. Let them roll around on your tongue. You can practically hear the sound of distant thunder as the Nutrition Establishment rises as one to proclaim: Bah, humbug!

Fad diets come and go, which is why they're called fads. But experts say all fad diets have several traits in common:

- ✔ They claim that you can lose lots of weight really, really fast.
- ✔ They promote "special" foods or a severely restricted diet.
- ✔ They claim you can lose weight without exercising.
- ✔ They quote sources nobody knows or use before-and-after pictures and anecdotes or testimonials.
- ✔ They have no long-term scientific back-up.

Before you bite, check out the following worms in these (diet) apples.

Promises, promises

If a diet claim sounds too good to be true, it probably is. The perfect example is a diet that promises to take off 30 pounds in 30 days, a formula chosen presumably because some months do have 30 days, and the numbers sound good together.

According to the American Society of Bariatric Physicians, a group of doctors specializing in weight control, losing 30 pounds in 30 days is an impossibility because:

- You need to cut your calorie intake by 3,500 to lose one pound.
- You need to cut out 105,000 calories (30 lbs x 3,500 calories = 105,000 calories).
- A person who consumes 2,800 calories a day — more than most American woman — only takes in 84,000 calories in 30 days.
- If this person stopped eating entirely, she would still have to get rid of another 21,000 calories to reach 105,000 — the number equivalent to 30 pounds.

Anyone here think that will happen?

On the other hand, a slow but steady loss of five pounds in that 30-day period means cutting back just 17,500 calories (5 lbs x 3,500 calories = 17,500 calories). Divide 17,500 by 30, and you come up with 583 calories a day, a reduction most serious weight-loss programs can handle.

So the next time someone says he knows how to lose 30 pounds in 30 days, tell him to take a hike. The exercise will do him good.

Funny food plans

A second hallmark of a fad diet is its reliance on strange food plans based on:

- "Fat burning" foods such as grapefruit, a perennial favorite
- Unusual meals such as fruit alone or grains alone or meat alone . . . whatever
- Special products, such as costly liquid or powdered food substitutes available only from the people pushing the diet

No one food will rev up your metabolism to burn fat. In addition, your body is perfectly equipped to handle all kinds of food at one meal. Restricting your food intake to one food or one type of food will not only bore you silly after a while, it will also cheat your body of essential nutrients.

As for "special," "high potency," or "high energy" liquids, powders, and other potions, they will certainly enrich your diet guru, but their value as a diet aid is questionable.

No hard work, no hard body

The only thing you need to know to judge a weight-loss program is that losing weight and keeping it off takes more than the brainpower required to identify a healthful diet. True, you need to exercise your intelligence, but you also need to exercise your muscles. The old song says, "Every little movement has a meaning all its own." The new tune tells you, "Every movement uses calories." The more you move, the easier it is to use up calories and melt away the pounds.

Who says so?

Finally, fad diets come naked, without the requisite recommendations from reputable health organizations such as the American Dietetic Association or the American Heart Association or an arm of the National Institutes of Health. Instead, a fad diet:

- Bases its advice on the results of one study, often a dubious one (65 overweight pet rats or five middle-aged men lost weight after three months on a diet of nothing but fresh apricots and peaches).

- Comes with endorsements from people who may be well-meaning but have no expertise (the rats' owners or the mother of one of those men).

- Contradicts the generally accepted advice of health and nutrition professionals (rats and people need nutrients other than those supplied by apricots and peaches).

Fad versus fit

No matter how you slice the food, healthful weight-loss programs require time and effort to melt away the excess pounds. Fad diets are so appealing because they promise maximum results with minimum investment (other than the dollars you may be asked to cough up for those miracle products).

Lose the weight, keep the money

Americans spend millions each year on diets and weight loss. But you don't need to join the money-burning frenzy. Here are budget ways to lose weight:

✔ www.ediets.com: E-diets lets you choose the diet focus best for you — heart healthy, soy, vegetarian, diabetic, or cholesterol lowering. Or take the free diet needs analysis, which analyzes your current health, habits, diet goals, and dietary concerns (whether you want low sugar, no red meat) to determine the right diet for you. Then for about $3–5 a week, you receive a weekly set of meal plans that adjust to your progress, a personal shopping list, and 24/7 online professional support. Stay motivated by talking with others in the program in chat rooms. Add on a weekly fitness plan for $1 per week.

✔ www.weightlosssoftware.com: If you're a bit of a nerd or just like to keep track of things, the Weight Loss Software Food And Exercise Diary For Windows analyzes your exercise and food consumption and then generates reports and graphs you can use to monitor your weight loss. The software analyzes your actual daily weight, daily diet, and daily exercise in order to suggest a daily caloric-intake limit and exercise-expenditure-limit for sensible weight loss. Of course, you can enter your own diet and exercise limits if you have a good feel for

your body's metabolism. The Weight Loss Software comes with a nutritional information database of nearly 10,000 different food items, including brand-name foods, so you don't have to look up all those annoying nutrition tables. It's about 40 bucks.

✔ www.healthyweightforum.org: This site is a free forum offering support, motivation, recipes, and fellowship for those trying to lose weight. It includes reviews of fad diets and helpful weight loss tools like a calorie counter, weight tracker, and online diary.

✔ www.shapeup.org: Shape Up America! is a national initiative to promote healthy weight and increased physical activity in America. Its program Shape Up & Drop 10 claims to offer real help for real people — just solid information and guidance. As a member, you can also access the CyberKitchen, which helps you build menu plans and provides you with recipes that are approved by a nutritionist/dietitian. All ingredients for the recipes are put into a convenient shopping list for you to print out and take to the store. The Shape Up Fitness Center helps you assess your readiness for physical activity, your activity level, flexibility, strength, and endurance, and then design a program to meet your goals. The first six months of membership in Shape Up are free.

Part III
Saying "I Love You"

The 5th Wave   By Rich Tennant

@RICHTENNANT

"I knew they were writing their own vows, but I expected quotes from Robert Frost poems, not The Geneva Convention."

In this part . . .

*W*hen most people reach their 50s, they find that the landscape of their lives — and especially their love relationships — has changed considerably. After years of raising children and focusing on careers, they suddenly have more time on their hands — time that they can and should devote to their spouse or loved one. The trouble is, after all those years of focusing on the kids and work, most couples find that they need to rekindle the romance in their relationship.

If you are one of these couples, we have great news for you! The chapters in this part describe some simple ways you can reconnect with each other in mid-life, adding an air of romance and renewing your commitment to each other. We even offer tips on keeping sex alive in your senior years.

For those who are looking to start a new love relationship, we have an entire chapter about dating in today's world. And for those who are looking for love in the form of a trusted pet companion, we have a chapter for you, as well.

Read on, and discover the love in your life all over again!

Chapter 10

Rekindling Romance
with Your Spouse

· ·

In This Chapter

▶ How to tell whether a marriage is working

▶ Overcoming empty nest syndrome

▶ Frolicking in the bedroom in your senior years

▶ Renewing your marriage vows

· ·

Half of all marriages end in divorce — and that's not a happy statistic. But when you think about all the hopes and dreams people carry into marriage, it's amazing that the divorce rate isn't even higher. After all, how can any relationship possibly deliver the complete love, great sex, never-ending fun, and permanent security that marriage is supposed to guarantee?

It can take one year, two years, or five years. But, whenever the inevitable disappointments occur, one or both partners may feel tempted to give up on the marriage. More often than not, calling a divorce lawyer is a mistake. A far better course is to figure out strategies that will make your marriage more satisfying.

This chapter offers some thoughts and valuable tools for keeping your marriage afloat through midlife and well into your senior years, beginning with the five building blocks of a marriage that works.

The Five Building Blocks of a Working Marriage

In this section, we show you how to develop the five building blocks of marriage, which can make the difference between a relationship that stays together and one that falls apart.

- ✔ **Developing a realistic view of marriage:** The reality of most enduring marriages lies somewhere between the glorious love song and the cynical joke. Sure, there are bound to be times when things are terrible. However, these times are usually balanced by other times when things are going great. Ultimately, the majority of married partners spend most of their time in an emotional space between the two extremes of ecstasy and agony.

- ✔ **Treasuring what the two of you have in common:** One of the best ways to become closer with your partner is to value and build on the things the two of you have in common. These common areas can be based on virtually any interest you and your partner share. Your shared interest can be spiritual or cultural. It can be something as profound as a religious conviction, or something as ordinary as playing cards.

- ✔ **Making room for separateness in your togetherness:** Every person needs a certain amount of personal space — and married partners are no exception. Many couples pursue separate interests in sports, films, and other hobbies. In many cases, they manage to find ways to work things out so that neither partner feels slighted or threatened, and their relationship thrives.

- ✔ **Making the most of your differences:** Everyone has strengths — as well as frailties and blind spots. The trick is to use your partner's strong points as motivators to stimulate growth in areas where you need improvement.

  That spark of excitement you and your partner initially felt toward each other can be recaptured — if you remember that the same differences that cause problems now may have played an important part in why you once found each other so attractive.

- ✔ **Accepting that not all problems can be solved:** Some problems between married partners are relatively simple to resolve; others take a good deal of work; some may never be solved. As you strive to build a stronger marriage, you have to accept that many of your incompatibilities will be constantly recycled in different variations throughout your marriage.

Making the Most of Marriage at Midlife

After 20 or more years of marriage, it may seem a little late to ask yourself if you picked the right person. After all, it's way past the warranty period. Still, midlife is the time when wives and husbands are likely to ask that question.

In midlife, married partners often find themselves sandwiched between two generations. Coming up behind the typical midlife couple are their adolescent children — who may require years of emotional and financial support before they become self-sufficient. Ahead of the married couple are their aging parents — who may be sick or dying. These changes come at a time when the partners are likely to be reflecting on their own mortality and on the choices that define their lives.

Becoming a couple again after children grow up

Even though husbands and wives can experience anxiety about their grown children leaving home, many find this initially painful transition to be a positive force in their marriage. Research shows that midlife couples who've launched their children have happier marriages and enjoy life more than those couples of the same age whose children continue to live with them, or those couples who've never had kids. Many couples actually look forward to their children leaving the house and find that this is one of the happiest times for their relationships.

Here's how you can set the stage for a positive empty-nest experience:

- **Prepare yourself for the inevitable.** Some parents have trouble letting go of their children. Spouses who've spent their entire marriage caring for home and family sometimes fret over what they'll do after their last child leaves. The vast majority of parents readily acknowledge that their children's leaving is an essential part of the life process. Parents usually understand that their children don't need them in the same ways that they used to.

- **Think of new ways to rechannel your energies — both as individuals and as a couple.** Your children may not have required your physical attention for years. However, once they're out of the house, the sense of freedom may seem more real.

- **Lay the groundwork with your children for maintaining close ties.** Research shows that parents who have positive relations with their children are best able to cope with this transition.

  If you don't stay close to your kids after they leave, the pain of missing them continues to linger. Staying close also smoothes the way for positive interactions with your grown child's spouse and his or her family.

- **Consider downsizing to a smaller home, or renovating your present home.** This can give you the feeling that you're launching a new lifestyle.

- **Allow time for an adjustment period.** After investing so many years sharing your home with your children, you're bound to feel some sense of loss when they go. Part of your pain may date back to your own leaving home — and the stresses you may have had with your family of origin during that period. Give yourself time to reflect on those feelings, and share your thoughts and anxieties with your partner.

Studies show that couples often experience a kind of second honeymoon after the children are launched. With the kids out of the house, the partners now have an opportunity to refocus their energies on each other — and on making their marriage more exciting.

Improving your topical tan

The two of you have no rules dictating whether you should share one interest or twenty. For example, you both might enjoy traveling, but if you have responsibilities, you can't be gadding about all the time together. The same is true for going to the theater or skiing. . . . But you *can* take action:

- ✔ Read up on subjects that interest you and discuss what you learn.
- ✔ Go online and discover stimulating facts to share with each other.

If you do these activities regularly when you have the chance, then you add to the shared experiences about which you can reminisce.

The two key words here are *share* and *stimulating*. If you both can talk about it, and you both become enthused while doing so, then it doesn't matter what "it" is, as long as *it* gets you communicating.

Steaming up the nest

With the kids out of the house, you're more free to engage in sex at the moment of your choosing. Make love before dinner. Or during half-time of the game. Or right after breakfast. You decide.

You may also decide in advance the time that you'll make love. When your kids were around, you could never be sure exactly what hour they'd all go to bed and fall asleep. You might have said to each other in the morning, "Let's make love tonight," but if Johnny had a bad cold or Suzie had to stay up late studying for a test, your plans wilted. As empty nesters, you can say, "This afternoon, let's shop for groceries; then let's make love."

What else can you do with all this new privacy?

- ✔ **Take your morning shower together.** Much of the time showering together doesn't lead to sex, but don't be afraid to be late for work once in a while.
- ✔ **Go for a moonlight drive.** Find a spot where you won't be interrupted and hit the back seat!

✔ **Rent erotic movies.** If you worry about what the neighbors think, drive to another neighborhood to rent them.

✔ **Greet the sunrise.** Don't fight the fatigue. When you both come home from work exhausted, have a light supper, set the alarm for dawn, and go to bed. In the morning, open the curtains, and as the light creeps into your window, compete with the sun for making the warmest glow.

✔ **Scent your world with flowers.** Buy a load of roses, cover your bed with petals, and settle down into the aroma.

✔ **Write an erotic story.** Spend a night writing together and acting out all the "good parts."

✔ **Rent some costumes.** Spend an evening playing Romeo and Juliet, Bonnie and Clyde, or Cleopatra and Marc Antony.

✔ **Create your own game show.** Watch your favorite quiz show and play along using the "at home" rules — the person who answers wrong has to take off an article of clothing.

The art of romance: Keeping love fresh

Before mankind visited space, people thought that space was filled with ether. Whatever this "ether" was, it was assumed to be quite delicate, which is where we get the word *ethereal*. Romance is very much like ether. It fills the spaces between two lovers, and it, too, is very delicate.

To keep your love fresh, you must tend to romance, repair any rips in its surface, and make sure that there's enough of this substance between the two of you to support as much love as you can possibly exchange.

Here are some thoughts on keeping romance alive:

✔ **Communicate:** Communication is the first and most crucial step toward solving the issue of too little romance. (Communication is crucial to most other problems that couples face, as well.) If the two of you want more romance in your relationship but sit there like statues never voicing your feelings, then you have no chance whatsoever of making any improvements. Only by talking about the issues can the level of romance start soaring like a hot air balloon rather than sinking like a rock.

✔ **Differentiate sex and romance:** There's romance — and there's sex. Obviously, the two have certain connections, but they're not synonymous.

People who barely know each other can have sex during a one-night stand, but you can't say that they're romantically involved. If you think back, you can probably remember being madly in love with someone before you had sex, proving that romance can exist even when sex isn't part of the picture. So while sex may eventually become an integral aspect of a romantic relationship, think of them as two separate ingredients, like lox and cream cheese, which complement each other when placed on a bagel but can also stand alone.

✔ **Find time to be together:** The old saying may state that familiarity breeds contempt, but these days too many couples just don't spend sufficient time with each other for romance to grow and flourish. No matter how full the appointment calendar is on your Palm Pilot, you must set aside some time to be together. Make this time a priority. It may not be more important than feeding the kids, for example, but sometimes you can order a pizza instead of cooking. The kids will love the treat, and you and your spouse will have an extra half hour to connect.

✔ **Seek out privacy:** Sitting together while the kids/your in-laws/the neighbors/the pizza delivery man are in the room isn't particularly conducive to romance. You need to be able to say what needs to be said, and maybe touch what needs to be touched, without interruption or observation.

Getting out of the house altogether may be helpful; a change in scenery can help to stimulate romance. At home, just catching sight of a pile of unpaid bills out of the corner of your eye can be enough to deaden any romantic impulses that may be stirring.

✔ **Concentrate on each other:** It's all well and good to have that perfect moment when you're together, alone, and there's nothing on the schedule for the next 20 minutes. But if one or both of you lets that moment carelessly slip away, you can become even more frustrated. No matter how tired you are or what crisis is on the horizon, force yourself to concentrate on the here and now and that person sitting next to you. If you find your thoughts drifting off, bring them back to the moment.

✔ **Increase the energy level:** Falling asleep in each other's arms may be considered romantic in some instances, but if you're trying to rekindle your romance, you need to put more energy into the process than that. Both partners have to take an active role. The more enthusiasm and spirit you put into any attempt to increase romance, the more likely your efforts will pay off.

In addition to increasing your private time together, getting out of the house can increase your energy level. Just going for a walk together helps to clear the cobwebs from your mind and gives you more energy. After you're out of the house, you'll be interacting with a dynamic world. That added stimulation keeps your energy up. Something as simple as a sunset can trigger the right emotions, as can some beautiful flowers or even a driving snowstorm (if you're in a romantic mood and not worrying about having to shovel the driveway).

✔ **Find your special romantic focus points:** To some people, reading poetry is very romantic. If your partner fits into that category, then go out of your way to read some poems out loud to him or her. Drinking a glass of champagne while watching the sunset may set someone else's heart on fire, so if that's the case, add such a toast to your daily (or at least weekly) agenda.

✔ **Hey, big spender:** We don't want to make it seem that being romantic necessarily involves spending big bucks. Yes, Carol Channing did sing "Diamonds Are a Girl's Best Friend," and some women love getting jewelry, but you have plenty of ways to be romantic that don't require much (or any) money at all. Here are a few:

- **Give a massage.** Massages are very romantic because they involve a lot of touching. It doesn't matter what type of massage you give — an all-over massage, a back rub, a foot massage, or just a few simple squeezes of the back of the neck. Any of these show you care and feed the romantic ether.

- **Pitch in around the house.** Do some of your partner's household chores without being asked.

- **Cook your partner's favorite meal.**

- **Watch your partner's favorite TV show with him or her.**

- **Support your partner's interests.** For example, go to the library to borrow a book on a favorite topic or one that's written by an author your partner likes.

- **Identify an annoying habit and try to stop it.** For example, stop leaving the toilet seat up or using all the hot water when you take a shower.

- **Show that you pay attention.** Even a small gesture, such as taking the telephone off the hook when your partner says "let's talk," shows how much you care.

✔ **Second that emotion:** Sharing emotions can be intensely romantic, especially if you don't normally reveal how you feel. Allowing your partner to peer down into your inner self, making yourself somewhat vulnerable, definitely pulls at the heartstrings.

✔ **Climb out of your rut:** Doing something unexpected can be romantic. Following the same routine can become boring, and boredom is definitely not romantic. If you do something to take your partner by surprise, like suggesting a walk in the pouring rain — without an umbrella or shoes — you'll definitely grab his or her attention. By putting yourself in a new light, your partner will see you differently, and that creates a positive impression.

✔ **Establish relationship rituals:** While some repetitive behavior can be boring, reenacting relationship rituals has the opposite effect. A second honeymoon to the same place you took your first one is very romantic. But a relationship ritual doesn't have to be quite that elaborate or expensive. Kissing each other hello and goodbye is such a ritual; when one party skips this peck, the other can sorely miss it. Going out to dinner on a certain night of the week can be a romantic ritual. Even doing the grocery shopping together could inspire closeness. *Together* is the operative word here; whatever the ritual is, if it involves the two of you and is done regularly, then the ritual can strengthen the bond that exists between you. And that will boost your romance.

✔ **Put your best foot forward:** Like it or not, what you look like does play a role in setting a romantic tone. If you live with your partner, you obviously can't look your best every second of the day. But you can't always look your worst and expect that not to have an effect on your relationship. Everybody likes to dress comfortably while at home, but clothes can be comfortable without looking ratty. And while our bodies do change as we get older, a little effort can go a long way toward minimizing those changes.

✔ **Create a pleasing environment:** The appearance of your environment is important to romance. That doesn't mean you have to put every single thing in your home away, but if you're so messy that you can't even find a place to lay down together . . . well, that isn't going to encourage romance, is it?

✔ **Tickle your partner's funny bone:** While those romance novels may make it seem like a person in love has to be dark and brooding, laughter lifts the spirits and can help make any relationship more romantic. You can't always be silly, and the guffaws don't drive romance anyway — good spirits do. So while you don't need to keep your partner doubled over with laughter, do make an effort to keep a smile on both your faces.

✔ **Become great friends:** It's definitely a plus if the two of you are great friends, which means that you enjoy being together and doing things as a couple. That isn't to imply that you do everything together, however. While living in such a cocoon may seem idyllic for a short time, eventually the two of you have to grow and act individually. If you do everything together, when one or both of you start to change, you may get the impression that a rift is growing between you.

✔ **The truth will set you free:** Being romantic is very difficult if one or both of you is living a life full of lies. Don't get us wrong: We're all for the little white lie that prevents hurting a loved one's feelings. White lies are told to protect the other person. If you're telling lies to protect yourself, or if your partner is being dishonest, that's a serious matter. Romance can only thrive in an atmosphere of trust.

✔ **The inner game of romance:** The concept was that if you tried too hard to hit the ball, you'd distract yourself and wouldn't play as well. The same concept works with romance. If you start thinking "should I do this" or "should I do that," then it's very difficult to be romantic. Romance is a feeling, and you have to allow it to envelop you. It's almost impossible to force yourself to feel romantic. So in order to rekindle your romance, the two of you should learn to luxuriate in each other's presence, drifting off into that tunnel of love.

✔ **Ego stroking:** In order to love someone else, you first have to be able to love yourself. That's sometimes easier said than done, so any help that a partner can give in that department will be well worth it. Both partners should be supportive of each other, exchanging compliments whenever appropriate. Try to keep track of your partner's mood. If he or she is feeling low, then make a point of coming to the rescue with some well-chosen ego boosting.

Having Great Sex in Your Senior Years

As you age, you may find that sex doesn't occur with the same intensity or frequency as when you were in your twenties, but it's a big mistake to look at older people and think that they're sexless. Sadly, some older folks see themselves as sexless and give up on lovemaking when there isn't any need to do so. After all, we recently entered a new era in medical history where drugs like Viagra can restore what once was lost.

Taking a fresh look at your romance

When you first started having sex, it was great. Then the natural result of sex came along — children — and sex may have taken a back seat. As your careers took off and your children became teenagers who stayed up late, sex may have tapered off even more.

Many changes occur as you age, including the following:

✔ Your children may go off to college or leave home to pursue other interests. Whether or not you missed the privacy you gave up when you had children, you should discover the joys of being able to walk around naked and have sex when the mood suits you.

✔ You may start to slow down in your work life even before you retire. Some seniors find that they have accrued a considerable amount of vacation time over the years. Having seniority at your company may mean that you can extend your weekends. Or your seniority could mean you have fewer responsibilities and can get home at a reasonable hour. Extra time together definitely helps in rekindling your romance.

✔ The new steps you need to perform before enjoying sex due to physical changes — playing with his penis, putting some lubricant in her vagina — may increase the intimacy between the two of you. Becoming closer is good for your sex life and your romance.

This time in your life represents a true crossroads for many couples. Some couples can't cope with the physical changes, and their marriages become sexless or their relationships don't survive. Others find ways to deepen their relationships because of the changes. You can choose the better direction when you approach that fork in the road, because you now know what physical changes to expect as you grow older.

Appreciating new sexual experiences

Sex is easy to take for granted when you are young. After all, when you are in your twenties, the orgasm you just had may be followed by another orgasm in an hour. As your sex life changes, you may find that you have a better appreciation for your sexual opportunities. Growing older means developing a maturity and a wisdom to appreciate life's pleasures — from watching a sunset to playing with grandchildren to enjoying sex.

✔ **Getting the most out of sex:** You need to know how to make the best use of the sexual powers that remain vital as you age. Knowledge definitely helps you maximize the return you get from each sexual episode. Even if the opportunities occur less frequently, a little know-how may mean you'll be just as satisfied.

✔ **Seizing the (break of) day:** Although a young couple may fancy having sex at any time, most couples tend to engage in sex at night. (For variety's sake, you might like to try making love at different times.) But an older couple may find that morning sex is the most enjoyable.

Sex in the morning is more enjoyable for an older couple for two main reasons.

• The first reason is that they're well rested and energetic after a good night's sleep. Thus, they're better able to exert themselves. Older couples don't need to start having sex the moment they wake up. We recommend that the couple get out of bed, wash their faces, have a light breakfast, and then go back to bed and make love.

- The second reason morning sex is more pleasurable for older couples is physiological. Testosterone, the male hormone, affects the man's ability to become aroused. This testosterone level goes up and down during the course of a day and is at its highest level in the morning. If a man has any trouble achieving an erection, morning sex makes it easier for him.

✔ **It's all in the timing:** When both partners are easily aroused, it doesn't matter much who initiates sex, because soon both are fully stimulated. Older couples may find that they both are *not* easily aroused. For various reasons, an older couple may not always be in synch. A man may have an erection in the morning, but a woman may take several hours to warm up due to her arthritis. Until her swollen joints are warmed up, she may not be in the mood to have an orgasm.

Although fighting off the effects of age would be great, you may find that you sometimes have to accept the physical changes that occur over the years. As the years advance, you have to adapt to all sorts of aids and habits in order to make it through each day. Much the same way, you have to make some adaptations in your sex life.

Don't think of having scheduled sex — when partners are satisfied at different times — as being strange; think of it as being very intimate. If sex is more fulfilling when you have separate orgasms, don't allow "convention" to stop you. Do what is necessary to stay vital and sexually active. We think you'll find that scheduled sex is worth the effort.

Sharing a slow and steady fire

Of course, sex is only one component of romance. You can't expect your spouse to give you an orgasm and ignore him or her the rest of the day. Finding other activities that bring you closer together like walking, dining, and reading to each other are essential. The process of rekindling your romance continues throughout the day.

The years bring on changes that require different approaches to keeping that romantic flame alive. For example, both partners are going to be sensitive about changes to their appearances. The physical changes may be subtle during the first few decades of the relationship and become more noticeable as the years add up. Gray hair, wrinkles, potbellies, loss of hair, and loss of muscle: All of these physical changes mean that you have to assure each other your love hasn't grown any dimmer because of the natural aging process. Give compliments to your partner and tell him how much you love him as often as you can; it's more important these days than ever.

Reasons for Saying "I Do" Times Two

You can look at a renewal as merely a further commitment to your original vows, but isn't it better to look at it as a chance to celebrate your marriage? If you've gotten past all the bumps on the road of life so far, why not congratulate yourselves with a public renewal of vows? We all can use a pat on the back for a job well done, and there's no better way to offer congratulations to each other than to renew your promises.

If your marriage isn't working well — if the two of you have issues to deal with — a marriage renewal is probably not the answer. Doing so may mask the cracks for a short time, but eventually those cracks will reappear. So don't look at a marriage renewal as a quick fix. If your marriage needs repairs, take care of the issues first. Let some time go by, and if it looks like your marriage is holding up, celebrate with some sort of vow renewal.

Here are a few other reasons to renew your vows — besides the desire to throw a party:

- ✔ **Strengthening a second (or third) marriage:** Not every marriage is a first marriage. If one or both of you have gone through a divorce (maybe even multiple times), the extra reassurance provided by a renewal of vows may be quite appreciated. In such marriages, you may not want to wait for the 10th or 20th anniversary to renew your vows. That's not to say your marriage is necessarily shakier because of past mishaps, but any added signs of commitment couldn't hurt. Plus, a renewal shows any people who warned you against getting married again that they didn't know what they were talking about.

- ✔ **Recognizing that your job is not done:** Another reason for renewing vows is that the job of a husband or wife isn't done until one of you goes to that great wedding hall of fame in the sky. Openly renewing your marriage vows can give you additional strength to continue to remain faithful to each other. Any promise loses power over time, and it becomes easier to make excuses for being weak. Besides, if you outlive your partner, you'll be thankful after he's gone that you did renew those vows. You'll know that you took at least that particular opportunity to tell your spouse, once again, how important he or she was to you.

- ✔ **Embracing a lifetime of change:** If the two of you have been married for quite some time, you've both gone through many changes physically, intellectually, and emotionally. These changes have been gradual, so they may be hard for you to see. If you look back at your wedding pictures and try to remember your emotional and intellectual selves back then, the changes will become quite apparent. If you love each other despite the changes you've both gone through, you have another reason to recommit.

✔ **Setting an example for the younger generation:** The example that you set definitely affects your children. The more often they can witness the two of you demonstrating your love for each other, the more likely that they'll imitate you and try their hardest to stick with their spouses. Your kids may even want to take part in the renewal ceremony. They could write something to recite, or (if they're old enough) each of them could get up and say a few words about your relationship.

✔ **Bringing years of experience to your vows:** The love that you have for your spouse now is inevitably different than it was when you got married. Although the intensity may have waned over the years, the ties that bind you have added up through those same years. Chances are that you feel more tightly connected than you did when you first married.

✔ **Sticking together through life's speed bumps:** If you've been together for a long time, there's no doubt you've hit some of life's little speed bumps. Actually, you may have even met some rather large bumps head on. For example, each of you may have lost one or both of your parents. This situation is to be expected if you stay together long enough, but the fact that your spouse takes on greater importance when you no longer have your parents to fall back on can't be denied. So while you may not have understood fully what your wedding vows meant the first time around, they'll have a much deeper meaning for the two of you now.

✔ **Celebrating shared memories:** If you're both 50 and you've been married for 25 years, then you've spent half of your lives together. Even if you haven't been together quite so long, you still have quite a bank of shared memories stored up. And if you have children, you've shared even more special moments that only the two of you can appreciate.

✔ **Taking a trip down memory lane:** A natural part of the process of renewing your vows is thinking back on all those memories that the two of you have accumulated over the years. Make a conscious decision about how this is going to occur. If you do so in a piecemeal fashion, the impact won't be the same. Try to set aside a block of time when you and your spouse can look over old pictures, movies, and videos, leaf through diaries, and just talk about the "good old days."

Your first marriage vows were probably not very specific because the two of you didn't know each other very well yet. This time around, you have X number of years as husband and wife under your belt. You know each other a lot better, and now that you're older, you know yourself a lot better too. Whatever ceremony you plan this time, you can be a little more specific with your vows.

Make an effort to let the good feelings from your renewal ceremony have more than a 24-hour life span. If you've made some specific promises to your spouse, try to live up to them. The next time you feel a little angry at your spouse, in the spirit of these new vows, release that anger and give him or her a hug instead.

Bargain gifts that say "I love you"

Unique, romantic gifts can go a long way toward sparking some passion in a relationship, but they don't have to cost a lot. Here are a few ideas:

- www.winecountrygiftbaskets.com: For something romantic yet sophisticated, try a wine gift basket like the Crane Lake Cabernet Sauvignon. In addition to the wine, this basket includes a zesty cheddar cheese spread and cheese knife, Tazo tea assortment, caramel cookies, cheese baguettes, and Ghirardelli milk chocolate with caramel. If you go to the "Specials" section, you find this and several other baskets for less than $30. Just don't forget to get the kids out of house or you'll spoil the effect.

- www.chocolatefantasies.com: If you're a little more daring, try erotically shaped gummies or a jar of chocolate body paint complete with brush. You can even get a low-fat version. Most of the gifts are inexpensive, with some of the smaller jars of "naughty chocolate sauce" under $5.

If the gifts just listed aren't appropriate, but you're drawing a blank on anything else, here are two sites that help you figure out what your loved one would want:

- www.findgift.com: FindGift helps you find unique gift ideas and then connects you to online stores where these gifts are sold. You can search by the person you're buying for, age, occasion, special interests, price, gift type (do you want it romantic or off the wall?), and the emotion you want the gift to express (such as thank you or crazy for you).

- www.gifts-and-gift-ideas.com: This directory is similar to FindGift, presenting gift ideas and suggestions organized by various categories including anniversary, baby, birthday, house warming, retirement, wedding, Mother's Day, and so on. The site also has a section that links to the bargain, special sales, and closeout sections of many of its merchant affiliates. If you find something you like here, act fast because gifts in these sections don't last long.

If you find the renewal process effective, why not make it a regular part of your marriage? We're not saying that you should make a big deal about it once a year. But you could have a small private ceremony, just between the two of you, every year on your wedding anniversary. When you make that toast to each other, say a few words that will fill in for a full renewal of your marriage vows. Rituals are a good way of acting out our feelings constructively.

Chapter 11

Practicing Great Family Relationships in a "Sandwich Generation"

In This Chapter

▶ Understanding the challenges of aging

▶ Providing care for the elderly — and the caretaker

▶ Planning a fabulous family reunion

*F*or most people, reaching their 50s means that they find themselves living in a "sandwich generation." Most middle agers' parents are now elderly and may require assistance to live independently, and at the same time, these middle agers are trying to stay connected with their children who are no longer children, but adults who may even have kids of their own.

This chapter gives you some tools for understanding the various generations (particularly the elderly) and the challenges they face, as well as some tips for taking care of yourself in the process. The chapter also gives you some ideas for how to plan a family reunion — a great way to have some fun and stay connected with all the generations.

Recognizing the Challenges of Aging

People over 65 are more diverse than people in any other age group. The varied life experiences of those who live a long time probably account for much of the individual uniqueness. People also age in different ways. Some folks remain healthy and active into their 80s, while others become frail early on. Even within every individual, organs age at different speeds. For example, Dad's ticker may be strong, but his digestive system may be falling apart. Here are some situations to be aware of:

✓ **Slowed reflexes, memory lapses, and "senior moments":** Even in the healthiest people, strength, flexibility, and reaction time diminish with age. The decline actually starts when you're a young adult but isn't noticeable until middle age, when knees aren't what they used to be and pesky memory lapses (senior moments) appear.

✓ **Diminished senses:** In the normal healthy older adult, the five senses (vision, hearing, smell, taste, and touch) tend to decline somewhat with age. A dulling in the perception of pain (the sense of touch) may cause an elderly person to ignore a bedsore, burn, or other injury increasing their risk of serious infection or disability.

✓ **Age-related disease and disability:** Lots of diseases strike older people more often than younger people. Interestingly, the same illnesses may produce different symptoms in older people than they produce in younger adults. For example, an underactive or overactive thyroid may cause confusion in an older patient but not in a younger one. When the confusion is mistaken as dementia, the elder may be unnecessarily institutionalized and the underlying illness left untreated.

✓ **Changed family relationships:** A parent who can't take care of himself or herself rattles the foundation of the family. Sometimes loved ones rise to the occasion with calmness and cooperation. More often, long-forgotten childhood rivalries and jealousies raise their ugly heads, creating chaos and strife.

Avoid the mistaken belief that taking care of your frail parent is "parenting your parent." Even though many eldercare tasks are the same as childcare tasks (feeding, bathing, toileting), *emotionally* your elder is still your parent. Trying to parent a grown-up (by speaking to him or her like a child, for example) ends up with the parent feeling insulted and angry and the caregiver feeling frustrated and ineffectual.

Acknowledging that help is needed

Sometimes, admitting to yourself that your older person is failing is tough to do, especially when that person assures you that everything is fine and dandy. But taking early action prevents more serious problems. If you observe the following warning signs, a thorough assessment of your older person's situation is in order:

✓ Extreme clutter, especially in a former neatnik's home

✓ Clothes strewn about

✓ Items that used to be in drawers and cupboards now crowding countertops and other surfaces

✓ Medication bottles left open

✔ Uncertainty about what medications he or she is taking, and when and why medications are supposed to be taken

✔ Unfilled prescriptions

✔ Unpaid bills

✔ Penalties for overdue bills

✔ Dunning bill-collection notices

✔ Disheveled and dirty clothes

✔ The same outfit worn over and over again

✔ Dangerous driving

✔ Unkempt hair

✔ Body odor (indications of loss of bowel and bladder control or difficulty bathing)

✔ Bad breath (inability to brush or floss, gum disease, or infection in nose, throat, windpipe, or lungs)

✔ Not much food in the house

✔ No nutritious or fresh food in the house

✔ Decayed food in the refrigerator

✔ Burnt pots and pans

✔ Confusion, sadness, anxiety, no interest in friends and former pastimes

✔ Evidence of falling prey to a telephone scam or door-to-door fraud

✔ Compensation for losses in sometimes clever but dangerous ways

✔ Bruises on body (could be a sign of falls)

You're always best to double-check. Ask neighbors and friends if they've observed similar problems or have concerns.

Making an assessment

When your elder appears to be struggling with some tasks but you're not sure if you have the full picture, the time is ripe for an organized assessment of his or her capabilities. The key to locating trouble spots is to list all the basic activities that people need to do to keep themselves healthy, safe, happy, and financially solvent. Then go down the list, one item at a time, determining whether your elderly person can manage each item without help.

Understanding your four options

Eldercare involves an ever-changing set of chores. Needs almost always grow. As frailty increases, more decisions about care need to be made, such as:

- ✔ **Remaining in his or her own home:** Most Americans want to "age in place," but doing so may take creative thinking. Like all adults, elders want to be surrounded by their own things and enjoy the freedom and privacy to do exactly as they please.

- ✔ **Living with you:** When worrying about your mom affects your work and a phone ringing late at night gives you the shudders, entertaining thoughts of moving your elderly parent into your own household is only natural. The arrangement has its benefits, to be sure. Providing care yourself is less expensive than hiring others. Having mom close by can alleviate your fears that she will burn her house down, not eat properly, or forget to take her medication. Such a move may seem especially right when a parent loses his or her spouse and is depressed and lonely.

- ✔ **Assisted living:** Approximately one million elderly reside in assisted-living facilities. The premise behind this option is that living in a home-like group setting (with a menu of services available) enhances and extends an older adult's ability to live with dignity. Residents have private or shared rooms and receive only the services that they need or want. Services (some requiring an extra charge) include meals, housekeeping, laundry, transportation, recreational activities, shopping assistance, and reminders to take medications. Assisted-living facilities do not provide medical care.

- ✔ **Nursing homes:** Some people go to nursing homes for a short while to recuperate after a hospitalization. For the elderly who become residents, the nursing home will be the last place they'll live. We know of no nursing home residents who live in nursing homes because they simply like the lifestyle. They live there because their medical conditions are such that they need to have skilled nursing care and supervision within reach 24 hours a day.

Four ways to enhance the quality of life

The average life expectancy in the United States today is 72.5 for men and 79.3 for women, which averages out to 76 years. By 2050, the average life expectancy will be 80 years. You may have to take an array of pills to control a collection of chronic illnesses — but life will be long.

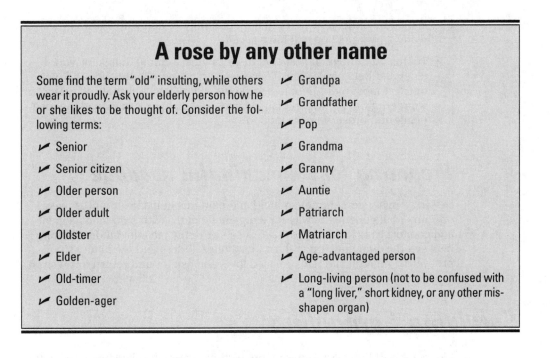

A rose by any other name

Some find the term "old" insulting, while others wear it proudly. Ask your elderly person how he or she likes to be thought of. Consider the following terms:

- Senior
- Senior citizen
- Older person
- Older adult
- Oldster
- Elder
- Old-timer
- Golden-ager

- Grandpa
- Grandfather
- Pop
- Grandma
- Granny
- Auntie
- Patriarch
- Matriarch
- Age-advantaged person
- Long-living person (not to be confused with a "long liver," short kidney, or any other misshapen organ)

The now-important area for research isn't to keep people living longer (that's pretty much been accomplished!), it's to help them to make those extra years as good as they can be by doing the following:

- **Retaining health:** Getting sufficient sleep, exercising regularly, eating a well-balanced diet (including breakfast), and not smoking help ward off disease — important advice at any age. Having a satisfying relationship with those closest to you has been shown to also be a factor in health promotion and disease prevention for the age-advantaged person and his or her caregiver.

- **Understanding emotions:** Sometimes it's clear why grandpa is depressed or worried — he's lost his spouse, his health, or his confidence. On the other hand, it's sometimes a mystery. Sadness and apprehension can come without warning, seemingly unrelated to anything in daily life. Identifying and treating emotional upsets takes some investigation, perhaps medical intervention, and a whole lot of love and patience.

- **Keeping your loved one out of harm's way:** A kitten underfoot, throw rugs, appliance cords tangled up like spaghetti, and shag rugs on stairs are accidents waiting to happen. A kitchen fire or a broken hip can signal the premature end of independent living. Elder-proofing mom's home can add months and years to her autonomy — and who knows how many gray hairs you will have saved!

✔ **Taking advantage of assistive devices:** Resist doing things for your elder and help him or her devise ways to be more independent. Point out that most older people have some difficulties, but that today is a wonderful time in which many gizmos and gadgets can extend independence and preserve personhood.

Preparing for a meaningful goodbye

Helping a dying person remain lucid and pain free in his last months, weeks, or hours of life opens the way for a dignified death. With pain management and comfort as priorities, the stage is set for richly meaningful discussions between the dying person and his loved ones. Elders and the family share past hurts, regrets, and unexpressed love, and ask for and return forgiveness.

Surviving Caregiving

Eldercare is difficult. Shouldering the work by yourself is like being "it" in the game of tag. If you're lucky or swift, someone else will take his or her turn. Lots of caregivers remain "it" simply because no one else is within tagging distance or because they don't know how to get anyone else involved in the game. As your elderly person grows ever more frail, the health, sanity, and well-being of you and your immediate family depend on getting others to pitch in. Anticipating the situations you're likely to encounter can help a lot, too!

Unlike professional caregivers who go home after their shift, you're always "on call," facing some of the following situations:

✔ **Handling a resentful spouse and angry children:** Every hour spent on caregiving represents an hour you don't have available for family and friends (for example, less time to attend hockey games, less time to help with homework, and perhaps less time to share a hobby or interest with your partner). It's natural for your family members to start to feel cheated, even if they don't admit it.

One solution is to include a spouse and kids in eldercare to enhance their understanding of the demands you face every day. Make it fun. For example, grandchildren love assisting with exercise. They count the repetitions and cheer Grandpa on. Young teenage girls may get a kick out of doing their grandma's nails. Not only does it lighten your load a bit, it helps young people become more compassionate human beings.

✔ **Feeling unappreciated by the rest of the family:** If you're the one who takes care of most of your elder's needs, others may eventually take your hard work for granted — especially when you do the job so well. Over time, you may begin to feel unappreciated and believe that sacrificing your life is your only option. You may find yourself dwelling on all the things that you're missing because eldercare dominates your days.

Consider joining a support group. Your despair will be met with emotional support and helpful resources and ideas.

✔ **Feeling unappreciated by your elder:** A lack of appreciation by family members stings, but criticism, complaints, and the lack of gratitude from your elder cuts even deeper! If you're in this situation, you may find yourself visiting less and offering less care, even though the age-advantaged person needs it as much as ever.

Share your pain with someone close and take an objective look at the situation. If the older person has always been ungrateful, it's unrealistic to expect anything different now. If the oldster is newly unappreciative, cruelly critical, or apathetic, it's her *illness* making her so.

✔ **Making do with lower future earnings:** Eldercare responsibilities lead to stress-related illness, lost time from work, lost career opportunities, and poor productivity on the job — all bound to affect earnings. Approximately one-third to one-half of all caregivers are employed.

Under the 1993 Family and Medical Leave Act, companies with 50 or more employees must allow up to 12 weeks of leave for employees to care for a seriously ill parent or spouse. The leave is unpaid, but your job is secured. If your elder's problem is a time-limited acute illness (heart attack) or condition (broken hip), and you can manage 12 weeks without pay, take advantage of family leave. Ask your boss whether you can take your 12 weeks in small chunks. Ask the Human Resources department at work for information about family leave, flexible work hours, or job sharing.

✔ **Suffering from unemployment:** Approximately 12 percent of working caregivers eventually find they have to quit their jobs to provide full-time care. Sometimes the people receiving the care want to make up the lost wages but they don't have the money. Even if they do have the money, an unwritten code says that accepting pay for family care is wrong. A study actually attempted to tally up how much all this free care (to impaired relatives of all ages) would cost if families had to pay for it. They estimated that the services provided each year are worth a whopping $196 billion.

A full accounting of your lost income as well as the cost of care (food, medication, transportation, and formal services) should be on the family conference agenda.

✔ **Dealing with feelings of guilt:** The bane of eldercare is that no matter how much you do, you always feel that you could have done more. Even worse is the guilt felt when angry words toward the elder occasionally leap from your lips in the frustration and fatigue of the moment.

Be realistic — you can't change your feelings. Nasty feelings are occupational hazards. All caregivers have them! Realize that you're doing the best you can with what's available. Think of unpleasant emotions as clouds that float in and float out. One goes away only to be replaced by another. Your guilt will flow in and out along with other negative and positive feelings.

When you live far away

The following suggestions are for the far-away caregivers who are trying to do it all:

✔ Resist the "relocation reaction." Before moving your elder to your home, allow lots of time to consider other options.

✔ Do an on-site comprehensive assessment of your elder's situation.

✔ Arrange for home healthcare providers and special programs like Meals on Wheels and transportation services for the frail elderly.

✔ Enlist family members and friends to fill in the gaps.

✔ Ask neighbors, friends, or relatives to visit your elder regularly to spot problems impossible for you to detect by phone, such as mail or newspapers piling up outside the home.

✔ Contact the local postmaster. Informing the local letter carrier that a frail elder is on her route may encourage her to report worrisome signs on the property.

✔ Tell the local police department that an elder lives alone in the community. This knowledge may encourage officers (especially in small towns) to give the oldster a little extra attention, like checking up on him during heat waves, cold spells, earthquakes, hurricanes, and *tsunamis* (huge sea waves caused by under-ocean disturbance).

✔ Check with local utility companies, which may have "elder-watch" programs designed to be sensitive to signs that something may be amiss with an elderly person or couple.

The following suggestions are for faraway caregivers who play second fiddle to the primary caregiver but nevertheless want to help:

✔ Save vacation days and personal holidays for emergency visits.

✔ Squirrel away funds for crisis air travel (or save frequent-flier miles).

Check your airline to find out how to get a ticket on short notice. Frequent-flier programs vary, and airline policies change frequently, but agents will try to help you plan for emergency travel — before the emergency!

✔ Don't wait for eleventh-hour predicaments. Visit as much as possible.

✔ Call often.

✔ Give the primary caregiver a welcome break by bringing the elder to your home or staying with her in her home.

✔ Avoid stepping on the primary caregiver's toes. She is closest to the situation and knows things you don't. Be diplomatic. Tread lightly when disagreeing or intervening.

✔ Offer to research these areas:

- Medical conditions (a task made in heaven for Internet surfers!)

- Assistive devices (a task made in heaven for technology freaks!)

- Benefits and entitlement programs (a task made in heaven for number crunchers!)

- Health and social services providers (a task made in heaven for born organizers!)

Rotating care when necessary

Handing off caregiving chores to others can help you survive. As long as Mom agrees and doesn't get stressed out by travel or adjusting to different settings, six months at her daughter's home and then six months at her son's place can be fun for her and doable for both families. Family members can also take turns helping Mom in her own home. Here are some tips for making it work:

✔ Don't allow offers of help to dry up. Every time someone offers, respond graciously with a specific task. Keep a list in your pocket or purse for just these occasions and add to your "chore list" whenever you think of something that needs doing.

✔ Keeping uninvolved relatives in the loop about medical conditions, treatments, and finances increases the likelihood of their involvement. At the very least, it prevents later complaints that "nobody told me" or "I'd have never agreed to that had I known."

✔ For elders who suffer from confusion, don't rotate personal care (bathing, feeding, dressing) unless absolutely necessary. Otherwise, you may find that your older person's symptoms worsen, and his or her emotional upsets become more frequent. Instead, focus on rotating behind-the-scenes activities (making doctor's appointments, keeping financial records, hiring help, shopping, and emotionally supporting the primary caregiver).

Organizing the Perfect Family Reunion

Family reunions are a great way for all the generations to reconnect and reestablish family ties. You may have elderly parents, children, and grandchildren — and maybe even great-grandchildren — who would enjoy the opportunity to spend a day learning more about each other.

Family reunions come in all shapes and sizes, from small groups of immediate family to large groups pulled together from all corners of the globe. Family reunions can be as simple as a handful of kinfolk getting together for a backyard barbecue or lakeside picnic, or something as elaborate as a catered affair for hundreds of family members in a convention center or hotel ballroom.

Great reasons for having a family reunion

Having a family reunion is a simple way for kinfolk to reestablish family ties. But most families have a "big why" — a main reason — to hold a reunion. Some families have a big why because it makes the amount of time and money spent on the reunion easier to justify.

You can choose from many big whys to have your reunion. For example, suppose that

✔ Granny is celebrating her 100th birthday.

✔ Beth is graduating from medical school.

✔ Pops is retiring.

✔ Aunt Suzie and Uncle Joe are celebrating 50 years of marriage.

These examples are terrific reasons to hold a family reunion.

Consider having a theme for your reunion. Simply getting a bunch of people together for a meal or a barbecue can be boring. Having a theme livens things up. Perhaps your great-grandparents came from the "old country," or maybe your relatives are chicken eaters and like to get together for grandma's famous fried cluck. Use these common bonds to your advantage.

Seven steps for planning the big event

The type of reunion that you plan depends on the number of people attending and the activities involved. For example, activities like a friendly game of croquet or kick-the-can call for a casual atmosphere, whereas a ballroom-dancing competition calls for more of a *shooshefafa* (a silly pet term for a gala affair) atmosphere complete with black ties and evening gowns and some cute little finger sandwiches that barely fill a hole in your tooth.

Here's a list of things to plan for:

- **Figuring out who to invite:** Here's a simple trick for formulating a guest list for a reunion: Compile the guest list based on a common or unifying factor. Having a common factor makes the reunion more enjoyable because everyone shares something special.

- **Locating everyone:** Sometimes finding the clan can make the reunion planner (you) feel like a gumshoe in a detective movie. Folks move or disappear from the family holiday card list without a trace. Start with your immediate family and folks you know, and you may be surprised who among the missing turns up. The Internet is a great tool for finding people, too.

- **Pondering the time and location:** Most family reunions take place during the summer, which makes it easier for families with kids and *usually* means that the weather will cooperate. For the location, you can choose from a wide range of options, from hotel ballrooms to campgrounds or the good old backyard. Wherever you decide to hold the reunion, be sure that the place can accommodate the guest list.

- **Organizing the big event:** Family reunions are big events — usually too large for one person to manage efficiently. You may need some help. You can find that help in the form of *reunion committees,* which are groups of fellow kin that you put together to help you hash out all the reunion details.

- **Keeping everyone busy:** A successful reunion needs activities. These activities can be as simple as storytelling and scavenger hunts or as energetic as carnival-sized games and the family Olympics.

- **Feeding the tribe:** Everyone loves to eat. Your family reunion is a great time for everyone to show off their cooking skills by participating in a potluck meal. If you're not into potlucks (or cooking), you can hire a catering service to provide the eats.

- **Cleaning up the mess:** Reunions are messy affairs, so prepare yourself for some hefty cleanup! Keeping your reunion site tidy makes the cleanup easier; for example, consider setting up areas for recycling and diaper changing.

Planning a family reunion on a budget

Staying close to family is a high priority, especially as you get older and all your kids spread out across the country. Check out these sites for bargain ways to bring them all back home:

✔ www.family-reunion.com: Just being well-organized can save you money. Use this helpful site to create a budget, secure food options (potluck, restaurant, or caterer), plan activities, decide on the guest list, find a location, select the date, choose a theme, form committees, and find lodging and travel. And if the info here isn't enough, post to the message board to get help from others. Don't you feel more organized already?

✔ www.family-reunion.com/software: If your family reunion is quite large and the details are getting out of hand, you might want to check out this family reunion software. It helps you organize family and individual information in an address book, track your budget and expenses, make a schedule, create a family reunion Web site to let everyone know what's going on, plan themes and activities, and keep track of each person's assignments. You can review the free trial version or spend $30 for the full software.

✔ www.familyreunion.com: This site lists resources for caterers, hotels/lodging, decorations, party rentals, and other essential reunion needs. You can also post announcements or have family members take a poll to give you helpful feedback.

✔ www.lexyl.com: Finding lodging for everyone can be a trying experience. At Lexyl.com, you can post your family's lodging reservation needs and let hotels begin bidding rates for your rooms. Compare direct price quotes from over 50,000 hotels worldwide without any obligations — and it's free.

✔ www.famware.com: An important part of many reunions is recording family history and memories. Take a look at this easy-to-use system for organizing and documenting your family's history. The system tracks all types of information about your family — dates, places, facts, and events of all kinds! You can then create pedigree charts, descendant charts, and family group sheets, as well as address labels, anniversary lists, and photo charts. The system runs about $30.

✔ www.bargaintravelcruises.com/group_travel.html: If you really want to plan as little as possible, consider a family reunion cruise. Cruising can be a great vacation value because the price includes all meals and entertainment.

Chapter 12

The Dating Game

*T*iming is crucial in many things in life, and dating is certainly no exception. Finding the right person at the right time increases the probability of a cool experience; finding the right person at the wrong time is going to be a problem; and finding the wrong person at the wrong time? — well, heaven help us.

For the wrong person, no time is right. Trust us on this.

This chapter gives you some tips for meeting people and planning a first date. We also address second dates and briefly cover the challenges that remarried spouses and their stepfamilies face.

Making Sure That You're Ready

So how do you know the right time to launch yourself into someone else's orbit and try to convince them to try your trajectory (and no, we're not talking dirty)? As is true of much in life, first understanding the wrong time not only can give you insight into what to avoid and the warning signs, but it can also help you to tell when the right time is just about to arrive so that you can be ready.

Ten times not to date

The wrong time to date is any time when you're feeling blue and lonely and sad and sorry for yourself, which is, of course, the time when all of us decide, "Okay, I *need* to find someone." You may be particularly susceptible to this type of thinking when the following applies:

- ✔ You've lost your job.
- ✔ You've lost your housing.
- ✔ You've lost a friend.
- ✔ You've lost a parent.
- ✔ You've lost your cat or dog . . . or any other special pet.
- ✔ You're lost.
- ✔ You're married.
- ✔ You're still involved.
- ✔ You're separated.
- ✔ You've been divorced less than a year.

Five reasons to start dating

The best time to begin dating is when your life is really in gear, your friends think you're swell, you're relatively content with the way you look, work is going well, you're on speaking terms with your parents, and you can think of exes without raising your blood pressure. But, if you're so all-fired happy, "why go through the hassle of dating?" you ask. Good question. Here's why: The right person can make a good day great and a great day simply fabulous, and there *is* something about that chemistry thing.

Following are some scenarios that may motivate you — happy, well-adjusted person that you are — to jump into the dating arena:

- ✔ **Your friends are involved.** Often the trigger to get you going is that all your friends are involved, and they seem really happy. Equally important, they also don't have a whole lot of time for you these days, or at least not as much free time as you find yourself with — good motivating factor.

- ✔ **You're feeling great.** Feeling much better about your life than you have for a long, long time — cheerfully assuming you're stone cold sober when you notice the feeling — is also a great time to begin. Remember, it's always easiest to borrow money when you seem to not really need it, and the same is true with relationships. You're your coolest self when you're happy and relaxed. If you could bottle it, you'd be rich. You don't have to bottle it, but you may want to spread it around.

✔ **You're in a new city.** Moving to a new city is a really good time to get in the swing. You'll learn the city faster and have someone to share it with, someone who knows the sites taking you around. Be sure to leave some time for you to be by yourself. Although having someone along is great, time alone to explore your new surroundings is important, too. And when you're alone, you get to concentrate on the parts of the city that really interest you.

✔ **It's New Year's Day.** While a New Year's Eve party is a really treacherous first date experience, New Year's Day itself can be a good reminder that time is marching on and, if you want someone marching with you in your parade, it's a good time to push yourself a bit. (Also, a New Year's Day introduction can make a great opening line: "I decided that meeting *you* was going to be the first terrific thing I did for myself this year. . . .")

✔ **A big event is coming up.** A big-deal event coming up in your life — a wedding, a party, an anniversary — can be a useful motivation to offset your lethargy or fear and inertia when it comes to dating. The event can be a good opening gambit. If you feel compelled to take a date to the big event, do be a bit careful about making the big event the very first date. Having a couple of date-ettes to break the ice before the big event is always a good idea. If possible, give yourself enough time to have a couple of dates or even a couple of months before the event.

The Confidence Game

So let's talk about this confidence thing. Are some people — the gorgeous, smooth, successful among us — born with it? Nope! These people got to be successful and smooth by *appearing* to be confident. And what about those who were smart enough to choose the right parents or get dipped in the gorgeous-gene pool? Well, I know some of the most stunning people on this earth, and most of them are surprisingly *insecure* and *frightened* — of losing their looks, of appearing stupid and superficial, of growing old, of putting on weight, of having no one love them for any reason other than their cheekbones, or having no one love them at all.

We're not suggesting that you petition to be hit upside the head with an ugly stick, just that you have to get on with it, whatever you look like. Accept the ride home with the too-cute guy from your building who you never thought would ask you out — rather than worry why he'd ask *you* out. Introduce yourself to the fascinating woman you'd really like to know better. Or at least say "hi" to the person you see daily at the bus stop. If you're smart, you do the best you can with what you've got, and you don't whine too much in the process.

Square breathing

Breathing is the key to calmness. The fight-or-flight response — our age-old response to real or imagined threat — depends on delivering oxygen quickly and efficiently to rapidly metabolizing muscles by increasing the heart rate, closing down the bronchioles in the throat, diverting the blood supply, and sweating. Real or perceived danger (anxiety) throws the body into overdrive, literally. Calming the breathing slows everything down.

Ordinarily, we parallel breath, in and out. To enter into a more relaxed state, practice square breathing, which is inhaling to the count of four, *holding* to the count of four, exhaling to the count of four, and *holding* for four. With practice, you can increase the intervals and slow things down even more. Square breathing is not only good for confidence-building, but it's also good for relaxation, talking to the boss about a raise, preparing for a speech, and — *ta da* — going out on a date.

Five ways to exude confidence

Confidence is the ability to trust yourself and convey that sense to others, and appearance is half the battle. If you want to appear confident, whether you feel confident or not, try the following:

- ✔ **Stand up straight.** Posture counts. A straight spine denotes purpose and strength (*spineless* means cowardly, after all). Face forward. Think military bearing rather than the bent over hag from *Snow White,* and you'll get the picture.

- ✔ **Smile.** A smile is not only a good umbrella to the slings and arrows of outrageous fortune, but it also convinces others you're happy and healthy and wise. A frown makes you look like you're worried or frightened.

- ✔ **Make eye contact.** It's all in the eyes. Showing that you're not afraid to look someone in the eye means that you're strong and truthful and willing to meet their scrutiny.

- ✔ **Lean slightly forward.** Whether you're standing or sitting, leaning forward rather than pulling back denotes energy and forthrightness — and *that* signals strength and willingness. It also lets your energy move forward. Leaning forward is a bit aggressive or at least assertive, rather than defensive or passive.

✔ **Shake hands firmly (yeah, women too).** Upon entering a new situation, walking confidently into someone else's space and putting out your hand and firmly — not crushingly or limply — offering a part of yourself in a friendly but assertive way says gobs and gobs of good things about you: You're unafraid, you're an equal, you're friendly, you're engaging. A firm handshake while you look someone in the eye works wonders in business and personal situations.

Three great confidence builders

This section gives you some ideas about how you can go about building your confidence.

✔ **Catalogue traits you like about yourself.** Start with a pencil and paper and write down the things you like best about yourself. Be specific: No sentences like, "I'm really a nice person" — what does *that* mean? It may mean that you're really good to animals, handle a calculator like you were born with it in your hand, make a mean burrito, have a great singing voice, or always clean your plate. So if you mean that you don't fly off the handle every time something goes wrong, write that down. The more specific the items, the better for confidence building.

✔ **Help someone else.** The ability to do something for someone else builds confidence because the person you help says thank you and appreciates not only what you did for him, but that person appreciates *you* in the process. So if you feel your confidence is a bit too soggy for serious inter-action with the opposite sex, do someone a favor, find a volunteer activity, or deal with kids (so that you can feel more powerful). The other terrific advantage of volunteer work is that you're not locked in: You can feel good quickly and not feel like you have to stay doing something forever.

Keeping some do-good stuff in your life is a way to be connected and keep a balance in your life, as well as feeling good about yourself and helping out.

✔ **Try a challenging activity.** Try doing something you didn't think you could do. Even if you don't do a great job, you'll feel much better about yourself when you try something really difficult. Even succeeding at something that's easy often doesn't feel as good as attempting some-thing hard. And if you succeed at the hard stuff? Well, gangbusters!

Doing something that you know you can do is okay, too; you still get a sense of accomplishment and it's a good start for gaining confidence. Just as feelings of incompetence seem to spread, so, too, can the more positive feelings. So get out there and get started.

Finding a Date

The best places to meet people are ones in which

- You can see clearly, hear clearly, and respond honestly.
- You have an interest in what's going on, increasing the likelihood that you'll have something in common with anyone you meet there.
- The atmosphere feels safe and familiar.

A place you enjoy, where you feel comfortable and safe, solves the problem of what to talk about. The key is to be light-hearted about approaching a stranger. Think of it as a soufflé that needs to be treated gently; no loud noises, early peeks, or banging doors. Otherwise, you'll end up with a dessert that nobody wants, despite the effort you put into it — flat, ugly, and unappetizing, even with the right ingredients.

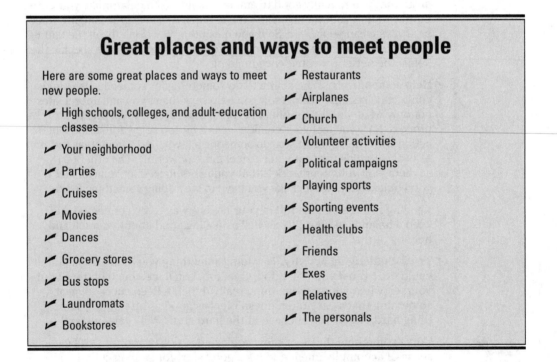

Great places and ways to meet people

Here are some great places and ways to meet new people.

- High schools, colleges, and adult-education classes
- Your neighborhood
- Parties
- Cruises
- Movies
- Dances
- Grocery stores
- Bus stops
- Laundromats
- Bookstores
- Restaurants
- Airplanes
- Church
- Volunteer activities
- Political campaigns
- Playing sports
- Sporting events
- Health clubs
- Friends
- Exes
- Relatives
- The personals

Exchanging Phone Numbers

The phone is quicker than pony express, less traumatic than a telegram, more personal than e-mail, more fun than smoke signals, and the first major step toward moving from strangers to something much bigger and better.

The following are the rules for getting, giving, and using phone numbers:

- ✔ If you want a number, ask and be willing to offer your own.

- ✔ If you don't want to see the person again, don't ask for a number and don't give a number.

- ✔ If you're not sure, build a time frame into your response so that nobody is sitting around waiting for you to call.

- ✔ This part is fun and easy, so relax a bit and don't get too involved before you've even had a first date. It's not worth the stomach acid.

- ✔ Calling and hanging up is not okay; neither is driving by. All states now have antistalking laws, and they are enforced. Playing games could get you in serious trouble, so don't be silly here. Plus, caller ID has made hang-ups traceable. You don't need police on your doorstep as part of your dating experience.

Three tips for getting a phone number

When you know that you want to call someone, it's a great idea to ask for the phone number. One of the best ways to approach getting someone else's number is to demonstrate your good faith and show that you're not Jack or Jacqueline the Ripper:

- ✔ Smile, talk softly, and make eye contact.

- ✔ Ask for the number in a friendly, nonthreatening way. For example, rather than saying, "So, can I have your number?" try something like, "I'd really like to stay in touch. Is there a number where I can reach you?"

- ✔ Offer your own number. Offering your number is a great way to deflect suspicion by putting the proverbial ball in the other person's court. Offering rather than asking also allows you to be vulnerable first.

  You can win sensitivity points by saying, "Look, I know that these days a gorgeous woman like you has to be careful, so if you would prefer, I can give you a way to get in touch with me. I'd love to court you the old-fashioned way and call you, but I don't want to make you feel uncomfortable by asking you to give me your number if you're not ready."

Giving your phone number

If someone wants to contact you, think about whether you want to hear from the person. You may be tempted to give your phone number for these reasons:

- ✔ **You want him or her to get in touch.** If you're interested and want to stay in touch, give out your number, but also get the other person's number. If you only give your number and don't get a number in return, you're setting yourself up to hang around the phone, waiting for a call. (Of course, if you have no intention of calling him, don't ask for the number. It's just as nasty for you to ask for his number and not call him as it is for him to ask for your number and not call you.)

- ✔ **You're not sure that you're interested, but you want to keep your options open.** When you're not sure that you want the person to call, you can always say that you're about to change your number because you've received too many hang-ups; the number used to belong to an escort service; or you want a cuter number.

  Another alternative, if you're not sure whether you want to give out your phone number, is to get their number. Of course, doing so means you have to call them.

- ✔ **You wouldn't spit on him if he were on fire, but you don't want to appear rude.** If there's no way that you'd ever want to see this person again, don't be tempted to give your number. Doing so may be easy for the short term, but it actually makes the situation more uncomfortable. You'll end up causing yourself and the other person heartache not very far down the line.

Advice from the animal kingdom

Yes, even at our most well-behaved, we're still animals — human animals, but animals nonetheless. As a result, the same rules that apply to the larger animal kingdom sometimes apply to us.

Lionel Tiger, who has done a lot of work on animal behavior, indicates that to show that their intentions are honorable, animals bare their necks, the most vulnerable part of any animal's body. (Where do you think we got the phrase "Go for the jugular [vein]"? And you thought it came from a Dracula movie.)

Therefore, the best way to show how honorable your intentions are is to bare your neck, metaphorically, of course: In other words, to get a phone number, offer your own.

Consider online dating

Traditional dating is fundamentally random. Consider this:

By sheer luck, you're invited to a party. By chance, you meet a friend there. The friend is talking to someone who is single. You find the person physically interesting. He or she also shows signs of interest. You start a conversation that goes well. The party ends. One of you has the courage to propose exchanging phone numbers. You have a second date. You find out more about this person. You like what you see. So does he or she. And so on and so on.

If, at any step along the way, you realize that you're not a match, quit and wait until another random event (like a party) occurs. Then try again.

Considering the advantages of online dating, especially when compared to finding a mate in the nonvirtual world, we're amazed that the human race ever managed to propagate without the benefit of computers.

Internet dating offers these benefits:

✔ **An almost limitless supply of people are online.** Online, you're surrounded by age-appropriate singles every time you log on. And if you don't find enough people at one site, you can go to any of hundreds of other sites, or you can simply wait a while and a new crop of singles will sign on.

✔ **Internet dating is way more convenient than traditional dating.** When was the last time you prospected for dates in your pajamas at 3 a.m.? The whole concept of virtual dating is that the community of single prospects is available to you whenever you want to meet them. For people with day jobs, children, and other social obligations, prospecting online at odd hours is the only way to go.

✔ **You can parallel-date at warp speed.** You can certainly initiate contact with multiple prospects at the same time because the process of initiating contact is so simple. Then you can engage them in e-mail and phone exchanges until you can determine which, if any, are worth dating. If none, you just go back to the trough.

✔ **Internet dating eliminates the awkwardness of first introductions.** Are you good at walking up to a stranger and saying hello? Not too many people are and we weren't either. In online dating, the effort of making first contact is so slight that the fear of rejection simply melts away. After you initiate an e-mail exchange, a reply arrives and the ice thaws. For many people, just getting past the initial encounter successfully makes the rest of dating easier.

Phone number alternatives

Here are a number of ways to give out a phone number without actually *giving out* a phone number:

✔ **I'm listed.** If you want them to get in touch, make sure you've made the listing clear as it appears in the phone book. In many cases, though, directing someone to the phone book means that you've given out your home address as well.

✔ **Business card.** A business card usually has a work phone number, often a fax number, a business address, and an e-mail address.

If you don't have a business card, for very little money, you can have one printed up that gives out whatever information you want to share. (You can usually get around 500 business cards for between $15 and $25 or less.) If you're self-employed or work at home, having a business card can make you feel a little more professional as well.

✔ **Home address.** Giving out a home address is a bit risky. Of course, sooner or later, if the two of you hook up, you'll both very likely know home addresses. The question is sooner or later? Our advice is later — when you're sure that this is someone you trust to behave respectfully and appropriately after they know where you live. If you have even the most minor inkling of this person "surprising you" by lurking on your doorstep, trust your instinct for heaven's sake, and don't give out your address.

✔ **E-mail.** For many folks, giving out an e-mail address is a safer alternative than giving out a phone number. Of course, each of us has to balance our sense of safety and our need for intimacy. We may be old-fashioned, but we think actually hearing a voice is a nice way to begin to connect with someone.

Ten Rules for Your First Date

A first date may never be a relaxing experience (after all, no matter how down-to-earth you are, you'll still worry about the broccoli in your teeth), but it doesn't have to be ulcer material either. This section outlines the basic rules. In fact, these rules are so basic, they sound silly, but you'd be surprised how often they're disregarded, with dire consequences. So a word to the wise: To make your first date as comfortable as possible, follow these ten rules:

✔ Pick an activity that you enjoy.

✔ Pick an activity that you can easily afford.

✔ Do something that doesn't require new clothes.

✔ Go where you can talk without getting thrown out.

✔ Go to a place that's easy to get to.

✔ Do something that isn't competitive.

✔ Pick an activity that doesn't involve a lot of alcohol.

✔ Leave time to get to know each other.

✔ Do something that doesn't involve *high-ticket others* (includes friends, family, exes, kids, animals, or colleagues).

✔ Find an activity that doesn't last more than a couple of hours.

Four great places for a first date

Some places and events lend themselves to successful first dates, and others practically scream, "What could I be thinking?!" Would you believe that Valentine's Day is a first-date no-no?

Following are the cream of the first-date-ideas crop:

✔ **Museums:** At a museum, you get to meander through the halls, look at exhibits, and chat about anything that inspires you. It's a great place to get to know each other and to see each other's tastes in art — or whatever. Also, most museums are usually easy to get to and offer a place to eat (even if overpriced for what you're getting, they won't break the bank). A museum is relaxed, easy, inexpensive, and doesn't bump into any of the ten rules for first dates.

✔ **Amusement park:** Unless it's really hard to get to, going to an amusement park is usually fun and makes everybody feel young and carefree. The only real problems? Sticky fingers from cotton candy and rides that make you so queasy you'd give up your first born for an antacid tablet, but all-in-all, a good choice.

✔ **Walks:** You can take walks (almost) anywhere: parks, zoos, botanical gardens, and so on. It's cheap, fun, and pressure-free. Plus, you can often hold hands.

✔ **Outdoor activities in general:** Sporting events, concerts, and picnics are great places for first dates. You can talk, and being outside, everything feels less claustrophobic. It's easy and relaxed, and clothing usually isn't a problem.

Doing the restaurant thang

Going out to eat is one of the most common first date activities. But you don't have to make the date routine. To make your date a notch above ordinary, put a spin on the restaurant theme:

✔ **Go to a coffeehouse.** Unless you're meeting at a coffeehouse and order-ing two grandé skim lattes and roasted pepper and goat cheese sand-wiches (which is about the same amount as the national debt), this is a pretty cheap date, compared to a traditional restaurant. It's the '90s ver-sion of a singles bar: relaxed, casual, and no time pressure.

✔ **Go to an interesting restaurant.** Food is good. Good food is even better. Good, unusual food is the best and is often less pricey than the usual, boring steak or fried chicken. The event doesn't have to be the culinary experience of your life, but fun and interesting food (maybe ethnic, but easy on the spices) on a first date is a cool idea. We're partial to weekend lunch and brunch dates, ourselves. They're relaxed, liquor's not required, you have plenty of time to get to know each other, and they're in the daytime.

Five things to consider

There are some cool ways to enhance the enjoyment of a restaurant date. For any restaurant you consider, think about the following:

✔ **Noise level:** You got together so that you can get to know each other. It makes sense to be able to hear what your date has to say and talk with-out seriously harming your vocal chords.

✔ **Price:** Go to a place you can afford. You can't enjoy yourself if you worry about your date ordering an appetizer *and* a dessert.

✔ **Service:** You want the service to be attentive, without hovering. And who wants to be rushed out the door?

✔ **Spaciousness:** Adequate space is an animal need. That's why we all feel a little uneasy in a packed elevator or an overcrowded restaurant.

✔ **Lighting:** You don't want the restaurant too dark or too light. Too dark and he can't see the great job you did on your makeup, or she won't notice that your tie matches your eyes; too light, and no matter what you did, you'll still end up looking like a delivery to the morgue.

Picking the place

After you've narrowed down your list of potential restaurants to those that meet your economic and ambiance requirements, narrow down the list even more by doing the following:

✔ **Pick a place you know.** Menu familiarity reeks of confidence. You'll sound like Cary Grant if you lean over and say, "Try the duck. It's out of this world." Also, knowing a restaurant well means that you're comfort-able with the service, the all-important table spacing, the lighting, the wine list, the taste, the presentation, and payment procedures. This way, you can insure a good time. If you're happy, your date stands a better chance of being happy, too.

✔ **Pick a place that knows you.** What could be cooler than a maitre d' smiling widely when you walk in or a waiter saying, "Nice to see you again!"? Better, though, is the fact that "regulars" usually get the best tables and most prompt service — both of which go a long way in creating a great first date.

✔ **Pick a place where your date can eat.** Obviously, don't take a vegetarian to a steak house, and if his cholesterol count is above 300, steer clear of the Wisconsin Cheese Fest. Chances are, unless you already know each other well, you won't know the intricacies of your date's dietary preferences. Simple solution: Ask ahead of time. Less simple: Keep everyone's options open by selecting neutral territory, such as a restaurant with a large menu or a coffeehouse with a small one.

Six ways to enjoy yourself

You don't need the Fourth of July to have a great time on your first date. The sky doesn't need to erupt in fireworks to consider your date a winner. What *does* need to happen is that you create an environment that allows both you and your date to relax a little, let your hair down, get to know one another, and have fun. The basics of enjoying yourself are fairly straightforward:

✔ Be relaxed.

✔ Be yourself.

✔ Be prepared to talk — and listen.

✔ Be prepared (think Boy Scout — money, time, place, way, and so on).

✔ Be okay about silences (if they don't go on too long).

✔ Be realistic about expectations.

Don't sweat it — screwing things up is pretty hard to do. Besides, it's only one date. And with a bit of pre-planning on your part, this date can be a really cool one.

What to Expect on a Second Date

A first date is *takeoff* — your seatback is in the upright position, your tray table is stowed, your seatbelt is buckled, and you are listening intently to make sure that the engines are on full throttle. A second date is *climbing to cruising altitude*. You're on the way to your destination. You're up in the air. You hope the pilot didn't have a martini with her lunch, the flight attendant didn't have a fight with his girlfriend, and the skies are not cloudy all day. In other words, a second date is the beginning of a settling-in period.

Big date do's and don'ts

It's your 50th birthday, New Year's Eve, a retirement party at the firm . . . whatever. When it comes to a BIG date, as in not-just-any-old-Saturday-night date, these guidelines can help you have a great time:

✔ DO plan ahead. Big dates are almost always dates you know are coming weeks in advance. Arrange your date as soon as possible so that he or she can mark a calendar, rent a tux, buy a great present.

✔ DON'T make a first date a big date. It's too risky and too loaded.

✔ DO ask someone with whom you're really comfortable. Big dates tend to be longer than your average date and often include family members. The last thing you want is a high-maintenance date.

✔ DON'T make your big date such a big deal that your companion feels like it's a premarital date, too. It's okay to go out on a big date with Mr. or Ms. Kinda Right or Right for Now.

✔ DO substitute a platonic date when a great date isn't in the cards. You're better off to have a fun time with a friend (or alone!) than have a miserable time.

On a second date, you'll have

✔ **More communicating:** You move from neutral conversational territory like census data, to more personal stuff like family history, favorite movies, the school you went to, the school you go to, your hometown, work life — stuff you'd put in a personal ad, stuff your next-door neighbor knows but not as much as your best friend knows. It's also a good time for follow-up. You asked the opening questions on your first date; now get a bit more detail.

✔ **More testing the compatibility waters:** You want to make sure that you and your date are a good fit. Your attention shifts away from how you look, act, feel, talk, eat, and slurp to the kind of person your date is.

✔ **More probing for shared interests:** While you want to express yourself on a first date, a second date is for allowing, encouraging, desiring, and listening to your date express what he or she likes and dislikes.

✔ **More sexual innuendoes:** Nothing overt, but playful flirting is good.

✔ **More gazing into each other's eyes:** Most important, a second date is one step further along on the intimacy scale. You're stripping away the outer layer of superficiality and beginning to know your date's soul. Few things are more intimate, or soulful, than prolonged eye contact. Don't stare. But don't be afraid to connect with the window to your date's soul — the eyes.

Four good places for a second date

Given that a second date is about delving deeper, getting to know someone better, flirting a bit more, and just plain being more intimate, pick a place that lets you do those things:

- ✔ Quiet restaurant or café
- ✔ Public park
- ✔ Sporting event
- ✔ Museum

Bargain second dates that don't let you down

Your goal on the first date is to impress your date, but also to get to know what his or her interests and hobbies are. You then use the information when planning the second date — who cares how little money you spend if you show your date that you understand and value what he or she likes to do. Here are some ideas to jumpstart your planning skills (and if you're a senior, don't forget to discreetly ask for a discount everywhere you go):

- ✔ If you're both a little new to the city you live in, go to the visitor's center in your town and pick up brochures on area attractions and museums. Many are free or have certain days when prices are lower.

  Sometimes the local library gives out free day-passes to the more expensive city museums and art galleries. Call ahead in case you have to reserve the pass or pick it up early.

- ✔ If your date likes music, check the local symphony's schedule — the "nosebleed" seats are often very reasonably priced. Follow the concert with a cup of coffee at the local barista or at a club on half-price martini night.

- ✔ Community theater productions are often reasonably priced — far more so than professional theater companies. Check the schedule of upcoming plays.

- ✔ Matinee movies can save you up to ten bucks for the two of you — go to a 5:00 show and afterwards have dinner together. If your date likes foreign films, go see one at an art house cinema and then go for a specialty meal from that country for dinner.

- ✔ Check your local library's bulletin board. You can often find local entertainment postings for things like community theater, concerts, poetry readings, and lectures. Universities also have lectures or readings open to the public.

- ✔ Not much is cheaper or more enjoyable than packing a picnic lunch and driving to a state park or lake within reasonable driving distance. Take your camera, hike or stroll, and enjoy your picnic.

- ✔ If you and your date enjoy dancing or at least trying something new, go out swing or contra dancing. Many cities have dance clubs with weekly dance nights. Prices are usually under $15, and you can get a free lesson beforehand.

When distraction is your best option

Should you find yourself on a second date fantasizing about gene pools or doodling your first name and his last name, stop immediately and distract yourself. Though we wouldn't recommend whipping out a crossword puzzle, you might want to try doing what you initially set out to do: Get to know your date. Not your future marriage partner or the potential mother of your kids or even the guy you want to take home to meet mom. Just relax, realize there's no substitute for time, no excuse for shortcuts, and no way to really know someone without listening, learning, caring, sharing, and being there.

A Second Date Is	A Second Date Isn't
A next step	A relationship
A continued search for compatibility	A pre-spouse interview
A chance to reveal yourself	A confessional
A time to flirt	A time to have sex
A shift of focus onto your date	A time to obsess about yourself

Six not-so-good places for a second date

Following are some not-so-good places for a second date:

- ✔ Noisy bar
- ✔ Quiet bar
- ✔ Movie marathon
- ✔ Your parents' house
- ✔ Your date's parents' house
- ✔ Your place

Ten Tips for Happy Dating

Here are our ten best tips for happy dating:

✔ **Be realistic:** Ask yourself about your expectations: Are you being reasonable? Are you asking too much of yourself, too much of your date, too much of the situation? Best friends are really helpful in the reality-check department, so when in doubt, it's okay to say, "Am I being realistic here, or have I overdosed on romance pills?"

✔ **Be specific:** Often, when we talk about the opposite sex, we either go all gooey and soft or we become harsh and judgmental. Neither stance is particularly helpful. Look carefully at the details. Being specific is one of the best ways not only to problem solve but to be realistic as well.

✔ **Take responsibility:** This is a cool rule for life as well as for dating. Nothing makes people angrier than the "who me?" routine. All of us make mistakes — sometimes because we are thoughtless, sometimes because we are clueless, often out of ignorance. But when it's clear we blew it, even though every instinct is saying play dumb, we need to accept responsibility: If you're late, 'fessing up — saying "I'm late. I'm sorry. I didn't leave enough time" (or "I got caught up and lost track of the time") — is still much better than playing dumb.

✔ **Be active:** In our society, we seem to have become a nation of crybabies and busybodies. We've all become professional victims. The best way to not feel victimized is to do *something,* anything (almost). Don't wait for someone to call you. Call them, take a walk, scrub the floor, scrape gum off your shoes, or jog. Don't wait for them to make your day or make you happy or get the ball rolling. *This is your life;* it's not a dress rehearsal.

✔ **Don't settle:** Being flexible is neither bad nor wrong. The trick is knowing when to compromise and when to go for it! To do that, you have to know what's really important to you, and once you know that, don't settle. If you don't have what you want, make sure that you know what you want — being both realistic and specific. You can always reevaluate. What most people regret is not the mistakes they made, but the chances they didn't take.

✔ **Reevaluate often:** Something that made you happy, or behavior that pleased you, or someone who rang your chimes once may or may not be in for the long haul. The only way of knowing the short-term from the long-term is to be willing to take your own emotional pulse from time to time.

✔ **Write stuff down:** A log (not a Captain James T. Kirk kind of log, but a feelings log) can be really useful and helpful to pinpoint important times, beginnings of issues, and changes in the relationship. *Journaling* is a great way to keep us honest and focused, and as long as it isn't left around for someone to find and read, there's no downside here. A log is also a way of taking responsibility privately so that you can practice before you take it "publicly."

✔ **Be creative:** You're not like anybody else on the planet, and neither is your date, so why do the two of you have to follow anybody else's rules or precedents about what you want, how you act, where you go, or how you communicate? If it's okay with the two of you — and it's not illegal — then why not?

When it comes down to it, isn't the point to fashion our lives, individually and together, as something precious and rare and meaningful to each of us?

✔ **Be aware:** Sophocles said that the unexamined life is not worth living, and we say that the unexamined date is a waste of time. Pay attention to your date and to your own responses. You don't have to constantly monitor as though your date were in dating ICU and liable to expire at any moment, but be willing every once in a while to step out a bit and see what's going on. How are you? How does the date seem to be doing? Are you happy? Is it fun? Are you being attentive? Do you need more sleep? Are your senses being dulled? Being dense is a tough way to lead your life and dangerous when you're dealing with someone else who wants you tuned in.

✔ **Analyze Fear:** Fear! It's buried and it's old and it's kinda nasty, but it's pretty familiar. Whatever our fear, it's likely gotten moldy because it's been around for so long. Fear is often left over from childhood or adolescence and pops up at the most inconvenient times — like when we're trying to let down our guard and feel close to someone and let them know the true us so that we can feel loved.

When You're Considering Remarrying

First-time spouses are often driven by romantic passion and go to the altar with unrealistic expectations of how great things are going to be. However, people rarely enter second marriages with the same fantasies, because these relationships necessarily follow a divorce or the death of a first spouse. After going through divorce or widowhood, remarried partners tend to be more realistic and less bright-eyed than first-timers. But that doesn't mean that a second or even third marriage can't be wonderful. Read on for tips and guidelines to make the transition as smooth as possible.

Four suggestions for making a second marriage work

Here are some suggestions for achieving the kind of closeness that may have been lacking in your first marriage:

✔ **Truly get to know each other.** Perhaps you and your former spouse never fully opened up to one another. Now you have a second chance to know someone on a deeper level — and to allow that person to know you.

✔ **Don't be afraid to share your most important thoughts and feelings with your partner, and encourage him or her to do the same.** Listen carefully to what your spouse tells you, and allow that person to open up at his or her own pace.

✔ **Develop new routines and rituals that don't mirror those of your previous marriage.** When wives and husbands have been married for a number of years, they develop certain patterns that come to define the relationship. People who've been single for a long time often become set in their ways. It's quite natural to want to continue these routines and rituals — and to expect your new spouse to follow suit. These expectations can be a source of conflict — especially if your spouse is also bringing in a completely different set of expectations from his or her former marriage. Sitting down and rewriting the rules in a way that reflects both of your needs and desires is important to do.

Changing your expectations about how things are supposed to get done takes time. You probably had to make similar adjustments in your first marriage — remarriage is an opportunity to be more flexible in how you and your partner negotiate the terms of your relationship.

✔ **Make a fresh start.** Try not to live in the home where either partner resided with a former spouse. Ghosts can haunt your new relationship if you do. If at all possible, move into a home where neither of you have lived before. Doing so gives each of you the sense that you're truly starting over.

Remarried couples often have the maturity to form deeper, more-intimate relationships than first-time partners. Hopefully, you and your new spouse have both profited from your experiences and mistakes. If so, you have a much better chance to make marriage work this time around.

Understanding the complex issues that stepfamilies face

When a childless couple divorces, the partners generally go their separate ways — unless they voluntarily choose to remain in contact. However, when children are in the picture, estranged husbands and wives have to negotiate any number of financial and emotional issues with each other for many years to come.

Exes in this situation have no way they can get rid of each other. Should one or both spouses subsequently remarry, the cast of characters expands dramatically — and so can the potential complications.

Three financial issues remarried spouses face

Remarried partners tend to see money differently than first-time spouses. In the majority of first marriages, the partners agree to pool their money. However, second marriages have a different set of realities — especially when children are involved. The following are some of the most common financial issues remarried spouses face:

- Remarried families are often strapped for funds.

- Child support arrangements can be tricky — even when both spouses have money — because of the many different ways that custody is shared.

- Remarried partners usually want money accumulated during the first marriage to be passed to their own children.

Five tips for avoiding misunderstandings about money

You can avoid many misunderstandings about money if you set down some ground rules early. We recommend that remarried couples take the following steps, preferably *before* getting married:

- Be aware of all of the financial implications of entering into the new marriage. Start out by having a series of discussions about the exact amount of money each of you plans to contribute to maintaining the household.

- Talk about any monies that you're not willing to contribute to the common pool, as well as any legal ties and obligations each of you may have to your former spouse or to major pre-existing debts.

- Be sure to take notes and make calculations so that you can make accurate decisions about your financial future.

- If either or both of you have children from a previous marriage, talk about how each child will share in assets accumulated in the first marriage, as well as assets the two of you accumulate together.

- Consider drawing up a marital agreement. *Prenuptial agreements* are legal documents that are signed before a couple marries. *Postnuptial agreements* are signed afterwards. These contracts, which spell out the financial arrangement between a husband and wife, are far more common in second and third marriages than in first-time unions.

Four techniques for forming a successful family unit

In a first marriage, the bond between the husband and wife has time to develop before children are brought into the picture. However, in a remarried family, the child/parent relationship predates the marital connection. Families who recognize that all the resulting difficulties are part and parcel of stepfamily life are able to ease this transition. You can communicate your understanding by using the following techniques:

✔ **Encourage an open expression of feelings.** Instead of becoming defensive when family members express their concerns, show that you understand what they're going through.

✔ **Don't ever badmouth your child's absent parent — however much you may despise that person.** Research shows that children of divorce have a much harder time adjusting to a stepfamily when their parents are in open conflict.

✔ **If you're a stepparent and your partner admits that he or she feels torn between you and her biological or adoptive child, don't accuse her of being disloyal.** Instead, acknowledge her conflict by saying, "That must be tough. If I were in your position, I might have the same kind of mixed feelings."

✔ **Foster open lines of communication among ex-spouses, children, their biological parents, stepparents, grandparents, and other relatives.** The more cut off people feel from those they love, the more conflict and hostility will exist between family members, and the more difficult it will be to have a smoothly functioning stepfamily.

Children need the love and support of both their parents. You and your estranged spouse have an obligation to maintain enough civility to provide for those needs.

Five strategies for managing the household

Having a house full of kids with mix-and-match parents and stepparents (with visits from each of their extended families) can be a complicated business. You may find a built-in ambiguity of roles and relationships that has little resemblance to a traditional first-time family.

While you won't find a model for how each uniquely structured family is supposed to operate, try sticking to the following guidelines:

- ✔ Take the primary responsibility for raising and disciplining your own children.

- ✔ Remarried spouses often find that the relationship between their children and new partner is not what they'd hoped it would be. Keep your expectations modest.

- ✔ Be prepared to deal with unfamiliar situations. Stepfamily relationships have many sides to them — some of which can cause unanticipated complications.

- ✔ Hold regular family conferences.

- ✔ Make special time for the two of you to spend alone.

Chapter 13

Loving a Pet

. . . .

. . . .

*T*his chapter is for folks who are considering a pet companion. We help you pick the best pet to fit your needs, whether it be male versus female cat, or puppy versus full-grown dog. We discuss the advantages (and disadvantages) of birds as pets, and we tell you a little about the different types of aquariums available.

Considering the Canine Possibilities

Every dog may be a wolf at heart, but we've certainly done plenty to change the rest of the package, to soften some traits and strengthen others. No species on earth shows such diversity of size, shape, and purpose.

Dog breeds and breed types differ in size, activity level, shedding level, and trainability. That means that becoming a canine expert is a good idea. Not for the opportunity to impress the family when you see a dog show on TV — "the Schipperke, a Belgian breed, first became popular as a watch dog for use on canal boats," you can say with authority — but for the ability to analyze how any particular breed or breed type will work as a member of your family.

Choosing the right dog for you, your family, and your lives is the first step in acquiring the dog of your dreams.

  ✔ **Letting go of love at first sight:** In dogs, as in humans, the one you're immediately and most powerfully attracted to may not be the best bet for a long-term companion. You may have grown up with Collies in a suburban home with a large yard and your mother home all day, and you may still consider the Collie your favorite breed. But a Collie may not be the best choice for you today if you live alone in an apartment and are fond of expensive clothes in dark colors. So start fresh, with a fair appraisal of your life and of the dogs who offer the best fit.

✔ **Starting from scratch:** Choosing a breed or breed type is one of the most enjoyable aspects of adopting a dog. You have a chance to window-shop on a grand scale, to discover dogs you've never heard of and imagine life with breeds you've never seen before. Start with an open mind, and be honest about your own life, your own preferences, your own expectations. Keep these factors in mind:

- Size and space requirements

- Activity level

- Fur factor

- Trainability and dominance

✔ **Sizing up a breed type:** For the sake of practicality, size is the first factor you should look at when choosing a dog, if for no other reason than figuring out the cost difference between keeping a dog that eats one-quarter cup of food a day versus one that eats seven cups.

- **Large dogs:** For some people, only a large dog will do. Large dogs are the perfect choice for active people: joggers, hikers, and cross-country skiers. And even the friendliest large dog is a bigger crime deterrent than the surliest small dog. Still, there are trade-offs. The bigger a dog gets, the more food she eats and the more waste she produces. Big dogs can be more difficult to handle, more likely to knock over your toddler or your grandmother, more capable of destroying your home, and more likely to inflict a serious injury should they decide to bite. A pushy small dog is amusing; a pushy large one is dangerous. Large dogs are harder to travel with and more expensive to kennel. If you don't own your own home, you may find securing housing that accepts a large dog nearly impossible.

- **Small dogs:** They may get their share of snickers, but little dogs don't care. They live a life big dogs can only dream about. Only a small dog can sneak into a department store hidden in an oversized purse. This kind of portability, the go-anywhere functionality, combined with adorable faces and shoe-button eyes, makes the small dog a whole lot more fun to own than a lot of "real dog" people can imagine. Some practical advantages exist, too. You can give a small dog a bath in the kitchen sink, without straining your back lifting the animal. A small dog can sit in your lap while you watch TV. They're no trouble to walk, even for small children. Food costs are low. Your walk is a rapid trot for them, so exercise is easy.

On the negative side, toy breeds can be yappy, and they're definitely fragile, which makes them unsuitable for homes with boisterous children. They have to be protected, too, from large dogs, some of which may consider a powder-puff dog an appetizer.

✔ **Keeping up with your dog:** You can sometimes gauge a breed's activity level by looking at the work it was bred to perform, but still, all you're getting is an overall impression. Each individual dog varies by breeding, age, and health, although the general rule holds true: If a dog was bred to go all day long, a sporting breed, for example, it's going to be more consistently "up" than a large, heavy, guarding breed that only worked when intruders arrived. Dogs such as Dalmatians, bred to run for miles alongside carriages or horse-drawn fire trucks, aren't likely to take a laid-back attitude toward life. Terriers, developed to keep vermin at bay, are always on the alert and ready to rumble.

✔ **Facing up to fur:** There's no such thing as a dog with fur that doesn't shed. (The slight hedge is for such breeds as the hairless variety of the Chinese Crested, a tiny little dog that can't shed what it doesn't have.) The corollary is that there's no such thing as a dog that's hypoallergenic. Some dogs do shed less and may be manageable for some asthmatics and allergy sufferers, but if you're not prepared for or capable of handling fur, you're better off with goldfish (not a cat and not a bird, because those can be even worse for many allergy sufferers).

✔ **Factoring in intelligence:** People are always asking about how smart a particular dog is, as if that's good for anything more than bragging rights. Intelligence is fairly irrelevant when predicting how well a dog is going to work as a member of your family. What's more important is trainability or biddability, qualities that describe how much — or how little — a dog concerns herself with what you want her to do.

Consider three of the breeds most often touted as highly intelligent — the Border Collie, Golden Retriever, and Doberman Pinscher. These dogs — which are bred to move sheep around, retrieve downed game, and patrol with a police officer or soldier — come prewired to look to a human for guidance. If the human knows enough to provide that guidance, these breeds will gladly serve. That's their job, after all.

✔ **Puppy or grown dog?** The advantages of a puppy are obvious: Puppies are adorable, sweet, and cuddly. To look at them is to smile. A puppy is yours to work with, an almost-clean slate you can mold to fit perfectly into your life. (Or completely ruin it if you're not careful!) Yours will be the only family she knows, as long as you keep up your part of the deal. That said, choosing a grown dog has some real advantages. They're often less expensive to acquire, and certainly less expensive to maintain, since their puppy shots and wormings are behind them. If you choose carefully, you can find one that's already house-trained, and maybe knows a little basic obedience, too.

✔ **Male or female?** Does a male or female dog make a better pet? There's no way of settling that question for sure, so for most people the choice comes down to personal preference. Do consider their differences, however, because even spaying and neutering doesn't make males and females the same.

If you don't plan to spay or neuter your pet, the differences are more distinct. Unspayed females are generally moodier than unneutered males, and they come into heat twice a year. Although males tend to be more constant in temperament, they can be annoying in their constant pursuit of such male-dog activities as sex, leg-lifting, and territory protection.

Spaying or neutering generally evens things out a bit. Females become more emotionally constant and males are less likely to fight or roam. But differences remain.

✔ **Cost considerations:** How much should a puppy or a dog cost? Prices vary so widely that you can pay anything from "free," to the (generally) "less than $50" that shelters charge, to the "deal-of-the-century" price that breed-rescue groups charge for purebreds, to several hundred for an "ordinary" purebred, to several thousand dollars for a show-quality dog of a rare or red-hot breed.

Gaining a New Appreciation of the Cat

In ancient times, the cat was worshipped. In more recent history, the cat was used to keep farms clear of rodents. Although you still find cats plying their trade as rodent-killers on farms all around the world, the cat's greater role today is strictly as a companion. And in this, too, the cat excels, for the following reasons:

✔ More of us are living in smaller quarters — in apartments, in condominiums, in houses on smaller lots — than ever before. Although such conditions aren't conducive to the keeping of dogs — even though many people make it work anyway — such living conditions are in no way a deterrent to keeping a cat, especially an indoors-only one.

✔ Many of us have little time or money for a pet, but a greater need for companionship than ever before — and cats are the ideal pets to fill this need. In our middle years, we're nearly pulled apart by the demands of job and family. Our older years may be more active than ever before but can also be a time where we long for companionship.

The indoor versus outdoor controversy

With the evolution of the cat from semi-wild hunter to loving companion animal, has come a change not only in how cats are loved but also where cats are kept. Increasingly, more cats are living indoors.

The truth is that all cats are living dangerously if you allow them to go in and out at will. With correct diet and preventive care, an indoor cat can easily live for 15 to 20 years — or more. A cat with outdoor privileges is lucky to live a fraction as long, although many exceptions do exist, of course. The decision is really a judgment call that the pet owner needs to make.

As for the question of whether cats can be happy living an indoors-only life, the answer is a resounding "Yes!" Kittens raised indoors become cats who don't miss the outdoors, and with patience, you can convert even grown cats. Toys, scratching posts, indoor gardens, and screened patios or balconies all make the indoor cat's life special — as may the addition of a second cat (or even a dog) for companionship.

Kitten or cat: Which is a better choice for you?

When people think about adding a cat to their lives, they seem to automatically think "kitten." And why not? A kitten seems to make perfect sense, a little fluff-ball who'll grow into your household and your heart. For some people, though, an adult cat is a better option. And even if you're perfectly set up for a kitten, you ought to consider an adult as well, for you'll find many wonderful pets among the ranks of grown cats, and most will never get a second chance to show how perfect they can be.

Don't rule out either before you fairly consider each one.

- ✔ Kittens can be a lot of work and aggravation. They can result in a lot of expense, too, because many a kitten seems to use up nearly all of a cat's nine lives, which means you may end up seeing the nice people at the emergency veterinary clinic a time or two in the first year.

- ✔ With a kitten, you also need to put more effort into training, from making sure that the kitten understands what's expected regarding the litter box, to helping your kitten learn to stay off the counters.

- ✔ You need to kitten-proof your home — or keep the kitten confined in a safe part of the house whenever you're not watching him — and then spend months during which, every day, you're picking your little tiger off the drapes, off the kids, off the back of the couch, or off your slippers every time you walk down the hall.

- ✔ The most serious disadvantage to adult cats is simply that they aren't as "baby cute" as kittens!

✔ Kittens get away with all their endearing goofiness because they measure way off the adorability scale, but if you suspect that you're going to tire of having your feet attacked, if you worry about your children not being gentle enough, or if you don't want to be figuring out what your little kitten is into every second of the day and night, an adult cat is a better option for you.

✔ If you adopt an adult cat, you know exactly what you're getting. Body type, coat, and eye color are set. Laid-back or active, quiet or vocal, cuddly or demanding, an adult cat has already settled into his own persona. These considerations may not be as important in a pedigreed cat, because you know, based on your kitten's background and the breeder's knowledge and reputation, what your kitten is likely to grow into in terms of body type and temperament. But in a no-pedigree kitten, these qualities are really anybody's guess. If you want to make sure that you're getting, say, a mellow pet, choose a cat beyond the ants-in-his-pants kitten stage.

✔ The easy care and generous affection of adult cats make them perfect pets for people for whom walking dogs would be difficult or impossible. And study after study confirms the importance of a cat in the lives of those who feel isolated by age or disabilities.

✔ One of the most compelling reasons to adopt a mature cat is that many of these adults have little hope of getting a second chance after they hit the shelter, no matter how healthy, beautiful, and well mannered they are. Kittens are so adorable they're hard to pass up, so many people never even look at the cages of adult cats when they're at the shelter.

✔ The possible disadvantage of adopting an adult cat is that you may be choosing a pet with behavioral problems — not using a litter box, for example. A good shelter, rescue group, or breeder practices full disclosure of any known health or behavior problems with the animals up for adoption. Remember, however, that many animals are given up for behavior problems that can be resolved or aren't their fault — such as the cat who's looking at a filthy litter box every day and decides to do his business elsewhere.

She-kitty, he-kitty: Which one's better?

You're not going to get a definitive answer out of us on this one, even if we had one, which we don't. Males and females make equally good pets, under one very important condition: altering.

Male or female, a cat who is what the experts call *whole* or *intact* — in other words, fully equipped to reproduce — is a royal pain to live with.

✔ When females are "in season" — which happens several times a year, for a couple of weeks at a time — they're yowly escape artists who attract noisy suitors from miles around.

✔ Some people think males are even worse. By the time they're sexually mature, they begin *spraying* — marking territory with a special pheromone-spiked urine with a smell that's not only foul but also nearly impossible to eradicate. They're also roamers and fighters.

The experts — even reputable breeders who keep intact cats for their breeding programs — all agree that neutering is the key to a cat's being a good pet, no matter the gender. An important contribution that those involved in the sport of showing cats have made is to ensure that animals who can no longer breed can still compete — in classes for "altereds." This aspect of showing is wonderfully progressive and supportive of those who like to show their lovely cats but not breed them.

The Beauty of Birds

Pet birds bring so much into the lives they share — color, song, speech, and a relationship that, at its best, approaches what you would find with a mate or a child. (And at its worst, approaches what you would find with a mate or a child.) And there, for some people, is the problem. Birds give as good as they get. Sometimes birds are a joy to live with, and other times . . . they're a big pain in the tail feathers.

For your own sanity, and for the health of the bird you hope to introduce to your world, you need to ask yourself whether you're really up to the challenge. Forewarned is forearmed, after all.

Along those lines, here are some of the pros and cons of owning a pet bird:

✔ **Of song and speech:** Birds use song and mimicry to protect their territory, warn of danger, and attract mates, and throughout history, their fascinating music has also engaged a human audience. Such birds as the canary and the singing greenfinch have long been prized for their song, and the members of the *psittacine* family — otherwise known as parrots — are extremely well known for their vocal talents.

✔ **A charming companion:** Although birds have lived as part of the human family for tens of thousands of years, the here and now may be the best time to enjoy an avian companion. Laws enacted to conserve birds in the wild and to stymie the worst sins of the importation trade (in which thousands upon thousands of birds died, either in transit or after entering the public realm as pet birds) have put the focus on breeding. The birds that come out of the best breeding programs make the very best quality pets, better than any a Roman Caesar could have known.

Socialized since infancy to see humans as part of their "flock," many of today's pet birds have companionship potential that can amaze anyone who believes the old stereotypes about wild-caught birds. Every bit as beautiful as their wild relatives, breeder-raised babies are loving and intelligent, and improvements in what we know about their care keep them healthier than ever before. Our newfound knowledge, combined with centuries of experience and perspective, means that if you educate yourself to care for your pet, you can expect a phenomenal relationship — better than you may have imagined when you decided to become a bird owner.

✔ **Putting in the time . . . and time again:** Forget any notion you ever had about birds being low-maintenance pets. Although canaries and finches can fall loosely into that category, the same cannot be said of all the other birds we love as pets. From budgies to cockatiels to the flashiest of macaws, birds can be — how shall we say this politely? — demanding. You can't just put them in a cage, change the papers, add food and water, and ignore them. They won't let you.

Cared for properly, birds can be as time-consuming as dogs. Really. They need to be loved, handled, trained, fed, and cleaned up after — a lot! If you don't have that kind of time and energy, be sure that the bird you choose is a finch or a canary. Or maybe a tank of fish.

✔ **Shelling out the bucks:** Birds are expensive to care for properly, much more so than most people anticipate. The price of acquiring the bird itself can run from the downright inexpensive — and, we advise, better avoided — loss-leader price for finches, canaries, and budgies to the monthly-salary figures that some of us are willing to shell out for large, flashy parrots.

And that's just the beginning.

Safe, roomy caging isn't cheap, nor is a proper diet. Preventive veterinary care to keep your pet healthy is a pricey must, and if your pet gets really sick, be prepared to dig deep. All of these factors must be figured in, along with such necessities as toys, which a large parrot can go through with awesome efficiency. It all adds up.

✔ **Dealing with the noise and mess:** To hear some people tell it, the best tools for anyone who wants to keep a bird are earplugs and a handheld cordless vacuum. And it's true some birds can give a rowdy rock band a run for their money when it comes to decibel levels and the ability to trash a room.

Some of the problems are natural and normal, and some are caused by humans, but either way, the potential for noise and mess is an important consideration when you're thinking about a bird.

But then again . . . these problems shouldn't stop you, unless ultimate peace, quiet, and a clean house are the things that matter most to you in life.

The Practice of Aquarium Keeping

Okay, it's time to snag a comfortable chair and travel through the marvelous world of aquarium-keeping. Here are some great reasons for having tropical fish:

- Fish-keeping is a hobby that the whole family can participate in and enjoy together.

- Scientific research shows that aquariums can help lower stress and prolong life.

- The tanks don't require a lot of space and are perfect for apartment dwellers who may be prohibited from owning larger, roaming pets, such as dogs and cats.

- Fish don't bark at the neighbors, caterwaul at the moon, chase the letter carrier, make unsightly messes on the floor, or whimper all night. You probably will never have to bail a renegade goldfish out of the local pound, either.

- An aquarium encourages your artistic side to run wild when it comes to aquatic decorating, and you won't find another hobby quite as soothing — nothing compares to dipping your tired arms into nice cool water to do a little underwater planting or rearranging.

- Daily care and maintenance of a home aquarium is simple, and really doesn't require a great deal of time or money. You can set up a complete aquarium system with a relatively small amount of money as long as you don't go overboard at the beginning, and are content to add to your system as you go along.

Are you sold? The next thing you need to do is decide which type of aquarium you want. The following sections describe each type.

Freshwater systems

The most popular type of aquarium is a *freshwater* system. It's probably the most practical system for a beginning aquarist for several reasons:

- A freshwater system is not quite as expensive to set up as a saltwater system.

- Freshwater fish are generally less expensive than marine fish. It's much better to work with less expensive fish when you're just starting out, and still learning the ins and outs of the hobby.

- Freshwater fish are readily available at most aquarium shops and offer a wide variety of colorful species to choose from. Many hardy species, such as guppies, platys, and swordtails, are very forgiving of beginners' mistakes. Marine fish are much more sensitive to water conditions and don't tolerate mistakes as easily.

✔ Many varieties of freshwater fish breed quite easily and may provide you with opportunities to sell your overstock (don't quit your day job, though) and a chance to experiment with new breeds.

✔ You can keep significantly more freshwater than marine fish in the same amount of space.

You can set up either tropical or coldwater freshwater systems. Each system has slightly different equipment requirements and houses different types of fish.

✔ **Freshwater tropical aquariums:** Freshwater tropical aquariums house the largest majority of retail freshwater fish. If you choose this system, you can set up a community aquarium with a variety of species that can coexist peacefully, or you may decide to try a species tank for a few of the more aggressive species, such as cichlids. A freshwater tropical aquarium offers the greatest number of choices in livestock and plants out of all the systems discussed in this chapter.

Popular species of tropical freshwater fish include platys, guppies, mollies, neons, swordtails, catfish, angelfish, algae eaters, bettas, tetras, and barbs.

✔ **Freshwater coldwater aquariums:** A coldwater aquarium usually houses species such as goldfish, sunfish, shiners, and bitterlings that normally live in lower temperatures in their native habitat. Large koi are often kept in coldwater ponds. The equipment you need for a coldwater aquarium is similar to that for a tropical aquarium, except that coldwater tanks don't require a heating system. Larger tanks are better for this type of system because coldwater species are generally larger than most tropical species and they consume more oxygen. Take care in choosing plants for this system because many plants can't survive the lower temperatures.

Aside from goldfish, most coldwater fish are difficult to obtain in many areas of the country. Setting up a coldwater system drastically reduces your choices of fish and live plants.

Marine systems

Marine, or *saltwater,* systems require saltwater. You see marine fish on most scuba and underwater programs. The most popular of these fish includes the coral reef species often found living in close proximity to various *invertebrates* (animals without backbones); they are often very colorful and quite beautiful. But don't fool yourself, beauty has its price. Saltwater fish can be very expensive.

The saltwater used in a marine system is usually obtained by mixing fresh water with a manufactured salt mix. A good filtration system is important in marine tanks to keep the oxygen levels high and the ammonia levels low. Marine fish have a lower tolerance to ammonia (a fish waste product) than freshwater species do, and an inadequate filter soon leads to disaster in a saltwater tank.

Like freshwater, marine aquariums can be broken down into a few subcategories.

- ✔ **Coldwater marine.** Many tanks of this type house animals such as lobsters and rockfish that are native to colder Pacific areas.

- ✔ **Tropical marine.** These tanks generally contain fish native to coral reef areas, such as tangs, clownfish, and damsels.

- ✔ **Reef tank.** Some reef tanks contain only invertebrates, such as anemones, scallops, organisms growing on live rock, and clams. Other tanks may have both invertebrates and fish.

You can set up a saltwater system in a variety of ways. Invertebrates are a little more difficult to care for, so if you do set up a saltwater system, you may want to start with a fish-only tank, or choose your invertebrates carefully.

Gaining a little experience with a freshwater system is a great way to prepare yourself to enter the marine side of the hobby. Don't get me wrong. A beginner can maintain a successful marine tank, but the lessons you learn can be very expensive. We see many new hobbyists become disheartened with fish-keeping because they start out with a marine setup that's just too much for them to handle. If you have a close friend who's experienced in marine systems, ask her for advice — she may be able to help you get started successfully.

Many marine fish are social time bombs waiting to explode all over the other fish in your tank. In fact, saltwater fish can be downright rude. Most community freshwater fish have reached a state of enlightenment or something like that, and are pretty cool with each other.

Brackish systems (reading between the lines)

The *brackish aquarium* is the least popular of all three systems, simply because the fish are generally unavailable from local pet stores, and are usually more expensive than freshwater tropical fish. The water in a brackish aquarium lies somewhere between fresh and marine in salt content. Popular species for this type of system include monos, archers, puffers, and scats. The equipment for a brackish system is similar to that for a freshwater setup, but only specific plants can tolerate a brackish system.

Financing a furry friend on a budget

Pets are great company, but keeping them alive, healthy, and happy can be a bit costly. Here are some sites to help you find, feed, and train a pet affordably:

✔ www.hsus.org: The cheapest way to get a pet is to adopt. Whether you want a puppy or a more mature dog, a purebred or a one-of-a-kind mixed breed, the local animal shelter probably has the best selection of animals anywhere — and they're all screened for good health and behavior. Most shelters will even help you with spaying and neutering. The Humane Society site gives you information on finding your nearest shelter, adopting purebreds, choosing the right pet for you, preparing for a pet, and bringing it home. The site also gives advice on healthy places to buy pets, if that's the way you want to go.

✔ www.simplypets.com/pet-recipes: Check out this site for nearly 200 reader-submitted recipes for food and treats for birds, dogs, cats, fish, and rodents — you'll even find three recipes for feeding llamas.

✔ www.pet-grub.com: This site is more than just recipes — it clearly explains the why, the what, and the how of making homemade pet food quickly and easily.

✔ www.virtualvet.com: If you're new to pet ownership, this site is a good starting point for caring for the health of your pet, with special sections on kittens, puppies, and even senior dogs and cats. You can search for a local veterinarian, find pet products for both dogs and cats, and peruse tips for traveling with pets. It also provides the latest information on alternative pet healthcare and medicine, forums to chat about your pets, and an "Ask a Vet" e-mail service.

✔ www.perfectpaws.com: Train your pet with the helpful articles at the Perfect Paws site. The list of topics includes housebreaking a puppy; leash training a dog; training pets not to bite; training the shy dog or puppy; training dogs on chasing, running away, and jumping; and litter box training.

Part IV
Money Matters for Folks over 50

The 5th Wave   By Rich Tennant

"Oh, her? That's Ms. Lamont, our Plan Administrator. She's going to help me determine your eligibility in our 401(k) Plan."

In this part . . .

*I*n the United States today, many people are finding that they spend the last third of their lives in retirement. That's a lot of time! That means that once you reach 50, you really need to start thinking seriously about planning your retirement (if you haven't already).

This part prompts you to ask yourself the questions you need to answer to plan effectively. You see how to create a simple budget to manage your spending, and you get an overview of the different types of investments you can make to save up for those golden days. We add a modern twist and give you a brief rundown on the benefits of online banking, too.

And for folks who have already reached retirement age, we impart investing and spending strategies to help you stretch your money as far as it will go. We also give you some ideas for planning your estate, including the inside scoop on trusts and life insurance.

Chapter 14

Fabulous Secrets for Planning and Financing Your Retirement

*N*o matter where you stand on the retirement timeline, inevitably you have to ask yourself this question: Am I investing wisely enough to get where I want to go? Smart investing, however, is only part of the equation. The age you begin saving seriously is also important. So too are the retirement benefits you may be entitled to at work. Even your family tree could influence your savings strategy. Did your parents or grandparents live long enough to celebrate the births of great-grandchildren? If so, you may be one of the increasing number of Americans who spend a third of their lives in retirement.

This chapter helps you plan for retirement. We offer guidance on how much you can expect retirement to cost and outline your investment options for earning the money you need.

The Costs of Retirement

Financial planners often suggest that most retirees can live comfortably with 60 to 80 percent of their preretirement income. Once retired, many people's expenses decline. After all, they don't have to buy work clothes or pay Social Security and Medicare payroll taxes or wear down their car in a long commute. They also may have paid off the mortgage by then. Later in retirement, medical costs, particularly prescription drug bills, can strain a budget, but by then, other expenses, such as money devoted to entertainment, often decline.

Looking past the money

Many people's retirement daydreams end happily with a huge pile of cash at the finish line. Some people, bent on stockpiling lots of money, behave as if they have a savings scoreboard riveted to their forehead. In calculating what they have and what they'll need, eager-beaver savers postpone gratification until they retire, letting the money issue drive retirement decisions instead of being just a part of the preparation process.

Yet you can't fully enjoy the money you've diligently squirreled away if you don't focus on what you'd like to do when the alarm clock is no longer a necessity. Some affluent folks continue to work past retirement age not because they relish working, but because they don't know how else to fill the void. Many aren't sure what to do with their financial freedom beyond spending time with grandchildren and traveling. For those that remain puzzled, consider answering this question: What you would like to do if you had only five years to live?

You'll probably need to save more for retirement if

- ✔ You invest conservatively, primarily in bonds and cash.
- ✔ You want to retire early.
- ✔ You expect to spend 70 percent or more of your preretirement income after leaving the workforce.
- ✔ You face children's college costs.
- ✔ You don't start saving seriously until your 40s or 50s.

You can probably save less if

- ✔ You invest more aggressively.
- ✔ You plan to work part-time during retirement.
- ✔ You'll receive a pension.
- ✔ You can live on less than 70 percent of your preretirement income.
- ✔ You began saving at least 10 percent of your income in retirement accounts before hitting 40.

Eight key questions to ask yourself

Whiz-bang computer software is only as good as the information that you plug in. Before you can intelligently determine your needs, you must fill in some huge blanks. The older you are, the more you should be paying attention to these retirement questions.

✔ At what age do you want to retire?

Some retirees ultimately return to work because they've miscalculated how far their money will stretch. Most experts agree that if you want to retire quite early, say at 55 years of age, you'll need enough assets to last at least 30 years.

✔ How much can you expect from Social Security and any pension?

✔ How long do you expect to live?

✔ Can you survive financially if your spouse dies?

✔ How much money, if any, do you want to leave to heirs?

✔ What kind of investment return can you expect?

✔ How much investment loss would you be willing to take?

If you're not sure whether you have nerves of steel, consider visiting the Bear's Cave, a cozy Internet spot devoted to demonstrating the crushing power of a bear market. You'll find the Cave at the 401Kafe (www.401kafe.com), a Web site devoted to 401(k) participants. At the Cave, you'll discover how bloodied and bruised your portfolio would have been during one of the worst bear markets ever.

✔ Are you (and a spouse) protected by long-term-care insurance?

Seven ways to play catch-up

What if you haven't started saving enough? What if you haven't saved at all? If you fit this description, you're not alone. According to one survey, the typical age when Americans who are 55 or older begin saving for retirement is age 42. At this point, your biggest challenge may be convincing yourself that starting to save isn't futile. This section provides some drastic and some relatively painless catch-up techniques to show you that all hope is not lost.

Here are some ways to do so:

✔ Delay retirement.

✔ Max out your tax-deferred contributions.

✔ Commit to saving a certain amount each week — and invest it wisely.

✔ Carefully evaluate retirement benefits and other perks in a compensation package at a potential new workplace before deciding to change jobs.

✔ Trade your house for a cheaper one.

✔ Seek outside advice from a certified financial planner.

✔ Find a bridge job to help you transition out of full-time employment.

Protecting Your Money before Retirement

Like it or not, you deal with money every day. Some people deal with it better than others do. The difference is in their money-management skills. You're not born with these skills; you acquire them over time. And improvement comes with practice.

Where are you now?

Your budget is a financial map to help you reach your financial goals, and it's useless unless you know where you are now and where you want to go. Determine your current financial situation by taking a thorough survey of your current financial status and then creating a worksheet to keep track. Include everything from your salary, your checking account, and your savings account, to your stocks, bonds, and mutual funds. Also include IRAs, 401(k)s, and any other retirement funds you have. Don't forget real estate, insurance policies, and personal property.

As you remember other assets, return to this worksheet and enter their values, adding more lines as necessary.

Creating a budget to get you there

Here are the steps for creating a budget that works:

1. **Create goals for yourself.** You need to create short-term, mid-term, and long-term goals.

2. **Assign a dollar amount for meeting each of those goals.**

3. **Keep a spending diary.** Track every dollar, every cent you spend for at least one month.

4. **Based on your spending diary, create a worksheet that indicates the *categories* in which you spend.** For example, most people spend money on rent, utilities, and doctor's appointments, as well as nonessential items such as movies, magazines, and hobbies.

5. **Examine where you are currently spending your money, and figure out where you *want* to be spending your money.**

Table 14-1 is a sample budget to show you what your budget might look like. Using the information from your spending diary, insert the values for what you paid in each category last month in the Last Month Actual column. After you determine what you should be spending in each category, put those amounts in the This Month Budget column. At the end of another month, put the amount that you actually spent in each category in the This Month Actual column. This budget leaves you space in the Over/Under column to compare each item's real value to its real cost. When you compile your budget, you want to be able to compare real versus projected values.

Table 14-1	My Monthly Budget			
Expense	*Last Month Actual*	*This Month Budget*	*This Month Actual*	*Over/ Under*
Housing and Utilities				
Mortgage or rent	$_____	_____	_____	_____
Homeowners' or condo assn. fees	$_____	_____	_____	_____
Home maintenance	$_____	_____	_____	_____
Electricity	$_____	_____	_____	_____
Gas	$_____	_____	_____	_____
Water	$_____	_____	_____	_____
Garbage removal	$_____	_____	_____	_____
Sewer fees	$_____	_____	_____	_____
Telephone	$_____	_____	_____	_____
Subtotal, Housing and Utilities	*$_____*	_____	_____	_____

Creating a Foolproof Financial Plan

Face it: Very few people achieve financial security by inheriting a lot of money, winning the lottery, or marrying a very rich person. If you look around, however, you'll find many financially secure people. How do they do it? The answer is probably investing.

You're ready to make the move from saver to investor when you're free of credit card debt and other major obligations, and after you've saved for an emergency fund. That emergency fund covers six to nine months of expenses in case you're laid off or without work.

Investing in a 401 (k)

If you earn employment income from a for-profit company, you may have the option of putting money in a 401(k), a retirement account that appreciates without taxation until you retire or leave the company. (Not all companies sponsor plans, especially small companies, and 401(k)s are not available to state and municipal workers — check with your employer to see if your company offers this plan.)

Here are the facts about investing in a 401(k):

- With a 401(k), the employee contributes pretax salary to the plan. Generally, a 401(k) allows you to contribute a certain percentage of your income each year to the plan.

- Companies often match a portion of their employees' contributions to the 401(k). Many employers add 25 cents or even 50 cents more to each dollar an employee chooses to contribute. A typical formula is for an employer to match 50 percent of what an employee puts in, up to 6 percent of his or her salary. The plan may also allow an employee to make after-tax contributions.

- Money that is contributed to the company's 401(k) is then invested in various, predetermined ways. Many plans typically provide between four and seven investment options, including mutual funds, stocks, and bonds. Usually, a plan offers at least one stock fund, a balanced fund, a bond fund or fixed income account, and maybe a money market account.

- Many plans offer an automatic payroll deduction feature. You never miss the money you contribute and payroll deduction makes investing easier.

- Your money can go with you from job to job. Even after you leave your employer, you can roll your retirement money into other tax-deferred retirement accounts, such as an IRA (see the section "Investing in Individual Retirement Accounts," later in this chapter).

- Unlike a traditional pension plan (which promises a set dollar figure in benefits when you retire), the amount of money your 401(k) provides upon retirement is determined by how much is invested and the way it grows. The regular account statements you'll receive offer an indication of your likely return, but there's no way to predict how much you'll get until the day you actually retire.

- Deciding not to participate because you don't want to cut back on your take-home pay or telling yourself retirement is a long way off may prove to be a big mistake. You risk ending up without enough money after you retire.

The six worst 401(k) mistakes

Here are the six worst mistakes you can make when managing your 401(k):

✔ Mistake #1: Failing to diversify

✔ Mistake #2: Loading up on company stock

✔ Mistake #3: Failing to double-check the accuracy of your 401(k)

✔ Mistake #4: Borrowing from your 401(k)

✔ Mistake #5: Fumbling the handoff

✔ Mistake #6: Ignoring estate-planning options

Exploring the 403(b) world

Although weird and potentially confusing, 403(b) plans can be worth the headaches. Once you understand the convoluted rules, your 403(b) can provide far more flexibility than a 401(k) ever could. For instance, if you don't like the investment choices at your workplace, you may be free to shop for a better provider. In some cases, you can also make up for years when you contributed little or nothing to the plan.

If you're participating in a 403(b), chances are you're a teacher, school administrator, or a professor. Doctors, nurses, and others working in nonprofit hospitals are also enrolled in these plans, as are those on the payrolls of charities and churches. The six million people with 403(b) accounts have been enticed by the same golden promise: They can save retirement dollars without getting hammered by taxes.

Here are the pluses and minuses of investing in a 403(b):

✔ Just like in 401(k)s, the money contributed to a 403(b) is not taxed up front, and earnings grow tax-deferred. It's only when the money is withdrawn that the 403(b) participant must pay taxes based upon his or her tax bracket.

✔ Some employers provide matching contributions.

✔ Nobody screens the choices — or the salespeople.

✔ Employers don't like to get involved.

✔ Many 403(b) investment plans are invested poorly.

Investing in Individual Retirement Accounts

An Individual Retirement Account (IRA) is a tax-saving program (established under the Employee Retirement Security Act of 1974) to help Americans invest for retirement. Anyone who earns money by working can contribute up to $2,000 a year, or 100 percent of your income, whichever is less. If you don't have access to a 401(k) or other retirement plan, or if you've calculated that your current plan won't completely cover your retirement needs, then an IRA can help.

Here are the facts:

- ✔ An IRA offers tax-deferred growth — you don't pay any tax on it or the money that it earns for you until you withdraw it during retirement.

- ✔ You set up your IRA on your own with a bank, mutual fund, or brokerage firm. Like a 401(k), you can invest your IRA money in almost anything you can think of, from aggressive growth stocks to conservative savings accounts.

- ✔ Some financial planners advise that you use your IRA for investments that produce the highest income, such as stocks paying high dividends, because you defer the taxes. Another tactic is to put the IRA funds into riskier high-growth investments, such as stocks or certain types of mutual funds, because you don't touch the funds until retirement and can always switch them to safer investments as you get older.

Why invest in an IRA?

Here are just a few reasons to invest in an IRA:

- ✔ If your employer doesn't offer a 401(k) plan

- ✔ If you've calculated that your current retirement plan won't completely cover your estimated retirement needs, consider investing in an IRA — if you qualify

- ✔ To invest in high-yield investments — such as stocks paying high dividends — because your investment dollars are tax-deferred

- ✔ To invest in higher risk investments, such as stocks and certain mutual funds, if you don't plan to retire for years to come (by doing so you commit to taking the chance of receiving higher gains for your investment dollar)

Choices, choices: The two types of IRAs

You can choose from two types of IRAs: the traditional IRA and the Roth IRA. Use Table 14-2 to help you compare traditional and Roth IRAs and decide which type of IRA is best for you.

Table 14-2	Comparing Traditional IRAs and Roth IRAs	
Feature	*Traditional IRA*	*Roth IRA*
Tax deductible contributions	In some cases	None
Penalty-free withdrawals	After age 59½	
Withdrawals	Required at age 70½	Never required
Income level	No requirement	Must have income under $110,000 if single; $160,000 if married filing jointly
Tax-free earnings	Earnings taxed upon withdrawal	Earnings never taxed
Annual contribution limit	$2,000	$2,000

Inherited IRAs: What you should know

In a sudden and surprising move, the IRS issued new IRA regulations in 2001 that dramatically simplify the rules for millions of Americans and give a second chance to elderly people who made mistakes when calculating what is officially referred to as their *required minimum distributions*. These required minimum distributions kick in after someone reaches the age of 70½. At that point, a person is required to take at least a minimum amount of money out of his or her IRA each year. In the past, inadvertent errors made at this crucial age were most often irrevocable.

The new regulations have created something else to cheer about. In some cases, family and friends who have already inherited flawed IRAs may be able to undo the damage.

Making the most of the new regulations is crucial both for retirees who are contemplating passing along assets to family, friends, or charities and for folks who expect to inherit an IRA or other retirement plan proceeds. The trouble is that IRA inheritance rules can be confusing. This quick list highlights what you need to do, whether you are the IRA owner or an heir.

Advice for an IRA owner:

✔ See how the new IRA rules might affect your IRA beneficiary decisions.

✔ Avoid naming your estate as the IRA beneficiary.

✔ Insist that your financial institution acknowledge in writing that it received your IRA beneficiary paperwork.

✔ Consider using customized IRA forms if no standard forms cover your situation.

✔ Double-check whom you've listed as IRA beneficiaries, and name contingency beneficiaries.

✔ Seek out professional advice on IRA inheritance issues.

✔ If you're currently making mandatory withdrawals from your IRA, calculate your new minimum required distribution. It may be considerably less than what you are now forced to take out.

✔ You can begin taking out the lower mandatory withdrawals beginning in 2001.

Advice for an IRA beneficiary:

✔ Keep your inherited IRA alive as long as possible.

✔ Discuss with your parents their intentions for passing along their IRAs.

✔ If a relative dies, don't move or touch the loved one's IRA without receiving tax advice.

✔ Explore how IRA mistakes may be rectified after the IRA owner has died.

✔ Don't erase the benefactor's name from an inherited account.

✔ If you inherited an IRA in or after 2000, you should be able to use the more favorable IRA payout schedule.

✔ Make provisions to pass on an inherited IRA to your own kids.

Using the Rule of 72

A quick way to calculate how long it will take an investment to double — at any steady interest rate — is to use the Rule of 72. Simply divide 72 by the interest rate, and you have the number of years it will take for your investment to double. For example, if you have an investment earning 8 percent, divide 72 by 8 percent to find that it will take nine years for your investment to double in value.

Just think: If you made an initial investment of $10,000 when your child was born and earned 8 percent interest on that investment, that child would have $40,000 at age 18. That money could help pay for a college education!

Defining mutual funds

A mutual fund is managed by an investment company that invests (according to the fund's objectives) in stocks, bonds, government securities, short-term money market funds, and other instruments by pooling investors' money.

Here are the facts about mutual funds:

✔ Mutual funds are sold in shares. Each share of a fund represents an ownership in the fund's underlying securities (the portfolio).

✔ By law, mutual funds must calculate the price of their shares each business day. Investors can sell their shares at any time and receive the current share price, which may be more or less than the price they paid.

✔ When a fund earns money from dividends on the securities it invests in or makes money by selling some of its investments at a profit, the fund distributes the earnings to shareholders. If you're an investor, you may decide to reinvest these distributions automatically in additional fund shares.

✔ A mutual fund investor makes money from the distribution of dividends and capital gains on the fund's investments. A mutual fund shareholder also can potentially make money as the fund's share per share (called *net asset value,* or *NAV*) increases in value.

NAV of a mutual fund = Assets – Liabilities ÷ Number of shares in the fund

(Assets are the value of all securities in a fund's portfolio; liabilities are a fund's expenses.) The NAV of a mutual fund is affected by the share price charges of the securities in the fund's portfolio and any dividend or capital gains distributions to its shareholders.

✔ Unless you're in immediate need of this income, which is taxable, reinvesting this money into additional shares is an excellent way to grow your investments.

✔ Shareholders receive a portion of the distribution of dividends and capital gains, based on the number of shares they own. As a result, an investor who puts $1,000 in a mutual fund gets the same investment performance and return per dollar as someone who invests $100,000.

✔ Mutual funds invest in many (sometimes hundreds of) securities at one time, so they are diversified investments. A *diversified portfolio* is one that balances risk by investing in a number of different areas of the stock and/or bond markets. This type of investing attempts to reduce per-share volatility and minimize losses over the long term as markets change. Diversification offsets the risk of putting your eggs in one basket, such as technology funds.

✔ A stock or bond of any one company represents just a small percentage of a fund's overall portfolio. So even if one of a fund's investments performs poorly, 20 to 150 more investments can shore up the fund's performance. As a result, the poor performance of any one investment isn't likely to have a devastating effect on an entire mutual fund portfolio. That balance doesn't mean, however, that funds don't have inherent risks: You need to carefully select mutual funds to meet your investment goals and risk tolerance.

✔ The performance of certain classes of investments — such as large company growth stocks — can strengthen or weaken a fund's overall investment performance if the fund concentrates its investments within that class. If the overall economy declines, the stock market takes a dive, or a mutual fund manager picks investments with little potential to be profitable, a fund's performance can suffer.

✔ Unfortunately, unless you have a crystal ball, you have no way to predict how a fund will perform, except to look at the security's underlying risk. If a fund has existed long enough to build a track record through ups and downs, you can review its performance during the last stressful market.

Fortunately for all investors, some companies use a statistical measure called standard deviation, which measures the volatility in the fund's performance. The larger the swings in a fund's returns, the more likely the fund will slip into negative numbers.

Companies that track funds' standard deviations include Morningstar Mutual Funds and Value Line Inc., which are mutual fund reporting and ranking services whose newsletters are available in most libraries. You can visit their Web sites at www.morningstar.com and www.valueline.com, respectively.

Investing in stocks

Why invest in stocks? Back in the 1990s, this question wasn't one that many people pondered. The answer appeared self-evident. Techno-geek millionaires bought Lamborghinis on their lunch hour. Secretaries with stock options retired before the first gray hairs ever appeared in their combs. And the 401(k), that unlyrical subsection of the U.S. Tax Code, infiltrated the public's consciousness to become a household name. When the 20th century ended, the longest bull market in American history stampeded across the fallen confetti and charged right into the new millennium — at least for a little while.

Even with market changes, the following advantages of investing in stocks remain:

✔ **Stocks have been top performers over time.** Throughout modern history, stocks have clearly outperformed bonds and cash by an impressive margin. Since the eve of the Great Crash in 1929, the stock market has been up more than twice as many years as it has been down.

✔ **Investing is easy.** The explosion of discount brokerage services has reduced the average transaction fee that investors pay for buying a block of stock to less than the price of a tank of gas. Valuable research that used to be the exclusive domain of institutional investors is now free. Index funds, which were once ridiculed by financial pundits, are enabling amateur investors to soundly beat the pros with better investment returns. Wall Street has even created a new way to invest in equities for those who are torn between individual stocks and mutual funds: the exchange-traded funds. Such funds provide a great option for reluctant investors who love the idea of owning individual stocks, but lack the desire or the knowledge to go the distance with individual stock trading.

✔ **You don't need a lot of money to begin investing in individual stocks or stock mutual funds.** You can now open a trading account at a discount broker for as little as $500, and some mutual fund companies will get you started for $50 provided that you commit to investing a small amount of cash each month.

Investing in bonds

A bond is an IOU. When you buy a bond, you're essentially lending cash to a debtor, such as the U.S. Treasury, an airport authority, a wireless startup, or some other organization or company. How well you'll profit from your loan partially depends upon how desperate the borrower is to generate cash. If the borrower isn't terribly trustworthy, you should be rewarded upfront with a better deal.

WARNING!

Avoiding the roller-coaster approach

You've probably heard the horror stories and triumphant tales of investing. Somebody just made millions by following a hot tip overheard on the golf course. Somebody else just lost everything when she borrowed a bundle to invest in real estate in Florida.

You want to avoid the roller-coaster approach to investing. Roller coasters belong in amusement parks. Good, steady growth over the long haul is your goal for investing.

Here's the rundown on bonds:

✔ Most bonds are priced at $1,000. Even when a pension fund or some other huge institutional player buys a multimillion-dollar block of bonds, they are doled out in $1,000 increments. The amount of money you lend is called the *principal;* the bond's face value is referred to as *par.*

✔ Of course, when you lend money, you want something in return. A bond provides that through its coupon. A *coupon* is the amount of money or interest that the issuer agrees to pay each year over the life of the bond. Coupons make bonds ideal for those investors who desire a predictable income stream from their investments.

✔ Neither you nor the debtor wants your money tied up forever, so every bond eventually expires. In fixed-income jargon, the time when the bond expires is called the bond's *maturity.* You can choose from a wide assortment of maturities. Treasuries, for instance, peddle their debt with maturities as short as 3 months and as long as 30 years. In extremely rare cases, some corporations, such as Disney, have issued 100-year bonds. These bonds are typically bought by pension funds and other institutional investors. When a bond reaches maturity, the investor gets back the original $1,000 investment.

✔ Bonds are classified by their maturities:

  • Short-term bonds last 1 to 3 years.

  • Intermediate-term bonds last 3 to 10 years.

  • Long-term bonds last more than 10 years.

✔ Usually, investors who are willing to lend money for the longest periods (which is often not a wise move) can expect more compensation. Consequently, someone investing in a 30-year Treasury bond expects a higher coupon than somebody lending the Treasury money for 5 or 10 years. There are occasionally periods, such as the year 2000, when the coupons for the shorter Treasuries were greater than the longest ones.

✔ You expect extra compensation because you are assuming more risk with a long-term bond. If you tie up your money in a 30-year bond with a 6.5 percent coupon, you may find that five years later interest rates climb, and now everybody else is grabbing bonds yielding 10 percent or 12 percent. If you want to bail and latch on to a more tantalizing bond, you can. Plenty of people will happily buy your sorry bond, but they will do so only at a fair sale price. Consequently, the price of your bond will plummet, which means the yield skyrockets for the next owner. You will lose some of your original principal, but that's the only way to unload the bond.

✔ Because investors can't accurately predict interest-rate movements, many financial experts suggest that long-term fixed-income fans, who desire the highest interest rates with the least amount of risk, stick with bonds that mature in the 7 to 10 year range.

Most Frequently Asked Questions about Social Security

Here are answers to some common questions about Social Security:

✔ **What do I pay?** All of us who work are doing our part to keep the Social Security system solvent. Currently, 7.65 percent of our paychecks is siphoned into Social Security and Medicare. The Social Security portion of the tax is 6.2 percent; Medicare swallows the rest. Your employer picks up the other half of the tab, which brings the total tax to 15.3 percent.

Under this system, the self-employed get dinged twice. They must pay the 15.3 percent tax all by themselves. The self-employed, however, can claim half of this obligation as a tax deduction.

Social Security can't extract an unlimited amount of money from any one person or employer. There is a cap, which is adjusted annually, on how much Social Security can extract. In 2001, the maximum that a worker on somebody's payroll has to pay is 6.2 percent of $80,400. The Medicare portion of the tax, however, has no ceiling.

✔ **Are all workers covered by Social Security?** Most workers are covered by Social Security, but a few pockets of holdouts remain, thanks to past legislative action. Some federal, state, and local government employees still work outside the system, as do railroad employees and some church workers. Usually these people are covered by some other type of pension system.

Keep in mind that just because you're contributing to Social Security through payroll deductions doesn't automatically entitle you to future benefits. To qualify, you must earn 40 calendar quarters of coverage. As a practical matter, anybody who has contributed to Social Security for 10 years, which breaks down to 40 quarters, is covered. You don't have to work a decade to earn those 40 quarters, however. You can pocket four quarters quickly by meeting a minimum income requirement, although you can't earn more than four quarters in one year.

✔ **How are my benefits calculated?** In computing your benefits, the government averages for most workers the 35 highest-wage-earning years of an individual's salary history. (It is indexed to reflect the average increase in national wages during the same period.) Of course, not everybody has such a lengthy work record. Suppose you worked 25 years. The amount you earned during those 25 years will be averaged with 10 years' worth of zero income. Obviously, this method of calculation will shrink your benefit.

✔ **How much can I expect from Social Security?** To its credit, the Social Security Administration has made a stab at eliminating some of the guesswork concerning your future benefits. The federal government now mails yearly four-page statements that estimate what a worker's benefits will be upon retirement. Every worker who is 25 years of age or older should get one of these statements. You can expect the yearly mailing about three months before your birthday.

✔ **Does Social Security protect against inflation?** Social Security does offer one tremendous advantage over most private pension plans: It's designed to beat inflation. After 1974, cost-of-living adjustments (COLAs) have been automatic. Since that time, COLAs have ranged from 14.3 percent in 1980 to 1.3 percent in 1986 and 1998. In 2001, a 3.5 percent COLA bumped the average check up by $29. The government calculates the COLA every October, and the checks are adjusted in January.

Claiming Social Security benefits at age 62

Most people claim their benefits at this age, but before you join the crowd, consider these issues:

✔ **If your health is failing.** Morbid as this fact is to contemplate, some people aren't going to live long after retiring. If you have a history of heart disease or you're fighting a cancer diagnosis, you may want to take the money now. Your family's health history may also play into your decision. Maybe your grandparents, parents, uncles, and aunts tended to die at relatively early ages. Smokers, alcoholics, the grossly overweight, or those who haven't been conscientious about taking care of themselves may also want to claim their Social Security stake as soon as possible.

✔ **If you need the money.** If you're struggling financially, you may want to take the money and run, particularly if you are in poor health or have been laid off, with little chance of finding a new position in your field. If you have no desire to jump back into the work force or circumstances make that impossible, then Social Security could be your only way to stay afloat.

✔ **If you plan to invest the money.** Some people who don't need the money may opt to postpone payments, but some financial planners urge their clients to take the cash and invest it instead. Sinking the money into the stock market could earn a greater windfall. Of course, investing in the stock market in your later years is also more perilous. If you plan to divert the cash into CDs, a savings account, or money market, you might be better off postponing Social Security.

✔ **If you continue to work.** You could pay a heavy price if you begin taking Social Security benefits while you're still on the job. In 2001, federal law allows a Social Security recipient who is between 62 and full retirement age to make only $10,680 a year without being penalized. Once that limit is surpassed, workers forfeit $1 for every $2 they earn.

✔ **If your spouse would suffer financial hardship if you died first.** Social Security is plagued by a gender gap. Because women live longer, they are the ones who usually face dramatic cutbacks in Social Security when a spouse dies. A widow (or widower) will receive a check that is just one-half or two-thirds of the couple's combined benefit.

What hurts women is their historically lower salaries and their periodic absences from the workforce. Although Social Security retirement benefits are usually calculated upon the highest 35 years in a career, the typical woman works only 27 years. (The average man's career lasts 39 years.) All those missing years hurt when a woman's benefit is calculated.

✔ **If you're a woman.** If you will receive benefits based upon your own work record, you may want to start those benefits early. (This advice assumes you are not continuing to work.) As previously noted, women enjoy an actuarial advantage over men because they live longer. Chances are a woman will remain alive long enough to overcome the built-in financial penalty for taking the money early because she'll draw many more checks over the years.

Claiming Social Security benefits at full retirement age or older

Back when Social Security was launched, people often worked almost until their deaths because there was no national safety net. The retirement age that Congress originally envisioned for workers to claim their checks was 65, and it was assumed that many people would die before they reached this age. If you want full benefits and you were born prior to 1938, the age to claim full benefits is 65. For everyone else, the full retirement age keeps creeping up.

If you decide to postpone Social Security when you reach 65, you should still sign up for Medicare. There is no financial incentive for delaying Medicare.

If you delay retirement until age 70, the amount of your ultimate monthly checks will increase anywhere from 4.5 percent to 8 percent a year. There is absolutely no point in waiting beyond age 70 because the benefits stop escalating. There's now even less need to wait until a 70th birthday because fewer retirees are being penalized for returning to work.

Merging pensions and Social Security

If you're vested in a pension, you're entitled to your full pension, right? The answer for millions of Americans could be no. This terrible surprise can be explained by a practice that experts call "integration." While controversial, this practice is completely legal. Here's how it works: In certain circumstances, a company can subtract a portion of your Social Security benefit from your pension.

What can you do about pension integration? Here are some suggestions:

✔ Find out your company's policy. Ask your human resources department and request a copy of your pension program's summary plan description. This document, which federal law requires to be easy to read, lays out how the plan works. It must precisely document how the integration is calculated.

✔ If your corporation uses integration, chances are most or all of your colleagues won't be aware of it. If enough people are angry by the arrangement, workplace sentiment might encourage the company to revisit the issue. You can also lobby Congress to outlaw integration altogether. U.S. Sen. Olympia Snowe (R-Maine) and Rep. Rob Andrews (D-N.J.) are both trying with their own legislation to banish integration from the workplace.

✔ If you face the prospects of getting your pension reduced, find out how the calculations were made. If a company has used an estimate of your Social Security benefits in its calculations, you can ask for a recalculation. Consider consulting an actuary or an accountant to see how integration will affect you.

Two ways to avoid taxes on Social Security benefits

Social Security checks can be taxed. Some retirees are shocked when they discover this nasty surprise. Many people will never pay taxes on their Social Security checks, but plenty do. Whether you owe money depends upon whether your income reaches a high enough level.

Okay, that's the bad news. The good news is that some of this tax may be avoided. Here's how:

✔ **Postpone Social Security benefits.** Affluent Americans can dodge or reduce the tax bite by postponing their Social Security benefits. As mentioned earlier, anyone under the age of 65 who is working and receiving benefits can get hit with a huge tax bill as well.

✔ **Time IRA distributions carefully.** Many retirees are stunned to learn that their mandatory yearly withdrawals from traditional IRAs can trigger Social Security taxes. How does this happen? Large enough withdrawals can bump up someone's modified adjusted gross income and catapult that person into a higher federal tax bracket. In many cases, however, you can control how much of your Social Security will be taxed by thoughtfully controlling your IRA distributions.

To learn more about Social Security benefit taxation, you can order the IRS's Publication 554, *Tax Information for Older Americans.* Call the Internal Revenue Service at 800-829-3676 or go to www.irs.gov.

An Online Banking Primer

Simply stated, the term *online banking* describes the technology, tools, and processes that give you access to your bank accounts and banking transactions from your personal computer. The specific capabilities of an online banking system depend on the features of the computer software that you use to access the system and on the services that your bank chooses to provide, but typically you can do things like check account balances, get a list of transactions affecting your account, and perhaps transfer funds from one online account to another.

You need only a little imagination to think of the many ways that you can use online banking capabilities, such as:

✔ Getting an up-to-date balance for your bank account

✔ Identifying which checks have cleared the bank by reviewing a list of recent transactions that affect your account

✔ Checking the transaction details for ATM cash withdrawals, debit card purchases, and other transactions that you may have forgotten to record

✔ Confirming the date and amount of direct deposits (paychecks, tax returns, government checks, and so on) into your account

✔ Transferring funds from one account to another

✔ Making a payment on an installment loan or credit card account at your bank

✔ Sending a check to a creditor to pay a bill

✔ Downloading transaction information and automatically inserting it into personal finance manager software

✔ Simplifying the process of reconciling your records to your bank statement by automatically comparing information in your personal finance manager software to online data from the bank

✔ Doing all this and more, and doing it any time of the day or night, including evenings and weekends

All the capabilities in the preceding list may not be available from your bank, and some of them require personal finance manager software such as Quicken or Money.

TIP

Ten tips for using online bill payment

Here are ten indispensable tips for using online bill payment:

✔ Get the payee name right.

✔ Remember that the account number is critical.

✔ Test the system by sending yourself a sample payment.

✔ Understand that recurring payments save time.

✔ Confirm that your payment arrived.

✔ Look for a bill-payment guarantee.

✔ Update your payee information routinely.

✔ Don't overreact when you suspect a problem with a payment.

✔ Allow adequate time between pay date and due date.

✔ Set up online bill payment once, and the rest is easy.

Online banking enthusiasts often bandy about the following terms that you may want to be familiar with:

✔ **Electronic banking:** Electronic banking is any system that offers automated access to your bank accounts using electronic media (that is, information conveyed by wires instead of by paper); it includes *ATMs* (automated teller machines) and those automated *telephone banking* systems that allow you to make selections by pressing numbers on the telephone keypad in response to recorded prompts.

✔ **Online personal finance:** Online personal finance goes beyond simple banking to encompass other finance activities that you can perform online. Examples include researching investments, buying and selling stocks, applying for mortgages, and shopping for life insurance.

✔ **Online bill payment:** Online bill payment enables you to send online instructions to your bank so that the bank can make payments on your behalf. Basically, this means that you can write electronic checks by simply filling in an on-screen form.

TIP

Online banking sounds like everything you need, doesn't it? But don't toss your ATM card yet. You still need the ATM (or a human teller) when you want to get cash and make deposits.

Great ways to get free financial advice

Are you one of those people who doesn't start planning financially until you're running low on funds? If so, the last thing you want to do is shell out more money for advice. Instead, take a gander at the great, and free, advice in the following Web sites:

✔ www.free-financial-advice.net: Free Financial Advice helps you get a hold of your personal finances by explaining fundamental rules of money management and showing you a new way to look at your spending, investing, and debt management decisions. Advice topics include living within your means, understanding the time value and the compounding effect of money, beginning and prioritizing investments, retiring early, and saving money. Take advantage of helpful financial tools like the debt payoff calculator and the financial advice forum.

✔ www.fool.com: You may have heard the NPR financial radio show Motley Fool. This is the show's Web site. The site contains free newsletters, financial news, and discussion boards. Article topics include broker comparison, index funds, mutual funds, 401(k)s, IRAs, credit reports, insurance, and — believe it or not — financial advisors.

✔ www.kiplinger.com: The step-by-step guides at Kiplinger's give you the lowdown on investing, saving, financial planning, and money management. Some great tools are the finance-to-English dictionary for deciphering key financial terms, the financial forums, and the calculators for financial decisions. Or gather your 401(k) and IRA statements and your retirement planning questions and make a free phone call on Fridays to Kiplinger's financial planners who are experts on investing, insurance, estate planning, tax planning, and retirement planning.

✔ www.womenswallstreet.com/WWS/: Free financial advice for professional women dealing with divorce, raising children, and planning for retirement. Talk with other women in forums and make use of the financial checklists for big spending purchases, investing, retirement, IRAs, and interest.

✔ www.ihatefinancialplanning.com: This great site states that it's for everyone who loves money, hates planning, and wants answers. Is that you? It cuts through the jargon of financial planning, helping you analyze your own situation with real-world explanations. Some of the topics covered are divorce, college saving, finances for gays and lesbians, life insurance, and long-term care. Get free online advice or complete a plan over the phone or with a financial professional face to face.

Chapter 15

Welcome to Retirement!

- -

In This Chapter

▶ Investing and spending strategies for retirees

▶ The smart way to withdraw money from your retirement funds

▶ The role of annuities in retirement

▶ Estate planning

▶ A primer on trusts

▶ Insuring your financial health

- -

*T*raumatic. That's probably the first adjective that many people conjure up when they contemplate the inevitable. After saving for decades, reversing the process and spending for possibly decades can be a nerve-wracking prospect. In this chapter, you learn your best defense against the all-too-real possibility of portfolio erosion. Your best bet is to start thinking like a tax accountant. Planning your withdrawals in a way that avoids taxes can significantly boost the buying power of your nest egg.

In addition, this chapter covers the different types of annuities and the role they can play in your retirement. A list of resources to find out more about these complicated investments is included, as well.

This chapter also highlights some of the basics of estate planning, including the advantages of setting up a trust and an overview of the different types of life insurance. Having this knowledge is crucial whether you expect to receive an inheritance or plan to give one away.

The Great Guessing Game: Retirement Planning

The weak link in retirement planning has always been human error. You can easily project how long your nest egg will last by crunching numbers on a calculator, but although the math may be correct, the conclusions could be terribly wrong. How is this possible? One simple reason: You are forced to guess a lot. When devising retirement withdrawal strategies, you must make big assumptions about three unpredictable factors:

✔ **Your retirement spending needs:** Perhaps the only assumption you can make a reasonably accurate stab at is your retirement spending needs. To some extent, you can base your future spending on your previous patterns. As a general guideline, many planners estimate that retirees will spend 70 to 75 percent of what they did during their preretirement years. Spending is expected to decline as people move into their mid-70s and beyond, but other costs (such as nursing care and drugs) could keep costs from shrinking much. These generalities, however, are just that. Costs may go up or remain the same.

Many people assume that Medicare will pay all the medical bills, but it doesn't cover such things as drugs, nursing homes, dental bills, hearing aids, and glasses.

✔ **The future of inflation:** Inflation, another one of the big unknowns, is completely beyond your control or your best estimates. You just have to fudge this number. During most of the 1990s, inflation averaged just over 3.5 percent, so it would seem safe to plug that figure in to your equation. But inflation gets downright ugly during some periods. From 1973 through 1978, for instance, inflation soared by 48 percent. Although Social Security is indexed for inflation, this adjustment wouldn't nearly make up for the impact on a person's lifestyle.

Even when inflation is muzzled, it can still dangerously erode the buying power of somebody on a fixed income. Assume that a retiree is living comfortably on $50,000 a year. Even if inflation were a mere 2.4 percent (as it was between 1994 and 1998), the retiree's income would have to double in 30 years to prevent backsliding.

✔ **Future market performance:** Predicting market performance is fiendishly difficult. Not knowing what else to do, many retirees determine their yearly withdrawal rates based upon the historic performances of stocks, bonds, and cash. Since the mid-1920s, the stock market has posted a yearly annualized return of 11 percent, bonds have averaged about 6 percent, and cash has averaged 4 percent. In recent times, investors have been treated to even higher gains. During the past decade, the Standard & Poor's yearly return has averaged nearly 17 percent; the broader stock market, which also includes smaller stocks, did about the same. During the same period, government and corporate bonds averaged about a 9 percent return while cash generated 5 percent returns.

You can use some strategies to help offset these uncertainties. For one, you can invest wisely so that you can spend more. Here are some tips:

 ✔ **Withdraw modest amounts:** Traditional wisdom holds that retirees can earn 10 percent a year on their investments, take out 7 percent annually, and pretty much guarantee that they will die with an impressive chunk of money left behind in a brokerage account.

A super-safe strategy could limit yearly withdrawals to 4 percent of a portfolio's value. But 4 percent of $1 million is only $40,000, and a retiree with a $300,000 nest egg could withdraw only $12,000, which is hardly a princely sum to supplement Social Security and a pension.

You may think that if you remain loyal to stocks, such a modest withdrawal rate doesn't have to apply to you because a portfolio that's all stocks can grow fast enough to take bigger withdrawal hits. But remaining aggressively committed to stocks can catapult even the brightest investor into trouble.

 ✔ **Mix it up:** Many studies suggest that an all-bond portfolio in retirement is courting danger. A retiree cannot be sure that a fixed-income portfolio would last 25 to 30 years unless the annual payout is limited to a modest 3 percent, 4 percent, or possibly 5 percent. But the survival odds improve noticeably if $1 out of every $4 in a predominantly bond portfolio was invested in stocks.

For many retirees, suggesting that bonds make up no more than 50 percent of their holdings is nearly sacrilegious. It's understandable why seniors have clung to their bonds. With an income portfolio, traditionally only the interest is spent; the principal remains intact. Knowing that the principal isn't being touched can be incredibly reassuring. But what people fail to realize is that they need growth to balance the certainty of the bond income. A bond's worst sin is that it fails as an inflation slayer. Whereas stocks are valued for their ability to increase in value (sometimes quite dramatically), you generally can't expect much price appreciation from bonds.

Tax-Savvy Withdrawal Strategies

Here are some tactics to help you minimize the taxes you pay when you withdraw money from your retirement funds:

1. **Empty your taxable (nonretirement) accounts first.**

   The taxable money should usually go first. Remember that you're already paying the IRS for any earnings that your taxable accounts generate. The cash that you have sitting in a bank account, a mutual fund, or a brokerage account is subject to yearly income taxes and possible capital gains taxes as well. By spending this money first, you eliminate the federal tax liability that can soar as high as 39.6 percent if you're in the highest tax bracket. The tax bite is even bigger if you live in a state with its own income tax.

2. Be choosy when you drain your taxable portfolio.

Not all the investments kept in taxable accounts are tax hogs. Consider keeping your more tax-friendly holdings until you absolutely must withdraw funds from them. Municipal bonds fit into this category. The owners of *munis,* which are issued by state and local governments, avoid paying any federal taxes on the interest income. Some munis even permit you to skip state taxes and, in certain cases, local taxes.

3. Tap into retirement accounts funded by after-tax contributions.

Need more money? Be just as selective when cracking open your retirement accounts. Your best bet could be drawing cash from accounts whose tax hit won't be so high. One logical place to start is with a nondeductible IRA (refer to Chapter 15 for definitions of IRA types). This type of IRA is a good bet because a percentage of your withdrawals avoid taxes. Because you can't deduct your contributions to this type of IRA from your income tax return, you won't be expected to pay taxes on the original contributions when you start your withdrawals. (This approach works only if all your IRAs are nondeductible ones.)

4. Access the rest of your retirement accounts.

Retirement accounts that don't contain any after-tax money, such as 401(k)s and deductible IRAs, should be left until the end. That's because every dollar you pull out will be hit with a tax because you didn't pay the tax at the time of deposit into the account.

5. Tap into your Roth IRA.

If you've concluded that you won't need all the money sitting in your retirement accounts, don't touch any money that you might have in a Roth IRA. Unlike all other IRAs, the Roth owner never has to withdraw money from the account. Everyone else must begin mandatory IRA withdrawals after age 70½.

In addition, Roth withdrawals for retirees are tax-free if the money has been in the Roth for at least five years. If you do need to tap into your Roth IRA, don't withdraw all the money at once. Instead, take out only what you need — once the money leaves the Roth's tax-free oasis and is deposited into a regular bank or brokerage account, you'll pay taxes on any capital gain or income that the money generates in the future.

Four withdrawal options for your 401 (k)

You won't always be chained to your desk, and neither will your 401(k). When you retire, both of you will walk out the door. When you do, you'll face several options:

✔ **Keep your 401(k) at your old employer.** Before deciding to leave your 401(k) where it is, find out how easily the account can be moved in the future. This may be a satisfactory interim move if you aren't sure what you want to do with your account. Later, you ideally should transfer the money into an IRA rollover account, which provides unlimited investment options.

Here are some other things to keep in mind when considering this option:

- If you leave your 401(k) money where it is, after your death, a spouse is the only beneficiary who can roll the money into a tax-protected IRA. If you leave the 401(k) money to your kids, as a practical matter, they won't be able to stretch out the payments through their lifetime. The reason is that corporations don't want to bother with this hassle. By law, companies can limit payouts to beneficiaries for five years. After that, a 401(k) must be disbanded and the tax benefit is lost.

- On the other hand, if you discover later that you need to prematurely withdraw money out of your retirement account, the 10 percent early withdrawal penalty can sometimes be avoided if the cash remains in a 401(k) rather than in an IRA rollover. That's because anybody who is at least 55 when leaving a job can begin drawing down a 401(k) without getting dinged by the 10 percent penalty. The penalty, however, applies if the worker transferred the 401(k) money into an IRA rollover and then began siphoning it out before the age of 59½.

- If you'd rather not disturb your 401(k), learn how flexible the plan will be after you're gone. Ideally, the access to your 401(k) should be the same as you'd enjoy with an IRA rollover.

✔ **Deposit all the money in an IRA rollover.** If you crave the freedom to invest your 401(k) proceeds any way you like, establishing an IRA rollover is the best option. You can establish an IRA rollover account at just about any financial institution.

When you transfer money into a rollover account, the account is classified as a traditional IRA. That means that the money is shielded from taxes until you begin withdrawing the money. At that point, the taxes are based upon your income tax bracket.

In a rollover account, your money grows much faster than it would if you had cashed out the 401(k), paid the taxes, and put what was left in a taxable account.

✔ **Put everything in an IRA rollover except company stock.** Although stashing your 401(k) in an IRA rollover is almost always the best move, sometimes it's better not to roll over any company stock. You may want to consider this strategy if you're at least 55, the age at which taxpayers can avoid the 10 percent early withdrawal penalty on 401(k) savings.

If you place the stock in a rollover, no taxes are owed immediately, but when you begin pulling out this money, the cash will be taxed at your ordinary income tax rate. The tax bite can be less onerous if you segregate the stock in a taxable account. If you do this, you'll owe upfront taxes only on the cost basis. The *cost basis* represents what you paid for the company stock during your years in the 401(k) plan. At this point, you won't pay any taxes on the appreciation. Suppose that you paid an average of $30 a share for your company stock over the years, and now it's worth $400 a share. You won't owe taxes on that $370-a-share profit until you unload the stock. When you begin selling it, you'll pay tax on this appreciation, but here's where keeping the stock out of the IRA will pay off: You will owe only long-term capital gains taxes on the windfall, which are no more than 20 percent. And that rate is scheduled to decrease further in the future.

✔ **Take the money and run.** Many people love this idea, but they do it at the wrong time. According to one survey, 57 percent of workers cash in their 401(k) chips when they leave their company for another job. They may buy a car, remodel a kitchen, pay tuition, or spend the money in ways that they won't even remember by retirement time. If you follow the herd, you will not have the money when you really need it. And by then, you'll have no more salary increases and job promotions to bail you out.

Cracking the IRA nest egg

If you live long enough, someday you will crack open your IRA whether you need to or not. The IRS, which has waited patiently for this day, requires that you begin mandatory withdrawals shortly after reaching the age of 70½ (if you haven't tapped into the account already).

Here are some things to keep in mind:

✔ The federal bureaucracy didn't make the mandatory disbursement age an easy one to remember. You must begin siphoning money out of your IRA no later than April 1 of the year following the year in which you turn 70½. For example, if you were born on October 1, 1933, you will reach the age of 70½ in 2004, so you must withdraw your first payment from your IRA by April 2005.

✔ Roth IRA owners can avoid this mandatory withdrawal rule. If they never touch their IRA, that's their prerogative. One of the other charms of a Roth IRA is that owners can make tax-free withdrawals during retirement.

Two options for receiving your pension

Cashing in on a pension may seem like a no-brainer. After retirement, pension checks begin automatically arriving in the mailbox. What could be easier? Well, like so much in retirement, cashing in a pension is not that simple.

For starters, your company might throw you off balance by giving you two choices: a lifetime supply of checks or a lump sum. When presented with these two possibilities, workers often grab the windfall. The money is just too tantalizing to ignore. But you need to explore your options before deciding which alternative is best for you.

If your company doesn't offer a lump sum option, you might have little to agonize about. If you're married, however, you'll encounter more choices. The following list discusses what you need to know about all your possible pension options.

- ✔ **Receiving regular pension checks:** If you're single when you retire, you'll begin receiving what's called a single-life pension or single-life annuity. When you die, the pension dies, too.

   Married workers face an extra option. A husband or wife can also choose the same single-life pension. Again, when the retiree dies, the pension vanishes. If you want your pension to continue after your death, you'll want the joint-and-survivor alternative. This pension lasts for two lives: yours and your spouse's. However, when the worker dies, the pension check is typically cut in half for the widow or widower.

   You might be wondering why a husband or wife would opt for a single-life pension. That's simple: The monthly pension check is fatter. The payments are more generous because they last for only one life rather than two.

- ✔ **Taking a pension lump sum:** When you retire, should you take a lump sum instead of a pension? A lot of people don't give this issue much thought. They are hypnotized by the dollar signs and want that money now rather than watching it trickle in through monthly checks.

   In some circumstances, taking the money in a lump sum may be a good idea:

   - **You're an investing whiz, or you hire someone who is.** Some people assume that they can invest a lump sum so intelligently that its value will exceed that of a lifetime of pension checks. This is not as easy as it sounds, however.

   - **Your health is poor.** If you're single and in poor health when you retire, your heirs will lose out if you opt for a series of pension checks. If you die a few months into retirement, your pension benefit disappears. If you chose the lump sum and die early in retirement, you'll pass a tidy amount on to your heirs.

Consider these compelling reasons to pick the stream of checks instead:

- **You're tempted to blow it.** If you take the cash, you should safe-guard it in a rollover Individual Retirement Account. By taking this step, you allow the money to continue to grow tax-deferred. The worst thing that you can do is begin to spend the money. Any cash that you don't put into an IRA is taxed at your income tax rate. If your state has an income tax, you'll owe the state as well. What's more, if you haven't reached the age of 59½, you'll probably be hit with a 10 percent early withdrawal penalty.

- **You're entitled to a subsidized pension.** Suppose that at age 55 you're offered an early retirement package that provides you with the same pension you'd get if you slaved away at your cubicle for another ten years. This pension is called a *subsidized pension*. The Pension Rights Center suggests that it's not uncommon for an early retiree to lose 35 percent to 40 percent of the pension benefit when taking the lump sum in this circumstance, rather than a stream of sweetened pension checks.

WARNING!

Beware of pension maximization insurance

If you discuss your retirement plans with a stockbroker or an insurance agent, you may be encouraged to take the single-life pension (even when it doesn't appear to make sense) in favor of something called pension maximization insurance. In the vast majority of cases, this life insurance strategy is a bad idea.

Here's the pitch: With pension maximization insurance, you can enjoy the biggest pension benefit possible without jeopardizing your spouse's final years. In theory, you pull this off by purchasing life insurance for yourself. If you die first, your pension disappears, but the surviving spouse won't be condemned to poverty because he or she will receive the life insurance windfall. The life insurance coverage that's necessary to pull this off is based on the amount of money needed to replace the lost pension checks. This scenario uses the assumption that the insurance premiums will be smaller than the extra cash that you'd pocket with the biggest pension benefit. In many cases, this assumption is incorrect. For one thing, the pensioner might not be healthy enough to buy a policy at a standard or preferred rate.

A pension maximization insurance policyholder may not be able to continue paying the premiums throughout retirement. Some couples have been forced to cancel their policies, with tragic results: The pension disappears if the breadwinner dies first.

Considering Annuities

What separates annuities from other types of investments is insurance. Annuities are created by insurance companies, which can extend certain promises about the security of your investments. For example, if you're contributing to an annuity and abruptly die, the insurance company will make sure that your heirs, at the very minimum, receive your initial investment. They'll pay up even if your investment has plunged in value. A similar reassurance is made to retirees who are receiving monthly income from an annuity. The insurance company promises the payments will continue as long as you live and sometimes even longer, even if the money you originally invested in the annuity runs out.

Here are the different types of annuities:

✔ **Deferred annuity:** The vast majority of annuities sold every year in this country are deferred annuities, a product usually tailored for investors who still have many years before they retire. You can invest either a lump sum or add regularly to a deferred annuity over a lengthy period. The interest generated grows tax-deferred.

Some people who have already maxed out their contributions to an Individual Retirement Account, a 401(k), or other workplace plan gravitate to this type of annuity because of the tax protection. Like a 401(k) or traditional IRA, the tax reprieve evaporates when the cash is eventually withdrawn. At that time, income taxes are due. If you're under the age of 59½ when you tap into your annuity, you'll probably be subject to a 10 percent early withdrawal penalty. Unlike a workplace retirement plan or an IRA, you can shovel as much money as you want into a tax-deferred annuity.

✔ **Immediate annuity:** With an immediate annuity, you deposit your cash into the investment, and your monthly payments can start immediately. Part of the money you receive each month is tax-free because it represents a return of a portion of your premium. An immediate annuity relieves you of the burden of investing a chunk of your retirement savings on your own. The insurance company assumes this responsibility and promises to send you monthly checks for life. The insurance company makes a bet that you won't live long enough to pull out more than what you originally deposited. Of course, you're hoping that you beat the actuarial odds.

An immediate annuity can be ideal for someone who is retiring with a 401(k) plan, but is uncertain how to invest it.

Annuity resources

Some of the best sources for annuity information are the following:

- **Insure.com:** This consumer-friendly media site covers a wide variety of insurance issues, including primers on annuities. Go to www.insure.com.

- **National Association for Variable Annuities:** This trade group maintains a separate Web address for consumers who are interested in learning more about annuities and finding out about specific products. Contact the association by mail at 11710 Plaza America Dr., Suite 100, Reston, VA 20190; by phone at 703-707-8830; and on the Internet at www.navanet.org or www.retireonyourterms.com.

- **U.S. Securities and Exchange Commission:** You can obtain a copy of the SEC's cautionary publication, *Variable Annuities: What You Should Know,* by calling the commission or going to its Web site. You can also call the SEC with annuity complaints. Contact the Office of Investor Education and Assistance, 450 Fifth St., NW, Washington, DC 20549-0213; 202-942-7040; www.sec.gov.

- **National Association of Insurance Commissioners:** This nonprofit organization represents insurance regulators in the 50 states and Washington, D.C. The organization's Web site provides links to the home page of each state's insurance commissioner. You may want to contact your state commission with questions or complaints about annuities. Contact the national association by mail at 2301 McGee, Suite 800, Kansas City, MO 64108-2604; by phone at 816-842-3600; or on the Internet at www.naic.org.

An immediate annuity, with its dependable income stream, can be a godsend for retirees without a pension or whose investing skills are shaky. If your only steady monthly check is coming from Social Security, you may want to consider investing some of your assets into an immediate annuity.

Immediate annuities are also appropriate for retirees who need monthly income and otherwise would be drawing cash out of money markets and certificates of deposit. That's because the income from the latter-two investments is fully taxable. In contrast, the income in those monthly annuity checks is partially protected from taxes.

Age, gender, and payment options influence how big your monthly check from an immediate annuity will be. Women, for instance, receive smaller checks than men of the same age because they're expected to live longer.

- **Fixed annuity:** The fixed annuity is marketed to the sort of people who get white knuckles when the stock market is bouncing like a ping-pong ball, such as retirees who need a steady income. When you opt for a fixed annuity, you're guaranteed a set rate of return for your investment. The rate of return can never slip below the guaranteed floor set at the time of purchase. Although the rate floor never moves, the actual rate may change as often as every month, and these changes do affect how much money builds up in the account. Whether the rate creeps up or down depends on such factors as the interest rate climate and the performance of a company's typically conservative investment portfolio of government and corporate bonds.

Some people feel safe with the guaranteed rate, but this rate doesn't provide assurance that a fixed annuity will keep up with inflation. Yet a fixed annuity may be suitable for someone who willingly surrenders the potential for higher returns that stocks can provide in exchange for a sure thing.

TIP

A fixed annuity can be quite attractive for retirees who are investing a portion of their nest eggs in Certificates of Deposit (CDs) or Treasuries.

Fixed annuity rates can be significantly higher than CDs or Treasuries. What's more, the fixed annuity grows tax-deferred. In contrast, an investor must pay yearly income taxes on the interest that a CD generates. Treasury investors must pay federal, but not state, taxes. The tax on a fixed annuity is due only when the money is withdrawn. If you have a CD that's about to mature, you should check out competing fixed annuity rates.

✔ **Variable annuity:** The variable annuity is a popular choice for persons who are still saving for retirement. This annuity shares a lot in common with a mutual fund, but an annuity offers an insured guarantee against losing even a fraction of your original investment. No regular mutual funds can make such a promise. As the name suggests, the returns on variable annuities fluctuate because there's usually a heavy reliance upon stock funds. Consequently, the value of your investment hinges upon how well the underlying funds are performing. Variable annuities are vastly more popular with Americans than the fixed ones. This situation wasn't the case just a decade ago; when interest rates were higher, the fixed annuity looked more appealing.

Estate Planning: Doing It Right

Everyone in America has a will. Even if you have never paid for or written a will, you have one. The reason is simple. Your state has laws dictating how your bank account, car, furniture, all the junk stacked up in the garage, and your other worldly possessions will be divided if you die without an estate plan. Trouble is, you might hate the way the bureaucrats slice the pie.

A lot of people don't seem spooked by the specter of bureaucrats deciding who gets grandfather's gold-plated pocket watch or a lifetime accumulation of General Electric stock. The American Bar Association estimates that 70 percent of Americans die without a will. Delinquents who never bothered to draw one up include such famous people as Abraham Lincoln, Pablo Picasso, and the reclusive Howard Hughes.

The best reasons to plan ahead

A good estate plan enables you to accomplish the following tasks:

- Increase the windfall you leave family and friends if you use estate tax-evasion strategies
- Divide your assets as you see fit
- Allow your estate to possibly skip probate court
- Name surrogate parents for minor children
- Arrange in advance to have your estate's assets invested well
- Avoid or minimize estate and income taxes
- Protect loved ones' inheritances from lawsuits, divorce, and bankruptcy
- Establish trusts for any number of beneficiaries
- Leave lasting gifts to favorite charities
- Provide for a disabled child
- Direct how you'd like to be medically treated during your final weeks
- Designate someone to act on your behalf if you become incapacitated
- Keep your financial affairs confidential after your death
- Disinherit undesirable family members

Assessing your assets

Do you know how much you're worth? How much is your estate worth? If you died tomorrow, the two figures could be vastly different. Many people don't realize this fact when they dismiss estate planning as crucial only for the rich. Large amounts of term insurance, for instance, can make someone worth considerably more dead than alive. For example, in 2001, any estate worth more than $675,000 was hit with federal estate taxes.

Consequently, you need to know just what assets you have before you begin the estate-planning process. Include these commonly held assets in your calculations:

- Individual Retirement Account
- 401(k) plan or other workplace retirement accounts
- Insurance policies

✔ Home equity

✔ Other real estate

✔ Valuables such as cars, jewelry, and boats

✔ Household furnishings and possessions

✔ Bank, brokerage, and mutual fund accounts

✔ Pensions

✔ Business assets and insurance policies

✔ Annuities

✔ Trust income

✔ Royalties, patents, and copyrights

After you've compiled an inventory of your assets, keep the list with your other estate-planning documents.

Writing a will

Although the debate rages on about the merits of living trusts, this much is clear: Every adult needs a will. Even someone who favors using a living trust to pass along a fortune needs a backup will.

Here are the facts about wills:

✔ A *will* is the document that directs where you want your property to go after your death. In a will, you can leave your property to people, charities, schools, churches, or any organizations you please. In addition to major assets, such as a house or a brokerage account, your will can dictate who gets your sentimental possessions. For instance, you might give your personal journals to a daughter, your World War II medals to a son, and a rocking chair to a favorite niece.

✔ You also use a will to appoint an *executor* who'll be responsible for carrying out your final wishes. The executor, who can be a spouse, friend, relative, attorney, accountant, or some other third party, handles the inevitable paperwork that's triggered by a death. The executor locates your will upon your death, files a final tax return, writes checks to creditors, and pays the funeral expenses. After all the bills are paid and all the assets are tracked down, the executor passes along what's left to the heirs.

Don't be weak-willed

If you write your own will, you'll want to make it bulletproof. The chances of your will being contested or thrown out decreases if you avoid these types of wills:

- **Fill-in-the-blank wills:** You can find boilerplate will forms in stationery stores, but relying on them is unwise. These forms may not come with instructions and can be oversimplified.

- **Handwritten wills:** A judge once accepted a will scrawled with lipstick on a cocktail napkin. Nonetheless, typing the will on white paper is the preferred method. Most

states do not consider *holographic* (handwritten) wills legitimate. At the very least, all the handwriting on the will must match the penmanship of the signature.

- **Video wills:** States haven't caught up with newer technology. At this point, no state allows a multimedia will.

- **Oral wills:** Most states refuse to honor spoken wills. You may get some leeway with a spoken will if you're dying on a battlefield, but otherwise, write it down. Only a minimal amount of property would be allowed to be effectively disposed of in this way.

- Overseeing the whole process is probate court. One of the probate judge's most important tasks is determining that your will is authentic. The probate process also officially gives the executor the authority to represent the estate. Unless the will specifically waives the requirement, often the judge requires that this person post a bond just in case he or she disappears with the money. (If you don't feel a bond is necessary for your hand-picked executor, say so in your will.) The probate court is expected to make sure that the executor carries out all of his or her responsibilities.

- Many people believe that naming an oldest child or a trusted friend as an executor is a great honor. Think again. An executor's job often boils down to menial paper shuffling that requires a phenomenal commitment of time. Think long and hard before you select somebody to do the grunt work. Because of the responsibility involved, ask the person's permission before making the designation official in your will.

Creating a trust

After deciding which potential heirs make your final cut, you can proceed down one of two paths:

- The first option is the direct bequest. This option means that you pass along your hard-earned money and property to family, friends, charities, churches, or others outright. Once your heirs receive that cash, investment portfolio, or vacation home in the Rocky Mountains, they can do whatever they desire with these gifts.

✔ The second option is to bequeath all or some of your worldly possessions through trusts. Trusts, which come with an extra legal layer, aren't
as simple as direct bequests. With a trust, you attach strings to your
generosity. A trust established for a grown child, for instance, might stip-
ulate that the money is parceled out over the course of a decade or two.
Some trusts are intentionally designed to endure for two generations or
more. The first heirs in line, who are often the adult children, receive the
income generated by a trust's investments. Discretion is often given to
the trustee to also distribute principal as required. They're sometimes
referred to as *income beneficiaries.* The grandkids, or whoever are the
backup heirs, receive what's left of the estate after their parents are
dead. These heirs are called *remaindermen,* which makes sense because
they get what remains.

A trust's language contains the distribution rules, which dictate how much
money the beneficiaries will receive over the years or under what circumstances. Some trusts are written broadly so that the beneficiaries have
greater access to the assets; others can be infuriatingly restrictive.

Here are the advantages and disadvantages of putting your assets in a trust:

✔ **A trust can reduce estate taxes.** Many trusts can be used to sidestep
estate taxes. The bypass trust, which is also referred to as a shelter
trust, is the most common one used for this purpose.

Many people think that a living trust can be used to avoid estate taxes,
but that's a huge misconception. See the sidebar, "A trust glossary," for
descriptions of various trusts and to identify the tax shelter-ready trusts.

✔ **A trust can protect against creditors, court judgments, and ex-spouses.**
Inheritances are meant for loved ones. But without the protection of a
trust, heirs may end up sharing money with people they detest, such as
an ex-spouse or a legal adversary. Suppose that you leave your fortune
to your daughter, who marries a ne'er-do-well. Maybe he's an alcoholic,
a wife abuser, an adulterer, or in some other way just plain bad news.
Even if your daughter divorces the bum, he could still be entitled to a
share of her inheritance depending on the state in which your daughter
lives. If the money is left to her in a trust, however, this money-grab
might be impossible.

✔ **A trust can stretch out the money for more than a generation.** Some
benefactors love the idea of making their money outlast their children.
Consequently, trusts can be tailored to ultimately benefit two generations. With a trust, for example, you could leave money for your children
and grandchildren. The kids would receive whatever income the trust
spins off during their lifetime, and eventually the grandchildren would
pocket whatever is left at the end.

A trust glossary

Whether you're creating or inheriting a trust, you should know the terminology:

- **Executor:** Person or institution named in a will to carry out its instructions. A woman selected for this job is called an *executrix*.

- **Fiduciary:** A person who holds a position of trust. Trustees and executors are called fiduciaries because the law requires that they responsibly carry out a will and/or trust's dictates. A bank or trust company that serves this role is called a corporate fiduciary.

- **Grantor:** The person who creates a trust; also can be called a settlor or trust creator.

- **Irrevocable trust:** A trust that can't be canceled or changed by its grantor after it's established.

- **Remaindermen:** The people who receive what's left of a trust when it terminates.

- **Revocable trust:** A trust that can be changed or dismantled while the grantor is still alive (such as a living trust).

- **Successor trustee:** Person or institution who takes over as trustee when the original trustee(s) has died or become incapacitated.

- **Testamentary trust:** A trust created by a will.

- **Trust corpus:** Name for property that's put into a trust.

- **Trustee:** Holds legal title to the trust assets for the benefit of the beneficiaries.

- A trust can provide for heirs who aren't capable of managing the money themselves. Trusts may be a logical way to leave money to beneficiaries who you fear aren't capable of handling a windfall outright. You may worry that they'll waste the money on jewelry, vacations, cars, gambling, drugs, or frivolous purchases. A trust can guarantee that an inheritance won't be blown during one terrible night at a Las Vegas blackjack table by functioning as a spigot that releases the funds gradually over a person's lifetime or at specific ages.

- A trust can benefit your favorite causes. Although you can donate directly to a charity or church, there are benefits to tucking the money, stock, or other assets into a trust. With a sophisticated trust, you and the charity can both benefit financially. After a donation into a charitable trust, for example, you could receive a stream of income for the rest of your life.

- A trust ensures privacy. When you leave your possessions through a will, anyone can trot down to the courthouse and find out who has what. This doesn't happen when assets are tucked away in a revocable living trust. Often the creators of the trust are more worried about protecting their privacy from their own families than nosy outsiders. They may not

Disability insurance

You insure your car, your house, your health, and your life. What about your career? Most people ignore that one, but insuring your career can be extremely important. Imagine the fate of a pianist diagnosed with progressively worsening osteoarthritis or a carpenter who has muscular dystrophy. How about a reporter or software programmer who is crippled by carpal tunnel syndrome after years of typing on a keyboard? Could you survive financially if an injury or disease kept you away from your job for long stretches of time or perhaps forever? And, of course, if you can no longer work in your profession, your retirement savings goals can be obliterated.

Here are some factors to consider:

✔ The chances of becoming disabled are greater than you might assume. The Health Industry Association of America says that 30 percent of Americans between the ages of 35 and 60 will become disabled for at least 90 days. Although interest in disability insurance has picked up recently as the baby boomers feel less invincible, most Americans still aren't buying. Those who do purchase policies are primarily white-collar workers.

✔ Some people pass on the coverage because they think that they're already protected through a workplace policy, workman's compensation, or Social Security. However, most corporate coverage lasts only for a brief period, from a few days to no more than six months. A few states, such as New York, New Jersey, Rhode Island, and Hawaii, require six months of coverage; California insists on one year. Worker's compensation covers only disabilities that occurred on the job or were caused by it.

In all likelihood, you'll want to supplement your workplace coverage with your own personal policy, which can be expensive. Prices should be cheaper if you go through a professional or trade association.

✔ Social Security is not a sure thing. It imposes extremely tough standards in winnowing out those who qualify for disability payments. Those eligible must be unable to perform any job. Suppose you were a teacher before suffering partial brain damage in a car accident. If the only job you can now handle is sweeping the floor at a fast-food restaurant, that's your tough luck. Social Security won't help. Recently, the average monthly disability payment from the government was just $733.

Like all insurance, you can mix and match disability coverage in many ways. Some features cost more than others. The trick is finding an affordable policy that can realistically provide for your needs.

Free advice on putting your retirement finances in order

If you thought you could stop planning and worrying about money when you retired, sorry. But you can get some free advice on the process:

✔ www.estateplanninglinks.com: This site links you to hoards of well-organized, timesaving Web sites on estate planning, elder law, trusts, and taxes. Some of these sites are selling books and software, but many are free forums, articles, and advice.

✔ www.nolo.com: Nolo is a large publisher of do-it-yourself law. You can browse through tons of encyclopedia articles on retirement planning, elder care, power of attorney, 401(k) plans, Roth IRAs, Social Security benefits, wills, trusts, and funeral planning. You can also ask questions online.

✔ www.efmoody.com: This site claims to be the Internet's largest (over 1,500 pages and 1,500 links) and most comprehensive independent financial site for consumer knowledge. You can't help but find what you need

at this site — although you may have to do some extensive reading. The topics covered are similar to those in the other financial sites listed here.

✔ www.smartmoney.com/estate: This site covers everything from trusts to funeral plans. Use the handy net worth calculator to help you figure out how significantly your estate will be hit by taxes and what you can do now to protect it.

✔ www.nafep.com: The National Association of Financial and Estate Planning site offers some helpful articles on proper ways to hold on to legal title to property during your life and pass it on to your heirs the way you want to, all with minimum taxes and intervention by you know who. Send away for more detailed info. Reading the site is free, but talking to an actual financial planner is going to cost you.

Part V
Fun, Fun, Fun: Hobbies

The 5th Wave   By Rich Tennant

"In his later years, Capt. Hook gave up on chasing Peter Pan and took up knitting."

In this part . . .

What better time to take up a new hobby than after the kids have left home, or when you finally retire? You can entertain yourself with a lively game of Bridge, get out of the house and onto the golf course, or relax at home *or* on the go with your new knitting project. With some hobbies, you can even make some money!

The chapters in this part offer some ideas for active and relaxing hobbies you may decide to take up. Whether you're looking to exercise your legs, tease your brain, or get some rest, you'll find what you're looking for in this part.

Chapter 16

Getting Up and Going: Active Hobbies

Many people find that their time frees up when their kids are older or — naturally — when they retire. They find that this time in their lives is ideal for returning to a favorite hobby or even taking up a new one. To help you get started with a hobby that you'll enjoy (and may even become a favorite!), this chapter provides an overview of some hobbies that require you to get up and moving, from gardening to golfing, cooking to carpentry, and much more.

Stepping into the Antique Boutique

The antique supply fluctuates constantly. Every day, fewer older antiques are available, and a few new "just turned 100" antiques become available. Before you buy, look at a lot of antiques, talk to dealers and other experts, and read a few price guides, auction catalogues, and books. Dealers, curators, and collectors all gave us this same advice: Buying antiques is like searching for buried treasure — if you don't know what 16th-century doubloons really look like, you may not see the treasure even if you stumble over it.

So how can you stop and smell the doubloons? Finding dealers and other specialists you can trust is one key to successful antique buying. You also have to get enough experience to figure out the difference between old stuff that isn't worth the lace on your tennis shoes and an antique that you should mortgage your stationary bike over. You need to know the difference between an antique, an antique-in-waiting, a collectible, and an antiquity. Read on.

- ✔ **"A" is for *antique*:** A legal antique is something that's 100 years old; this definition was created so that the customs people would know how to tax things.

- ✔ **Stepping up to the collectible plate:** A collectible is just about anything people want to collect that's younger than 100 years. Collectibles include items such as Hummel figurines, collector's plates, Depression glass, various toys, and baseball cards. Just about anything is fair game.

- ✔ **Those charming pre-century antiques-in-waiting:** Just to keep things from being too cut and dried, a certain 20th-century crowd exists that is simply too magnificent to accept the word *collectible*. These "antiques-in-waiting" are truly masterpieces and are valued more highly than many antiques. This beauty-before-age syndrome applies primarily to work from the Art Nouveau, Art Deco, and Art Moderne periods in the early 1900s. A Tiffany lamp that goes at auction for a quarter of a million dollars — well, it's definitely an honorary antique.

- ✔ **Digging into antiquities:** Finally, there's the stuff that is unearthed. This stuff includes work from ancient cultures such as the Roman, Greek, and Egyptian cultures and is called *antiquities*. You might come across these ancient articles: ancient Egyptian/Syrian glass, little pottery jars, bowls and vases from Greece and the Middle East, ancient bronze coins and miniature bronze figures from old Persia, the Middle East, and Italy (not in the excellent quality/condition that the museum pieces are, but collectible and great conversation pieces).

What's your game plan?

Before you embark on an antique shopping spree, you need to figure out your goals. What do you want to collect and how much do you want to spend and how do you want the antiques to fit into your home? Your goals may change as you get to know more about antiques and as your own tastes develop.

- ✔ Do you want to own a few antiques of great quality or more of lesser quality?

- ✔ Do you want to specialize in a particular period or style?

- ✔ Do you want the aesthetic, the functional, or a combo?

- ✔ How do you want to budget your antique purchases?

- ✔ Where do you plan to put your antiques?

Five signs of a really great antique

We like to tell novice (and experienced) antique collectors to keep their "RADAR" out for values. RADAR is an acronym that stands for Rarity, Aesthetics, Desirability, Authenticity, and Really great condition.

✔ **Rarity.** What constitutes a *rarity?* If no one else on your block owns one, you know that it's worth something. If no one in your zip code has one, it might be worth even more. And if no one in your area code has one, chances are, you have a piece that's pretty valuable.

✔ **Aesthetics.** Visiting art galleries and museums is one great way to see antique objects of art that are considered aesthetically pleasing. Books on your areas of interest also will show the better pieces.

✔ **Desirability.** Desirability is defined by what's in vogue in the current market. A few decades after Tiffany created his now-famous lamps, some people thought of them as gaudy, and so prices were steals by today's standards. Now people covet the artistry that Tiffany displayed.

✔ **Authenticity.** Part of the mystery and fun of antiques is separating truth from fiction. As technology and the ability to reproduce items become more advanced, identifying the authentic antique becomes more difficult.

✔ **Really great condition.** Here's the best way to define "really great condition": The less that was done to the original item to alter it, the more it's worth. That is, the fewer the additions or deletions over the years, the better.

Strategies for spending your antiquing dollars

We recommend a purchasing strategy that many collectors endorse: Always buy the finest piece that you can afford at the time. The theory behind the strategy is this: As you get more knowledgeable, the flaws in a piece that is not well-made become more apparent. You will get more long-term enjoyment from an antique that is truly well-made and wonderfully designed.

Here are some tips for getting the most out of your investment:

✔ You're generally better off, investment-wise, to own one top-quality porcelain piece than three lesser-quality pieces or even than three quality pieces in poor condition. The finest quality work usually maintains its value and resells more easily. Lesser quality antiques are harder to sell and may not hold up as well physically.

✔ "The best you can afford" does not necessarily mean the most expensive piece. It means purchasing the best example of the type of antique that you love. If you feel insecure about choosing high-quality antiques, consult with a trusted dealer or an antique-loving friend.

✔ Sometimes people weed through their collection, trading or selling pieces of lesser quality. Other people keep every object that they ever buy. Then they have a timeline of antique acquisitions and maybe a story to go with each piece.

Carpentry (From Wagons to Cabinets)

The earliest "carpenters" were wagon makers by trade, but over the centuries, the term carpenter has come to mean a tradesperson who builds (or repairs) wooden things, especially structures.

The work of the house carpenter (or the homeowner/would-be carpenter) divides into rough carpentry and finish carpentry.

✔ **Rough carpentry** covers all the work beginning with the construction of a wood frame on a foundation and ending with the completion of the skin on the exterior walls and roof, and the installation of the subflooring. This type of work must be done to code (available from your local building inspection), and often requires permits and inspections.

✔ **Finish carpentry** includes wood-related cutting, fitting, assembly, and installation that follow. Finish carpenters also install accessories such as towel bars, closet shelving systems, shower doors, and other non-wood materials and products.

Stocking a good toolbox

Although power saws have all but replaced the handsaw and other non-powered saws for most cutting operations, there are still times when using a hand tool is more efficient or better.

✔ **Small combination saw and a *hacksaw*.** You can buy a *coping saw* (looks like a "C") and *compass saw* (looks like a swordfish) or a similar *keyhole saw* (looks like a skinny sword) or *drywall saw* (a keyhole saw with a thicker, coarser-toothed blade) as needed.

✔ **⅜-inch variable-speed reversible drill/driver.** These are available in plug-in or cordless models.

✔ **Drill/driver.** This tool can perform both high-speed and low-speed drilling operations and, most significantly, it can drive and remove screws easily.

✔ **Screwdrivers.** The first rule for driving screws is to use a driver that matches the type and size of screw that you're driving. The majority of screws are either Phillips screws, which have a cross-shaped recess in the head and require a Phillips screwdriver, or slotted screws, which have a single slot cut across the diameter of the screw head and require a standard driver.

You get the best deal and are prepared for most screwdriving situations if you buy an assortment of screwdrivers. At minimum, your collection should contain two standard drivers (a ³⁄₁₆-inch cabinet and a ¼-inch mechanics) and two Phillips drivers (a 4-inch #2 and a 3-inch #1).

Alternately, buy either a 4-in-1 or 6-in-1 driver. The 4-in-1 has a double-ended shaft (two ³⁄₁₆-inch and ⁹⁄₃₂-inch standard, and #1 and #2 Phillips interchangeable bits, or tips). In the 6-in-1 model, the two ends of the shaft serve as a ¼-inch and ⁵⁄₁₆-inch nut driver. Buy other size screwdrivers as needed. One advantage of these multidrivers is that they accommodate different bits; when you run across screws with square holes, star-like holes, or other tip configurations, you need to buy only the appropriate tip, not another tool.

✔ **Hammers.** Nail hammers come in two basic types: the curved-claw, which has a curved nail-pulling claw, and the ripping-claw, which has a straight claw.

✔ **Long pants and long-sleeve shirt.** The right work clothes will protect you against cuts, scrapes, and scratches — the kind of minor (but painful) injuries that will make you crazy.

✔ **Heavy-soled shoes or ones with special gripping soles**. If you've ever dropped a 2-by-4 on your toes or stepped on a board with a nail sticking out, you know why sturdy shoes with strong soles are important. And grippy, sticky soles will prevent nasty falls and slips.

✔ **Heavy work gloves and chemical-resistant gloves.** Leather work gloves will protect your hands against splinters and blisters, and, most important, from cuts caused by sharp, rough materials. Chemical-resistant gloves will keep you from discovering the acute discomfort that can be caused by cleaning fluids, solvents, and such seemingly innocent but caustic materials like tile grout.

✔ **Coveralls.** This one-piece garment protects you from paint splatters, dirt, and drywall dust. Inexpensive, disposable ones are available. Of course, you could wear your old leisure suit, but you would scare little children.

✔ **Kneepads.** These cushioned rubber pads, held in place with elastic strips, protect your knee joints from the inadvertent bumps and constant pressure of kneeling on hard surfaces. (Pretend that you're rollerblading, and you won't feel so silly.) Kneepads are especially important to wear when you're crawling around on hard, debris-strewn surfaces.

✔ **Hard hat.** While you rarely see a D-I-Yer (do-it-yourselfer) don a hard hat, proper headgear is very important when heavy construction work is going on around you. (If you don't want to buy one, how about using your bike helmet? It's better than cracking your skull!)

✔ **Goggles.** Goggles, or safety glasses with side shields, are inexpensive investments that may save your eyesight. Just remember to put them on! And make sure the goggles or glasses are well-vented or they may fog over.

If you wear prescription glasses, choose a pair of safety goggles that fits over your glasses or invest in a pair of prescription safety glasses.

✔ **Ear protection.** If you typically use a noisy tool in one location, such as a garage shop, hang a pair of earmuff-style protectors near your workstation so that they are convenient.

More often, you need protection-to-go. We'd be the first to admit that it's often inconvenient at best to put on ear protection every time you pick up a circular saw, especially if you're in the attic and your ear protectors are in the basement! The answer? Little, very soft foam earplugs that mold to your ear canal. You hardly know you have them in, and you can keep a little container full of them in a tool belt or toolbox so you'll have them when you need them.

✔ **Dust mask.** Wear a dust mask whenever your work raises dust (sawing, sanding, sweeping, insulating, and so on).

✔ **Shop vacuum or a wet/dry vacuum.** Shop around. All models are noisy, but some are unbearable. Compare any noise ratings or simply try it out before you buy. Some models collect debris in bags, which is more costly, but they can handle fine dust such as the powder that sanding drywall leaves behind. Shop vacuums without bags tend to choke on fine dust and spew more back into the room. The wet pick-up capability is handy for spills and floods that result from leaky pipes or foundation.

Choose a shop vacuum that has hoses and attachments that allow it to be used as a dust-collection system for your power tools that are similarly equipped. You'll stay healthier and your house or work site will stay cleaner.

✔ **Push broom.** You don't want to haul out a big vacuum all the time, so keep a sturdy push broom — preferably one that has a reinforcing plate that braces the handle where it joins the head to prevent breakage. And get a good dustpan!

✔ **Ladders.** These can be made from several materials. For most home carpenters, a good-quality wood or aluminum ladder is more than adequate.

TIP

Nine ways to put your carpentry skills to work

The great part about carpentry is that you can put your skills to work in so many ways. Here are nine ideas to get you started:

- ✔ Teaching your kids
- ✔ Helping your neighbor
- ✔ Making your home safer
- ✔ Accessorizing your kitchen cabinets

- ✔ Making a bath vanity more useful
- ✔ Organizing attic and garage clutter
- ✔ Installing a whole-house fan
- ✔ Making simple furniture
- ✔ Making wooden toys and gifts

Ten-plus-one great ways to use the Web for carpentry

Having been involved in the growth of the Internet and particularly the World Wide Web, we know what a great resource this collection of electronic files, networks, and services can be. Of course, there's a lot of fluff and misinformation, too. So consider the source before you act on advice or information.

Here's a list of some of our favorite Web sites with reliable information on carpentry, woodworking, and related subjects:

- ✔ **Thinking of buying a power tool?** Before you buy a tool, read the Tool Reviews at www.augusthome.com to get the latest news and reviews.

- ✔ **Associating with the right people:** Who knows better about working with redwood than the California Redwood Association (CRA) at www.calredwood.org, about plywood and engineered wood products than APA, The Engineered Wood Association, at www.apawood.org, or about cedar siding, paneling, and roofing than the Western Red Cedar Lumber Association (WRCLA) at www.wrcla.org and the Cedar Shingle and Shake Bureau at www.cedarbureau.org?

  The CRA offers a great deck-planning kit, outdoor project plans, and technical information relating to redwood construction and finishing. Turn to the APA for literature about basic wood-frame construction and recommendations for floor, wall, and roof construction. In addition to the information on the installation, repair, and care of wood siding, the WRCLA site features how-to information and D-I-Y plans on outdoor projects such as fences and gates. The Cedar Shingle and Shake Bureau is the online source for information about installing, repairing, and maintaining cedar shingle and hand-split cedar shakes on sidewalls or roofs.

- **Don't get stuck in the mud:** For anyone interested in hanging, repairing, or finishing drywall, take a look at www.usg.com. USG is the leading manufacturer of drywall in the country. Its brand name, Sheetrock, like Band-Aid, Kleenex, and Skilsaw, is often synonymous with the product.

- **Getting in the pink:** Looking for a way to save big bucks and make yourself more comfortable at the same time? Well, if your home is uninsulated (or under-insulated) or if you're refinishing a basement or attic, then be sure to check out the Pink Panther at www.owenscorning.com. This Owens Corning site has the most in-depth coverage we've seen, called "Around Your House," that helps you visualize how and where and why to insulate. While you're there, take a look at the information about windows, roofing siding, and a host of other building materials that the company manufactures.

- **Conquering closet clutter:** If closet clutter has gotten the best of you and you're hell-bent on getting organized, get help at www.homebase.com. In addition to information on installing prefabricated wire closet organizers, this Web site has particularly useful step-by-step advice that you can print about installing both prefabricated and custom-built closet organizers.

- **This site will floor you:** Check out www.pergo.com, the site of the Scandinavian company that's invading home centers with its extensive line of floating floors. Floating floor installations are perhaps the easiest floor system to install and Pergo offers a premium plastic laminate flooring that they claim is 30 times more abrasion-resistant than laminate countertops (and backs its claims with a solid warranty).

- **Working the Wood Web:** For the ultimate woodworking resource, look to www.woodweb.com, the information resource for the woodworking industry. The ever-growing site includes a database of woodworking machinery, supplies and services, an online bookstore with hundreds of titles, and interactive forums where you can get your specific questions answered.

  It's great fun to find all the resources in one place on the Net. Although Wood Web is designed for professionals, even wannabe-woodworkers will learn from this extensive site.

- **Motivating couch potatoes:** Inspired by projects they may have enjoyed watching on Dean Johnson's *HomeTime* on public television, fans of this program will appreciate having an online source for all the step-by-step information that makes it more likely they'll make the move from the couch to the workshop. Take a look at www.hometime.com even if you don't catch the show. It's good stuff.

- **Working with hardwoods:** If you're a more skilled craftsman, you'll appreciate the installation instructions the Hardwood Council offers on its site, www.hardwoodcouncil.com. This trade group has taken its extensive line of color brochures and placed them online, just waiting for you to download or print. There's a booklet on hardwood lumber grades and one on various hardwood flooring installations. The council's built-in cabinet is a showstopper we'd love to build.

✔ **Mail ordering made easier for woodworkers:** Browsing these woodworking mail-order catalogs is always a revealing experience. You'll discover neat tools, hardware, and other woodworking supplies that will make your tasks easier to accomplish with more professional results. Many of the nation's leading woodworking mail-order companies are online. Here are some that are ready to serve surfers:

- **Rockler:** 800-279-4441 or www.rockler.com

- **Constantines:** 800-223-8087 or www.constantines.com

- **Garrett Wade:** 800-221-2942 or www.garrettwade.com

- **Woodcraft Supply:** 800-225-1153 or www.woodcraft.com

✔ **Getting caught in the Net (HouseNet, that is):** We couldn't talk about Web sites without mentioning www.housenet.com, the site we founded. Some of the best carpentry advice comes from the visitors who share their best tips here, with hundreds of clever ideas. The Project of the Week provides simple, step-by-step instructions for a variety of carpentry-related home improvement and maintenance projects. The ever-popular Project Calculators help you figure out how much material you should buy for a job. Browse the message boards to get help and help others. There's tons of info here to use right away for a project you're about to undertake or to file away for future reference.

Our Compliments to the Chef!

Whether you're planning a romantic dinner for two or preparing meals for a small army, nothing beats the sense of accomplishment you feel after cooking a fine dish. Imagine the joy when your family and friends start asking for your best dishes by name, or spend an entire evening trying to wrangle your secret tomato sauce recipe from you. There are so many reasons to learn to cook. Here are just a few:

✔ When you dine in restaurants, you can complain with authority that particular dishes aren't made the way you make them at home.

✔ You get to use all kinds of amusing implements — and actually know what to do with them.

✔ You can control your diet rather than depend on the dubious victuals churned out by carryout places or frozen food purveyors.

✔ At home, seconds and thirds are permissible.

✔ Feeding friends and loved ones is inherently more intimate than going to a restaurant.

✔ Establishing a connection with the food chain allows you to distinguish quality food from what's second rate. Who knows, you may even be inspired to plant a vegetable garden next spring.

✔ You start hanging around the cookbook section in bookstores, fertile terrain for opposite-sex encounters.

The following sections describe the essential tools you need to complete your kitchen, and ten ways to think like a chef. Much more information about cooking techniques is available in *Cooking For Dummies* (Wiley).

Tools you can't live without

If you're just getting started or are on a tight budget, here are some essential tools you'll want to buy. As you become more proficient, you may want to expand your repertoire, but for now, we'll start with the bare-bones-all-you-can-spend-now kitchen equipment you should have:

✔ **10-inch chef's knife:** You can perform more than 80 percent of all cutting and slicing chores with this knife.

✔ **Paring knife:** For peeling, coring, and carving garnishes from vegetables and fruits.

✔ **10-inch nonstick frying pan:** The all-around pan for sautéing, making egg dishes, braising small quantities of food, and more.

✔ **3-quart saucepan:** For cooking vegetables, rice, soups, sauces, and small quantities of pasta.

✔ **Expandable steamer attachment (to fit the 3-quart saucepan):** For steaming vegetables, fish, and shellfish.

✔ **10-quart stock pot with lid:** For making stocks or large quantities of soup, pasta, and vegetables. You'll be surprised by how often you use this pot.

✔ **Electric blender:** This machine does not slice and chop like a food processor, but it's terrific for making quick, healthful sauces, soups, purees, and drinks.

✔ **Heavy-duty roasting pan:** For all kinds of roasting.

✔ **Liquid and dry measuring cups:** So you don't botch up recipes by using too much or too little of something.

✔ **Strainer:** Essential for certain sauces, pastas, salads, and soups.

✔ **Meat thermometer:** Why guess?

✔ **Vegetable peeler, pepper mill, hand cheese grater, rubber spatula, and wooden spoons:** Don't go off the deep end buying little kitchen gizmos; these tools are all you need to get started.

Ten classic cookbooks

Following are ten wide-ranging cookbooks that have stood the test of time. Lots of great cookbooks are out there, but if you own the following books, you'll be set for years:

- ✔ ***The Best of Craig Claiborne,*** Craig Claiborne with Pierre Franey (Times Books, 1999): Hundreds of well-written and reliable recipes from the famous culinary duo from *The New York Times.*

- ✔ ***Better Homes and Gardens New Cookbook,*** Betters Homes and Gardens Editors (Better Homes and Gardens Books, 1999): This is a great all-around book for home cooks. Most recipes are easy and well-suited for everyday cooking.

- ✔ ***The Cake Bible,*** Rose Levy Beranbaum (Morrow, 1988): An exhaustive, authoritative guide to baking any kind of cake imaginable.

- ✔ ***Essentials of Classic Italian Cooking,*** Marcella Hazan (Knopf, 1992): If you buy only one book on Italian cooking, you might well choose this one. Hazan, an easygoing and thorough teacher, covers all the techniques involved in Italian cuisine. The fresh pasta and gnocchi chapters are particularly well done.

- ✔ ***How to Bake,*** Nick Malgieri (HarperCollins, 1995): Nick Malgieri is a highly respected cooking instructor based in New York City. This book has an easygoing and authoritative approach to baking everything from baguettes to brownies.

- ✔ ***James Beard's American Cookery,*** James Beard (Budget Book Service, 1996): A broad look at American culinary styles through the impish personality of the larger-than-life James Beard. Recipes are traditional and solid.

- ✔ ***The New Joy of Cooking,*** Irma S. Rombauer, Marion Rombauer Becker, and Ethan Becker (Scribner, 1997): This best-selling classic is an excellent primer for beginning cooks, filled with lucid illustrations and instructions. This book tells you how to make the classic version of a dish — you take it from there.

- ✔ ***Larousse Gastronomique: The New American Edition of the World's Greatest Culinary Encyclopedia,*** edited by Jenifer Harvey Lang (Crown, 1988): This book is more an encyclopedia of food than a cookbook. Filled with color photos and illustrations, it is the definitive resource for answers to cooking questions. The book does not give recipes per se but rather descriptions of how to make something as if you were telling a friend. Its historical notes are interesting, too.

- ✔ ***Mastering the Art of French Cooking, Volumes I and II,*** Julia Child, Louisette Bertholle, and Simone Beck (Knopf, 1983 and 1991): Not an everyday cookbook, this two-volume classic is where you go to learn how to do something the way it was originally intended. If you have a strong interest in French cuisine, this book is indispensable. Particularly interesting are the step-by-step instructions for making pastries, dough, bread, and cakes.

✔ **The New Doubleday Cookbook,** Jean Anderson and Elaine Hanna (Doubleday, 1990): This amazingly comprehensive book belongs in every cook's kitchen. For a tome of this size (967 pages), it is stylish and light on its feet. Instructions are well written, and illustrations are easy to follow. Every aspect of American and international cooking is covered. Whenever we couldn't find something in other references while researching this book, we found it in *The New Doubleday Cookbook.*

Ten ways to think like a chef

In observing and interviewing many chefs, we found a consensus among them about how to progress as a cook. Here are our ten favorite tips from the chefs who know:

✔ **Know the basic techniques:** Cooking is so much more fun — and successful — when you approach it with confidence. Chefs say that confidence arises from knowing your techniques so well that they are second nature.

✔ **Use only the freshest ingredients:** Use only the freshest ingredients and buy in-season fresh fruits and vegetables. Seasonal produce offers the highest quality and supply and the lowest price. Why make an apple pie in the summer from mealy apples held in storage all year when you can make a pie with fresh, ripe peaches or juicy plums? Let what's fresh and available at the market help you spontaneously decide what's for dinner.

✔ **Get it together:** So much of cooking, even for professionals, is preparation — slicing, peeling, dicing, and so on. Get the chopping, mincing, deboning, and washing chores out of the way in order to create an even, efficient flow of cooking steps. That way, when the butter or oil is hot and sizzling in the skillet, you don't need to stop suddenly to peel and mince onions and garlic that are supposed to be sautéed in the hot fat.

✔ **With this basil, I thee wed:** Learn about herbs, both fresh and dried, so that you can season without always relying on a book or recipe. Chefs base some of the world's great cuisines on the combination of a few simple herbs and spices.

✔ **All the plate's a stage:** Think of the choreography of food on a plate. People eat with their eyes first. The food should be colorful and attrac-tively arranged, with fresh herbs as a colorful garnish.

✔ **Plan your menus in advance:** Before cooking, think about contrasting flavors, textures, and colors. If the appetizer is a salad of grilled Portobello mushrooms, then mushrooms in the entree is not an interesting choice. Keep the courses balanced and don't overload yourself. If you serve a time-consuming and complex appetizer, serve a simple entree or one that needs only reheating, like a tasty stew. If your appetizer is cold, be sure that the entree is hot.

Take a good look at the timing of the meal, too. Figure out how much cooking and preparation time are needed so that your diners don't feel they are getting the bum's rush or have to wait too long between courses.

✔ **Be thrifty:** Throw out nothing (unless, of course, it's spoiled). Every morsel of food is usable for soups, stocks, salads, and so on. You can sometimes make great meals from leftovers. Also, learn about different cuts of meat and how to cook them so that you don't have to rely on more expensive cuts. Hone your knife skills so that you can save money by purchasing whole chickens, ducks, fish, and so on and then cutting them up yourself.

✔ **Don't be a slave to recipes:** Use a good, basic recipe that you like as a starting point, but don't consider it written in stone. Say you have a recipe for basic stew. You make it once and decide that it could use more garlic, so the next time you double the amount. Or instead of turnips, you think that the sweet effect of chopped carrots would work, so you substitute one vegetable for the other. With experience and good technique, and by learning how ingredients work together, you can simply glance at a recipe and make adjustments to suit your taste.

✔ **Simplify, simplify:** It's not what you decide to put into a dish that's important, it's what you decide to keep out, says Jan Birnbaum, owner and chef of The Catahoula Restaurant and Saloon in Calistoga, California. Start with a product that's fresh and flavorful and add only those seasonings that complement the food.

✔ **Above all, have fun:** Take a cooking course, buy yourself a cookbook, or make a new dish that you've always wanted to try. Cooking, like golf, should be fun — something you look forward to. So what if you slam one into the rough every now and then? It's all part of the game.

Growing a Green Thumb

If you want to learn more about gardening, just where do you start? We could start with some heavy-duty science, tossing around terms like *cotyledon, cambium,* and the ever-popular *pith.* Or we could start talking about beautiful gardens like critics of fine paintings — employing words like *composition, energy, focal point,* and such.

We don't mean to suggest anything but respect for scientists and artists. In fact, the chance to combine science and art is what draws many people to gardening in the first place — especially if you throw in a little farming and a few old wives' tales (of course, you should or shouldn't plant sweet peas at the full moon).

All we really want to do here is to get you through a few basic principles of plant growth and garden planning so that you can rush out into the yard when the weather's right for planting and the soil is ripe for digging.

What a plant needs

Like other living things, plants have certain requirements for good health. For example, they require the right amounts of sunlight, moisture, and nutrients. Plants also need an equitable range of temperatures — neither too hot nor too cold.

When selecting plants, you can meet their requirements in one of two ways:

- You can select your favorite plants and then do your best to alter the growing conditions at the planting site to meet their needs. You can change the growing conditions by adding sprinkler irrigation, incorporating fertilizer, hauling in fresh topsoil, pruning some trees, or covering plants with blankets in winter. But this is the backward approach.

- A better way to make sure plants grow well — and need less care in the process — is to learn about the conditions at the planting site first and then choose plants that grow under those conditions. Of course, some of the plants that you want to put in are accustomed to conditions different from what you have in your yard, and those plants are going to need some attention to stay happy. But the better you match plants to the planting site, the longer the plants will live, the better the plants will look, and the less work (watering, pruning, fertilizing, and controlling pests) you'll have to do to care for them.

What can I use my garden for?

True, you can go buy plants and stick them in the ground — and let it go at that. But many of us want a "garden," which, by our definition, contains enough organization and space to allow room for growing plants plus other purposes — playing, relaxing, outdoor dining, entertaining, and more.

A garden can make your life more comfortable, healthier, more colorful, and more convenient. A garden lets you expand your living area to the outdoors, harvest fresh food, and pick your own flowers. Take a look at the different ways that a garden can enhance your life:

✔ **A private getaway.** Imagine taking a vacation in your own backyard or relaxing in a shady spot, secluded from the hustle and bustle of daily living. This dream can be yours, if you begin by creating a private area for your own pleasure.

✔ **A place for entertaining.** Whether you like large get-togethers with the extended family or business associates or a quiet dinner with a few friends, your garden can provide an ideal atmosphere. You need a few key ingredients to make your garden perfect for entertaining.

✔ **Don't forget Junior . . . or Spot.** Who will use your garden? Take into account children and pets — they have different garden interests than grownups.

✔ **Your own flower shop.** Cutting an armful of flowers from your own garden and bringing them indoors is so satisfying. If you like freshly cut flowers, be sure to leave space to grow your own.

✔ **Harvesting the fruits of your labor.** One of the most delicious aspects of your garden is that it can produce wonderful vegetables, fruits, and herbs. You can grow gourmet produce, rare and special crops, and grow them organically.

✔ **A practical work area.** Being outdoors means more than fun and games. You may need a place in your yard to keep your garden tools, heating fuel tank, firewood, clothesline, or garbage cans. Organize all of these less-than-attractive outdoor necessities into the same out-of-the way location — a workstation separate from your entertaining and play areas. Ideally, the location should be handy, near the garage or driveway, but far enough away from handsome views or gardens so that the workstation is not a distraction.

✔ **Take time to relax.** Anywhere that seems cozy and pleasant is a great place to put a sitting nook. The area doesn't have to be fancy, just a place for you to relax and, perhaps, watch the kids play. Start with a comfortable bench or chair and position it in shade beneath a magnificent oak, at the end of your vegetable garden, or at the back of your yard near the swing set. If you put in all-weather footing — gravel or mulch, for example — you can sit outside regardless of the soil conditions.

The possibilities for your garden are almost endless. Take some time to jot down everything you may possibly want in your yard.

The two types of plants: Annuals and perennials

Annuals are the shooting stars of the garden universe. They burn brightly indeed, but briefly. Perennials are the phoenixes of garden plants: Every winter they die only to rise from the ashes the following spring, fuller and more beautiful than before. Perennials are essential in cold winter climates because they grow and sometimes begin flowering while annuals are still warming up and getting started.

- ✔ An *annual* is a plant that undergoes its entire life cycle within one growing season. You plant a marigold seed in May, the seedling sprouts quickly, it starts blooming in July, frost kills it in October, and seeds scatter and (we hope) sprout the next spring to start the process again.

  Annuals are versatile and just about foolproof. You don't need to be born with a silver trowel in your hand to achieve some beautiful effects in your yard:

  - Plant entire beds and borders in swaths of color.

  - Create a combination of annuals for your pots and window boxes that blooms all summer long.

  - Mix annuals into borders of trees, shrubs, and ground covers to add seasonal color, fragrance, and texture.

- ✔ A *perennial* is a plant that can live for several years, sprouting new growth and making new blooms cyclically year after year. If you start a typical perennial, such as columbine, from seed in May, it spends the summer growing foliage and dies back completely to the ground when winter arrives. The following spring, it starts growing again, blooms that summer, dies back again, and repeats the pattern of blooming and dying back for years.

Creating a perennial border

The classic use of perennials is to combine many of them in a large planting bed, known as a *perennial border*. A well-designed perennial border has something in bloom throughout the growing season. This type of border not only has a well-thought-out color scheme, but also relies on plant texture for visual interest. Designing a spectacular planting can take years of experience, but even beginning gardeners can create a workable, pleasing border, adding to it over the years as their knowledge increases.

For most gardeners, a perennial border is constantly evolving, which is part of the fun of creating it. If certain plants don't work, you can replace them with something else. If the border has some downtime when nothing is in bloom, add some flowering annuals to fill in the gap or plant some flowering shrubs, such as floribunda roses, which bloom over a long season. When your border consists of a medley of flowering plants, including small trees, shrubs, bulbs, annuals, herbs, and even vegetables, you have a *mixed border*.

Beds and borders

Flower beds come in two basic configurations:

> ✔ A *border* is a flower bed located alongside a wall, fence, hedge, or pavement. Border gardens are usually long and narrow as they follow the contours of the backdrop.

> ✔ An *island bed* is a free-standing flower bed surrounded on all sides by lawn, gravel, or pavement. The edges can be straight or curved. Island beds can be any shape or size.

The Simple Game of Golf

Golf is a simple game. You've got a bunch of clubs and a ball. You have to hit the ball with a club into a series of holes laid out in the middle of a large, grassy field. After you reach the 18th hole, you may want to go to a bar and tell lies to anyone you didn't play with that day about your on-course feats. If you're like most people, you play golf for relaxation and a chance to see the great outdoors. If you're like Arnold Palmer, Jack Nicklaus, and Greg Norman, you do this and make a bazillion dollars on top of seeing the great outdoors.

Of course, you do have some obstacles. To paraphrase Winston Churchill, who called golf "a silly game played with implements ill-suited for the purpose," the game isn't always so straightforward.

Goals of the game

Simply stated, the goal of golf is to get the ball into each of 18 holes in succession with the fewest number of shots possible by hitting the ball with one of 14 clubs. After you hit the ball into all the holes, you add up your score from each hole to figure out your total score, which usually comes out to some number IBM's Big Blue couldn't calculate. The lower your score, the better your game. That is golf. That is the goal.

The best advice that we can give you is to take the game slowly, make prudent decisions, and never hit a shot while contemplating other matters. Golf is a game to be played with total concentration and a complete disregard for your ego.

Golf balls — what to choose

Take a look around any golf professional's shop, and you'll see a lot of golf balls and a lot of different brands. And upon closer inspection, you'll find that every type of ball falls into one of two categories: Either the manufacturer is claiming that this ball goes farther and straighter than any other ball in the cosmos, or it's telling you that this ball gives you more control than your other brand.

Here are some tips for picking out the best golf balls for your game:

- **Basic types:** Golf balls come in only three basic types: one-piece, two-piece, and three-piece. Go with a two-piece ball.

  We wouldn't recommend a three-piece, balata-covered ball to a beginning golfer. *Balata* is a relatively soft, rubber-type material designed to give advanced players better feel and therefore more control — not what a beginning golfer needs.

  And you can forget one-piece balls. They tend to be cheap and nasty and found only on driving ranges. So that leaves two-piece balls.

- **Material:** Unless you have very deep pockets and more cash than Greg Norman, go the surlyn, two-piece route. (*Surlyn* is a type of plastic first developed by the Dupont Corporation.) Most amateurs with double-digit handicaps use this type of ball.

- **Compression:** Golf balls also come in three compressions: 80, 90, or 100 compression. The 80-compression ball is the softest, and the 100 is the hardest. All balls go the same distance, but each one feels a little different. How hard or soft you want the ball to feel has to do with your personal preference.

How to choose the clubs in your bag

If you're just starting out (and you've played with the rental clubs for a while), find cheap clubs to use as an interim set during your adjustment period. You're learning the game, so you don't want to make big decisions on what type of clubs to buy yet.

Here are some factors to consider when choosing your clubs:

- **The grip:** Determine how thick the grip on your clubs should be. The grip is very important. Grips that are too thin encourage too much hand action in your swing; grips that are too thick restrict your hands too much. Generally, the proper-sized grip should allow the middle and ring fingers on your left hand to barely touch the pad of your thumb when you take hold of the club. If your fingers don't touch your thumb, the grip is too big; if your fingers dig into the pad, the grip is too thin.

- **The shaft:** Consider your height, build, and strength when you choose a club. If you're really tall, you need longer (and probably stiffer) shafts.

What does your swing sound like? If your swing makes a loud swish noise and the shaft is bending like a long cast from a fly-fishing rod at the top of your swing, you need a very strong shaft. If your swing makes no noise and you could hang laundry on your shaft at the top of your swing, you need a regular shaft. Anybody in-between needs a medium-stiff to stiff shaft.

✔ **Loft:** Then there's your typical ball-flight. If you slice, for example, you can get clubs with less loft — or perhaps offset heads — to help alleviate that problem.

✔ **The clubhead:** Consider the size of the clubhead. Today, you can get standard, midsize, and oversize heads on your clubs. We recommend that you get bigger clubheads for your early days of golfing. Bigger clubheads are more forgiving and can help psychologically, too.

✔ **The iron:** Advanced players choose irons that are best suited to their swing. Forged, muscle-backed irons are for good players who hit the ball on the clubface precisely. Cavity-backed irons (hollowed out in the back of the iron) are for those players who hit the ball all over the clubface.

The bigger the clubface, the more room for error — hence the bigger-headed metal woods that are popular today for all you wild swingers out there.

Try all sorts of golf clubs — ones with steel shafts, graphite shafts (which are lighter and therefore easier to swing), big-headed clubs, forged clubs, cavity-backed clubs. You have more choices than your neighborhood Baskin-Robbins. Remember: You're in your experimental stage.

Ten questions to ask when you buy clubs

Don't be shy; after all, you want the clubs that best suit you when shelling out your hard-earned cash. Ask these questions and you're sure to get a good fit.

1. Do you have a club-fitting program?
2. What's the price of club-fitting?
3. What shaft length do I need for my clubs?
4. What lie-angle do I need on my clubs?
5. What grip size do I need?
6. What material — leather, cord, all-rubber, half-rubber — do you recommend for my grips?
7. What kind of irons should I buy — investment-cast, forged, oversized, or cavity back?
8. Should I use space-age materials like boron, titanium, or graphite in my shafts? Or should I go with steel?
9. What type of putter should I use: center-shafted, end-shafted, or a long putter?
10. Can I test them for a day?

Ten timeless golf tips

Having been around golf for a while, we've noticed certain bad habits that our friends constantly repeat on the golf course. Just knowing not to repeat these habits will help the average player live a long and peaceful life on the links.

We've racked our feeble brains and jotted down ten tips so that you won't repeat these common faults that we see repeated on golf courses all over the world.

- ✔ **Take enough club to get to your target:** We're constantly playing with amateurs who consistently come up short for their approach shots to the green. For whatever reason, they always choose a club that — even if they were to hit the most solid shot they've ever hit — would get their shot only to the front of the green. Take a club that you can swing at 80 percent and still get to the hole. Conserve your energy; you have a long life ahead of you!

- ✔ **If you can putt the ball, do it:** Don't always use a lofted club around the greens. We've got a friend at home called "flop-shot Fred" who is always playing high sand wedge shots around the green, regardless of what the shot calls for. We think his idol is Phil Mickelson, who can hit these shots straight up in the air. Leave this kind of shot to guys like Phil who can handle them. Our best advice is to use a club that can hit this shot with the lowest trajectory possible. If you can putt the ball, do it.

- ✔ **Keep your head fairly steady:** You're going to move your head a little during the swing, especially with the longer clubs. But try not to move your head in excess. Moving your head too much leads to all sorts of serious swing flaws that make this game very difficult to play. Have someone watch you to see whether you move your head, or watch yourself in the mirror while you take practice swings.

- ✔ **Keep your sense of humor:** If everything else fails, you can keep your sense of humor and still survive, or at least die laughing.

- ✔ **Bet only what you can afford to lose:** You can cause some serious problems among friends by betting for more money than you have. Never bet on your golf game what you can't afford to lose. Our theory was to bet everything in our pockets except for $10, and that was to pay for the gas home.

- ✔ **Keep the ball low in the wind:** When the wind starts to kick up, we see golfers play their normal shots and fail to hit the ball lower to allow for the conditions. Play the ball back in your stance, put your hands ahead of the ball, and keep them ahead when you make contact. Keep the ball as low as you can, and you can manage your game much more efficiently. You probably won't lose as many golf balls, either.

✔ **Take some golf lessons:** If you really want to have fun playing this game, start off with a few lessons to get you on the right track and, of course, read *Golf For Dummies* (Wiley) in its entirety. It's amazing what you can do with a clear concept in your mind of how to make a golf swing.

✔ **Don't give lessons to your spouse:** Giving golf lessons to your spouse can be a federal offense. Don't do it! Doing so can only lead to disaster. Invest some money in lessons. Get good instruction and reap the benefits (peace of mind).

✔ **Always tee it up at the tee boxes:** Whenever it's legal (in the teeing area), tee the ball up. This game is more fun when the ball's in the air.

✔ **Never blame yourself for a bad shot:** Give yourself a break. This game is hard enough without blaming everything on yourself. Find creative ways to blame something else. We like to blame our bad shots on the magnetic force field from alien spacecraft. Let your mind go and see how crazy your excuses can be. Save your sanity!

Ladies and Gentlemen: Start Your Point-and-Shoots!

Your point-and-shoot camera is practically an invitation to just start taking pictures. A wonder of automation, it uses advanced electronics and tiny motors to quickly execute the many separate steps that photographers used to have to do manually each time they wanted to take a picture. Point-and-shoots automatically advance the film from shot to shot, or, if they're digital, automatically store your pictures in their onboard "memory." And film or digital, they automatically compute the correct exposure — the exact amount of light that your film or digital camera needs to properly record the subject — and adjust their settings accordingly. They automatically turn on the flash in dim light. And they automatically focus the lens. Digital cameras take things a step further, using a built-in computer to convert each scene you shoot into a "file" of tiny dots of varying color and tone.

Actually, your particular point-and-shoot may not perform every one of these functions. And which ones it does perform depends partly (though not entirely) on what type of point-and-shoot you have. So this section — a section otherwise devoted to getting you started taking pictures as quickly as possible — begins by describing the four different types of point-and-shoot cameras.

The four types of point-and-shoot cameras

Like people, point-and-shoots have more in common than they do differences. This is especially true of the way you operate the cameras — what you push, slide, or twist to make them do specific things. But while they're operated in pretty much the same way, point-and-shoots differ both in the way the image is captured and in the mechanical and electronic complexity they bring to the job. Those differences make it possible to divide these cameras into four main types:

- **The 35mm point-and-shoot:** Granddaddy of the point-and-shoot movement, the 35mm point-and-shoot uses 35mm film — the film that comes in the funny-looking little cassette with the perforated tongue sticking out at you. You grab that tongue of film to start the roll through the camera, as this chapter explains in detail. 35mm point-and-shoots come in every form from cheapo, check-out counter specials to expensive, full-featured models that rival 35mm single-lens reflexes (those professional-style system cameras) in their sophistication.

- **The Advanced Photo System point-and-shoot:** A younger generation of point-and-shoot cameras, Advanced Photo System (APS) models look pretty much like their 35mm counterparts. But they take a different, smaller-than-35mm film cassette that has allowed manufacturers to create smaller cameras. The system also simplifies film loading, makes storage and reprinting easier, and gives you a shot-by-shot choice of three different print sizes, which you pick with a switch on the camera.

- **The one-time-use point-and-shoot:** One-time-use cameras are by far the most popular type of point-and-shoot, outselling reloadable models many times over. These inexpensive (usually $5 to $15, depending on the type) models are in some respects the ultimate point-and-shoot because they're the easiest to use. You don't have to insert film or batteries, for example. In fact, you don't even have to remember to bring your camera along, because you can buy a one-time-use camera on the way or on the spot.

- **The digital point-and-shoot:** Unlike the other types of point-and-shoot cameras, a digital point-and-shoot neither contains nor accepts film. A digital camera stores photographs as digital files that can be downloaded directly and immediately to a computer for various purposes, including retouching, e-mailing, and printing. And most digital point-and-shoots store these files on *memory cards,* small plastic-and-silicon wafers that are (in some respects) the digital equivalent of film. In terms of operation, digital point-and-shoots are essentially like film-using cameras — and again, most of the shooting advice in this and other chapters applies to them as well.

Finding a film that's your type

You can choose among several types of film when making your purchasing decision — all will work with your point-and-shoot camera. The key is knowing what film is best for the special circumstances you will be photographing under.

Photofinishing has as big an influence on the quality of your prints as the film you choose — sometimes bigger. Lack of care or attention, whether on the part of a minilab or a mass-market processor, can make prints from great film look terrible. Good photofinishing, on the other hand, can pull excellent prints from run-of-the-mill film. A good brand-name film will give you rich color and detail, even with a pretty inexpensive camera. If it doesn't, then you should consider switching to a different photofinisher or minilab.

Color versus black-and-white film

Here are the two types of film:

- ✔ **Color print film:** Most snapshot photographers use color print film because it gives them both color and prints — color for the sake of realism, prints for the sake of viewing convenience and ease of sharing. Therefore, color print film is the film on which both minilabs and mass-market photofinishers base their voluminous business. It is also the film in which manufacturers invest the most money, time, and effort. So color print film is, generally speaking, the most technologically advanced film you can buy.

- ✔ **Black-and-white film:** Color pictures have become the norm pretty recently in the grand sweep of photographic history. Before color became practical and affordable, black and white *was* photography. The great photo-essays that appeared in the first decades of *Life* magazine were all in black and white — and no one questioned their realism. In its grittiness, black and white actually seemed more true-to-life — less decorative — than color. That perception persisted even after color became the norm for magazine reproduction.

How fast is fast enough?

In addition to color considerations, you must choose a speed for your film. Table 16-1 contains a film speed buying chart to help you choose the best film speed for your needs.

Table 16-1		Film-Speed Buying Chart (Color Print Film)	
Film Speed	*Pros*	*Cons*	*Best Subjects/Light*
ISO 100	Finest grain of all; improves smoothness and detail in big blowups (11 x 14 and larger); helps soften distracting backgrounds in outdoor portraits	Increases the risk that hand tremors blur or soften the entire picture; reduces flash range and background detail in indoor flash shots; may not stop action outdoors	Landscapes in sunlight; beach and snow scenes; portraits in bright light; close-ups with flash
ISO 200	Reasonable compromise between fine grain and speed; less risk of blur due to hand tremors than with ISO 100 film; increases flash range by 40 percent over ISO 100 film	Still too slow for much low-light shooting; considerable risk of blur due to hand tremors at long zoom settings	All-around outdoor shooting in moderate overcast to bright sun; outdoor portraits in soft light; flash shots at medium distances
ISO 400	Best all-purpose film; fine-grained but *fast,* provides excellent picture quality in standard-sized prints; permits higher shutter speeds for better action stopping and reduced risk of blur from hand tremors; more faithful color in mixed (indoor/ outdoor) light; doubles the flash range of ISO 100 film	May suppress flash in indoor shots, making you *force* the flash when you don't want to shoot by existing light; shows grain in big blowups (11 x 14 and larger)	All-around shooting in conditions ranging from deep shade and existing indoor light to bright sun; indoor flash shots at greater distances from subject
ISO 800	Excellent all-purpose film combining high speed and surprisingly fine grain; good fail-safe film for must-get shots; provides two-and-a-half times the flash range of ISO 100 film; offsets hand tremors due to long zoom settings; best film in mixed light	Expensive; may suppress flash in indoor shots or create flash *ghosts;* shows grain in blowups (8 x 10 or larger)	All-around outdoor shooting from dawn to dusk; outdoor portraits in less favorable light; indoor existing-light shots; distant flash subjects

Can film go stale?

When we buy a carton of milk, we dig around for the one that's stamped with the latest "sell by" date. Actually, film has similar dating information stamped right on the box. Called the *expiration date,* it appears next to printed words such as *Develop before.*

You should definitely shoot and develop a roll of film before the date stamped on it. If you don't, it may not give you the best quality, diminishing your pictures' contrast and color brightness.

Some merchants discount film that's past its expiration date; if we were you, we wouldn't buy it. It's not worth gambling on your pictures to save a buck.

Refrigeration can help keep film "fresh" both before and after you actually shoot it. But never, ever store film in a place where it can get hot; this actually accelerates its aging, and may even cause prints to be discolored or otherwise flawed.

Ten simple ways to make your pictures better

Thanks to point-and-shoot technology, you don't have to be the slightest bit technical to get good picture quality. Exposure, focus, flash — you name it, it's all handled for you, and the results are remarkably consistent.

You don't even have to be artistic to take good pictures. You just have to use some visual intelligence. You have to think with your eyes, in a sense. And much of that visual thinking can be reduced to the simple notions in the following list.

These pointers apply to *any* kind of point-and-shoot, from fancy "designer" cameras to simple, one-time-use models — digital point-and-shoots included. You don't have to have a pricey point-and-shoot to make them work for you; you don't even have to have an auto focus model.

✔ **Capture the moment:** Not to co-opt Kodak, but most of personal photography is about moments. Keep in mind, though, that moments can be unique or everyday. Don't wait for a specific occasion to take your pictures; find the telling moments in seemingly ordinary events. Also remember that moments are by definition fleeting. To catch that perfect expression or charming interaction, you have to anticipate it — keeping your finger on the shutter button, your eye to the viewfinder, and your patience.

✔ **Don't use the viewfinder like a gun sight:** "Shooting" is an apt description of the way most picture-takers compose — by placing their main subject dead-center. (There might as well be crosshairs in the camera's viewfinder.) The most common instance of this is the way people's heads always seem to end up smack in the middle of the picture, with empty space above. For people pictures, vertical or horizontal, try placing heads near the top of the picture area.

✔ **Get close:** Try to fill the frame with your main subject. Most pictures suffer from the subject being too small. In most cases, the best way to fix this — and the only way, if you have a nonzooming camera — is simply to move in closer. Unless you're shooting a tight portrait, zooming to fill the frame is often not a good idea. In fact, your own two legs are the most important photographic tool at your disposal: Use them to move in and out, and thus to control the subject's size in the frame.

✔ **Shoot from a low or high angle:** There's nothing sacred about your own eye level. If you've ever stooped to shoot pictures of kids, you know this instinctively. Shooting from a child's eye level helps you make more intimate contact. And with taller subjects, human or inanimate, aiming the camera up from a low angle can create an interesting monumental effect. (Again, legs are your tool here. Squat!)

Shooting from a high angle is a little trickier. You may have to get up on a wall or a car hood, or perhaps shoot from a deck or window. But even a little extra elevation on a subject can keep foreground and background elements from overlapping confusingly, and add depth to an image.

✔ **Use flash outdoors:** Your point-and-shoot automatically fires its flash in dim light, but you shouldn't think of flash just as a way to add light to a subject when there isn't enough to shoot by already. Flash is actually a great idea when you must shoot in direct sunlight, because it "fills" the dark, unattractive facial shadows created by a subject's eye sockets and nose. Flash also helps brighten a "backlit" subject that would otherwise end up too dark.

On the other hand, if an outdoor subject has delicate lighting that you think might be overpowered by flash (rosy light at the end of the day, for example), don't use it. And if you're shooting a landscape, don't bother — it's too far away for the flash to make any difference. When in doubt, shoot pictures with *and* without flash and then compare the final results.

✔ **Use a fast film:** Don't be talked into a print film that has a lower "speed" than ISO 400 unless you plan to make big blowups from it. Current fast films — ISO 400 or even ISO 800 — give you prints of exceptionally high quality. And their extra sensitivity to light not only reduces the risk of slow, image-blurring shutter speeds, but lets you shoot without flash in a wider range of existing light. Just as important, it improves background detail in flash shots.

A digital point-and-shoot doesn't use film, of course, but its image sensor's sensitivity to light is still measured by ISO numbers. Ordinarily it adjusts this sensitivity automatically, depending on the light level. But some models allow you to adjust their ISO setting manually, a useful feature.

✔ **Place the main subject off-center:** Whether you're shooting a person or a mountain, try not to center the subject in the viewfinder unless you have a compelling compositional reason to do so. A centered subject makes the picture more static in feeling. A subject placed to one side of the frame usually creates a more dynamic design.

✔ **Move from side to side:** A small shift sideways can make a huge improvement in a picture, preventing objects at different distances from overlapping horizontally and creating visual confusion. Study the viewfinder as you move to see how a change in lateral position can change the relationships among elements of the scene.

✔ **Experiment with the horizon line:** Usually, anything is better than placing a landscape's horizon line midway up the frame. Put it at the bottom instead, and you can emphasize a sky, for a "big" effect. Place it near the top, and you can create a strong feeling of depth.

✔ **Take lots of pictures:** Film is cheap, and digital pictures are free. Photography's great pleasure is that you can find out what works by trying it, for the cost of a 4-x-6-inch print.

Putting the Horse before the Spark: Fundraising Starts with Passion

Fundraising is Big Business — to the tune of more than $174 billion a year. That's one heck of a lot of hot meals, you may think. Or free condoms. Or community leadership seminars. Or tithes.

Four fundraising terms you need to understand

Before going any farther, we need to clearly define the terms we bat around. You'll see and hear these terms again and again as you proceed to raise money for the causes you believe in:

✔ **Philanthropy:** In the fundraising field, one standard definition of philanthropy is "voluntary action for the public good," meaning any action one takes — with or without a financial component — that is an act to make life better for someone else. When you tithe at church, it's philanthropy.

When you drop coins in the container on the counter at 7-Eleven, you're a philanthropist. When you include your local theater in your will, you're practicing philanthropy.

✔ **Gift:** In fundraising, *gift* may mean any number of things.

- You may hear about a *lead gift,* which is the first, usually sizeable, gift of a capital campaign.

- A *major gift* is another type of large gift that a donor may give in order to support a particular program, launch a campaign, further a cause, or be applied in another specific area.

- A *general gift* is one a donor gives to an annual fund or contributes to operating expenses.

Still, a gift is a gift, freely given, with no theoretical arm-twisting and no product or service given in return.

✔ **Fundraising:** Fundraising is the intentional and strategic activity of acquiring contributions for support and growth. Those contributions can include money, time, services, labor, donations of hard goods, in-kind contributions, or something else we haven't thought of yet.

✔ **Volunteer:** At a basic level, a volunteer is someone who works for no monetary payment. As a volunteer, you get other benefits, to be sure — the ability to help build something you believe in, acquire new skills, forge new relationships, and more.

Types of nonprofits

Nonprofit organizations (NPOs) exist to battle every imaginable ill — from environmental to health to human service issues. And don't forget animals, arts, and political groups. Most organizations fall into one of the following categories:

✔ Arts or cultural organizations

✔ Educational organizations

✔ Environmental organizations

✔ Health organizations

✔ International aid and relief organizations

✔ Public policy or social benefit organizations

✔ Religious organizations

✔ Social service organizations

Six tips for successful fundraising

Here are some tips for successful fundraising and for keeping your agency alive and growing:

- **Know your mission statement inside and out.** A crystal clear why-are-we-here mission statement helps keep everyone focused on the vision of the organization.

- **Be different.** You need to differentiate yourself from other similar organizations: Many opportunities abound for giving, but not so many that it's okay to duplicate services — not for the long term.

- **Know what's out there.** Be sure you stay plugged in to your environment. Be active in local fundraising groups — know who else serves the population you serve. When possible, work with as opposed to against other agencies so that you both can complement and not duplicate the others' practices.

- **Be responsive to the people you serve.** The ever-changing world presents us with opportunities for refocusing and retooling at every turn. If the social ill you battle is no longer viable, step back and reconsider the needs of your clients. If the language of your mission statement is outdated, be willing to speak in terms that will reach your constituents' hearts.

- **Be willing to change.** Especially for large, unwieldy organizations with a vested power structure and a bureaucratic bent, change is resisted at the board table. But populations, needs, and services change. Be willing to change with them. Doing so is one of the things that will help protect your agency's existence.

- **Ask the tough questions.** Does your organization meet today's needs? Fifty years ago, an agency created to provide lodging to unmarried pregnant women was a much-needed agency. In today's climate, programs exist in many places to help young women get the help they need and single pregnancy no longer carries the same crippling social stigma it once did. An organization that hasn't changed the focus of its mission is left in the dust in this type of situation.

Boarding the hobby club train without paying a fare

Joining a hobby club can be a great way to meet people, learn more about your hobby, and often get discounts on hobby-related items. Maybe one of the following clubs will pique your interest. If not, just do a search on www.google.com for your state and your particular hobby to find a club near you.

✔ www.vegetable-gardening-club.com: Vegetable gardening can be a year-round hobby that gets you out of the house — and you can't get a much better hobby as far as health is concerned. Whether you're growing vegetables for personal consumption or entering vegetable gardening competitions, this club provides new gardeners and the more experienced vegetable grower with the tips and tricks of vegetable gardening and a forum for discussing great topics like bug/pest control and growing help with other gardeners. And you can join for free.

✔ www.ichef.com: Gourmet cooking may not have been something you had time for when you were raising kids, but it makes for a great way to entertain the friends you have time for now. iChef is a free, Web-based cooking club with several unique tools. With the Menu Planner, you can plan recipes around specific meals, days of the week, or special occasions. The eCookBook allows you to keep track of your favorite online recipes and organize them to your heart's desire. If you step into the iChef.com discussion forum, you can post new discussions or reply to an existing discussion, such as saving meat from freezer burn. Exciting! As an iChef member, you can also create your own Recipe Club — a free Web site listing recipes, articles or stories, favorite links, a calendar of events, and a specialized discussion forum all focused on your particular cooking interest (such as cake decorating or French cuisine).

✔ www.cflphotoclub.com: Although this photography club is for central Florida, it's a great example of what such a club can offer the budding photographer: regular meetings to share and critique photos, workshops to hone skills, contests, fieldtrips, and discussion forums. To find a club in your area, go to http://dir.yahoo.com and search for photography clubs.

✔ www.virtualstampclub.com: Find current *philatelic* (that's stamp-collecting if you don't know the lingo yet) news, information, and discussion at the Virtual Stamp Club. The VSC was the first electronic chapter of the American Philatelic Society and all you have to do to join is participate. Enter the message board or chat away in one.

Chapter 17

Great Hobbies to Help You Relax

*T*his chapter discusses some of the greatest hobbies for relaxing either alone or in the company of your family and friends. Many of the hobbies described, such as knitting, crocheting, and even bird watching, are ready to travel wherever you want to go, be it the train station, the library, or a different room of your own home. Some even have proven psychological and physical benefits, such as resting your mind and easing the symptoms of arthritis.

Bird Watching: From Guns to Binoculars

Bird watching (or birding) is a hobby enjoyed by millions and millions of people. Birds are fun to look at, birds are beautiful, many birds sing beautiful songs, and bird behavior is fascinating. Birds foretell the changing seasons by their northward and southward migrations. And birds sometimes have feeding frenzies just before or after a blast of bad weather. So if you want to throw out your calendar and the local meteorologist, go right ahead. You don't need either — you have the birds.

Bird watchers come in many types, from casual backyard looker to rabid, globe-trotting birder, and everything in between. Today, an estimated 80 million people of all ages and physical abilities point their binoculars toward feathered creatures. Bird watching is second only to gardening as a favorite leisure time activity among North Americans. What's more, bird watching is considered the number-one spectator sport in North America!

Why watch birds?

Cheep and easy fun. That's bird watching. Once you have some optics (binoculars) and a field guide to the birds, you're ready to go. Unless you want to get into a private preserve, a state park or national wildlife refuge that has an entrance fee, or go on a guided tour, you've spent all you need to spend to be a bird watcher. (Okay, you do still have to eat, and wear clothes, and of course, pay your mortgage, but you'd be paying for those things anyway.) Perhaps only plant watching is cheaper — you don't need binoculars to identify plants.

Two essential tools for watching the birds

As we say in the preceding section, you need only two basic essentials to begin bird watching in earnest:

✔ **Binoculars:** Binoculars let you get a closer look. And a closer look lets you see clues to the bird's identity. With these clues (and a field guide), you can solve the mystery of just about any bird's identity.

Bird watchers use many different terms for their binoculars. Two of the most common are *binocs* and *bins*. Generically, binoculars and the telescopes used for birding are called *optics,* which is easier to say than optical equipment. We've also heard bird watchers use some unprintable names for their binoculars, often after they missed seeing a bird because their binocs were fogged or of poor quality.

✔ **Field guide:** The second piece of very useful equipment for bird watching is a field guide to the birds. If you're a beginning bird watcher, the field guide can be a big help as you learn to identify birds.

A field guide is like a family album of birds, but even better. It contains color images of birds, maps showing where the birds can be found during certain seasons of the year, and descriptive text that covers information about the bird that can't be conveyed by either images or maps.

Don't leave home without your field guide! We know it seems like we're trying to talk you into spending your money, but trust us: You *will* want more than just one field guide. Try keeping one in the car, one at the office, and several at home. You just never know when something unfamiliar will turn up, or when the field guide will provide the clinching bit of information to solve the day's greatest bird identification mystery. You'll find, however, that as you get more familiar with bird identification, you'll need to refer to the field guide less and less.

Three Great Card Games

Card games offer some of the most fascinating challenges that you may encounter. In most games, you can manipulate those 52 pieces of pasteboard into infinite permutations and combinations. Working out those combinations is the fun of card games — in almost every game of cards, you don't know what the other players have in their hands. During the course of the game, you use strategy, memory, cunning, and a whole host of other qualities to put together the best hand possible.

At the same time, you don't have to play cards all that well in order to enjoy yourself. Card games allow you to make friends with the people you play with and against. In addition, figuring out the fundamentals of a new card game can bring untold satisfaction.

Here's a description of three of the more popular games:

✔ **Bridge:** Bridge is built on the concept of taking *tricks.* A trick is created when all the players take a turn to play a card from their hands. Whoever plays the highest card in the suit that was *led* (the suit of the first card played in the trick) takes all the cards and wins the trick. If you're playing a game that has a *trump,* or boss, suit and you have no cards in the suit originally led, you can play a trump card and win the trick that way. If more than one player plays a card of the trump suit, whoever plays the highest trump card wins the trick.

Bridge is a partnership game, in theory, with partners sitting opposite one another — for the principal reason that they can only hurl verbal abuse at one another from that relatively safe distance and can't resort to physical violence. The players are traditionally allotted compass directions to distinguish them; therefore, North and South take on East and West.

The two partnerships vie against each other, trying to win as many of the 13 tricks available on each hand as they can. Ultimately, the team that most accurately predicts the number of tricks that they will win on each hand scores points that go toward winning the contest.

If you successfully make as many tricks as you promised to, the points you get go toward a *game.* The first partnership to win two games wins the *rubber.* After a rubber, the players can either quit or start another rubber.

✔ **Euchre:** Euchre is a trick-taking game. A *trick* results when each player plays a card; the player who plays the highest card in the suit of the first card played or the highest *trump card* collects all the cards together and stacks them in front of him — he takes the trick.

In Euchre, you win a hand and score points for taking the majority of the tricks in a hand, which means winning three or more of the five tricks available (Euchre is a five-card game). You get a special bonus if you manage to take all five tricks.

You play the game with partners, but under special circumstances, a member of a partnership can elect to go solo — if she thinks that going alone is worthwhile.

✔ **Poker:** Almost every game of Poker shares some common elements. To start with, Poker is a gambling game and a game of money (or chip) management. The aim on each hand is to win money — or, at the very least, to avoid losing too much money. Your object may just be to have fun, but if that's your sole aim, it probably won't come cheap!

To win a hand in Poker, you must achieve a hand of cards that has a higher rank than any other player at the table. (Hands are ranked by the combination of cards they contain, such as whether they're a *flush* or a *straight*.) You win by forcing the other players to drop out of competition or by outranking their cards in a showdown. If you do so, you collect all the bets — commonly known as the *pot* (or *pool* in England).

Fun with Money: Coin Collecting

Numismatics (pronounced new-miz-*mat*-ics) is the study or collecting of coins, medals, tokens, and the like. Therefore, a *numismatist* (pronounced new-*miz*-ma-tist) is someone who studies or collects coins.

You don't have to know how to pronounce or spell these words to be a coin collector, but if you do decide to take up coin collecting, you'll be wearing them like badges of honor. After all, you'll be joining a rich company of kings and queens, presidents, industrialists, robber barons, brewers, and millions of other folks who have been proud to be known as numismatists.

Are you a collector?

Here's a great way to find out whether you're an accumulator or whether you have the potential to become a coin collector: Visit your local coin store and purchase a folder made for the pennies from the '70s, '80s, and '90s. (A *folder* is a cardboard holder with holes for every different date.) Raid your change jar or go to the bank and buy $20 worth of pennies. Sort the coins out and fill as many different holes as you can. If possible, find the best-looking coin to place in the folder.

What makes a collection complete?

Completion is in the eye of the beholder. Many years ago, collectors were interested only in collecting by date. Therefore, in order to be complete, a collection had to include one coin from every year that coin was minted. Later, collectors developed an interest in *mintmarks* (the tiny letters that indicate where a coin was minted). Suddenly, to be complete, a collection now had to include a coin from every year and every mint. Then came collecting by variety (major or minor changes in the design of a coin) and the definition of completion expanded even further.

Obviously, completion is an ever-changing standard. Taken to the extreme, the only complete collection of coins is one that includes every coin ever made! Striving for completion will drive you nuts, especially if you allow others to define completion for you. Therefore, decide your own goals and set your own standards for completion. When you've completed that collection, consider a new definition of completion and go for it!

After you've gone through all the coins, sit back and take a look at your work.

- ✔ Do you wonder why some coins were harder to find than others?
- ✔ Do you wonder why you couldn't find even a single example of some coins?
- ✔ Are you interested in completing the set?
- ✔ Did you have fun searching through the coins?

If you answered, "yes" to any of these questions, you've discovered the difference between being a collector and being an accumulator.

Four great coins to collect

The most popular coins among collectors today include:

- ✔ **50 states quarters:** In 1999, the U.S. Mint began the 50 states quarters program, a series of 50 special quarter dollars, each one representing an individual state (see Figure 17-1). The new coins share a common *obverse* (coin front); the *reverses* (coin back) are chosen from designs submitted by each state. Each year, five new quarters are issued, thus spreading the program over a total of ten years. The United States Treasury reports that over 100 million Americans are collecting the state quarters, many of them completely new to collecting.

✔ **Sacagawea dollar:** In what was perhaps the biggest and most expensive advertising campaign ever seen for a new coin, the U.S. Mint introduced a new one-dollar coin in 2000 (see Figure 17-2). The new dollar featured the Native American guide Sacagawea (and her infant son) on the front and an eagle on the back. In order to make the coin distinctive, the edge was left flat and plain, and the entire coin was given a coating the color of gold. In a stroke of genius, the U.S. Mint contracted with Wal-Mart stores throughout the country to distribute the new coins in limited quantities. Banks received very few of the coins, creating the false impression that the new coins were rare. In fact, billions of the Sacagawea dollars have been produced and they will never be rare, but try to find one at your local bank or store. On top of that, many people thought the coins were made of real gold!

✔ **New commemorative issues:** The U.S. Mint issues one or more commemorative coins each year in a variety of metals, set combinations, and price levels. New commemorative coins are available in gold, silver, and copper-nickel on subjects that appeal to a broad audience. Each new issue creates excitement among existing collectors and brings new collectors into the hobby.

✔ **Error coins:** In 2000, a number of spectacular error coins stunned the numismatic world. One such error was a coin with the front of a 50 states quarter and the back of a Sacagawea dollar. This was the first U.S. coin ever to bear two denominations. Because the two dies differ in diameter, no one believed it was even possible for such an error to exist. This error received tremendous publicity in the national media, causing millions of noncollectors to begin examining their change. You can bet that many of them have become coin collectors.

Figure 17-1:
The Delaware quarter — first of the 50 states quarters.

Figure 17-2:
The 2000
Sacagawea
dollar.

The Joy of Crafting

The crafting experience has many rewards. Crafting is a relaxing way to unwind at the end of a busy day. You can craft at home, so you can work on a project while enjoying the company of your family — or even including them! The very act of crafting can give you a sense of well-being. But crafting also provides benefits you may never have thought about. Any one of the following benefits may appeal to you:

- ✔ Pride of accomplishment
- ✔ Self-fulfillment
- ✔ Saving money with "do it yourself" projects
- ✔ Personalizing your home
- ✔ Making money by selling your work
- ✔ Finding a new career (teaching your craft to others, for example)

Five paper crafts anyone can do

Here are some paper crafts to tickle your fancy (or would those be "feather" crafts?):

- ✔ **Decorative paper:** You make decorative paper for pretty wrappings. You can also buy decorative paper to cover a plain notebook or a box. Some decorative paper crafts are simple enough for kids to make, like their very own découpage box.

✔ **Rubber stamping:** The simplicity of creating designs with rubber stamps has led to an enormously popular activity. You can use rubber stamps for greeting cards, announcements, invitations, memory books, and anything else you can think of. You can create designs on fabric, on wood, and even on ceramic coffee mugs.

✔ **Photo crafts:** Photographs are the basis for this craft. You can crop snapshots, mount and preserve your photographs, and use them as the main design element in a craft project. You may even want to make a special frame for a holiday photograph.

✔ **Memory book crafts:** Creating a memory book means preserving memorabilia in a scrapbook that you design from your personal collection of keepsakes. Your memory book can include photographs, birthday cards, love letters, a child's drawings, wedding invitations, ticket stubs, announcements, newspaper articles, or scraps of pretty wrapping paper or wallpaper. Memory book crafting is about putting it all together in creative ways.

✔ **Découpage:** This French word literally means *to cut out* and is pronounced *day-coo-pahj*. Découpage is the art of applied cutouts. Using small scissors, you simply cut out designs from materials such as wrapping paper, greeting cards, or wallpaper, arrange the elements on a flat or three-dimensional object such as a plaque or a box, and glue them in place. Many coats of varnish preserve the designs and create a smooth surface.

Two fun paint crafts

This section gives you a couple of ideas for using paint crafts to beautify your home.

✔ **Stenciling:** Stenciling is the process of applying paint to a surface through a previously cut-out pattern. Although the process is as simple as that, you can use it to produce beautiful and dramatic results. Stenciling is one of the most popular paint techniques because it's so easy to master and the results are so rewarding. Furthermore, the design potential is limitless, and you can stencil a design on almost any material.

✔ **Faux finishing:** Faux (a French word meaning *false*) finishes simulate the look of something else: real leather, marble, wood, tortoise shell, stone, or another interesting, irregular texture on a surface, most often walls and furniture. When artfully applied to furniture, for example, it can be difficult to tell whether the finished piece is made of real marble or inexpensive pine.

To achieve these faux finish textures, you use ordinary materials like brushes, rags, paper towels, or plastic wrap to apply two or more paint colors or glazes to a surface. Other faux finishing techniques include spatter painting, sponging, ragging, and combing.

Seven places to find the inspiration you need

Maybe you aren't sure which craft you'd like to try first. Or perhaps you're interested in knowing about a specific craft but aren't sure what project you'd like to make. Many avenues can spark your imagination and get you fired up to begin. Before delving into any one craft, take a little time to look around for ideas. Here are some great places to look:

- ✔ Take a tour through a craft store
- ✔ Browse through fabric stores
- ✔ Take advantage of designer boutiques
- ✔ Look through magazines
- ✔ Check out cable TV shows
- ✔ Wander around a home center
- ✔ Scope out flea markets and yard sales

Four easy fabric crafts

You probably already have in your home everything you need to start a fabric craft project, and if not, all the tools and materials are readily available at craft stores, fabric shops, and even the fabric department of your local discount department store. Check these out:

- ✔ **No-sew** projects work great for those times when you need a fresh look or a quick solution to a decorating problem. Perhaps company's coming and you don't have time to stitch up new pillows to disguise your shabby sofa. Don't despair. Whipping up attractive fabric pillows with clever folds, tucks, and ties — and not one stitch — is quick and easy.

- ✔ **Patchwork** is the process of stitching together, either by hand or on a sewing machine, small pieces of colored fabric in a predetermined pattern to make a whole cloth, such as the top of a quilt or pillow. The same patchwork pattern can look completely different, depending on the choice of fabric colors and prints you use.

- ✔ **Appliqué,** a French word meaning, "to put on," entails applying cut-out fabric pieces on top of a fabric background. You usually design the fabric pieces that create the appliqués to portray something realistic, such as flower petals, a basket, or leaves. You can apply appliqué with hand sewing or a sewing machine.

- ✔ **Needlecrafts** include needlepoint and cross-stitch. Both these needlecrafts require a needle; wool, cotton, or acrylic threads; a background fabric (upon which you do the stitching to create a pattern or design) known as *canvas* or *even-weave;* a thimble (which is optional); and scissors.

Three basic materials from nature

Collecting the materials for a craft is half the fun, and turning the collectibles into decorative projects and gifts is the other half. In this section, you discover what bits of nature's bounty to collect for your craft projects.

- ✔ **Finding seashells:** You find the greatest variety of shells along tropical beaches, but every beach, even those lining freshwater lakes, can offer the crafter something of interest. If you crave exotic shells, they're easily obtained from shell shops and mail-order catalogs.

- ✔ **Collecting flowers and herbs:** Even if you live in a city, you can find flowers for crafting in every season. Most wildflowers are considered weeds and usually grow in the poorest soil and under the worst conditions. However, you can use some of the loveliest wildflowers, such as blue chicory, Queen Anne's lace, buttercups, daisies, and dandelions, to make the prettiest craft projects.

- ✔ **Gathering grasses, leaves, and pinecones:** Grasses, all sorts of leaves, and pinecones are great craft materials to gather from fields and forests. You can press blades of grass to use in a natural collage. Press leaves to decorate boxes or to make decorative cards and place mats. Honeysuckle vines and dune grasses from the beach are also good materials for crafting.

  You can usually find pinecones and pine needles blanketing a woodland floor in the summertime; in the fall, pick up the dried needles from the trees in the backyard. Use pine needles to make elegant little sachet pillows to keep your drawers smelling sweet. You can also combine the fragrant pine needles with dried flower petals and herbs for a potpourri.

After picking or gathering dried pine needles, break them up into small pieces to release their fragrance.

Hooking into a Life of Crochet

You don't have to become an expert in this craft to take advantage of the many beneficial qualities crochet has to offer.

- ✔ The soothing rhythm of creating stitches can calm even the most frazzled nerves.

- ✔ If you're one of those people who can't stand to be idle, crochet is a wonderful way to let your body get a bit of rest, while still feeling like you're not wasting time.

✔ If your family is always clamoring for you to sit down and watch a TV show or a special movie at night, go ahead, but bring along your hook and yarn. This way, you can still feel productive, and at the same time, satisfy your family's needs.

✔ Crochet is a wonderful take-along project. If you're planning a long car trip, bring it with you. You can crochet on trains and planes as well, although these days, you'll have to use plastic hooks when using public transportation. Not to worry though, because they're readily available as well.

✔ Psychological studies have been done on the benefits of crochet. The focus needed when creating something helps to take your mind off the myriad little things that require your attention and gives your brain some much needed down time. It also serves as an outlet for your creativity and provides a sense of satisfaction when you complete your design and can look at it and say, "I created this myself."

✔ Aside from the psychological benefits, physical gains are to be had as well. Crochet has been used as a form of physical therapy for those suffering from various forms of arthritis. The constant movement required helps keep the hands limber and the joints from stiffening up.

So you see, the reasons to enjoy this craft are many. We hope that at least one of these reasons is enough to get you on your way.

Gathering all your tools

This task is as simple as a quick trip to your local craft store. To start with, all you'll need is one or two hooks (preferably by different manufacturers) so that you can determine which style you're most comfortable with, and a skein of yarn. The other stuff that you'll need, such as a pair of scissors and a bag to keep all this stuff in, you're most likely to already have.

Ten tips to help you get started

Everyone has a different way of mastering a new skill. The following list gives you a number of things to keep in mind as you proceed to crochet:

✔ **Find the way of holding the hook and yarn that feels the most natural and comfortable to you.**

✔ **Use a size H-8 U.S. crochet hook and worsted-weight yarn when you're beginning and for practicing new stitches.** These sizes are the best to use when you're first getting started.

✔ **Choose a light to medium, solid-colored yarn.** If the yarn is too dark or multicolored, you may have a hard time seeing the stitches.

✔ **Pick a place to work where there are few distractions.** As when mastering any new skill, being able to focus is important.

✔ **Practice each new stitch or technique by working a swatch until you're comfortable with the stitch before moving on to the next stitch.**

✔ **Different publications may use different names for stitches.** Crochet hasn't been standardized, so you may come across names that you're unfamiliar with. Always read the stitch descriptions at the beginning of each pattern.

✔ **Patterns published in Great Britain or Canada use different terminology for even the basic stitches.** Check to see whether you're working from a British or an American pattern before you begin. You could end up crocheting something completely different from what you intended.

✔ **If you start to feel frustrated with a new skill that you're trying to master, put your hook and yarn down and come back to it later.** Sometimes, a little distance can clear up a previously difficult section.

✔ **If you're really having a hard time understanding a new technique, try to find an experienced crocheter to help explain it.** If you don't know anyone else who crochets, try contacting your local yarn shop. You can usually find someone in a yarn shop who's well versed in the craft, and she's usually more than happy to help someone with a new skill.

✔ **Mark the pages of the books that you feel are most important to you.** That way, you can easily find the reference that you're looking for.

Breaking Out of Crossword Gridlock

Crosswords and other grid games amuse, distract, teach, and — above all — gratify. Puzzles let you expand your mental horizons in concentrated spurts without requiring a big time commitment. They give you an icebreaker at the office or anywhere you may find yourself. They test your powers of recall and challenge your wits.

You can start exploring this exciting universe of puzzles by taking an insider's look at the standard crossword — the well-known checkered grid with clues.

Anatomy of a crossword puzzle

Think of the American-style crossword as a friendly Q&A quiz — kind of a skewed vocabulary test spiced up with a dash of pop culture trivia. Specifically, the following three elements make up the common crossword puzzle:

✔ **Clues:** The question part of your friendly Q&A, the numbered clues appear beside or below the grid. A crossword consists of 37 to 55 clues in each direction, depending upon the grid size.

✔ **Entries:** Think of entries as the answer part of your Q&A. Entries read in two directions: Across answers read from left to right, and Down answers read from top to bottom. The way the entries interlock to spell out answers in both directions gives the grid a kind of beauty and elegance.

✔ **Grid:** You fill in the entries (answers) in their assigned places indicated by a number in the grid. Black squares show you where the entries end. Why black in this age of Technicolor? Because most reading materials are still printed in black ink. (If you're lucky enough to have access to the Internet and the World Wide Web, you can visit some sites that treat you to multi-colored puzzles. A great place to start is Ray Hamel's Index of Crossword Puzzles, at `www.primate/wisc/edu/people/hamel/cp.html`.)

Solving a puzzle

Here are the general steps for solving a crossword puzzle:

1. **Walk through the clues, picking out the clues you can easily answer.**

2. **After you answer one clue, work on the clues that connect to the clue you already answered.**

3. **Scout around for other three- or four-letter entries in the grid.**

4. **Investigate one of the corners, such as the bottom-right corner.**

5. **Check out the mirror image of a corner that you've already solved.**

6. **Continue through until you've successfully filled each square.**

Tuning in to the most popular letters

If you ever tune to *Wheel of Fortune,* you see Vanna White turn over the letters E, S, and R with amazing frequency. These letters may appear anywhere in a word, while letters such as J and M appear more often at the beginning of words. Other letters appear most often at the end of words, while a small group of letters rarely appears at all. Use this knowledge to your advantage!

The crossword alphabet's most (and least) popular letters are

✔ **Most used letters:** S, R, E, T, D, A, I, L

✔ **Least used letters:** J, Q, X, Z, F, V, W

Sometimes you may complete a puzzle without reading and answering every clue. That's the way interlocking letters work: By answering the clues in the opposite direction, words begin to emerge even before you get a chance to read the clue.

Genealogy: You Gotta Have Groundwork

Tracing your family tree is a gratifying challenge for the person doing the research and an exciting project for everyone who helps that person. You're bound to unearth secrets and gain a feeling of closeness and understanding with both your ancestors and your living family.

The following sections offer a few ideas for where you can start digging for information. Perhaps the greatest resource, however, is the Internet.

Where to start

Sometimes, beginning genealogists start their search by trying to discover the identities of their great-great-grandfathers or their families' first immigrants. Such a strategy often becomes frustrating because they either can't find any information or they find something that they assume is true, only to find out later that the information doesn't apply to their family branch. To avoid this mess, we recommend that you conduct your genealogical research one step at a time — and that you begin your genealogical research with yourself by writing a biographical sketch of yourself.

After you complete your biographical sketch, try these places:

- Interviews with family members
- Love letters, laundry receipts, and other similar documents
- Old photo albums
- Birth records
- Marriage records
- Divorce records
- Death records
- Civil records
- Court records

Marching to a different drummer: Searching for military records

Although your ancestors may not have marched to a different drummer, at least one of them probably kept pace with a military beat at some point in life. Military records contain a variety of information. Here are the major types to look for:

✔ Service records

✔ Pension records

✔ Draft or conscription records

✔ Discharge certificate

✔ Copy of orders

A useful guide to military records is "Military Service Records in the National Archives," General Information Leaflet 7, available from the National Archives and Records Administration, Room G-7, 700 Pennsylvania Avenue, NW, Washington, DC 20408.

Coming to your census

Finding genealogical records in your relatives' attics can take you only so far in the pursuit of your ancestors. Although vital records such as those described in the preceding sections can fill in some of the gaps, eventually you need a set of records that provides information on your ancestors that was taken at regular intervals. This type of record is called a *census record*.

Here's a list of such records:

✔ United States Census schedules

✔ Land records

✔ Libraries, archives, and historical societies

Knitting Up Good Karma

The repetitive movements of needles and yarn truly knit up the raveled sleeve of care. Have you ever noticed a knitter's face while working away on the needles? Did you see the expression of relaxed alertness? It's the look we'd all be wearing if our alpha waves were lined up properly. The rhythmic movements of knitting, together with the mental focus needed for building a fabric stitch by stitch, make for a kind of meditation. It's real. Ask anyone who knits.

If you carry your knitting wherever you go, you always bring along a little well-being with you. In a world giving way to things global and anonymous, a knitting project at hand reminds you of the comforts and familiarity of things small, local, and individual.

Calling on your creativity

Knitting is a process of combining yarn, needles, pattern, and color. Even if all you do is follow a sweater pattern by using the exact yarn and needles it calls for, each stitch is of your own making, and no two sweaters from the same pattern worked by different knitters are ever exactly the same.

Chances are, after your first project or two, you'll be venturing with pleasure into the wonderland of new combinations of yarn, pattern stitch, color, and embellishment. You'll be wondering how you'll ever find the time to make all the things you have ideas for.

Ten great knitting books

The ten books in this section comprise a sampling of books that we consider the classics. Most are currently in print, and where we have been able to, we list the most recent edition. Some are out of print but are still available through libraries, the interlibrary loan service, and used book dealers. (Amazon.com can put you in touch with booksellers who have copies of specific out-of-print books.)

New books on various aspects of knitting are published all the time. You can find them in catalogs, local bookstores, and yarn shops. Knitting magazines regularly publish reviews, so look through their suggestions for books to seek out.

> ✔ *Mary Thomas's Knitting Book* and *Mary Thomas's Book of Knitting Patterns.* These books were originally published in 1938 and are now published inexpensively in their original format by Dover (1972). They're excellent reference books with lots of reference material and discussion on the structure of knitting.

> ✔ *Knitters Handbook,* By Montse Stanley, Reader's Digest (1999). Excellent reference with dozens of techniques and their variations.

> ✔ *Alice Starmore's Book of Fair Isle Knitting,* Alice Starmore, Taunton Press (1988). History of Fair Isle knitting, discussion of the use of color-ways, charted stitch patterns, and patterns for sweaters.

✔ *Patterns for Guernseys, Jerseys and Arans: Fishermen's Sweaters from the British Isles,* Gladys Thompson, Dover Publications (1971). A short history of the classic fisherman sweaters of the Aran Isles with charted patterns.

✔ *Knitting in the Nordic Tradition,* Vibeke Lind, Lark Books (1984). Wonderful book with information on specific knitting technique and general construction of hats, mittens, and sweaters.

✔ *The Complete Book of Traditional Scandinavian Knitting,* Sheila McGregor, St. Martin's Press (1984). Short histories of the knitting traditions in the various Scandinavian countries with lots of charted patterns.

✔ *Folk Socks,* Nancy Bush, Interweave Press (1995). Good basic sock book that explains sock construction, shows ways to vary them, and gives patterns for great-looking socks.

✔ *Knitting Lace: A Workshop with Patterns and Projects,* Suzanna Lewis, Taunton Press (1992). An absolutely thorough exploration of the structure of knitted lace and how to make it.

✔ *Designing Knitwear,* Deborah Newton, Taunton Press (1992). An inspirational book by a master knitwear designer.

✔ *Creative Knitting: A New Art Form,* Mary Walker Phillips, Van Nostrand Reinhold Co. (1971). An excellent exploration of the underlying structures of knitted fabric and their creative possibilities.

Meeting the Keyboard Family

Be it a piano, organ, or synthesizer, your keyboard is a wonderful and miraculous instrument. Keyboards come in all shapes and sizes. They can have many keys or just a few; they can be huge pieces of furniture or small little boxes. Whatever the size, shape, or makeup, the instrument is probably a keyboard if any of the following happens:

✔ Musical sound is produced via the pressing of a key or button.

✔ Blowing, bowing, strumming, or plucking it doesn't do much good.

✔ Anyone in the room says, "Hey, dude, nice keyboard!"

The following sections offer brief descriptions of a few types of keyboards that you may want to try. With a few lessons (okay, and a lot of practice, but hey, it's fun!), you'll be playing the "Michigan Rag" in no time!

The acoustic ones

Acoustic means *non-electric.* So, acoustic keyboards are great for starving musicians, because even when you can't pay the electric bill, you can keep playing.

✔ **Pianos:** Pianos, the most popular acoustic keyboard, come in three appropriately named packages:

- **Grand piano:** Think "night at the symphony." You may need a living room the size of a grand ballroom to house one of these instruments. If you don't live in a castle, you may want to consider a baby grand, the smaller version of the grand piano.

- **Upright piano:** These relatively small instruments sit upright against your living room wall. They are the most space efficient type of piano.

- **Baby grand piano:** A smaller version of the grand.

✔ **Harpsichords:** The harpsichord may bear a striking resemblance to the piano in many ways, but strike a key on the harpsichord, and you'll notice the difference between it and a piano immediately. The harpsichord achieves its different sound because of the way the strings are played inside the instrument. Pressing a key causes a corresponding hook (also called a *plectrum*) to pluck the string — much like you would pluck a banjo — tuned to the correct musical tone.

✔ **Pipe organs:** Pipe organs are the world's largest and most complex acoustic instruments. They are great monsters with many, many different-sized pipes. Each pipe has a unique sound. Several pipes played in combination can produce other, non-organ sounds — a trumpet, a flute, a violin, a pig squealing. Okay, so maybe not a pig squealing, but you can get a large variety of sounds. You can find pipe organs at churches, synagogues, universities, and some concert halls.

✔ **Other wooden boxes with funny names:** The centuries have seen the rise and fall of such ridiculously named instruments as the *psaltery,* the *virginals,* the *spinet,* the *hurdy-gurdy,* the *ottavina,* and the *harmonium.* Sounds like you're reading from a Dr. Seuss book, doesn't it? All of these acoustic keyboards were boxes of strings triggered in one way or another by a set of keys. Please send an e-mail to blakeneely@aol.com if you have one.

The electric ones

For considerably less money than you shell out for an acoustic keyboard — not to mention no delivery fees — you can own an electric keyboard that can sound like just about any other instrument on the planet (including an acoustic keyboard).

- ✔ **Synthesizers:** Like bakers, dancers, and burglars, synthesizers derive their name from the work they perform — they *synthesize* sound. (Burglars burgle, by the way.) Synthesizers can imitate virtually any instrument or sound effect you can think of plus tons of generic hums and buzzes that sound cool. Heck, you can make your synthesizer sound like the entire Vienna Philharmonic is in your living room — and without bringing in coffee or extra chairs.

- ✔ **Electronic pianos and organs:** Electronic pianos and organs became a huge success. Simply plug 'em in and have the kids gather 'round. Each comes in a compact size, even smaller than an upright piano, loaded with 10 to 20 different sounds — including piano, organ, trumpet, violin, and banjo.

A Stitch in Time: Sewing

Sewing is perhaps one of the most practical hobbies you can take up. From clothing to curtains to stuffed teddy bears, the possibilities for creation are limitless. We're going to jump right in on this one and give you the rundown on what you need to complete your sewing kit. With so many potential projects in the wings, you'll want to get started right away!

Eight essential tools

Like most hobbies, successful sewing projects begin with a few good tools and a little know-how. Sure, you can collect some of these tools from your household: those old scissors from the garage, the ruler from your desk drawer, and pins scavenged from freshly opened dress shirts, but you'll have a better sewing experience by using the tools intended for the job.

- ✔ Tape measure
- ✔ 8-inch bent dressmaker's shears
- ✔ 5-inch trimming scissors
- ✔ Fabric markers
- ✔ Long, fine, glass-head pins
- ✔ A good iron
- ✔ Needles
- ✔ Seam ripper

Working with a sewing machine

Many folks drag out their 75-year-old clunker from the garage or basement thinking it's good enough for a "beginner." The instruction book for their machine has long since disappeared, and just before completing a project, the machine becomes possessed with demons that sabotage every seam.

Just like your car, you want your sewing machine to be dependable transportation. The machine doesn't have to be a race car, and it doesn't need every modern convenience known to man. It just needs to work well — every time.

Your local sewing machine dealer can show you a wide range of models and prices. Many offer machines on a rental basis, and some dealers let you come into their classrooms and use a machine during open sewing time. You can also take your machine into a dealer, have an honest assessment made about its general working condition and life span, and see whether you can realistically count on using it.

Eleven sewing fundamentals to remember

This section gives you some tips that we wish someone had given us when we first started sewing. Post these hints on a bulletin board in front of you when you sew, or write them on stick-on notes and stick them on your sewing machine.

- **Buy the best fabric you can afford.** The better fabrics are easier to work with and give a better end result.

- **Know your fabric terminology.** Fabrics have selvages, a crosswise grain, a lengthwise grain, and a bias. You need to know what these terms mean in order to understand the pattern layout and cutting instructions, the basic project construction, how to buy the proper amount of fabric, and how to plan your project.

  - *Selvages:* These are the finished edges of the fabric. Selvages run the length of the fabric.

  - *Crosswise grain:* The width of the fabric, perpendicular to the selvages.

  - *Lengthwise grain:* The length of the fabric from one cut end to the other cut end, parallel to the selvages.

  - *Bias:* The 45-degree angle between the crosswise grain and the lengthwise grain.

- **Know the difference between right and wrong.** The *right* side of the fabric is the pretty side that faces to the outside of the project and usually has the brightest colors and more defined textures. The *wrong* side of the fabric is the side that faces to the inside of the project where the seams are.

✔ **Place right sides together.** When sewing, place the right sides of the fabric together to make a seam. This is as basic to sewing as the needle and thread. In other words, place the right side of one piece of fabric against the right side of another piece of fabric (usually matching the notches along the seamline).

✔ **Put the presser foot down before sewing.** The presser foot firmly holds the fabric under the needle. Without the presser foot, the fabric just flops around, and you can't sew straight. When the foot is lowered onto the fabric, the upper thread tension also engages so that the stitches form properly.

✔ **Stop and start sewing the right way.** Stop sewing at the end of the stitch cycle. If you don't, the take-up lever pulls out a length of thread for the next stitch and unthreads the needle. By stopping when the needle is out of the fabric and the take-up lever is at the highest position, you eliminate the problem. Newer sewing machine models have this feature built in.

When stitching a corner, stop with the needle in the dead-lowest position before pivoting at the corner to avoid a skipped stitch.

✔ **Righty, tighty; lefty, loosey:** This little rhyme refers to the tension knobs on your sewing machine and serger. Turning the tension dials to the right makes them tight. Turning them to the left makes them loose — this trick works with pickle and peanut butter jars, as well.

✔ **Test-stitch first:** The best way to make sure that the seamlines will behave is to test the stitch you intend to use for the seam on a scrap piece of fabric before you sew the real thing. This rule works with not only the straight stitch but also all the other stitches available on your sewing machine and serger.

✔ **Sew from bottoms up:** When you sew a vertical seam (like a side seam on a skirt or a pair of pants), sew from the hem edge up to the waistline. When you sew a horizontal seam (like a shoulder seam or a collar), sew from the outside edges toward the center.

✔ **Press seams flat and together — then open or to one side:** Proper pressing technique transforms homemade projects into custom-made masterpieces.

✔ **Clip with your scissors' tips:** Don't cut a hole in your project where you don't want one! Any time you cut from an edge into a seam allowance (for example, when you clip or notch a curve) and toward a seamline, use the very tips of your scissors or shears. This way, you won't accidentally cut into the seamline.

Drawing Inspiration from the Past: Quilt-Making

Quilt-making today is a hobby enjoyed by men and women alike (though women with their needle-nimble fingers still predominate). Machine techniques have replaced tedious hand-piecing and appliqué, but modern quilt-makers still take inspiration from quilts of days past, adapting those designs and techniques to today's lifestyles.

What makes a quilt a quilt?

A quilt — that soft, cozy, comforting hunk of fabric and filling — in its simplest sense is a textile sandwich; in fact, that's how the quilt layers are traditionally described — as a sandwich. This simple sandwich is what distinguishes a quilt from any other sewn object.

All quilts — whether intended for use on a bed or as a potholder — consist of three layers:

✔ **Quilt top:** The topmost layer of the quilt sandwich is the quilt top, which is typically made of fabric blocks that are pieced, appliquéd, or both. A pieced (also called patchwork) quilt top can be made up of tens to hundreds of small pieces of fabric, joined together by hand or machine to create a pattern or repeating design. Modern cutting and stitching techniques make the work of piecing both fun and easy to do.

✔ **Filling (called *batting*):** This layer is the middle layer, or filling, and is made of cotton, wool, or polyester. Batting adds depth and dimension to the quilt as it buffers the quilt top and bottom.

✔ **Backing:** The backing is the bottom layer of the sandwich. It is a large piece of plain or printed cotton that may or may not be pieced together from smaller pieces to create the proper size.

These three layers are held together (quilted) using a series of basic running stitches. The layers can also be tied together by stitching yarn, narrow ribbon, or pearl cotton through the layers at regular intervals and tying off the ends to hold the layers of the sandwich together. However you do it, your goal is to prevent the layers from shifting.

Two techniques for creating a quilt

Here are the two basic techniques for creating a quilt:

- **Patchwork** is the most popular form of quilt-making and uses basic shapes such as squares, triangles, rectangles, and hexagons to form patterns ranging from simple to complex. Various patterns can be pieced into one block, and each block is then pieced to another to create the overall quilt design. One block can be made of many pieces, or just one piece.

- **Appliqué** is another method of creating quilt tops. To create an appliquéd quilt top, you stitch various fabric shapes on top of a base fabric. Machine appliqué provides a variety of possibilities and is easy enough for even the rank beginner to master. Appliqué takes a bit longer to stitch than piecing, even by machine, but you can use it to create patterns that can't be pieced, such as dainty flowers with gracefully curving stems.

Stamps, Stamps — Everywhere

Before you collect, you accumulate. Yes, it's the same concept as crawling before you walk. An accumulation literally may be a pile of stamps, whether loose on a desk, in a drawer, or in a large envelope. You will not be able to find a given item instantly; you will not have any idea of what is included in the pile. A collection has been formed (very often from an accumulation) and has enough of a form that you're able to locate and identify items within it.

Here are a couple of attributes of a stamp *accumulation:*

- Current possessions are in no particular order.
- You don't plan on purchasing any more.

And here are a couple of attributes of a stamp *collection:*

- Orderly storing of items in album, stock book, or individual envelopes
- Purchases made to remain current with new issues and/or fill in previous issues

Four basic steps to creating a collection

Before you get to the stage of actually calling what you have a *collection,* you need to move beyond buying stamps at the post office and putting them into a drawer. Some basic steps will take you into the collector's arena:

✔ **Commit to caring for your stamps and finding a good home for them.** If nothing else, leaving those purchases in a drawer is not good for the stamps themselves. They need some sort of a home — an album, a glassine, or at least a box.

✔ **Strategize your purchases.** Beyond caring for the stamps, you need to develop some order to your collecting. This may be as simple as being certain you purchase each new stamp available at your post office. More items are available to you if your post office has a philatelic window.

✔ **Establish a relationship with one or more stamp dealers.** This relationship may extend to the point of having them send you material they believe fits your collection. You also may choose to shop from ads in stamp-collecting publications or online offerings, finding all items new to your collection by yourself.

✔ **Use a printed catalogue to note the stamps you have and (just as important) those you do not have.** The U.S. Postal Service annually publishes a colorful catalogue of U.S. stamps, *The Postal Service Guide to U. S. Stamps,* covering everything from 1847 to the present. A host of private publishers offers a wide range of such catalogues; some are even available on CD-ROMs that provide more detail.

The three types of stamp collections

In a nutshell, here are the three basic types of postage stamp collections:

✔ **Country:** You can create a stamp collection from the stamps available where you live or visit, the land of your ancestors, or even a travel fantasy. More than 650 countries have issued stamps from 1840 to the present, with many of those countries no longer in existence under the same name and/or government. Currently, more than 260 countries issue postage stamps. Each country's stamps are a possibility for a most interesting collection.

✔ **Thematic/topical:** A stamp collection may be based on the design of the stamp rather than what country it was made in. Orangutans depicted on stamps certainly are a possibility, as are spiders. And make your dreams come true with Ferrari racing cars. *Topical* is used in the United States; other countries use *thematic.*

✔ **Type of mail service:** Airmail, postage due, or one of an array of lesser-known services can also be the basis for a collection. Many countries issue stamps specifically for airmail service. The United States still has such stamps in its inventory, although the number is much less now that airmail service is limited to foreign mail. Airmail is no longer a domestic-mail service. The appearance of a postage-due stamp on an envelope you receive denotes that the sender did not pay the full postage cost. United States Post Office staff members hand stamp or even scrawl with a pen to show postage due, although there have been quite a few postage-due stamps over the years. The situation is somewhat similar with most other countries.

Where can I purchase . . . ?

Stamp-collecting periodicals are a good source of persons and places to purchase stamps. The World Wide Web is another excellent source of stamp-selling sites.

Fun freebies for your hobby

Some hobbies can get a bit pricey after a while, so here are some freebies to keep you in the black:

✔ www.rubyglen.com/crafts.htm: Print out free craft projects and patterns for basketry, decoupaging, stamping, kids' crafts, beading, candle-making, crocheting, painting, needlework, and woodworking. The site also lists special links just for crafters.

✔ www.freequilt.com: This site is a clearinghouse for all things free for quilters. Browse through quilt patterns and project categories like appliqué, baby quilts, blocks, mini-quilts, novelty quilts, paper piecing, and miscellaneous quilt tips and techniques. Check back often because the site is constantly updated.

✔ http://barbscraftbooks.tripod.com/barbscrochet: Check out this free needlecraft pattern site for crochet and knitting patterns, cross-stitch information, a needlecraft message board, and links to other sites with free needlecraft patterns. At least two new free crochet patterns or free knitting patterns are added monthly.

✔ www.paintingonjars.com/freepat.html: If you like unique painting projects that make great gifts, try out this site for free patterns, directions, and supply lists for jar painting.

✔ www.freecraftz.com: Print out free patterns for tole painting, scroll saw projects, woodworking, and other crafts. New patterns are added regularly.

✔ www.freesheetmusicguide.com: If you love playing the piano or guitar and want to expand your repertoire, you might want to explore this easy-to-use directory of free, downloadable sheet music. Here's a sampling of the directory categories: pop/rock, jazz, classical, Christian worship or hymns, Christmas folk, early American, and patriotic.

Part VI
Here You Go Again: Travel

The 5th Wave   By Rich Tennant

"Do I like arugula? I love arugula! One of my favorite vacations was a cruise to arugula."

In this part . . .

Many people find that mid-life and beyond is an ideal time to travel the country or even the world. The chapters in this part provide a reading tour of the most popular sunny hot spots in the United States to plunk down your beach chair and put up your feet, the most scintillating big cities that folks like to visit for a good time, and a whole slew of must-see cities and sites in Europe. You also get the rundown on cruise vacations, and places and vacation styles that reconnect you with nature.

Chapter 18

Following the Sun

In This Chapter

▶ Fun in the sun: America's hot spots

▶ All aboard! Cruise vacations

his chapter gives you the rundown on some of America's greatest hot spots to get away from winter and enjoy some warm weather. Whether you're an avid golfer or just looking to relax on the beach, you'll find what you're seeking in Arizona, California, Florida, or Hawaii.

And if that's not enough, we round things up by giving you a briefing on a way of vacationing that's gaining popularity at breakneck speed: cruise vacations.

Fasten your seatbelts: The tour starts here!

Arizona: Some Like It Hot

Some folks think Arizona is all desert and cowboys. But here are some facts about Arizona you may find surprising:

- ✔ Favorite activities among the locals include golfing, hiking, and mountain biking (not roping cattle).

- ✔ Arizona is home to many great spas — terrific for pampering skin that didn't benefit from quite enough sunscreen.

- ✔ Arizona's Sonoran Desert is lush with vegetation.

- ✔ Much of the income of the southern Native American nations comes from casinos.

- ✔ A long line often forms for the best Mexican restaurants, which tend to be in lively downtown barrios.

The scenery is as spectacular as anything you'd ever imagine (more than 80 percent of the state is undeveloped), ancient traditions are alive and well on the Indian reservations, and several cattle ranches are still active; some even rent their rooms.

Arizona has long stretches of open roads and a highway speed limit of 75 mph. Zooming down those long, wide roads in a convertible with your favorite tunes blaring on the radio is a great way to spend an afternoon.

Romancing the cities

Be prepared: Arizona's major urban areas are not the compact, strollable spaces that most travelers associate with the term *city*. Both Phoenix and Tucson came of age when the United States was romancing the auto and their original historic centers didn't hold. Take these two sprawling Sonoran Desert metropolises for what they are — the (heat) waves of the future.

- ✔ **Phoenix:** Arizona's largest, most populous city is actually a vast metropolitan complex. Phoenix, the state capital, and Scottsdale are its two best-known components. Growing rapidly and adding great restaurants, shopping centers, and resorts, but subtracting desert terrain, the Valley is quintessentially New West. Side trips from the Valley explore a far more pristine landscape (the Apache Trail), revisit Arizona's Hohokam past (Casa Grande), and provide a possible antidote against future shock (Arcosanti), among others.

- ✔ **Tucson:** The state's "second city" is first in terms of history and culture. Established almost a century earlier than Phoenix, Tucson still has Old West and Spanish character. The city also has more protected land, including a national park devoted to cacti (Saguaro National Park). But the urban math formula works here, too. Unbridled growth adds leisure amenities, while diminishing natural beauty. Side trips from Tucson lead to an observatory (Kitt Peak) and more cacti (Organ Pipe) and to a place where people once lived in a glass house (Biosphere 2).

Arizona's four regions

The east central and far northwestern portions of the state have their appeal but don't significantly add to a first-time visitor's experience. You can break down the state's remaining areas into the following prime touring regions. Starting from the south . . .

- ✔ **The Southeast:** The section southeast of Tucson has everything: Old West color, including Tombstone and several remote guest ranches; venerable Spanish missions and new wineries; outdoor activities, from horseback riding to bird-watching; the state's latest underground attraction, Kartchner Caverns; and great shopping down Mexico way.

- ✔ **Central:** Within the up-and-down area northwest of Phoenix, renowned for its red rocks, granite dells, and spreading desert, Sedona vies with Scottsdale for the state's "ritziest little town" title; Prescott, the one-time territorial capital, is rich with Victoriana; and Wickenburg keeps its mining legends alive through its many dude ranches. Near Sedona, the Verde Valley offers a lively ghost town, a great train ride, and two well-preserved Indian ruins.

✔ **Grand Canyon and the Northwest:** The Grand Canyon speaks — or should we say gapes? — for itself, but the rest of the northwest area may surprise you. For example, Flagstaff, Arizona's third-largest city, has a kickback college-town charm. Nearby, you can visit ancient dwellings that were left behind in a land ravaged, and then fertilized, by some not-so-ancient volcanoes.

✔ **The Northeast and Indian country:** One of Arizona's most remote and intriguing regions encompasses landscapes that define the Southwest, including Monument Valley, Canyon de Chelly, and Petrified National Forest; the native cultures of the Navajo and the Hopi that keep its spiritual heart beating; splashy attractions like Lake Powell; and the kicky Route 66.

Deciding when to go

How do you decide what time of year to travel to Arizona? This section lets you weigh the pros and cons of visiting during different times of year.

Because of Arizona's size and its varied topography, vacationing in the northern part of the state on the Colorado Plateau is a completely different experience from touring the Sonoran Desert in the south. Because of great temperature and altitude variations, the state's two sections are practically mirror opposites of each other — meaning Arizona always has great weather somewhere.

Southern Arizona

If you're like us and don't mind the heat — but, honey, when southern Arizona is hot, it's hot — you won't find a bad time of the year to visit. Spring — when the mercury hasn't peaked, but room prices have — is prime. Unless the winter's unusually dry, the desert blooms with wildflowers.

✔ **Winter:** The weather's glorious — sunny and warm — and perfect for sightseeing and anything else you want to do. Everything's happening — events, festivals, music, and theater programs — you name it. But keep in mind that room prices are at their highest, and crowds are at their largest — which means lots of traffic, too.

✔ **Spring:** The desert is usually a flowering wonderland, and room rates start to dip. Temperatures do begin to creep up, however; some days may be uncomfortably warm and you may enjoy better weather in your hometown.

✔ **Summer:** You can try the resort of your dreams for rock-bottom rates — and fancy restaurants run summer specials. The streets are uncrowded, thanks to the departure of students and *snowbirds* (long-term winter visitors). But keep in mind that the sizzling of summer is literal, and desert tours, hikes, and other activities slow or cease; many restaurants in the southeast close when their owners head for the hills.

✔ **Fall:** The room rates are still fairly low, and activities like concerts and shows come back on track. It takes a while to cure that heat hangover, however; temperatures may still be uncomfortable. Also keep in mind that the University of Arizona and Arizona State University freshmen are beginners at driving around the streets of Tucson and Greater Phoenix.

Northern Arizona

Northern Arizona doesn't have any loser seasons — even the cold isn't very cold. The fall is prime because the crowd's thin and the weather's crisp and comfortable. Stay away from the Grand Canyon in summer, though, if you want to bond with nature more than with your fellow human beings' elbows.

✔ **Summer:** The weather is great — sunny, warm, and clear — and everything's open and happening. Note, however, that everyone wants to visit in summer; the Grand Canyon is a zoo, and the room rates are as high as the sun in the sky.

✔ **Fall:** The crowds go back to school and work. The weather's still sunny and an actual autumn season begins — colored leaves and all. But keep in mind many places begin observing shorter hours; some facilities start to close. The rates aren't at their lowest yet.

✔ **Winter:** No scenery is prettier than the snow against the Grand Canyon (and Flagstaff is a winter sports mecca). If no snow is on the ground, the weather is crisp and clear. The room rates — and the crowds — bottom out; you enjoy your pick of lodgings. Note, however, that the Grand Canyon's North Rim is closed, and you can't swim in Lake Powell without freezing your patooties off. Fewer services are offered than at any other time of year.

✔ **Spring:** The weather warms up. Facilities reopen, but the crowds aren't present. But keep in mind that Mother Nature is erratic; snow may fall, the roads may close, and the temperature's still not warm enough to dip into Lake Powell. The rates begin to warm up, too.

California: The Golden State

With nearly 159,000 square miles of land and a 1,264-mile coastline, California is the third largest state in the United States. Sure, both Alaska and Texas are bigger — but California's uniqueness stems from much more than size. California is like the high school homecoming queen whose natural beauty and innate poise make the rest of the student body sneer at her while wanting to bask in her glow at the very same time. They don't call this the Golden State for nothing, after all.

California is really an awesome place, in the truest sense (not the surfer dude sense) of the word. Its jaw-dropping diversity is the real kick in the pants, more than anything else. Consider the following:

✔ With two of the nation's largest megalopolises — the San Francisco Bay area, which has grown beyond speculators' wildest dreams with the rise of Silicon Valley, and metropolitan Los Angeles, whose urban sprawl has a glamorous heart called Hollywood — California has the largest, wealthiest, and most urbanized population of any state in the nation.

✔ California is an agricultural wonderland whose bounty runs the gamut from artichokes, raisins, garlic, and asparagus to some of the finest winemaking grapes in the world.

✔ Even with its urbanization and agricultural foundation, California still manages to be home to some of the country's most striking and varied wilderness — from purple mountains' majesty to arid, marvelously barren desert.

✔ Within the natural landscape alone, the contrast is unparalleled. Take Mount Whitney and Death Valley as a case in point: At 14,494 feet above and 282 feet below sea level, respectively, they are the highest and lowest points in the continental United States — and just 85 miles separates them. Wow!

Four Regions to Visit

Unless you have a couple of months to spare for vacation (lucky you!) though, you're not going to see everything this marvelous, multifaceted state has to offer. You know what? Don't even waste time trying. Frankly, some parts of California are much worthier of your valuable time and hard-earned dollars than others. Here are some of our favorite regions:

✔ **The North Coast:** The wild and woolly coastal region north of the San Francisco Bay area offers some of California's most breathtaking scenery. It's quiet, remote, and ruggedly handsome, with spectacular nature broken only by the occasional picturesque village. Of those villages, none is more lovely than romantic Mendocino, a postage stamp of a town situated on a majestic headland. Mendocino serves as a good jumping-off point for exploring the regal Redwood Country, which starts just inland and north of Mendocino.

✔ **The Sierra Nevada:** Travel inland from the Bay Area or North Coast and you'll soon reach the Sierra Nevada, the magnificently rugged, granite-peaked mountain range that defines northeast and east-central California. This high-altitude region is so uniquely stunning that such geniuses as Mark Twain and Ansel Adams considered it one of their greatest inspirations. The Sierra Nevada stirred John Muir to do no less than found the U.S. National Park system.

Possibly the greatest of the national parks is spectacular Yosemite National Park, whose natural wonders include such record-setters as Yosemite Falls (North America's tallest waterfall) and El Capitan (the world's largest granite monolith).

Also in the High Sierra rests the United States' biggest and most beautiful alpine lake, sparkling Lake Tahoe — California's finest outdoor playground. Come in the winter to ski, in the summer to hike, bike, kayak, sail . . . you name it. If you're a history buff, consider taking a day to visit the Gold Country, the epicenter of California's 19th-century gold rush hysteria, on your way to or from Tahoe.

✔ **The San Francisco Bay Area:** The prime draw of the San Francisco Bay area is the loveliest and most beguiling city in America, San Francisco. "The city" (as locals call it — never "Frisco") is smaller than you may expect, loaded with personality in all corners, and pleasant to visit year-round. It's also the one destination in the Driving State where you can easily get around without a car.

If San Francisco is the ultimate urban destination, then the gorgeous Napa Valley — America's premier wine-growing region — is the embodiment of pastoral escape. This super-fertile valley brims with world-class wine-tasting rooms and some of the country's finest restaurants and inns. Some people consider it hip to prefer the neighboring Sonoma Valley, but if this is your first trip to California's wine country, start with the Napa Valley — the biggest, brightest, and best.

✔ **The Central Coast:** The central coast — that stretch between San Francisco and Los Angeles — represents California at its very best. The drive along Highway 1 — the world-famous Pacific Coast Highway — is one of the most scenic in the world. Keep in mind, however, that the drive is slow going and quite curvy — real Dramamine territory, so stock up.

Along the way down the coast, you'll find

- Santa Cruz, California's quintessential, and kinda wacky, surf town.

- The Monterey Peninsula, which cradles Monterey Bay, one of the richest and most diverse marine habitats on earth, and home to the Monterey Bay Aquarium, one of California's all-time top attractions, and the golf mecca Pebble Beach.

- Big Sur, where the spectacular wilderness and breathtaking views are unhindered by all but the most minimal development.

- Hearst Castle, one of the most outrageous private homes ever built and a real hoot to tour.

Driving farther down the coast puts you squarely in Southern California. If you have little ones in tow or a strong affinity for good pastry, head inland to Danish Solvang, a storybook town straight out of Scandinavia. Or visit Santa Barbara, a seaside jewel that embodies the Southern California dream — perfect for clocking in some top-quality relaxation time.

The big three: Southern California's cities

Southern California is where things get crazy, in a good way. Here are three great cities where you can get a little nutty, whether you're enjoying a good traffic jam or hanging with the Mouse:

- ✔ **Los Angeles (L.A.)** is by far the poster child for urban sprawl, the city we all love to hate — and it isn't for everybody. But think twice before you reject it out of hand. In addition to being celeb-rich and gloriously silly, it also happens to be the state's finest museum town. Really.

- ✔ **Anaheim (Orange County)** is home to Disneyland, the Happiest Place on Earth. This location is the original theme park, and it's an unadulterated blast for kids of all ages (even grown-up ones with jobs and mortgages). Consider visiting again even if you've been before, because you'll find plenty of new things to see and do — including a brand-new Disney park, California Adventure, set to open in mid-2001.

- ✔ **San Diego** is a significantly more easygoing city than L.A. — or even San Francisco, for that matter. This town's a real beaut, with a wonderfully mellow vibe, golden beaches galore, and plenty of memory-making diversions, most notably three terrific animal parks: the San Diego Zoo, SeaWorld, and the Wild Animal Park. If that's not enough to keep you and the kids happy and busy, also consider the multifaceted joys of Balboa Park (the second-largest city park in the country, after the Big Apple's Central Park) and the metro area's newest theme-park addition, groovy LEGOLAND.

Just deserts

California's desert is most fun to visit in any season but summer, when the scorching heat can be a bit much to bear. Still, some people enjoy summer in the desert, when prices are low and crowds are minimal (just pack your sunscreen — number 30 or higher, preferably). Here are some interesting sites to explore:

- ✔ **Palm Springs:** The Palm Springs area is the place to go for desert cool. This is the manicured side of the desert, where streets bear names like Frank Sinatra Drive, and where golf greens, swimming pools, spa treatments, and martinis rule the day. What's more, easy access to unspoiled nature makes Palm Springs appealing even to those who couldn't care less about the prefabricated glamour or retro-groovy stuff.

✔ **Joshua Tree National Park:** You can easily visit unspoiled Joshua Tree National Park on a day trip from Palm Springs. The stark, scruffy high-desert landscape upends traditional notions of natural beauty, forgoing leafy greenery for mind-bending shapes, majestic scale, and otherworldly hues.

✔ **Death Valley National Park:** Both shockingly barren and stunningly beautiful, Death Valley National Park pumps up the otherworldliness to new heights. Still, it's awfully remote; unless you have a lot of vacation time, you may be better off saving Death Valley for a future trip.

Understanding California's climate

Microclimates are small areas of uniform climate that generally differ from the surrounding climate — and California has lots of them. A perfectly plausible scenario sees you skiing in Tahoe in the morning, cruising around the Napa Valley in shorts and T-shirts in the afternoon, and bundling up against the damp, cold ocean breezes in Mendocino by evening.

Here are the rules to live by:

✔ The most important weather predictor is your location: coast or inland, north or south. As a general rule, the weather will likely be cool and windy along the coastline — even in July and August — and warmer and perpetually sunnier as you move inland.

✔ California weather is highly changeable. The bottom line: Be prepared for dramatic daily changes, even in summer. Layering your clothes is always a good idea.

Florida: The Sunshine State

If you want to come to Florida but don't know much about it, you're in good company. Even Florida natives are lucky if they get to know everything about their own backyards. The best way to tackle the sunshine state is to pick a region to explore, and go from there.

Diving into Florida's four main regions

Here are some areas of Florida you won't want to miss; pick one or all to visit, depending on the time you have to travel.

✔ **South Florida:** Miami, the unofficial capital of the South Florida region, is both picturesque and sophisticated, with a pulsating nightlife. With everything from the hot clubs of South Beach to the architectural marvels Villa Vizcaya and Coral Castle, you can't be bored in Miami. But Miami is a moderately expensive destination, and it has many of the other problems associated with a metropolis, including crime, congestion, and pollution.

Other great places to visit in the South Florida region include

- **The Keys:** The mood and the magic of the Keys are a little off-center, but that's just the Conch Republic's way of life. The Keys are best for those who want to kick back and forget about following a schedule.

- **The Everglades:** The Everglades are Florida's greatest natural treasure.

- **Palm Beach:** Palm Beach is the winter home of some of America's rich and famous. Even if you're not one of them, it's fun to window shop along Worth Avenue, known as the Rodeo Drive of the South.

  Fort Lauderdale: Fort Lauderdale has several of Florida's best golf courses, and the burgeoning yet historic downtown riverfront area, with shops, dining, and assorted amusements, is one of the region's most popular new tourist draws.

✔ **The Gulf Coast:** With some exceptions, this coast hasn't experienced the explosive growth that the Atlantic side has. The water is part of the reason. The Atlantic is alive with crashing waves, as good as the surf gets in Florida. Across the way, the Gulf of Mexico is calm and tepid, like a soothing tub.

Here are some places worth visiting at least once:

- **Tampa:** Tampa's Latin influence adds a welcome touch to the region's food, culture, and architecture. The city has a moderately good arts calendar, a dandy nightclub scene in Ybor City, and Busch Gardens, a theme park that rivals Orlando's offerings. St. Petersburg's signature attractions include its Gulf Beaches, the Salvador Dalí Museum, and the Florida International Museum.

- **Sarasota:** Sarasota's Asolo Theatre and the Ringling Museum of Art give the cultural community plenty of reason to crow. Gulf-view towns, such as Naples, Marco Island, and Fort Myers, are quieter than most of Florida's other beachfront cities. This stretch of the coast has more than 10,000 islands including Sanibel, Captiva, Gasparilla, and Boca Grande.

On the downside, this area is spread far and wide. There are few day-filling activities, and you'll have to drive a while to get to your next stop.

✔ **Central Florida:** If Orlando were a rock group, it would be called "Mickey and the Wannabes." In Central Florida, Walt Disney World is the lead vocalist, Universal Orlando and SeaWorld play the guitar and keyboards, and dozens of smaller attractions are behind the drums. This area truly is fantasyland, but the crowds, cost, and confusion can turn your trip into a frightful experience.

If ever there were a destination that virtually had it all, Orlando is it, which is why many people love it. It's a reasonably convenient place to park yourself: Much of the hoopla is in two areas, Lake Buena Vista and International Drive, and most of its neighborhoods have just about everything you need for a fantastic vacation.

On the flip side, traffic and crowds can be brutal, and the theme parks are expensive. (Most visits cost a family of four $180 — just for admission.)

✔ **The Great North:** Daytona Beach's calling cards are bikinis, bikers, and bullet cars. Daytona is a wide stretch of white sand, bathed in frothy Atlantic waters. Aside from the beach, Daytona's most popular tourist attractions are the Daytona International Speedway and Daytona USA, a high-tech, interactive, jump-and-shout exhibit in front of the speedway. But if you're not into sun, sand, and speed, Daytona may feel like you woke up in Wayne's World with a Southern twang. And if you arrive in March and aren't a member of the spring-break squad, you're likely to feel out of place on the beach.

Here are some other sites to check out:

- **St. Augustine:** The oldest city in the United States, St. Augustine (founded in 1565), is located a little farther north of Daytona on the Atlantic coast. If the idea of forts and other musty mysteries appeals to you, here's a chance to go back to the days of the earliest colonization.

- **Jacksonville:** Continuing north, Jacksonville is a Navy town that has traded paper mills for sprawl and interstate clutter. The Jacksonville Zoo and the natural beaches, such as the one at Little Talbot Island State Park, are pluses, but most tourists find themselves having to scatter to find things to do in the Jacksonville area.

- **Amelia Island Plantation:** One of northeast Florida's nicer resorts, Amelia Island Plantation is 30 miles north. This resort blends environmental consciousness with top-flight golf, tennis, and beach activities. At the other end of the island, Fort Clinch State Park, near Fernandina Beach, offers living-history presentations that are a joy to see.

- **Pensacola:** Pensacola's historic area is a blend of Spanish, French, and British cultures. The city also is the home of the National Museum of Naval Aviation and the Flora-Bama Lounge, where you may get to witness the world championship mullet toss. But like

Jacksonville, Pensacola isn't an especially popular choice among visitors.

- **The Redneck Riviera:** This area — basically, Fort Walton Beach, Destin, and Panama City — got its name because of its popularity among tourists from Georgia and Alabama. Expect beautiful beaches and great fishing, combined with honky-tonks, glitter, and spring-breakers — a combination that often makes this Riviera loud and rowdy.

The secret of the seasons

Seasons? You bet Florida has them.

- ✔ **Spring:** Spring is a popular vacation time for most travelers, and Florida is no different. In the spring, the weather is mild, and the flowers bloom. And accommodations that give discounts give them now. Without a winter, however, a long spring is rare. Temps can get warm and sticky in April (heat + humidity = Hades). Also, the pollen drives hay-fever sufferers crazy. Keep in mind that spring break cometh, as well. Avoid it unless you're a breaker.

- ✔ **Summer:** Florida bustles during the summer season, in spite of the sizzling temperatures. In the summer, you can enjoy picturesque 6 a.m. sunrises and 9 p.m. sunsets. August means back-to-school sales at malls and outlets, but with the crowds attracted by this season, don't expect discounts for accommodations or food. To beat the blaring heat of summer, savvy travelers spend the middle of the day indoors where it's air conditioned, whether it's in a cool attraction or their accommodations. Also keep in mind that summer is the heart of hurricane season, and thunderstorms are common.

- ✔ **Fall:** Florida has the same fiery reds, brilliant oranges, and screaming yellows as New England in the fall. The difference is that Florida's lasts about 17 minutes. Accommodations that give discounts do so in the fall, and lines and crowds begin to shrink. Although it's cooler in the fall, temps aren't as mild as those in spring until Thanksgiving or later. Also, the hurricane season lasts through November and activity can run high in September and October.

- ✔ **Winter:** Florida doesn't have a true winter, just a few days at or near freezing, followed by mild, sunny weather. Lines are short in many tourist areas during most of the winter season. The mid-December to early January holidays, however, are nearly as crowded as the dead of summer, and after mid-December arrives, prices rise.

The Hawaiian Islands

Hawaii isn't just one place — it's an entire island chain comprising eight major islands and 124 islets. Together they form a 1,500-mile crescent that slices a lush, volcanic swath through the sparkling Pacific waters just above the equator (in the north Pacific Ocean, not the south Pacific, as many believe).

Where to go: The main islands

Hawaii's eight main islands are

✔ **Oahu (oh-WA-hoo):** Oahu is the most developed of the Hawaiian Islands and its greatest population center — about 75% of Hawaii's residents (about 875,000 people) live on this gateway island. About three-quarters of Oahuans reside in Honolulu, the 11th largest city in the United States, and the only real incorporated city in the state.

Oahu is home to some of Hawaii's best sightseeing, including the

- **USS Arizona Memorial** in Pearl Harbor, the most moving tribute to World War II in existence.

- **The Bishop Museum,** the best little museum in the Pacific.

- **The Polynesian Cultural Center,** the world's best cultural theme park.

- **Waikiki Beach,** a fabulous beach where travelers from around the world regularly converge.

✔ **Maui (MOW-ee):** When people think Hawaiian paradise, they usually think Maui. Almost everyone who comes here falls in love with this island, and for good reason: It offers the ideal mix of unspoiled natural beauty and tropical sophistication, action-packed fun and laid-back island style. In fact, Maui has so much of that special something that the readers of *Condé Nast Traveler* have voted Maui "Best Island in the World" for eight years running, and "World's Best Travel Destination" five years in a row.

✔ **Hawaii** (commonly called the *Big Island*): Salt-and-pepper beaches, primal rain forests, stark lava fields as far as the eye can see — this otherworldly island simply may not be your idea of a tropical paradise. But travelers with a passion for adventure, an eye for the unusual, or a taste for luxury will think that they've found heaven on earth.

✔ **Kauai (ka-WAH-ee):** Of all the Hawaiian islands, Kauai is the one that comes closest to embodying the Hawaiian ideal — it's the ultimate in tropical romance and beauty. Even Hollywood thinks so, which is why Kauai has had starring roles as Paradise in movies ranging from *Blue Hawaii* and *South Pacific* to *Jurassic Park*. The island landscape doesn't get any more spectacular than what you find on Kauai. Every time we visit, we're newly wowed by how exquisite it all is. Kauai boasts the kind of natural beauty that cameras can't really capture, that even mere memory can't conjure up.

✔ **Molokai (mo-lo-k-EYE):** Sleepy Molokai is a rural island that's largely untouched by modern development (although, as residents like to boast, they do have KFC now). This lean, funky, scruffy little place is often called the *most* Hawaiian island because it's the birthplace of the hula, and it has a larger native Hawaiian population than any other in the chain. Although it offers some lovely, secluded beaches, the island's most famous site is Kalaupapa National Historical Park, a world-famous 19th-century leper colony that can only be reached by mule, prop plane, or helicopter.

✔ **Lanai (la-NAH-ee):** This tiny island (pop. 3,500) is featured on a few packages, but we don't recommend spending time here until you conquer the other islands. Staying on Lanai is less a Hawaiian experience and more a generic park-yourself-at-a-resort vacation, which you can do with more local flavor elsewhere in the islands.

✔ **Niihau (nee-EE-how) and Kahoolawe (ka-ho-ho-LA-vay):** Niihau is a privately owned island with a tiny population, and Kahoolawe is an unpopulated island that was formerly a U.S. military bombing target.

These islands make up more than 99 percent of the state's land mass. Of these, the first six are prime tourist destinations, each with its own personality, attractions, and tropical appeal. Of the six islands that are open to tourists, four are ideal choices for first-time visits to Hawaii: Oahu, Maui, the Big Island, and Kauai.

Understanding Hawaii's climate

Hawaii lies at the edge of the tropics, so it really has only two seasons: warm (winter) and warmer (summer). Temperatures generally don't vary much more than 15 degrees or so from season to season, depending on where you are. The average daytime summer temperature at sea level is 85°F, and the average daytime winter temperature is 78°F.

Here are some additional points to keep in mind:

✔ Temperatures stay even steadier when you consider the coastal areas alone: At Waikiki, the average summer high is 87°F, and the average winter high is 82°F — not much difference. Nighttime temps drop about 10 to 15 degrees — less in summer, a little more in winter. August is usually the warmest month of the year; February and March are the coolest months. Almost-constant trade winds bring a cooling breeze even in the hottest weather.

✔ Each of the islands has a *leeward* side (the west and south shores of the islands), which tends to be hot and dry, and a *windward* side (the east and north shores), which is generally cooler and wetter. For sun-baked, desert-like weather, visit the leeward side of an island. When you want lush, jungle-like weather, go windward.

✔ Locals like to say that if you don't like the weather, just get in the car and drive — you're bound to find something different. That's because each island also has many microclimates, which are highly localized weather patterns based on a region's unique position and topography. On the Big Island, for example, Hilo gets 180 inches of rainfall annually, which makes it the wettest city in the nation — yet only 60 miles away is desert-like Puako, which gets less than 6 inches of rain per year.

✔ Generally speaking, each island has a mountain (or mountains) at its center. The higher you go in elevation, the cooler it gets. Thus, if you travel inland and upward, the weather can change from summer to winter in a matter of hours. If you visit Maui's Haleakala National Park, for instance, you climb from sea level to 10,000 feet in just 37 miles — and it's not uncommon for the temperature to be 30 to 35 degrees cooler at the summit than it is at the beach.

✔ In general, November to March marks Hawaii's rainy season, and summer is considered the dry season. The weather can get gray during this season, but, fortunately, it seldom rains for more than three days in a row. Winter isn't a bad time to go to Hawaii; the sun's just a little less reliable, that's all.

The good news about Hawaii's rainy season is that it's almost never raining *everywhere* on an island, even in winter. So if it's raining on your parade, just get in the car and drive — you'll likely reach a sunny spot in no time. (The south and west coasts are usually your best bet.)

If you want guaranteed sunshine year-round — or, at least as close as you can get to a guarantee — base yourself in one or more of the following regions:

✔ Waikiki, on Oahu

✔ Maui's south coast (Kihei and Wailea)

✔ The Big Island's Kona-Kohala Coast

✔ The south and southwest coasts of Kauai (Poipu Beach and Waimea)

Getting on Board with Cruising

People choose a cruise vacation for a variety of reasons: It's easy to plan; their friends have told them great things about cruising; it allows them to go to several different countries instead of just one; they want to try something new; or they've found out about a great deal. Whatever led you to your decision to explore cruising, you're on the right track.

Ten reasons to take a cruise vacation

Of the nearly 8 million people who take a cruise in any given year, about 80 percent are likely to want to repeat the experience. Why? Well, consider these top reasons that first-time cruisers gave the Cruise Lines International Association (CLIA; the marketing group for the cruise industry) for preferring a cruise over other vacations:

✔ Being pampered

✔ Being able to relax and get away from it all

✔ Having the opportunity to visit several destinations in one trip

✔ Enjoying a variety of activities

✔ Getting good value for the money

✔ Enjoying high-quality entertainment

✔ Making the trip a romantic getaway

✔ Relaxing in comfortable accommodations

✔ Taking delight in the trip as a learning experience

✔ Trying out a vacation area with the thought of returning to it

The best part about cruising

Here are some of the best things about cruise vacations:

✔ Most ships currently catering to North American cruisers were launched in the past ten years, and bigger and better ships are appearing all the time. The new ships offer enticing extras such as cabins with private verandas (a wonderful feature worth the extra bucks), expanded spas, and alternative dining choices that include fancy restaurants (you usually pay an extra fee to dine at these) and casual venues for those nights when you don't want to sit through a five-course dinner in the dining room.

✔ The cruise lines are adding new destinations, new activities on and off the ship, new motifs, and more realistic cruise lengths (not everyone can take off for a week at a time), and they are bringing ships closer to travelers' doors by offering sailings from places including Baltimore, Boston, Charleston, Galveston, Houston, Long Beach, New Orleans, New York, Norfolk, Philadelphia, San Diego, San Francisco, and Seattle, rather than just from Florida and Los Angeles.

✔ You can see the world — you can cruise in North America, Central America, Europe, Greenland, Asia, Africa, South America, the South Pacific, Australia and New Zealand, and even Antarctica. Usually, you can also cruise in the Middle East, but in the aftermath of September 11, most of these itineraries were cancelled, with the ships moving to ports deemed safer. World cruises take those who have the time (we're talking months) to several of these regions.

✔ Most cruise ships, especially the newer and bigger vessels, boast lavish spas with beauty parlors (where for a fee you can splurge on a soothing massage or a manicure) and gyms, often with ocean views; extensive children's programs designed to keep your kids well occupied so that you have a chance to play; and organized activities that range from silly pool games to craft classes, art auctions, bridge tournaments, and lectures.

Sports enthusiasts may find (depending on the ship) basketball, racquetball, tennis, trapshooting, golf, rock-climbing, billiards, and/or in-line skating, as well as the traditional shuffleboard and ping-pong. Some ships even offer scuba classes. And at the ports, if you go to a warm-weather destination, you have ample time to enjoy the beaches and additional water sports offerings, including snorkeling.

Want more? How about video arcades and movie theaters showing first-run releases? You can shop on the ship for souvenirs and even diamonds and pearls (all duty-free). And thanks to satellite technology, you may even be able to watch a live sporting event. You can also stay in touch by sending and receiving e-mail at the ship's Internet cafe.

Or focus on eating: You can start with an early risers' continental breakfast at 6 a.m., followed by a full breakfast (buffet or sit-down), eat lunch at a buffet or in the dining room, and enjoy pizza and/or afternoon tea. But save room for dinner, and don't forget the midnight buffet!

✔ Nighttime is one of the liveliest times on a cruise ship. You have the multi-course dinner meal to look forward to, for one thing. And then, depending on the ship, you can dance, try your luck in a casino, sip drinks at a piano bar, light up a stogie at a cigar bar, see a Vegas- or Broadway-style show, or just walk on the deck and stare at the stars until sunrise.

Best of all, it's nearly all included in your cruise fare. You don't pay admission charges to any of the entertainment offerings; you pay only for your drinks (which are usually quite reasonably priced) and, of course, for any bets you place at the casino. If you're in a port at night, you can also partake of the local nightlife, including shows, casinos, and clubs.

✔ The best news for consumers is that the competition to fill all those new ships is keeping the prices low. In fact, given the spate of discounts, the price of cruising has actually gone down in recent years. Travel jitters due to world conditions, compounded by the recession, only added to this trend, bringing some of the biggest discounting ever (in March 2003, weeklong cruises were offered for as low as $299).

Choosing among the six types of cruises

Cruises come in all sizes, shapes, and designs. In the vast sea of possibilities, you can go for fun, rest, pampering, quality family time, education, excitement, or a mixed bag of pleasures. But first, you have to examine what's out there. That's why we created the following list.

- **Family cruises:** Some cruise lines specialize in family vacations, and they take great pains to plan for all age groups. If you want your vacation to be a family affair, look for a line that caters to adults *and* children. Expect a crowd during holidays and other school break periods.

- **Luxury cruises:** You say money is no object? If you can afford a top-of-the-line ship, you're in store for impeccable service, luxurious accommodations, first-class cuisine, and a sophisticated ambience.

- **Party cruises:** On these voyages, the passengers tend to party hearty, definitely at night (the disco hops until dawn) and sometimes during the day, too. People groove to the Caribbean steel-band tunes on the Pool Deck (even if the ship isn't in the Caribbean), and bar areas are crowded.

- **Resort cruises:** Activities and amusements are key to resort cruises, and these cruises are very popular with folks who want a vacation experience that includes the pool, the spa, aerobics classes, a state-of-the-art gym, sports offerings, kids' programs, and constant activities, such as scuba diving, snorkeling, water sports, golf, educational lectures, and a lot of goofy onboard contests.

- **Romantic cruises:** The romantic ambience on cruise ships is unmistakable. With the rolling seas as a backdrop, *amour* seems ever-present. Some lines promote romance with onboard wedding, honeymoon, or vow-renewal ceremony packages. If your idea of romance is privacy (or relative privacy), you may want to look at a ship where quiet time for the two of you is easier to come by.

- **Adventure and educational cruises:** If you rank exploring and learning about a destination first, an adventure/educational cruise is best for you. You can attend lectures having to do with the region in which you're traveling or participate in guided nature walks or history tours. Some cruises make kayaking, hiking, and nature observation the focus of the trip.

Most ships offer at least a taste of all the cruise categories discussed in the preceding list. But by knowing your priorities, you can more easily find the cruise that's right for you.

Think about what kind of hotel you generally stay in on vacation. If you're a bed-and-breakfast kind of person, you may be most comfortable on a smaller, more relaxed cruise ship; if Motel 6 is your thing, look for a budget cruise; if you're a Ritz-Carlton type, you probably want something more luxurious than a mainstream ship.

Eight great ways to find travel bargains on the Web

The Internet has a wealth of travel bargains if you're willing to look — from discount airfare to educational vacations to housing swaps. Here's a list of great places, both traditional and non-traditional, to start looking:

✔ www.travelzoo.com: TravelZoo lists sales and specials on airfares, vacation packages, lodging specials, and cruises available directly from over 200 airlines and travel companies. Some of the best deals are for the airfare/lodging packages. The site also lists great last-minute deals if you're adventurous and flexible. Or if you want a themed vacation, check out their unique escapes for something romantic, adventurous, or exotic. Register for a weekly e-mail of the top 20 bargains or visit the Web site when you're starting to itch for a trip.

✔ www.bargainbox.com: Go to the "senior" section of this site for special discounts on airfare, hotels, and car rentals. The Web site also has great bargains for families and helpful travel information on a wide range of topics from getting the most from frequent flyer miles to packing tips to terror alerts.

✔ www.silverwingsplus.com: If you are 55 or older, you can join the senior members center of United Airlines and book discounted airfare, find deeply discounted cruises that are tailored especially for last-minute or extended travel, and get 50 percent discounts with upscale hotels. Most other major airlines have similar programs for seniors, so make sure you check out their Web sites as well.

✔ www.senior-center.com: Recommended by AARP as a great place to get a bargain, Senior Center shows you how to buy wholesale airline tickets, lists airline ticket consolidation companies, links you to bargain Internet fares, and gives you lots of helpful tips on finding airfares you can afford.

✔ www.elderhostel.com: An educational and travel organization for older adults, Elder Hostel offers literally hundreds of great travel opportunities on every continent of the world — except maybe Antarctica. You can learn glasswork in New York, explore the Grand Canyon, or trace Mozart through Vienna, Prague, and Salzburg. The programs range from a three-day weekend to three weeks of travel and cover your food and lodging as well as program expenses. Prices range from budget to moderate.

✔ www.thirdage.com: This Web site links you to great vacation information specific to your needs. Maybe you're a senior wanting a romantic getaway for a moderate price or a family with teenage kids looking for an educational vacation on a budget. The site also has a lot of non-travel info, but if you go straight to the Travel link, it's pretty straightforward.

✔ www.eurapart.com: A great site if you're a family wanting to go to Europe on a budget. It gives you the lowdown on car touring and other transportation options, hostels and hotels good for families, self-catering apartments (in other words, no mints on the pillows — it's a fully-furnished apartment, but you do everything yourself) that you can rent for cheap, and the cheapest places to buy gas and food.

✔ www.4homex.com: A housing exchange makes almost any place affordable if you're flexible. For a low annual fee, you can post the dates you want to travel, list your own house and its amenities, and then list where you'd like to go — say France. If someone in France wants to vacation in the United States on those dates, you swap houses. Letting someone else stay in your house may sound a bit scary, but it's a well-established practice, and is about as cheap as lodging gets.

Chapter 19

Getting Back to Nature

• •

In This Chapter

▶ The exciting world of RVing

▶ Best national park vacations

▶ Camping essentials

• •

*W*hat better way to get back to nature than to plan a camping trip? Whether you pack a tent or pack up your RV, you can't go wrong with the park offerings in the United States and Canada. This chapter gives you some pointers on planning your best nature vacation, including picking the best places to go and knowing what essentials you need to pack along.

Discovering the Best of RVing

Freedom! If you want to sum up RV travel in one word, that's it. You're freed from fighting the battle of airports, from arriving at hotels only to find that your reservation was lost or your room isn't ready, and from waiting an hour past your reservation time at a restaurant or from tipping the host to get a better table. In your RV, you're the boss. You go where you want to go, when you want to go, and at whatever pace you please. *FREEDOM!*

We had enough trouble narrowing down our favorite RV drives to the 14 in this chapter, so we know you'll have trouble choosing among them. The following sections offer a rundown of each drive, including what you can see, the best time to go, who should go, who shouldn't go, and how much time to allow.

The coast of Maine: Lobster land

This drive follows Maine's rocky coastline along local roads and state highways, sometimes narrow and winding. Campgrounds are scenic and tree-shaded, many with small and narrow sites. Overall, you find high-moderate prices for goods and services.

- ✔ **Best time to go:** Summer and early fall.

- ✔ **Who should go:** Couples, families, retirees, lobster lovers, antiques shoppers, scenery buffs, and people who can plan ahead to reserve campgrounds for July and August.

- ✔ **Who should not go:** Anyone who gets nervous backing into a narrow, tree-lined campsite.

- ✔ **How far/how long:** Although the drive is only 225 miles, allow ten days to really relax and enjoy it.

- ✔ **Scenery:** Coastal views with rocks, crashing waves, lighthouses, lobster pots, and fishing boats.

- ✔ **Sightseeing:** Art museums, Acadia National Park, and trolley and transportation museums.

- ✔ **Food:** Fresh lobster, clams, chowder, and blueberry muffins.

- ✔ **Shopping:** Freeport factory outlets, teddy bear workshops, whirligig lawn ornaments, and antiques.

- ✔ **Offbeat:** The Moxie soft drink bottling company and museum in New Lisbon.

Western New York: Cooperstown to Niagara Falls

Highlights include the crashing, roaring waters of Niagara Falls and surprisingly scenic rolling green hills dotted with vineyards around the Finger Lakes. You encounter much history and several hands-on museums, plenty of good campgrounds, and high-moderate prices for goods and services.

- ✔ **Best time to go:** Anytime it's not snowing; late spring and early autumn are less crowded than summer.

- ✔ **Who should go:** Baseball fans, *I Love Lucy* nuts, feminists, honeymooners, photographers, player piano owners, couples, families, and those who know what a kazoo is.

- ✔ **Who should not go:** Anyone who doesn't like Buffalo wings, hot dogs, and roast beef sandwiches.

- ✔ **How far/how long:** The drive is 725 miles; allow a week or more.

- ✔ **Scenery:** Niagara Falls, the Finger Lakes, and the Erie Canal.

- ✔ **Sightseeing:** The National Baseball Hall of Fame, a carrousel factory, the Corning Glass Museum, the George Eastman House and International Museum of Photography, the Mark Twain study, the National Women's Hall of Fame, and Women's Rights National Historic Park.

- ✔ **Food:** Buffalo wings, beef on weck sandwiches, grape pie, fresh cheese curds, Italian breads and biscotti, Ted's red hots, and Nick Tanou's garbage plate.

- ✔ **Shopping:** Glassware at Corning and Steuben, New York State cheese, and American antiques.

- ✔ **Offbeat:** The Jell-O Gallery museum in LeRoy.

Blue Ridge Mountains: Skyline Drive and Blue Ridge Parkway

This leisurely, classic drive — avoiding commercial traffic, billboards, fast-food chains, and gas stations — offers frequent opportunities to pull off the highway for a short nature walk and many chances to leave the parkway for small towns with gas stations and cafes. Parkway campgrounds don't provide hookups and sometimes take no advance reservations. Prices are moderate to low-moderate.

- ✔ **Best time to go:** Spring, summer, and fall, with spring the least crowded; the roads are usually open in winter as well, but heavy fogs and sometimes icy roads can be dangerous.

- ✔ **Who should go:** Nature and scenery lovers, collectors of American crafts, Civil War buffs, lovers of home cooking, families, couples, and retirees.

- ✔ **Who should not go:** Anyone too impatient to stay within the parkway speed limit, which is 45 mph.

- ✔ **How far/how long:** The route covers 643 miles; allow one to two weeks to have time for camping and hiking.

- ✔ **Scenery:** Rolling hills and wooded hillsides, great shows of bloom, especially dogwood, rhododendron, and mountain laurel in springtime and autumn leaves in fall.

- ✔ **Sightseeing:** Great Smoky Mountains National Park, Shenandoah National Park, Manassas, Dollywood amusement park, and the Museum of American Frontier Culture.

- ✔ **Food:** Southern-style home cooking with country ham, fried chicken, hot biscuits, and a big selection of cooked vegetables, homemade relishes, pound cake, banana pudding, buttermilk pie, chess pie, and rich layer cakes.

- ✔ **Shopping:** American crafts, especially handmade quilts, wood furniture and wooden toys for children, pottery, and rag rugs.

- ✔ **Offbeat:** Snappy Lunch in Mt. Airy, North Carolina, where TV's Andy Griffith ate in real life and in TV's *Mayberry RFD*.

Is RVing for you?

So is RVing for you? See if you fit any of these personality types.

Garbo gourmets: Alone together luxuriating in the best that life can offer, these epicures carry their own wines and food, sleep in their own beds, and select their own surroundings by serendipity.

Sportsmen: Skiers, fishermen, surfers, golfers, and mountain bikers get into the heart of the action with all the comforts of home.

Weekenders: The stressed-out get out of the rat race and into the countryside to delete the pressures of the workweek from their hard drives.

Families on vacation: Offsetting the pricey amusement park, these families think of their motorhome as their own budget hotel and 'round-the-clock, self-serve restaurant; for the kids, RVing means no more "Are we there yet?," "I have to go potty!," or "I'm hungry!" Everything is here.

Eco-tourists: Going back to nature the easy way, eco-tourists bird-watch at dawn and spot wildlife during twilight. Photography and hiking lay fewer burdens on Mother Earth than heavy hotel and resort infrastructures.

The ultimate shoppers: Hitting all the antiques shops, estate sales, and the world's biggest swap meets, shoppers enjoy comfort and style with room to take all the treasures back home easily in the RV.

Pet lovers: Taking Fifi and Fido along for the ride and enjoying their company, animal lovers avoid facing rebellious and destructive pets after a spell of boarding them in a kennel.

Disabled travelers: A customized RV can open up the world with familiar and accessible surroundings.

Special-events attendees: Tailgating for a football game, or hitting a jazz festival or an arts festival on the spur of the moment, RVing fans sidestep overbooked hotels and restaurants and invite friends in for a meal.

Relatives: Visiting family and friends, RVers can take along their own bed and bathroom; when parked at home, they have an extra guest room with bath.

The Gulf Coast: Tallahassee to New Orleans

You can stroll along the coast's white sand beaches, fine and soft as powdered sugar. Scarlett O'Hara would feel at home among the region's antebellum mansions. Other highlights include an abundance of fresh seafood at bargain prices, Vegas-style casinos, plenty of campgrounds, and good takeout food. Prices are low-moderate to low.

- ✔ **Best time to go:** Early spring when the azaleas and camellias are blooming; enjoyable year-round, winter is mild but summer temperatures can get hot.

- ✔ **Who should go:** Anyone who's never had enough shrimp to eat, beach lovers, history buffs, garden growers, fans of TV's *Pensacola: Wings of Gold* series, families, couples, students, retirees, and snowbirds.

Springs National Park, Buffalo National River Park, and Ozarks Folk Arts Center.

✔ **Food:** Smoked meats and country ham, fried chicken, fried catfish and hush puppies, barbecue, and fried apple pies.

✔ **Shopping:** Antiques, country ham, and silly hillbilly souvenirs.

✔ **Offbeat:** Lambert's, "the home of the throwed roll," where servers toss hot homemade rolls to your table.

Montana and Wyoming: Tracking Buffalo Bill

Some of the most spectacular mountain scenery in the world lines this drive through regions where cattle outnumber people three to one. You find a world-class museum dedicated to Buffalo Bill and uncrowded campgrounds with wide open spaces (except at Yellowstone). Prices are moderate to low-moderate.

✔ **Best time to go:** Early fall from Labor Day to early October is the best time to visit, but late spring, summer, and early fall are all pleasant.

✔ **Who should go:** Lovers of the outdoors, cowboy fans, Western history buffs, families, couples, retirees looking for a summer hideaway, and hang gliders who love to catch great thermals.

✔ **Who should not go:** Anyone who hates traffic jams should avoid Yellowstone in summer.

✔ **How far/how long:** 772 miles, allow two weeks.

✔ **Scenery:** *National Geographic* comes to life with mountain vistas you won't believe; Yellowstone's geysers, waterfalls, and wildlife.

✔ **Sightseeing:** Yellowstone National Park, the Beartooth Highway, the Chief Joseph Highway, the Little Bighorn Battlefield National Monument, and the Grizzly Discovery Center.

✔ **Food:** Burgers and steaks from beef and buffalo; rainbow trout; homemade pies and rolls and gargantuan cinnamon buns; and meatloaf and Mexican dishes.

✔ **Shopping:** Museum shops, such as the one in the Buffalo Bill Center, stock outstanding Western craft items; antiques; Western clothing, and artifacts.

✔ **Offbeat:** Betting on the pig race at Bear Creek Downs near Red Lodge, Montana.

New Mexico: Billy the Kid meets E.T.

Old-West scenery of red rock canyons, mesas, buttes, rocks, and deserts fills your windshield in New Mexico. Uncrowded highways and scenic campgrounds are common. Prices are low-moderate to low.

✔ **Best time to go:** Spring and fall, but any time of year is acceptable, including winter; summers can be hot in the desert areas.

✔ **Who should go:** Fans of *The X-Files* and *Roswell* TV shows, history buffs interested in Native American culture, turquoise jewelry collectors, pottery collectors, chili-heads, families, couples, retirees, and snowbirds.

✔ **Who should not go:** Urbanites who get spooked when surrounded by plenty of empty space.

✔ **How far/how long:** 943 miles, allow two weeks.

✔ **Scenery:** Red rock canyons and sagebrush, misty blue hills and snow-capped peaks in the distance, and glistening white sand dunes and desert.

✔ **Sightseeing:** Carlsbad Caverns National Park, International Space Center in Alamogordo, International UFO Museum and Research Center in Roswell, and White Sands National Monument.

✔ **Food:** New Mexico cuisine blends Mexican and Pueblo Indian foods, fried breads turned into Indian tacos or sopapillas filled with honey; anything with chilies, particularly soupy red and green chile stews; chicken-fried steak; steaks; and homemade tortillas.

✔ **Shopping:** Cowboy boots, silver and turquoise jewelry, Pueblo pottery, and hand-woven rugs.

✔ **Offbeat:** Meeting (and buying) E.T. replicas at Roswell's UFO Museum.

The Oregon Coast: California to Washington

This stretch of coast offers beachcombing on uncrowded beaches with twisted driftwood, rocks, and surf. Although crowded on summer weekends, a generally good highway passes through the middle of most of the beach towns. You find wonderful local wines, cheeses, and seafood, and scenic state parks with hookups in this RV-friendly region. Prices for goods and services are high-moderate to moderate.

✔ **Best time to go:** Summer has the best weather and the least rain, but you can drive the coast year-round.

✔ **Who should go:** Laidback people who like casual clothes, boutique breweries, beachcombing, hiking, and biking; kite-flyers; sandcastle builders;

families with children; romantic couples; and retirees looking for a quiet hideaway.

✔ **Who should not go:** The uptight, the dressed up, and the fussy and demanding.

✔ **How far/how long:** 365 miles plus an optional add-on peninsula in Washington state; allow a week.

✔ **Scenery:** High sculpted sand dunes; rocky beaches with heavy surf and driftwood; and friendly, sometimes funky, little beach towns and fishing villages.

✔ **Sightseeing:** Sea Lion Caves, Oregon Coast Aquarium, Oregon Dunes National Recreation Area, Tillamook Cheese Factory, Columbia River Maritime Museum, and the Lewis and Clark winter quarters.

✔ **Food:** Fresh seafood, dig-your-own clams, Tillamook cheddar, Bandon cheddar, Blue Heron Brie, smoked fish, local cranberries, Umpqua Dairy ice cream, clam chowder, and fried oysters.

✔ **Shopping:** Cheeses, myrtlewood salad bowls, and smoked salmon.

✔ **Offbeat:** The snake-headed, insect-devouring carnivorous plants at Darlingtonia State Botanical Wayside that look like something out of *The X-Files*.

California Central Coast: Malibu to Monterey

Along the Pacific Coast Highway, you can listen to the distant barking of sea lions above the ocean roar and drive along cliffs overlooking the rocks far below. You find frequent scenic turnouts and good roads, except when rock or mud slides block the highway during storms. Campgrounds are frequent but also heavily occupied throughout the year. Prices are high-moderate to moderate.

✔ **Best time to go:** Anytime, but expect some coastal fog in summer, winds and occasional storms in winter; we like February, March, September, and October.

✔ **Who should go:** People who can make campground reservations in advance; spur-of-the-moment RVers who can make do with what's left; and romantic couples, families, and retirees.

✔ **Who should not go:** White-knuckled drivers; if you do go, follow the south-to-north route outlined in this book, as driving north-to-south puts you and your RV on the ocean side of the highway — on a cliff.

✔ **How far/how long:** 340 miles; allow three or four days to see all the attractions.

✔ **Scenery:** Dizzying overlooks above the pounding surf, treeless green hillsides and meadows that turn golden in summer, and elegant arched bridges spanning chasms.

✔ **Sightseeing:** The Big Sur coast, trees and bushes covered with monarch butterflies, old Spanish missions, the Getty Museum, the Hearst Castle at San Simeon, a splendid museum for John Steinbeck, and Monterey Bay Aquarium.

✔ **Food:** Cal-Mex cooking; real hamburgers; Santa Maria tri-tip roast beef with pinquito beans; the world's most famous taco stand, endorsed by Julia Child; Danish pastries in Solvang; and split-pea soup in Buellton.

✔ **Shopping:** Danish souvenirs in Solvang; out-of-date maps to movie star homes in Malibu; wineries around Santa Barbara; and antiques and collectibles in Cambria and Cayucos.

✔ **Offbeat:** Pieces of the Cecil B. DeMille movie set from the 1920s film *The Ten Commandments* buried under the sand dunes at Nipomo.

Route 66: OK to LA

You can visit what's left of old Route 66, long ago replaced by I-40 but popular again with back-road explorers. Bonus discoveries include Burma-Shave signs, the wild burros of Oatman, and the corn dog inventor. Road conditions vary widely so ask locally about present passability. Plenty of campgrounds and fast-food outlets line I-40. The prices are moderate.

✔ **Best time to go:** Spring and fall; summer is hot in some areas; winter brings the possibility of snow around Flagstaff.

✔ **Who should go:** Baby boomers who remember family road trips in the 1950s and 1960s; anyone who remembers the lyrics of the song.

✔ **Who should not go:** Anyone who's going to complain about potholes instead of admiring faded billboards and defunct gas stations.

✔ **How far/how long:** 1,435 miles, allow at least seven days.

✔ **Scenery:** Varied, from grassy prairies and ranch country around Tulsa to the windswept Texas panhandle, the rose-colored desert of New Mexico, the sun and golden sand of California's Mojave Desert beginning in Arizona, the highs of San Bernardino Mountains, the lows of San Gabriel Valley, the sprawl of Los Angeles, and the rolling surf of the Pacific Ocean at Santa Monica.

✔ **Sightseeing:** Grand Canyon National Park, Acoma Pueblo, National Cowboy Hall of Fame, Calico ghost town, Will Rogers Memorial Museum, Petrified Forest and Painted Desert, Oklahoma Route 66 Museum, Cadillac Ranch, and the Roy Rogers/Dale Evans Museum.

✔ **Food:** Onion-fried hamburgers, buffalo burgers, hillbilly chicken, sour-dough biscuits, chicken-fried steak, corn dogs, and beef jerky.

✔ **Shopping:** Minnetonka moccasins at roadside trading posts, and truly tacky souvenirs at Barstow Station.

✔ **Offbeat:** Exotic World, the Burlesque Hall of Fame, in California's high desert country.

National Parks: Heading East for History, West for Wilderness

All parks aren't created equal. You see, the national parks movement didn't begin until most of the eastern half of the country was thoroughly tamed, settled, and politically subdivided. As a result:

✔ The eastern parks are rich in America's cultural history — you know, George Washington slept here, there, and over there.

✔ The western parks preserved the country's magnificent and spectacular wild side.

That's not to say that eastern parks don't present spectacular landscapes, or that western parks don't recount pages of cultural history.

Vacationing at a national park

Here are some benefits of vacationing at a national park:

✔ **A bargain at twice the price:** A national park vacation is one of the best entertainment bargains around. Where else can $10 or $20 get you — and everyone else in your car, truck, or motor home — admission to someplace fun not just for one day but an entire week?

✔ **Bunking inside or outside:** The national parks offer several lodging options ranging from luxury digs to rustic campsites. You can expect to pay $100, $200, or even $300 or more per night at the more luxurious places.

If you're not looking for elegance, you can find rustic cabins in Yellowstone and canvas tent cabins in Yosemite for $50 to $55 a night. For considerably less (from free up to about $20 a night), you can stay in one of the parks' developed campgrounds.

✔ **Taking a walk on the wild side:** Ever feel the need to get away from the mundane concerns of day-to-day life? Who hasn't? You can quickly cut loose by heading down a national park trail. How far you trek — 1 mile or 10 miles or even 50 miles — is up to you. What's important is that you get out of your car and go!

- ✔ **Spotting bears and bison:** National parks host animals — lots of animals — and some creatures are incredibly easy to spot. Because so many animals live in national parks, they should be considered open-air zoos, although you definitely need to remember at all times that these animals are wild. When you reach the park of your choice, ask a ranger for the best spot to see animals.

- ✔ **Profiting from your park ranger's wisdom:** One of the best ways to brush up on your national park trivia is to spend some time with a ranger (but not because you're illegally parked or guilty of feeding bears). For years, rangers have offered campfire programs and hikes that explore an aspect of their parks' wildlife or geology or history, and these programs continue in full swing today.

Ten incredible national park vistas

By their very nature, national parks are incredibly scenic places. The old saying "beauty is in the eye of the beholder" doesn't seem to apply. You get a beautiful view just about everywhere you look. Sunsets? Parks virtually have a monopoly on the breathtaking ones. Purple mountains majesties? Got 'em by the truckload. Forests by the Brothers Grimm? Yep, you find these, too.

These parks have so many wonderful views that you don't even need to get out of your car to enjoy them — but do pull over and get out. Take a short walk, pull up a rock or downed tree trunk, and look around. You can thank us later.

- ✔ Badwater, Death Valley National Park

- ✔ Clingmans Dome, Great Smoky Mountains National Park

- ✔ Giant Forest, Sequoia National Park

- ✔ Glacier Point, Yosemite National Park

- ✔ Grand Canyon of the Yellowstone, Yellowstone National Park

- ✔ Hoh Rain Forest, Olympic National Park

- ✔ Oxbow Bend, Grand Teton National Park

- ✔ Paradise, Mount Rainier National Park

- ✔ Point Sublime, Grand Canyon National Park

- ✔ Zion Canyon Narrows, Zion National Park

Make the Visitor Center your first stop

Try to make the Visitor Center your first stop at any park. There you can find information on attractions, facilities, and activities, such as scenic drives, nature trails, and historic tours. Descriptive literature and exhibits will acquaint you with the geology, history, and plant and animal life of the area. The park staff will answer questions about accommodations, services, and accessibility of attractions.

Camping: Determining Your Interests and Needs

When you plan a camping trip, knowing what you want to do is just as important as knowing where you want to go. In fact, determining what you want to do should be the first item on the planning agenda because the answer may very well determine what choices you have in camping destinations. No sense planning a camping trip to the desert if fishing is high on the agenda — no matter how beautiful the spring wildflowers may be.

Beginning the firm planning

Your dreams of a great adventure are taking shape, but unless you want to end up like Gilligan, who only intended on a three-hour tour, you need to sweat the details. That means maps, permits, camping reservations, emergency planning, and more. Read on, and we'll lead you through the maze.

- ✔ **Obtaining maps of the area:** Purchase U.S. Geological Service (USGS) topographic survey maps, National Forest Service maps, trail guidebooks, and other privately produced maps of the area if available. You can't have too much information in this planning stage.

- ✔ **Making campsite reservations and obtaining permits:** Most public lands, including National Parks, Forest Service land, Bureau of Land Management (BLM) land, and Canadian Park land require you to obtain a permit before entering. If you're visiting a campsite, you need to make a reservation.

- ✔ **A few words on roads:** If your trip takes you onto the many unimproved and wilder roads that criss-cross the land in the United States and Canada, treat all official and unofficial terminology on maps — even recent ones — such as "improved," "graded," "primitive," "graveled," and so on, with a healthy dose of skepticism. While the road that leads into the great backcountry campground you heard about may very well have earned an "improved" designation several months ago, recent storms may have turned it into a rutted, soupy, quagmire capable of eating trucks, RVs, and any other vehicle you choose to place on the menu.

✔ **Plotting your route carefully:** After you make the arrangements for your camping trip, plot your route carefully on the maps (obviously, if you're only car-camping in park campgrounds, this is not necessary).

✔ **Planning for emergencies:** Always have an emergency plan in place. You never know when a real need or emergency will arise, so it's best to be prepared. Here's a quick checklist:

- Know where the nearest hospital emergency room is in relation to the place you will be exploring.

- Always tell someone responsible where you are going camping, and be sure to notify that person when you return so that she or he doesn't worry (or notify authorities to begin an unnecessary search).

- Learn basic first aid and CPR. Being in an emergency and having no idea how to proceed or what to do is a helpless feeling. The Red Cross is a good place to look for instruction in first aid.

National Park area: Camping facts to remember

The National Park system provides campsites to hundreds of thousands of people every month. Here are some pointers on using the system:

✔ Campsite use fees vary.

✔ Some parks offer year-round camping, while others have specific dates of operation.

✔ Backcountry camping requires a permit.

✔ You're allowed to camp only in designated areas.

✔ Developed area campsites have drinking water, toilets, fire containment devices, tables, refuse containers, and limited parking spaces. Generally, utility hookups are not available.

✔ Gathering of firewood is generally restricted, except in certain areas (check with a park ranger). In some parks, the use of campfires may be restricted to protect air quality or due to extreme wildfire danger.

✔ In parks where bears are present, the superintendent may designate areas where food must be stored in a specified manner to prevent its loss or to avoid an encounter with a potentially dangerous wild animal.

✔ Maximum lengths for trailers, campers, and motorhomes vary from park to park. The average maximum length permitted is 27 feet, but some parks can accommodate vehicles up to 40 feet in length. There are no electrical or water hookups at campsites. Some parks may have dump stations. Find out your park's specific maximum length so that you won't be disappointed when you arrive.

Is your dog welcome?

In general, you can expect agencies to have the following dog regulations:

✔ **All Parks:** Seeing-eye dogs and dogs assisting those with disabilities are allowed in all public places and in all public buildings.

✔ **National Parks:** No dogs are allowed except those on leashes within campgrounds.

✔ **National Forests:** Dogs are allowed, but consult ranger stations governing each National Forest area for specific guidelines.

✔ **Bureau of Land Management:** Dogs are allowed, but consult each district for specific regulations governing each management area.

✔ **State Parks:** No dogs are allowed except those on leashes within campgrounds, with a few exceptions.

That said, always check with the park you're visiting *ahead of time,* just in case they have different regulations

Outdoor gear and gadgets

Before heading out on any camping adventure, you need to equip yourself. Equipping yourself means selecting among many choices, potentially a tough task. To make it easier for you, this section covers some basic considerations and guidelines.

✔ **Tents:** A good shelter must be able to slip the wind without caving in, shed the rain without leaking, offer decent ventilation so that you don't feel as if you're sleeping in a steamy locker room, and be relatively easy to set up and take down.

✔ **Sleeping bags:** The key choice in sleeping bags is between synthetic fill or down. Down is lighter in terms of a weight-to-warmth ratio. Down is also more compact. However, only synthetic fills like PolarGuard 3D, Lite Loft, Hollofil, or Quallofil will maintain loft and warmth even when wet. Down turns into a heavy, soggy, cold mess that takes forever to dry out.

✔ **Backpacks:** When buying a backpack, the first decision will be whether to go with an internal frame or external frame.

  • **Internal frame backpacks** are an ideal choice for rock scrambling, off-trail work, winter ski touring, and mountaineering.

  • **External frame backpacks** are ideal for very large and bulky loads and for long backpacking trips. But they're not for mountaineering or skiing.

✔ **Stoves:** If you're going car camping or base camping with a larger number of people, a two-burner stove is probably a good idea. If you're preparing to backpack or trek, think single-burner.

After determining the stove size you need, decide on fuel. If convenience is your primary concern, use any of the pressurized gas canister fuel stoves because electronic ignitions are available with them and you won't have to deal with pressuring or pouring liquid fuels.

✔ **Kitchen kit:** Briefly, the camp kitchen items you choose to pack are a function of your menu. At a minimum, this means two pot sizes, small and large; a griddle; a skillet; a mixing bowl or two; and cooking utensils such as a spoon, fork, spatula, and knife. A cutting board is also very handy. If you plan to grill, bring a grate you can put over the fire — don't assume your campsite will have one.

✔ **Furniture:** A lightweight, portable table makes a great addition to your camping kit. If it turns out that you don't need it, you don't even have to unpack it. But if your site lacks a table, you'll be glad you brought one along!

The same is true of chairs. Rocks, stumps, and coolers can all be used for seating. But portable stools are far more comfortable. Lightweight folding chairs with full back support are even more comfortable, and having one or two at your disposal can really take a load off your feet.

✔ **Coolers:** Coolers are a great option to tote along if you are traveling by vehicle or boat. Look for a model that fits the space available in your vehicle and your food-storage needs.

✔ **Water carriers:** Collapsible jugs have been around for eons and come in a variety of sizes. We find the most convenient to tote and fill are the 2- to 2.5-gallon models — anything larger gets cumbersome.

✔ **Lights:** Here are five of our picks for brightening a slice of your nocturnal life, if not your world:

- **Headlamps:** Great for when you need both hands and have to use a flashlight at the same time.

- **Electric lanterns:** These are perhaps the safest of the lantern options, although the downside is battery consumption. Electric lanterns are certainly the only kinds recommended for use inside a tent or camper.

- **Gas lanterns:** Gas lanterns are very bright, although they have the drawback of being a tad on the noisy side, rather like camping near a jet engine running at half speed. We don't advise using a gas lantern inside a tent or camper.

- **Candle lanterns:** Candle lanterns do not throw off a great deal of light, but they are romantic. They burn for up to eight hours or more.

- **LED lights:** LED lights are more durable than any bulb as there is no filament to burn out or fragile glass casing to break. LED lights also burn in excess of 100,000 hours, far more than the traditional 40-hour life most flashlight bulbs now enjoy.

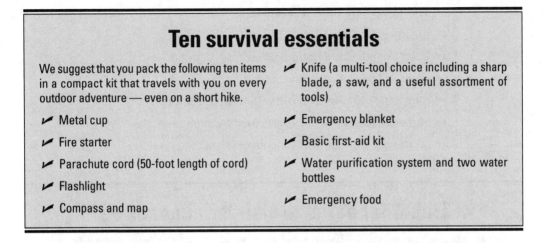

Ten survival essentials

We suggest that you pack the following ten items in a compact kit that travels with you on every outdoor adventure — even on a short hike.

✔ Metal cup

✔ Fire starter

✔ Parachute cord (50-foot length of cord)

✔ Flashlight

✔ Compass and map

✔ Knife (a multi-tool choice including a sharp blade, a saw, and a useful assortment of tools)

✔ Emergency blanket

✔ Basic first-aid kit

✔ Water purification system and two water bottles

✔ Emergency food

✔ **Water filter:** These days, you simply have to filter water before you drink. The current crop of handheld filters are compact, light, and easier to use than ever, and some, believe it or not, are dropping in price. A decent filter can be had for as little as $20 — less expensive than a week's supply of Pepto-Bismol and antibiotics.

✔ **Axe and saw:** Quite often, the wood you purchase from the campground or nearby areas is too big and needs to be cut down or split to make a good cooking fire. Logs that have simply been split in half or even quartered are still too big to produce good coals.

✔ **Comforts of home:** Though not necessary by any stretch of the imagination, the following items have been known to convince even the most anticamping family members to enjoy a camp outing or two:

- Portable toilet
- Solar shower

Ten best outdoor destinations

Trying to limit the selection of great outdoor camping adventures to ten is a bit like being asked to choose only ten favorite desserts from a table laden with hundreds of chocolatey and creamy concoctions: At best, you can sample only a few. Knowing, too, that many of us have limited time on our hands these days, we tried to select a variety of places where outfitted and guided trips were equally enjoyable as planning the trips yourself.

✔ Lightning Lakes: British Columbia

✔ Picture Rocks National Lakeshore: Michigan

✔ Glacier National Park: Montana

- The Temagami: Ontario, Canada
- All 'Round Ranch: Utah
- Cumberland Island National Seashore: Georgia
- Gates of Lodor, Green River: Utah
- King Range National Conservation Area: California
- Monongahela National Forest: West Virginia
- Strathcona Park Lodge: Vancouver Island

Beautiful parks to visit for almost free

The cheapest way to visit national parks and forests is to be 62 and get the Golden Age Passport for about $10. It gives you a lifetime entrance pass to the national park system and 50 percent off camping and other usage fees. You have to get the pass at a national park, so call ahead to find out what documentation you need to show.

If you're not quite 62, the National Park pass gets you into any national park for about $50 a year. However, it only covers admission, not camping fees.

If you're only planning one or two trips a year and want the budget option, stick to the national forests. They're a little more rustic than the national parks, but entrance fees are generally nominal or nonexistent and camping fees are usually in the $4 to $15 range. Here are a few great parks and forests to check out:

- **Gifford Pinchot National Forest** in southwest Washington state is an otherworldly landscape of craters, lava fields, volcanic caves, lava tubes, and pumice pits. One of America's oldest national forests, it covers a good portion of the area's Cascade Mountains, including Mount St. Helens National Volcanic Monument. The forest is surrounded by Mount Rainier National Park to the north, Columbia River Gorge national

Scenic Area to the south, and the extensive Yakama Indian Reservation to the east, so you won't lack places to visit.

- **Superior National Forest** is located on the border of Lake Superior in northeastern Minnesota and contains over 445,000 acres of water. Within the forest is the most heavily used wilderness area in America — the Boundary Waters Canoe Area Wilderness, which is a result of melting of glaciers during the late Ice Age. This vast area of water contains over 1,500 miles of canoe routes and more than 1,000 lakes and streams. But you aren't limited to water sports. Superior's forest is dense with fir, spruce, aspen, birch, and maple trees. And the wildlife includes moose, loons, black bears, and the rare gray wolf.

- **Chequamegon-Nicolet National Forest,** a huge swath of Wisconsin's north woods, is where you want to be come autumn. The rich mosaic of gold, scarlet, and auburn leaves and the crisp air may take your breath away. With the Peshtigo, Brule, Pine, and Popple Rivers, the Chequamegon-Nicolet is a magnet for canoeists and fishers.

- **Acadia National Park** in Maine was the first U.S. National Park east of the Mississippi. You can climb mountains, scramble along the rocky Atlantic shoreline, and hike and bike along the many paved and unpaved trails. Acadia's Cadillac Mountain, the highest point on the Atlantic coast north of Rio de Janeiro, is the first place sunlight strikes the United States each morning.

✔ **Sequoia National Park's** rugged beauty is within reach of Los Angeles, but unlike nearby Yosemite's crowds and overdevelopment, the lakes and mountain streams, snowfields, and scores of peaks that top 13,000 feet remain largely untouched. And of course there's the Giant Forest plateau, where you can find General Sherman, the tallest sequoia. It is 275 feet tall, the trunk weighs an estimated 1,385 tons, and the ground-level circumference is nearly 103 feet.

✔ **Rock Hound State Park,** near the city of Las Cruces in southwestern New Mexico, is known for its many lovely, semi-precious rocks that you can collect. Collecting rocks is usually forbidden in state and national parks, which makes Rock Hound unique, although it does have a 15-pound limit on the amount of rocks you are allowed to take home with you. Bring a pick and a shovel and wander the many desert trails to your heart's content.

Chapter 20

Heading to Town

In This Chapter

▶ America's most famous vacation cities

▶ A whirlwind tour of Europe's greatest cities

*W*hether you're traveling domestically or abroad, sometimes city life is the best way to go. The range of activities and cultural hot spots in such famous places as Boston and L.A. can't be beat. And where better to don your party shoes than Las Vegas or New Orleans?

With a little more planning, you can plan an invigorating European vacation. Take in history — real, old, ancient history — or cozy up in your favorite English pub. Either way, you can't go wrong with the European cities described in this chapter.

Boston: The Hub of the Solar System

Oliver Wendell Holmes gave Boston perhaps the city's most popular nickname: "The Hub of the Solar System" (which survives partly because headline writers love short words like "Hub"). The solar system may be an exaggeration, but eastern Massachusetts is an important destination for education, high-tech, financial services, and healthcare.

Don't be too quick to envision legions of pasty-faced techies glowing under fluorescent lights, though. Boston is downright beautiful. Redbrick buildings and cobblestone streets contrast delightfully with modern glass towers (and concrete boxes that seemed like a good idea at the time). Countless millions of dollars went into cleaning up Boston Harbor, and the result is worth every penny. The dot-com meltdown and the post–September 11 economic slump took a toll, but the city remains a vibrant, entertaining destination.

Five fun facts about Boston

This list is hardly comprehensive, but it covers some of the best reasons to make Boston a stop on your trip.

- ✔ With so many students residing in the city, you'll find noise, crowds, musical innovation, outlandish fashions, cheap diversions, and flat-out fun. Boston and Cambridge positively buzz with youthful energy.

- ✔ The city is home to some of the world's best and best-loved art, one of the finest symphony orchestras, and countless student efforts in every artistic field. Conversely, Boston is nearly as well known for bar bands, stand-up comedy, and street performance.

- ✔ Folks who come here to dine on fish and shellfish in every imaginable style come to the right place. From cutting-edge cuisine to down-home ethnic fare, nearly every menu includes succulent seafood.

- ✔ If you're like most visitors, you won't get out of Boston without at least a brief, painless history lesson. You can certainly immerse yourself in the past, visit innumerable colonial and Revolutionary landmarks, and stuff your head full of random facts. But you don't need to — merely walking around exposes you to the Boston of a bygone age.

- ✔ Peerless symbol of Bostonian ingenuity or unprecedented pain in the neck? The Central Artery/Third Harbor Tunnel project, better known as the Big Dig, is both. By 2005, when the Big Dig is over, Interstate 93, the main north-south route through downtown Boston, will be gone. (The demolition began in 2002, while construction was still raging.) Traffic will run through a tunnel and onto a gorgeous bridge over the Charles River.

The secrets of the seasons

Lots of places claim to be the inspiration for the weather cliché, "If you don't like it, wait ten minutes," but a few days in Boston will persuade you that New England's climate inspired the expression. Our advice: Think twice before letting the weather determine your plans. But here are some general guidelines to help you choose a time to visit:

- ✔ **Winter:** If you can't take bitter cold and biting winds, plan to concentrate on indoor activities. Snow sometimes overwhelms the city during these months, and some suburban attractions close for the winter.

- ✔ **Spring:** In April, spring comes to the mid-Atlantic states, but in New England snow can linger into the early part of the month. Reluctant outdoors people may want to note this is the height of mud season. (Pack shoes that you don't care about wearing again.) Full-blown spring usually doesn't arrive until early May, but that makes the first run of balmy weather all the more enjoyable.

- ✔ **Summer:** Graduation pandemonium lingers into June, when pleasant weather and the end of the younger kids' school year translate into a jump in occupancy rates at hotels and crowds all around town.

    June, July, and August are about the only months when you may encounter consecutive days of 90-plus temperatures, usually accompanied by debilitating humidity and abysmal air quality. Be ready to concentrate on indoor activities or willing to take it slow outside.

- ✔ **Fall:** In early September, college starts in earnest. The weather turns cooler, and humidity drops. Foliage season begins in late September and runs to mid-November. Many "leaf-peepers" stay in the Boston area or pass through on their way to northern New England, creating tour-bus gridlock.

    September and October are the months most likely to include a run of exhilarating weather, with comfortably warm days and cool to chilly nights. November is when convention business slows. The weather may turn cold and raw, but snow is seldom a problem.

Singing the Blues in Chicago

Chicago is the least pretentious and most livable metropolis in the United States — and maybe the most visitable, too. Chicago is basking in a cultural and building renaissance. Since the Great Fire of 1871, which destroyed much of the city, Chicago has been continuously rebuilding itself, and now is no exception. The city is at the tail end of its biggest building boom since the 1920s. Visitors and residents alike have benefited from this building fever. All over the city, shopping and theater districts have been expanded or restored, and new hotels and attractions have opened their doors to visitors.

Eight fun things to see and do in Chicago

Chicago does some things better than any other city: You just have to know what they are and how to find them. Read on for some of the activities that make Chicago a special place to visit.

- ✔ **Cheering on the Cubbies:** Baseball at Wrigley Field is a quintessential Chicago experience. The ivy-covered field is the coziest little ballpark in baseball.

- ✔ **Getting the blues — a good thing:** Chicago is the blues capital of the world. And if you get to know this style of music, you may gain a greater appreciation for other popular forms, such as jazz and rock 'n' roll.

- ✔ **Discovering the Third Coast:** While residents of the first two coasts (East and West, that is) may consider it a surprise, Chicagoans consider themselves residents of the *Third Coast* — Lake Michigan's shore. And you may be surprised to find 30 miles of sand beaches, green lawns, beds of flowers, and bicycle paths — no construction allowed here.

✔ **Soaking up some culture:** Chicago's Lyric Opera continually sells out 100 percent of the time, but don't fear. Subscription holders routinely hand in unused tickets before the performance, so you can still get some great seats. Other well-known cultural activities include seeing the Chicago Symphony Orchestra, the Joffrey Ballet, and local theatre companies such as the Goodman and Steppenwolf theaters. And nobody does comedy better than Second City, a training ground for comedians, such as John Belushi, Dan Ackroyd, Bill Murray, and Chris Farley.

✔ **Seeing "Sue" and other museum stars:** Yes, the biggest T-Rex fossil ever unearthed is now residing at Chicago's Field Museum of Natural History. As long as you're going to see "Sue" (if you're on a first-name basis with the famous T-Rex), you should know that an entire "campus" of museums is nearby, including

- The Adler Planetarium & Astronomy Museum

- The John G. Shedd Aquarium

- The Shedd, the nation's oldest and largest indoor aquarium

- The Oceanarium

- The Museum of Science and Industry

Downtown, the Museum of Contemporary Art was opened in the mid-1990s and features spectacular cultural programming. The Art Institute of Chicago is a great starting point to see masterpieces of art. And, a new natural science museum in Lincoln Park — the Peggy Notebaert Nature Museum — is an environmental museum for the 21st century.

✔ **Admiring the architecture:** One advantage to having your city burn to the ground: You can rebuild it with style. Thanks to the Great Fire of 1871, Chicago's architects were able to start over and "make no small plans," as city planner and visionary Daniel Burnham said.

Chicago is the birthplace of modern architecture and the skyscraper. Chicago is home to 45 Mies van der Rohe buildings and 75 Frank Lloyd Wright buildings, plus dozens by the first Chicago school and the second Chicago school. Enough said? The Chicago Architecture Foundation helps visitors discover the city's architectural gems.

✔ **Eating your way through town:** If you have to eat while you're here, you're in luck. Food doesn't get much better than the Mexican cuisine at Frontera Grill, the ribs at Twin Anchors, burgers at Mike Ditka's Restaurant, sushi at Kamehachi, or Italian at Tuscany on Taylor in Little Italy.

✔ **Tuning into the Talk:** Chicago has fostered a number of talk shows, including Jenny Jones, Jerry Springer, and, of course, Oprah Winfrey. If you want to check out a talk show and laugh, cry, or boo and hiss with the best of them, Chicago is the place to do it. After all, Chicagoans have been talking and dispensing advice for decades.

The secrets of the seasons

Most Chicago visitors find that the ideal times to visit are late spring and early fall. In the spring, you soak up blossoms, blooms, and equable temperatures. Fall, with its golds, reds, and browns, provides crisp, clear days with idyllic balmy interludes. Pleasant weather sometimes lingers into late November.

Here's a rundown of the pros and cons of each season.

- ✔ **Spring:** In spring, the weather warms up, but just because the days are warming up doesn't mean that the weather is necessarily nice. Strong winds can blow, and buckets of rain can fall during long strings of gray days.

  Also, you're a bit in limbo as far as events go. Festivals don't start until June, and you're too late for the holiday season and the decorations. And spring is the time of year (along with winter) when shows may close for a week; remember, performers need vacations, too.

- ✔ **Summer:** Summer is festival time. Chicagoans jam-pack summers full of outdoor activity — so much so that the choice of activities on weekends can be overwhelming.

  Because of the summer heat, everyone is at the lake, enjoying the off-shore breeze and making the area a congested free-for-all: inline skaters skating into bikers biking into runners running into Fido who just broke off his leash!

- ✔ **Fall:** Fall is a beautiful time of year — no matter where you are. In Chicago, you get the best weather in the fall — still warm enough, but not so hot and humid that you're going to have a meltdown. The cultural scene is back in swing, with openings for the opera and symphony seasons.

  However, convention season is in full swing. Getting a hotel room or restaurant table can be a challenge. You also need to be aware of unpredictable September or October Indian summer heat waves. (Don't forget the shorts and sunscreen — just in case.)

- ✔ **Winter:** During the holidays, the city looks beautiful. All of Michigan Avenue is lit up. Chicago goes all out with Christmas decorations. After Christmas, you can have Michigan Avenue to yourself on the weekdays. In February, WinterBreak Chicago fills the month with a series of blues concerts and more. Also, hotel prices sink during the slowest weeks of the winter, making the search for that good room at a great rate much easier.

  But bear in mind that the weather is *cold*, sometimes bitterly. December is a bad month for crowds, but (so far) the cold months are still the least crowded. Also note that winter is the other time of year (along with springtime) when shows may close for a week.

Loving Los Angeles

So it has smog. So it has traffic. So what? L.A. is a place where you can surf and ski on the same day!

El Pueblo de la Señora, la Reina de Los Angeles ("the city of Our Lady, Queen of the Angels") was founded by the Spanish in 1781. But truth be told, L.A. really wasn't on the map until the movie folks ventured there in search of outdoor locations that didn't suffer from snow.

And they keep on a'comin', though a few events, such as earthquakes and riots, have quenched migration enthusiasm, at least briefly.

Seven ways to entertain yourself in L.A.

Here are the highlights for fun in sunny L.A.:

✔ **Which way's the beach?** You can find a piece of that famous *Beach Blanket Bingo* vibe at places like the Santa Monica Pier, where you can stroll among the motley collection of souvenir shops, old carny rides, and a 1930s-era merry-go-round, or the Venice Ocean Front Walk, where the boys preen at Muscle Beach and pony-tailed gals zoom by on their in-line skates.

If you want to enjoy the ocean in a more pristine setting, head north into the Pacific Palisades and Malibu, where the waves get bigger and the houses get ritzier. North of that is Zuma, with its wild, cold waters.

✔ **All the stars in heaven:** The days of studio moguls like Louis B. Mayer and his stable of MGM stars may be long gone, but the city of Los Angeles remains synonymous with high-wattage celebrity. If you want to see stars — and they're out there, to be sure — you need to trek to the nether reaches of Malibu coffee shops and Beverly Hills clothing stores.

✔ **City of Museums:** L.A. has a number of museums with very high-quality collections, along with a few of the quirkier sort that folks like us tend to patronize. The big ones, of course, are the Getty; the Los Angeles County Museum of Art (LACMA); and the Museum of Contemporary Art (MOCA) at the Geffen Contemporary.

There are also a number of specialty museums, such as the Autry Museum of Western Heritage; the Japanese American National Museum; the Museum of Tolerance; the California ScienCenter; and the Petersen Automotive Museum.

✔ **Pillow talk:** Los Angeles has few atmospheric B&Bs or cunning little inns. What it does have are many standard-issue hotel rooms. You can find a measure of individuality, however, by staying at one of the venerable Old Hollywood establishments (such as the Hollywood Roosevelt, said to be haunted by Marilyn Monroe) or such hipster spots as West Hollywood's the Standard (where you can schedule a tattoo).

✔ **Fast food:** You can eat well in any number of inexpensive places all over the city — and often brilliantly. And L.A. wouldn't be L.A. without the quintessential old-school restaurants, where you can order a ring-a-ding-ding martini and a slab of red meat from crusty old waiters in dark wood-paneled environs. Need we say: Meet us at Musso & Frank.

✔ **Let me entertain you:** Nightlife in the City of Angels ranges from family-style sporting events like an evening at the Staples Center cheering on the world champion L.A. Lakers, to classical concerts under the stars at the Hollywood Bowl (the Beatles played here!), to finding your way past the velvet ropes into club land.

Rock historians will have a field day in L.A., visiting such seminal '60s and '70s clubs as the Roxy, the Whisky a Go-Go, and the Troubadour. You'll find saucy places to dance to any kind of music, as well as elegant cocktail lounges and real dive bars (but look who's sitting on the barstool next to you!).

And don't forget the opportunities to see major plays and musicals (the Music Center, the Mark Taper Forum, the Actors' Gang), symphony (the Los Angeles Philharmonic, in its new home at the Walt Disney Concert Hall), and opera (the Los Angeles Opera, at the Dorothy Chandler Pavilion).

✔ **The happiest place on earth:** The original Disney park, sprung from the fertile imagination of cartoonist Walt Disney back in 1955, is now the Disneyland Resort, a formidable enterprise consisting of two theme parks (including the latest, California Adventure), three hotels, a big shopping center, and lots of interesting restaurants.

The secrets of the seasons

People are fond of complaining that Los Angeles has no seasons. Sure, certain flowers bloom all year long, but the seasonal changes are there — they're just subtle, that's all. In the winter, the trees are bare (well, not the palm trees), and spring looks like spring almost anywhere.

Here's the rundown on the weather:

✔ If it's going to rain — and odds are, it won't, unless another El Niño snakes its way out of the tropics — it's most likely going to happen in spring. Even then, heavy rainstorms are unusual.

✔ It can get nippy in winter — oh, not Minnesota, 40-degrees-below-zero nippy — but it can get down in the 20s at night, so bring a coat if you visit in the cool months. A light wrap is always a good idea, thanks to temperatures that can drop significantly from day to night.

✔ Fall can bring the *Santa Anas,* the surprisingly strong, warm winds that are a bane to firefighters. And summer brings the real heat, and with that often real smog. Get in the car and head to the beach along with everyone else.

✔ Note also that the Westside neighborhoods (Santa Monica, Brentwood, Pacific Palisades, and even Westwood) always seem to be 20 degrees (or more) cooler than Hollywood, Pasadena, and the Valley (the latter two are the hottest places in the metropolitan area). We've spent many a day sweltering in 90-degree weather on the Eastside and then traveled west, only to find it 62 and foggy. Go figure. Thank the ocean breezes.

Be a Part of It: New York, New York!

New York has always been about traffic — traffic in money, in ideas, in trends, in commerce (and in the streets, of course). Visiting New York gives you a chance to participate in this long and rich history. Every group that has visited New York has brought something here and left its mark; even if all you leave behind is your vacation money, you're playing a part in keeping the merry-go-round spinning (and enjoying a pleasant ride yourself).

Six reasons why we love NY

Here are our favorite things about New York City:

✔ **A walking city:** Manhattan is a city to enjoy in the streets. The city offers a global assortment of people, outrageous outfits and personalities, street musicians, sidewalk artists, and hipsters. This abundant street life makes New York a great city for walking. Don't shortchange yourself on these pedestrian pleasures. (But to really enjoy yourself, you must bring comfortable shoes!)

✔ **Classic pleasures:** Classic New York experiences include crossing the Brooklyn Bridge at sunset, walking through Central Park on a summer day, making your way — slowly — up Fifth Avenue with the Christmas crowds, and inline skating or walking along the Hudson River on the new riverfront promenade.

✔ **International cuisine:** Because of its unique internationalism, New York has an incredible depth and breadth when it comes to cuisine. Visiting New York is a perfect chance to try Ethiopian, Tibetan, Turkish, Senegalese, or other cuisines you may not find at home. Italian is still the reigning ethnic cuisine, outnumbering all the others; and, of course, pizza is ubiquitous and available in many diverse styles.

✔ **Broadway:** For many visitors, seeing a Broadway show is the quintessential New York experience. Although the long-running musical *Cats* has closed, having finally used up all nine of its lives, *The Lion King* is still roaring, *Rent* is still being collected, and there will be no shortage of future blockbusters.

Off-Broadway and off-off-Broadway continue to produce experimental, challenging, and exciting shows. New York is in no danger of losing its primacy in American theater.

✔ **Cultural revolutions:** New York's cultural offerings have no end. If you enjoy art, New York's museums (the Metropolitan Museum of Art, the Museum of Modern Art, and the Guggenheim, to name the big three) rank among the best in the world.

Beyond theater, you have opera; beyond opera, ballet; beyond these, you find modern dance, performance art, poetry readings, and various new forms of exhibitionism. The premier institutions in these fields are in New York. Take music, for example: New York is the home of Carnegie Hall, Lincoln Center, famous jazz clubs like Blue Note and Birdland, world-renowned rock music clubs like CBGB, and newer clubs where the next phenomenon may be discovered.

Don't forget film, either. The Big Apple is seriously challenging Hollywood as the seat of the film and TV industry. Some 60 to 90 new productions are filmed in New York every day!

✔ **Shopping:** From high-fashion houses to designer sample sales, New York is the place for clothing, whether from known fashion superdesigners or from ambitious recent graduates of the Fashion Institute of Technology. Shopping can encompass visits to a few of the most famous department stores in the world, such as Bloomingdale's and Macy's, and some of the most high-end, such as Bergdorf Goodman. You can get everything in New York, from homemade goods to high-end imported Italian shoes and Persian carpets.

New York also has a thriving discount electronics business, huge CD and record stores, gigantic bookstores, a diamond district . . . the list goes on. At various times, the city has had entire stores devoted to fossils or maps. If you want it, believe us — it's here.

The secrets of the seasons

To catch New York at its best and brightest, consider visiting during the fall or the spring. Here's the scoop on the seasons:

✔ **Spring:** In the spring (April to June), temperatures are usually mild and pleasant.

- ✓ **Fall:** In the fall (September to early November), the sun almost always shines through crisp, chilly days. In mid-October, the city sometimes experiences an unseasonably mild spell known as Indian summer.

- ✓ **Summer:** Sometime between mid-July and mid-August, the city usually suffers through a period when temperatures soar to around 100°F (38°C), with 70 percent to 80 percent humidity. During this time, it's hard to be anywhere except an air-conditioned hotel room — the city literally stinks and people are often in a bad mood.

- ✓ **Winter:** In January and February, temperatures can drop to 20°F (–6°C) or lower. This post-holiday part of the winter is also a somewhat less busy time in New York. The cold seems to create a general chill-out effect, and as a result, the city sees fewer visitors and fewer cultural events — at least outdoor ones!

Anxious hoteliers and merchants court tourists and their dollars during the winter slow season. If you travel in January or February, getting tickets for a show or a discounted room in a hotel will be easier.

Leave Your Heart in San Francisco

With a wink and a wave to the past, San Francisco continues to reinvent herself. In her brief role as the heartbeat of the Internet economy, the city sashayed into the 21st century with an energy and style that caused even the old-timers to gasp in admiration.

Even after the dot-com bubble burst, some things stayed the same: The beautiful scenery continues to dazzle, the top-flight dining continues to garner raves, and the entertainment possibilities continue to grow in sophistication.

The best of San Francisco

Vibrant and alive, San Francisco offers a host of entertaining activities and scenic beauty. Here's the best of this great town:

- ✓ **Food lover's paradise:** San Francisco's reputation as a food-lover's paradise is both well-deserved and tested on a daily basis. You can find thousands of restaurants around town, from dives to divas, all with their loyal followings and all under constant scrutiny by critics and self-proclaimed gourmands.

- ✓ **The hills are alive:** The clatter and hum of cable cars, the huffing and puffing of out-of-shape joggers, the wooden stairways leading to hidden gardens — San Francisco's famous hills are most certainly alive and well. Gathered between the orange-hued Golden Gate Bridge and the silvery Bay Bridge, the hypnotic Pacific Ocean and the icy waters of the bay, these hills serve as the main attraction, as well as the backdrop, for sight-seers in the city, and they've worked their way into our collective imagination through the myriad books and films that have immortalized them.

✔ **Museums and parks:** For equally breathtaking, if less lofty, views, seek out the Palace of Fine Arts, the Museum of Modern Art, or Golden Gate Park. Ride the streetcar down Market Street to Fisherman's Wharf or in the opposite direction to the Giants' fabulous baseball stadium. Revel in the urban gardens at Yerba Buena Center and in the crowded sidewalks of Chinatown. In these places, you can catch a glimpse of what San Francisco was like during its formative years and where the city is headed in the 21st century.

✔ **Nightlife:** The music and club scene, especially around North Beach and South of Market, is thriving for those who want to shimmy as well as those who prefer to groove silently with the horn section. There's no lack of places to relax and make a toast to your vacation, and theater, dance, and classical music lovers can find a great many venues in which to laugh, cry, or clap wildly.

✔ **Shopping:** From the hallowed picture windows of Union Square to the curio-packed sidewalks of Chinatown, from the boutiques along Fillmore, Sacramento, and Union streets to the discounters of SoMa, if shopping is your bag, San Francisco can fill 'er up. Do you fancy fine wines? Do hand-made chocolate truffles have you making promises you have no intention of keeping? Would a unique objet d'art be just the right pick-me-up for your old coffee table? This is the town for you!

✔ **Urban renewal:** San Francisco never seems to sit still. Neighborhoods are developing in areas that at best were ignored prior to the dot-com revolution. Traffic, which will forever be a problem, hasn't lightened up, but public transportation is improving and expanding. With more and more people determined to call San Francisco home, gentrification is reaching every nook and cranny with both fortunate and unfortunate consequences.

The secret of the seasons

Because of its temperate California address, San Francisco hosts tourists and business travelers year-round. However, San Francisco is the most crowded between June and October. During this time of year, you need to make hotel and car reservations at least six weeks in advance, reserve a table at the more well-known restaurants three to four weeks in advance, and purchase your tickets to Alcatraz before you leave home.

✔ **Winter:** You're unlikely to see snow, but the weather won't exactly be balmy either. Still, a winter visit to San Francisco has its advantages. Hotel prices will be lower, especially on weekends, and overall, the city won't be as busy.

✔ **Spring:** Spring is a popular time for travel, but in San Francisco, it's also a popular time for conventions, bringing hotel costs up. Flowers are in bloom in the parks, and the major sites are less crowded than in summer.

✔ **Summer:** Many travelers are surprised at how cool and foggy San Francisco summers are. Kids are out of school, and it's the best time to plan a family vacation. Mimes are out in full force. However, foggy mornings are downers. Hotels are packed, and Pier 39 and Fisherman's Wharf are madhouses.

✔ **Fall:** If reliably warm, sunny days are a top priority for you, this is the best time to visit. Because of the nice weather, Napa Valley is booked, and the heavy events calendar lures additional crowds. But it's the nicest weather of the year.

Pledging Allegiance to Washington, D.C.

When most of the world thinks of Washington, D.C., the city's role as the nation's capital comes to mind: The president, the Congress, the Supreme Court, the Pentagon, and the State Department are all here. But, like all great cities, Washington is much more than just the government.

Nine ways to enjoy Washington, D.C.

Because Washington, D.C., is the nation's capital, it has a sense of history unlike any other city in the United States. It has a lively arts community, and offers an active nightlife and varied ethnic cuisine. Along those lines, here are some of our favorite things about Washington:

✔ **International cuisine:** As the world's capital, Washington has acquired restaurants that feature many of the world's ethnic cuisines. You can choose from Brazilian, Chinese, French, Indian, Italian, Malaysian, Mediterranean, Mexican, Moroccan, Spanish, Thai, and Vietnamese restaurants, as well as some others that feature dishes from all around Asia and Latin America. And, of course, you have many varieties of U.S. cooking to choose among, because Washingtonians come from every corner of the nation and bring their dining preferences with them.

✔ **Living history:** One of the most striking facts about Washington is that history really has been — and is being — made here. You can walk into and around the places you read about in your history books. And you can watch some of the history that's being created today.

✔ **Free attractions:** One of Washington's best selling points is that many of its top attractions, including the Smithsonian's many museums, are free. Unlike London, Paris, Rome, or other major capitals, you don't have to open your wallet before you can open the doors to most of the popular museums, galleries, and other sights.

✔ **Where are the skyscrapers?** In Washington, a high-rise is 180 feet tall. That's because no structure is allowed to exceed the height of the Capitol Dome. Plenty of interesting low-rises are there to capture your attention — the White House, the Capitol, and the Supreme Court, for starters.

✔ **Arts:** Washington has rich cultural, historical, scientific, and educational resources. The Smithsonian Institution's many museums, the National Gallery of Art, the John F. Kennedy Performing Arts Center, and the Shakespeare Theater are just a few examples.

✔ **Nightlife:** You can experience all the permutations of pop culture around town, from rock concerts at Robert F. Kennedy Stadium, to Broadway shows at the National and Warner theaters, to jazz, folk, bluegrass, country, and hip-hop at the city's clubs.

✔ **Sports:** Except for the egregious omission of Major League Baseball, Washington is a world-class sports town, with professional football, hockey, and men's and women's basketball and soccer teams, as well as some perennial college powerhouses. (Someday, maybe Washington will get a baseball team, too!)

✔ **Shopping:** Washington's merchants — in national department store chains or local boutiques — are ready and willing to lighten your wallet. Capitol Hill has an old-fashioned farmers' market, as well as upscale shops in gorgeously renovated Union Station. Georgetown boasts countless boutiques, as well as a traditional flea market. If you're into up-up-up-scale shopping, Upper Wisconsin Avenue has its own smaller version of Beverly Hills' exclusive Rodeo Drive.

✔ **Nature:** The District's climate is friendly to flowering plants in the spring. Azaleas join the cherry trees in bringing color to all parts of town. The Mall and other parkland give Washington a greenway that stretches west from the Capitol to the Potomac River.

The secret of the seasons

You can't choose a bad time to visit Washington if your primary goal is to see the sights and you're not concerned about the crowds. You can tour the museums, monuments, and government buildings any season. Cultural, entertainment, and sports activities are always going on. And the stores are glad to sell to you no matter what the season.

Here are the pros and cons of each season:

✔ **Spring and fall:** The best times to visit D.C. are spring and fall — April through mid-June and September through mid-November. Temperature and humidity tend to be moderate. The flowers are on display in the spring. The weather in the fall can be close to ideal. Congress is likely to be at work, and cultural and entertainment activities are running full force.

✔ **Summer:** You can find more bargains in hotter summer months, as hotels try to fill the rooms that empty during Congressional vacations by offering money-saving package deals. You can also enjoy a great deal of free, outdoor entertainment in the summer.

A strike against August is that, weather-wise, it can feel like an equatorial rainforest — excruciating heat, even more excruciating humidity, and regular, vicious thunderstorms.

✔ **Winter:** Washington does get a real winter most years, usually with snow and some periods of extreme cold in January and February. Washington looks gorgeous after a snowfall, especially when the congressional Christmas tree is on display at the foot of Capitol Hill. And D.C.'s latest administration has been doing a much better job of clearing the streets when the snow falls.

If you're anxious to see government in action, also keep in mind that Congress tries to take lengthy recesses in late summer and at the end of the year.

Glam and Glitz: Las Vegas

If a city exists that has its heart — and all sorts of other body parts — right on its sleeve, and all its goods in the shop window (which is, by the way, subtly outlined in blazing bright neon), it's Las Vegas. This isn't a coy metropolis nor an unassuming city. Vegas is a gaudy monstrosity of delight: a city designed solely to take your money and break your heart while making you love it and beg for more.

Las Vegas is the number-one tourist spot in America and the fifth most-popular destination in the world. Don't come here looking for culture and self-improvement, but do come here looking for a whale of a good time. You're sure to have it.

Las Vegas fact sheet

Viva, Las Vegas:

- ✔ **Lodging:** Las Vegas may well be the only city in the world where the skyline is made up entirely of other cities, and even countries. New York, Egypt, Paris, Venice — all are represented in the facades of extraordinary hotel-resort complexes, behemoths of more than 3,000 rooms.

  And their themes span the globe and the ages. Visit the Sphinx at Luxor, watch pirates battle at Treasure Island, ride a gondola through The Venetian, take in a joust at Excalibur, ride a Coney Island roller coaster at New York-New York, or climb the Eiffel Tower in Paris Las Vegas.

- ✔ **Food:** Vegas has a restaurant from many (if not most) of the celebrity chefs and name-brand eateries in America, and it can stand proudly alongside more traditionally lauded culinary cities. But if all you care about is stuffing yourself — and hey, we're right there with you — the famous Vegas buffets are still in action, presenting each and every diner with enough food to feed a small country, or at least several very hungry football teams.

- ✔ **Gambling:** You may have heard a vague rumor stating that there is gambling in Vegas. Boy, oh boy, is there ever! Get off the plane, and you see slot machines right there in the airport, just waiting for you to lay your eager hands on them. But don't; the gambling odds at the airports are notoriously bad. Try to control yourself; casinos beckon with numerous games of chance, from blackjack to poker to roulette.

- ✔ **Ditching the glitz:** None of Las Vegas's monumental hotels would exist without the modern marvel that is Hoover Dam. Just 30 miles outside the city, this feat of engineering provides the juice that keeps Las Vegas's cash cows running.

  For those who want to keep their bodies up and running, numerous recreational opportunities — from swimming to hiking — await visitors to Lake Mead. And for sheer natural beauty, you can't beat the almost otherworldly terrain of Red Rock Canyon and Valley of Fire State Park.

- ✔ **Crooners, giggles, and jiggles:** Frank Sinatra and his Rat Pack buddies made Vegas the hot destination. By the time Elvis established himself as a regular performer, Vegas shows were legendary. While those glamour days are somewhat in the past, top performers still consider Vegas a must-stop. At any given time, you can see a number of big-production shows, ranging from the exquisite artistry of the Cirque du Soleil to the high-kicking showgirls of *Jubilee!* and a host of other options — renowned magicians, comedians, and free lounge singers and bands. And yes, the topless revues, while no longer the main attraction, still have their place.

> ✔ **The club scene:** If sweating it out on the dance floor is more to your taste, Las Vegas's club scene will more than satisfy your appetite. Sashay your way into the city's appropriately snooty rendition of the legendary Studio 54, down almost any kind of rum concoction you can imagine as you dance the night away at rumjungle, rub elbows with the beautiful and the size zeroes at Ghost Bar, or party on at The Beach. If we can offer one sure bet when it comes to Sin City's after-dark action, it's that you'll find at least one club that caters to your demographic.

The secret of the seasons

Las Vegas is a year-round city. While the weather can be tricky and strange, you aren't going to get blizzards or tons of rain or other fun-dampening problems. Sure, it can get hot — oh, man, can it! — but that's why they invented swimming pools and air conditioning, both of which are found in Vegas in abundance.

Because Las Vegas is a year-round city, you may find that when it's off-season for other popular tourist destinations, Vegas's hotel rooms may be full thanks to conventions, a highly publicized boxing match, or some other crowd-drawing event.

Do remember that weekdays here are considerably less crowded than weekends, which means that you're likely to find the best hotel rates on weekdays.

Partying Down in Rockin' New Orleans

Somewhere in the verdant bayous of Southern Louisiana, nestled among the swamps, lies a magical, mythical city. Peopled by voracious Cajun men and exotic Creole priestesses, its streets are home to a constant, 24-hour party that begins in the streets of its storied French Quarter and ends in the sweaty confines of smoky jazz clubs. The festive hoards spend their days dancing in spontaneous public parades and dining on sinfully elegant seven-course meals. And somewhere close to all of this sits the city of New Orleans.

Five New Orleans highlights

New Orleans is a mix of French and Spanish cultures, with touches of African, Caribbean, and even a bit o' the Irish thrown in for good measure. This mish-mash of cultures serves as New Orleans's single most defining characteristic.

Here are some of its offerings:

✔ **Music:** From the drumming rituals of congregated slaves in Congo Square, which loosed African and European rhythms into the city streets, to the piano players hired to entertain customers in the parlors of Storyville's once-legalized bordellos, no city boasts a stronger link to its musical past than New Orleans. The syncopated shuffles that thundered out of those slave gatherings propelled stirring spirituals, work songs, and the blues, as well as the animated ruckus of marching brass bands. And this diversity of music sowed the seeds of jazz, rhythm and blues, and rock and roll.

✔ **Food:** If New Orleanians take one thing even more seriously than their music, it would have to be their food. The twin touchstones of local cooking are Cajun and Creole cuisine. You find elements of both styles of cooking on practically every menu in town, from the classic Monday-night staple red beans and rice to more sophisticated offerings such as Trout Almandine.

✔ **Historical sites:** New Orleans capitalizes on its historical influences to provide many interesting and educational activities for tourists, including:

  • The Cabildo, where the Louisiana Purchase was turned over to the United States in 1803, is now an entertaining museum focusing on life in early Louisiana.

  • On the site of the Battle of New Orleans stands Chalmette Battlefield, which celebrates that historic battle and houses a cemetery filled with Civil War soldiers.

  • The National D-Day Museum, which commemorates that watershed WWII event with a number of captivating exhibits, also highlights New Orleans's integral part in that struggle.

✔ **Mardi Gras:** While Mardi Gras is often billed, and not without cause, as the biggest free party on the North American continent, it's also both a major religious holiday and a study in cultural anthropology.

The big day itself (Shrove Tuesday, or literally, Fat Tuesday — the last day before Lent) is notable for being the culmination of Carnival season, capping a frenzied two-week window of accelerated hedonistic excess before the self-imposed sacrifices of Lent (the 40-day season that precedes Easter in the Catholic religion).

Don't feel guilty if you just come for the party, however. For one thing, Mardi Gras has certainly grown into a pop-cultural event all its own. And for another thing, it's filled with a number of fascinating aspects that reward close inspection, from the parades themselves to the pageantry and spectacle of the organizations (or *krewes*) that throw them.

  ✔ **The French Quarter:** No New Orleans travel guide worth its Cajun sea-
    sonings can afford to ignore the French Quarter, most often presented
    to the world as the face of New Orleans. Its mix of classic and modern
    ultimately gives the French Quarter its charm.

    The French quarter is also home to Bourbon Street. Dotted with loud
    music hangouts (most of them of the watered-down, tourist-trap variety),
    dance clubs, and strip joints, the entire boulevard serves as one long
    salute to the pursuit of unrestrained pleasure. The street is certainly a
    feast for the senses, which, despite the lowest-common-denominator
    appeal, can be oddly exhilarating.

The secret of the seasons

New Orleans really has only three seasons:

  ✔ Hot

  ✔ Cold

  ✔ "In between"

Except for late spring and early summer (when temperatures are just uniformly hot), the seasons tend to run together. That's because this port city,
a natural drop-off point for various cultures, also seems to be a way station
for just about every weather pattern visiting the North American continent.
A butterfly beating its wings in Kansas City seems to affect the weather in
New Orleans.

Discovering the Best of Europe: Sixteen Great Cities

Following is a brief — and hardly complete! — description of 16 cities that
everyone visiting Europe should see. Each of these cities is near famous
cultural and historical sites, and each is within easy traveling distance of
smaller interesting places to visit.

  ✔ **London** is the capital of the old British Empire. From the medieval
    Tower of London where Henry VIII's wives lost their heads to the neo-
    Gothic halls of Westminster, where you can watch Parliament in heated
    debate, London offers a wealth of sightseeing possibilities.

  ✔ **Edinburgh,** the capital of Scotland, is a vibrant university town whose
    old city is presided over by one of the best glowering castles in Europe,
    and whose Georgian new city is a genteel grid of streets for shopping
    and finding cheap town house accommodations.

- **Dublin** has its charms, such as admiring the Book of Kells at Trinity College, exploring Celtic history at the Archaeological Museum, following in the footsteps of James Joyce and other Irish scribes, and pub crawling through Temple Bar.

- **Paris** is considered by many to be the capital of European sightseeing. From seeing the masterpieces in the Louvre and the Impressionists collection of the Musée d'Orsay to climbing the Eiffel Tower, cruising the Seine, or simply whiling the day away at a cafe in the St-Germain-de-Pres or Marais neighborhoods, Paris has enough to keep you busy for a lifetime.

- **Amsterdam** is as famed for its examples of Dutch tolerance (from the libidinous — the Red Light district and "smoking" cafes — to the serious — the Dutch house that hid Anne Frank and her family during the Nazi occupation) as it is for its canals lined by genteel 17th-century town houses and artistic giants such as Rembrandt and van Gogh. And don't forget the Indonesian feasts in the Leidesplein district, rib-sticking dinner pancakes, and local brews Heineken, Amstel, and gin.

- **Munich** is the pulsing heart of life-loving, beer-happy Bavaria. This city is an industrial powerhouse packed with a bevy of fine museums and two outstanding baroque palaces — and host to the biggest fraternity party in the world, the annual September Oktoberfest. You can munch on bratwurst and pretzels in beer halls and stroll the old center and expansive Englisher Garten city park.

- **Vienna** retains its refined 19th-century air such as no other in Europe. Steep yourself in this heritage by climbing the cathedral towers, sipping coffee at a famous cafe, exhausting yourself on the masterpieces of the Kunsthistoriches Museum, or waiting in line for standing-room tickets ($3) at the renowned State Opera house.

- **Innsbruck** is another popular Austrian destination. It is a great little town tucked away in the heart of the Austrian Alps.

- In **Bern,** the capital of Switzerland, you can admire the masterpieces of hometown boy Paul Klee, see where Einstein came up with $E=MC^2$, feed the town mascots at the Bear Pits, and float down the river with the locals, where you can delve into the heart of the Swiss Alps, the Bernese Oberland region around the towering Jungfrau peak.

- **Prague** has come roaring out from behind the defunct Iron Curtain to become one of Europe's greatest destinations. This dreamy city of fairy-tale spires, castles, and churches is one of the world's top centers for sampling beer and classical music. You find a plethora of cheap concerts every night and in every venue imaginable — from symphonies playing in grand halls to street trios playing under an acoustically sound medieval bridge abutment.

- **Rome** has both ancient sites and over 900 churches, starting with St. Peter's and working its way on down through massive basilicas to tiny medieval chapels. The city's dozens of museums house everything from ancient Roman statues, frescoes, and mosaics to Renaissance master-pieces. You can also see Michelangelo's Sistine Chapel ceiling. The cityscape itself is a joy to wander, a tangle of medieval streets and Renaissance-era boulevards punctuated by public squares sporting baroque fountains and Egyptian obelisks, including Piazza Navona, Piazza del Popolo, and the Trevi Fountain.

✔ **Florence** is the birthplace of the Renaissance, with more world-class museums and frescoed churches than you can shake a Michelangelo at. Here you find his *David,* Botticelli's *Birth of Venus,* Leonardo's *Annunciation,* and other artistic icons. Florence is also a great place to chow down on succulent steaks, sample fine Italian wines, and wander Dante's old neighborhood.

✔ **Venice** floats like a dream city on its lagoon, a fantasy world of ornate palaces and tiny footbridges springing over a network of canals. The only modes of transportation here are boats and your own two legs. The interior of St. Mark's Cathedral glitters with more mosaics than you would think possible, and the works of great Venetian artists, such as Titian, Tintoretto, and Veronese, cover the walls of both the Accademia Gallery and Doge's Palace.

✔ **Madrid,** the Spanish capital, grabs you with its museums, from the masterworks in the Museo del Prado to Picasso's Guernica in the Reina Sofia. Tour the Royal Palace, take in a professional bullfight, or move from bar to bar sampling appetizer-sized *tapas* before indulging in a hearty 10:00 p.m. dinner and resting up to party in the clubs until dawn.

✔ **Barcelona,** the capital of Spain's Catalonia region, boasts a great Gothic quarter to explore, Las Ramblas (one of Europe's most fun pedestrian promenades), and the work of local early 20th-century greats. You find the work of Picasso, Joan Miró, and especially Antoni Gaudí, whose *modernisme* take on Art Nouveau architecture pops up in everything from town houses to a city park to the only great European cathedral still (slowly) being built, his Sagrada Famiglia.

✔ **Athens,** Greece, is the heart of the Mediterranean. It is the ancient Greek capital, a sprawling modern city still overseen by the ruins of the 2,500-year-old Parthenon atop the Acropolis Hill. Packed around the inexpensive *tavernas* and bargain-friendly shops lie more crumbling reminders of the Greek Golden Age such as Temple of the Olympian Zeus and Temple of the Winds. The city's archaeological museums high-light not only Classical Age remains but also statues from the Cycladic era and Kouros from the earlier age when ancient Egypt was the arbiter of artistic taste.

A few unique spots to visit on the cheap

At least at this point in time, food and lodging in Europe is cheaper the farther east you go. And although airfare to Bulgaria may be a little more expensive than a flight to Paris, if you watch for special deals, or have a travel agent who does, you can put together a pretty cheap — and unique — vacation. Here's a sampling of the many options available, with a couple places from Asia and South America thrown in for variety:

✔ **Sandaski, Bulgaria.** If you want a relaxing European spa vacation that's cheap, try Sandaski, a spa town built near some of the 500 mineral springs in Bulgaria that was once sought out by Roman emperors for its healing treatments. Stay in one of the many inexpensive resorts, and sample about every kind of spa treatment imaginable. And if you want to expend a little energy, visit some of Bulgaria's ancient monasteries and impressive mountain ranges.

✔ **Dubrovnik, Croatia.** With its magnificent stone walls, churches, palaces, and plazas, Dubrovnik is architecturally a living monument to the days when it was an affluent merchant state in the Roman Empire. Try to catch the open-air pop and classical concerts and street theater during the Dubrovnik Summer Festival, the biggest cultural event in Croatia. And Croatian food is always fresh and relatively inexpensive, with seasonal ingredients of the highest quality — especially the scampi and calamari.

✔ **Prague, Czech.** Once the capital of the Holy Roman Empire, Prague is famous for its architecture that stands mainly as it did a millennium ago. Attend inexpensive classical concerts in ancient churches nearly every night and browse through the endless crystal and ceramic shops and museums during the day. Although accommodations are starting to go up in price a bit, the food — and especially the alcohol — is quite cheap. One drawback to cheap alcohol is that Prague is filled with drinking students on vacation. But there is plenty for the more mature traveler.

✔ **Santiago, Chile.** Lying on the Pacific coast and surrounded by the impressive Andes mountains, the capital of Chile offers incredible scenery. You can swim in the sea in the morning and be on world-renowned ski slopes by afternoon. Bustling markets, charming old quarters, and beautiful parks with thriving artistic, social, and cultural scenes will occupy you all day. The city's museums, such as the Museo de Arte Contemporaneo, are definitely worth a visit, even though they are generally small. Lodging is fairly inexpensive, but the restaurants vary widely from very cheap to quite expensive. So look at the menu before you enter.

✔ **Ho Chi Minh City, Vietnam.** Still known to many locals and tourists as Saigon, this bustling, dynamic city is a budget way to see the beauty of Asia. See the sights of the city in a cyclo (part bicycle, part cart) or take a walk along the riverfront to enjoy the constant activity on the Saigon River or make your way down to Dong Khoi Street, which is packed with gift shops, tailors, jewelers, and restaurants. And check out the History Museum. Although it's a bit grimy, it houses a worthy collection of artifacts from Vietnam's two thousand years of recorded history. And with over 500 traditional dishes served up in innumerable little restaurants, you can eat all you want without breaking the budget.

Part VII
Going High-Tech

The 5th Wave — By Rich Tennant

"SINCE WE BEGAN ONLINE SHOPPING, I JUST DON'T KNOW WHERE THE MONEY'S GOING."

In this part . . .

In this part, you get up and running with your new computer — quickly and painlessly. Before long, you'll be creating documents with Microsoft Office and reconnecting with old buddies through the Internet. You even get the full scoop on eBay Internet auctions and distance learning online. Go on — get started!

The most popular operating system today is Microsoft Windows XP, covered in the next section.

✔ **Application programs:** These programs are the ones that do the work. Application programs include word processors, graphics editors, games, educational software, and so on. Whatever it is you do on your computer, you do it using an application program.

You can buy application *suites,* which contain several programs packaged together for one price. In addition, the programs typically look alike and use similar commands for common tasks, making them easy to use. Microsoft Office, the most popular application suite for the PC, is covered later in this chapter.

✔ **Utilities and programming software.**

✔ **Internet applications:** Web browsers, e-mail programs, and software of that ilk.

Getting to Know Windows XP

One way or another, you've probably already heard about Windows, created by the Microsoft company and owned by one of the richest men in the world. Windows posters line the walls of computer stores. Everybody who's anybody talks breezily about Windows, the Internet, and the World Wide Web. Weird code words, such as www.vw.com, stare out cryptically from magazines, newspapers, bus stops, and blimps.

Windows changed computing in several ways:

✔ Windows software updates the *look* of computers. Windows replaces the old-style words and numbers with colorful pictures and fun buttons. It's fun and flashy, like a Versace necktie.

✔ Windows XP is the most powerful of Microsoft's Windows software — software that's been updated many times since starting to breathe in January 1985. XP is short for *Experience,* but Microsoft calls it Windows XP to make it sound hip, as if Jimi Hendrix would have used it.

✔ Programmer types say Windows software is big enough and powerful enough to be called an *operating system.* That's because Windows "operates" your computer. Other programs tell Windows what to do, and Windows makes your computer carry out those commands.

Figure 21-2 shows a Windows XP desktop, with callouts to various elements.

Figure 21-2:
The
Windows
XP desktop.

Start button   Quick launch bar   Start menu   Icons   Windows trash can

Logging on to Windows XP

If your new PC came with Windows XP already installed (most do), Windows XP probably leaps to your screen automatically when you first turn on the computer. But before you can do anything, Windows XP throws you a fastball with its brilliant blue Welcome screen: Windows wants you to log on, as shown in Figure 21-3.

See, Windows XP allows bunches of people to work on the same computer, yet it keeps everybody's work separate. To do that, it needs to know who's currently sitting in front of the keyboard. The solution? You must log on:

1. **Click your *user name,* as shown in Figure 21-3.**

   A few seconds after you click, Windows XP shows you your desktop, ready for you to make a mess.

2. **When you're through working or just feel like taking a break, simply log off (explained in the next section) so somebody else can use the computer.**

   Later, when you log back on, your newly created mess will be waiting for you, just as you left it.

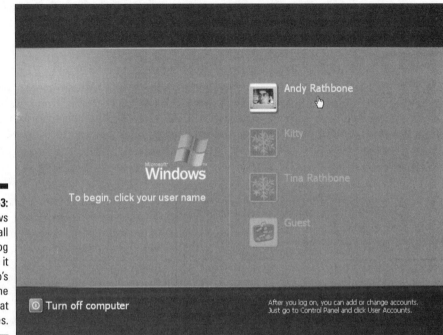

Figure 21-3: Windows XP wants all users to log on so it knows who's using the computer at all times.

Andy Rathbone

Kitty

Tina Rathbone

Guest

To begin, click your user name

Turn off computer

After you log on, you can add or change accounts. Just go to Control Panel and click User Accounts.

Although the desktop may be a mess, it's your *own* mess. When you come back to the computer, your letters will all be where you saved them. Someone didn't accidentally delete your files or folders while playing Widget Squash. Or, if you left your desktop tidy, it will be just as tidy when you return.

If you're the only person using your computer, you can set up Windows XP to skip the Welcome screen — there's no need to log on.

What's the secret password?

Windows XP lets bunches of people use the same computer without messing up each other's work. But how do you make sure Josh doesn't read Grace's love letters to Henry Rollins? How can you set up your computer so that nobody accidentally deletes your letters? How can Josh make sure Grace's pink background doesn't replace his spaceships when he logs onto the computer? A password solves some of those problems.

By typing a secret password when logging on, you enable your computer to recognize *you* and nobody else. If you protect your user name with a password, nobody can access your files (except for the computer's administrator, who can peek into anything — and even wipe out your account).

Starting your favorite program with the Start button

When Windows XP first takes over your computer, it turns your screen into a pseudo-desktop: a fancy name for a plate of buttons with labels beneath them. Click a button, and the program assigned to that button hops to the screen in its own little window. Click the Start button in the bottom-left corner of the screen, and you'll have even more buttons to choose from, as shown in Figure 21-4.

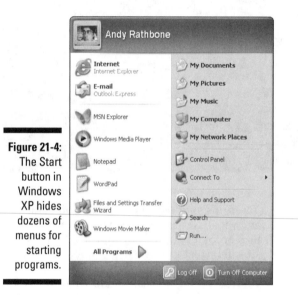

Figure 21-4: The Start button in Windows XP hides dozens of menus for starting programs.

Here's everything you need to know about the Start button:

✔ Because the buttons have little pictures on them, they're called *icons*. Icons offer clues to the programs they represent. Click an icon, and its program pops to the screen, ready for work. Click the icon of the stamped envelope, for instance, to launch Outlook Express, a program that lets people send and receive electronic mail on their computers.

✔ But wait — there's more! If Windows XP put all its options on the screen at the same time, it would look more crowded than a 14-page menu at the Siam Thai restaurant. To avoid resorting to fine print, Windows XP hides some menus in special locations on the screen. When you click the mouse in the right place, more options leap toward you.

For example, begin loading Windows' simple word-processing program, WordPad. If you spot the WordPad icon on the big menu, go ahead and click it. If it's not there, you need to dig a little deeper. Start by clicking the Start button. When the Start menu pops up, click the words All Programs at the screen's bottom. Wham! A new menu appears. Click Accessories from the new menu, and yet another menu appears. Finally, click WordPad to bring it to the screen.

Putting two programs on-screen simultaneously

After spending all your money for Windows XP and a computer powerful enough to cart it around, you're not going to be content with only one program on your screen. You want to _fill_ the screen with programs, all running in their own little windows.

How do you put a second program on the screen?

1. **Open a program, such as WordPad, by clicking its icon in the Start button's Accessories area (that area's listed under the Programs area).**

2. **Click the Start button and move through the menus, as described in the "Starting your favorite program with the Start button" section, until you find the program you want to start.**

   Suppose that you want to start the Pinball game.

3. **Here goes: Click the Start button, click All Programs, click Games, and click Pinball. Pinball rushes to the screen.**

To switch between the two open windows, you can click the appropriate buttons in the taskbar, or press Alt+Tab.

Logging off Windows XP

Ah! The most pleasant thing you'll do with Windows XP all day could very well be to stop using it. And you do that the same way you started: by using the Start button, that friendly little helper that popped up the first time you started Windows XP. There, along the bottom of the Start menu, are two options: Log Off and Turn Off Computer.

Which should you choose? Here's the scoop:

✔ **Log Off:** Choose this option when you're done working with Windows XP for the time being. Windows then asks if you want to Switch User or Log Off. Which option do you choose?

  • If you're _really_ through with the computer, choose Log Off. Windows saves your work and your settings, and returns to the Welcome screen for the next user.

- If somebody else just wants to borrow the computer for a few minutes, choose Switch User. The Welcome screen appears, but Windows keeps your open programs waiting in the background. When you switch back, everything's just as you left it.

✔ **Turn Off Computer:** Choose this when nobody else will be using the computer until the next morning. Windows XP saves everything and tells you when it's okay to turn off your computer.

Getting Acquainted with Microsoft Office XP

Microsoft Office XP is an application suite containing all the applications you need to do business, manage your life, or simply have fun. You can choose from several combinations of the following applications:

✔ **Microsoft Word:** As its name implies, Word lets you write words so that you can create letters, reports, proposals, brochures, newsletters, pink slips, ransom notes, and practically anything else that requires a rudimentary command of the written language.

✔ **Microsoft Excel:** *Spreadsheets,* such as Microsoft Excel, help you track budgets, inventories, or embezzlements (kidding!) on your own personal computer. With Excel, you can even create charts and graphs to help visualize your data.

✔ **Microsoft Outlook:** Outlook is a personal information organizer that helps you keep track of pressing appointments, pending tasks, and important names and addresses. Outlook also helps you write, send, and read e-mail, and it even can funnel all your e-mail from your Internet accounts into a central mailbox.

✔ **Microsoft FrontPage:** Microsoft FrontPage 2003 is designed for creating and editing Web pages — from creating frames to editing the HTML code that makes up your Web page.

✔ **Microsoft PowerPoint:** To help you create presentation slide shows on your computer, Microsoft Office XP includes a presentation program called PowerPoint. By using PowerPoint, you can show presentations on your computer or print them out as nifty handouts.

✔ **Microsoft Access:** Instead of racking your memory or hunting for slips of paper, try using Microsoft Access to organize your information. Access enables you to store, retrieve, sort, manipulate, and analyze information — making trends or patterns in your data easier to spot (so you can tell whether your company is losing money and may be thinking about another downsizing).

The programs in Microsoft Office XP share common commands to accomplish tasks such as opening, saving, and printing files, so after you see how to use one program in the suite, picking up another is easy to do!

Ten tips for using Microsoft Office XP

Here are ten indispensable tips for using Microsoft Office XP:

✔ **Customize the user interface:** To make Microsoft Office as easy to use as possible, take a few moments to customize the user interface. You can move toolbars to appear along the side, bottom, or right in the middle of the screen; zoom in to avoid eye strain; enlarge your toolbar buttons; and much more.

✔ **When in doubt, click the right mouse button:** When you want to rename, edit, or modify anything in Office XP, try right-clicking on the item. Chances are a handy menu will appear, and you can choose your command from there. Easy!

✔ **Use the What's This? feature:** Toolbars often display cryptic buttons that confuse even veteran Egyptian hieroglyphic experts. Rather than guess what these toolbar buttons do (or waste time experimenting), you can use the handy What's This? feature, which offers you a quick explanation of any toolbar button that confuses you.

✔ **Take shortcuts with macros:** A *macro* is a mini-program that records your keystrokes as you type. After you record the keystrokes in a macro, whenever you need to use those exact same keystrokes again, you can tell Microsoft Office XP to "play back" your recorded keystrokes. You can create and run macros within Word, Excel, and PowerPoint.

✔ **Protect your Microsoft Office XP files:** After you spend all your time learning how to use Microsoft Office XP, the last thing you want to happen is to lose all your precious data

that you sweated to create in the first place. So take steps now to protect yourself in the event of disaster, such as a computer virus, and you won't be sorry later. We highly recommend that you get an antivirus program, such as McAfee's VirusScan (www.mcafee.com) or Symantec's Norton AntiVirus (www.symantec.com) that can detect and remove viruses.

✔ **Encrypt your files:** In case you want to keep your Office XP documents private, you can use Office XP's built-in encryption program or buy an encryption program. Encryption scrambles your data so that no one else but you (and anyone else who steals or figures out your password) can read it.

✔ **Shred your files:** Because of the way computers delete files, when you erase a file, someone can "undelete" that file by using a utility program, such as The Norton Utilities. So if you want to permanently delete a file, you need to get a special file-shredding program. These file-shredding programs not only delete a file, but they overwrite that file several times with random bits of data. That way, if someone tries to unerase that file at a later date, all they see is gibberish. Two popular file-shredding programs are Eraser (www.tolvanen.com/eraser) and East-Tec Eraser (www.east-tec.com/eraser).

✔ **Back up your files:** If you happen to lose or delete a file by mistake, a back-up copy of your files enables you to continue working even though your original file may be history. The most reliable method is to use a back-up program and a back-up device

(continued)

(continued)

such as a tape drive, Zip drive, rewritable CD, or similar mass storage device. If you configure it properly, the back-up program automatically backs up your entire hard drive to your back-up drive without any extra effort on your part.

✔ **Use Pocket Office:** Rather than lug a laptop computer around the country, many people are opting for smaller, cheaper, and lighter handheld computers that run a slightly different operating system called PocketPC. PocketPC comes with a miniature version of Microsoft Office dubbed Pocket Office that includes Pocket Word, Pocket Excel, Pocket PowerPoint, and Pocket Access.

✔ **Use Smart Tags:** Smart Tags are a new Office XP feature that provides shortcuts for sharing and transferring data between the various Office XP programs.

Top free programs to download

Whether you're just figuring out the world of computers or have been savvy for years, you can always appreciate some free programs to get you where you need to go and protect you along the way:

✔ www.all-free-isp.com: Want to find a cheap or free Internet access service provider (ISP) in your local area? With this comprehensive database of free ISPs with local dialup access numbers, you can quickly find all free Internet service providers in your local calling area throughout the USA and Canada. You can also compare the free ISPs with the detailed information and ratings provided for each listing.

✔ www.zonelabs.com: A personal firewall is what stands between the outside world and your computer with its passwords, account numbers, and valuable data. Firewalls are absolutely necessary if you spend a lot of time on the Internet, and the free Zone Alarm from Zone Labs is a quality one. Just go to the download section at this site and get started.

✔ www.javacoolsoftware.com/spy wareblaster.html: Hackers can embed something called spyware into your system, which can wreck your system and programs. Spyware Blaster clears any spyware from your computer immediately and prevents it from ever becoming installed on your computer again. Download for free.

✔ http://housecall.trendmicro.com: No anti-virus software catches everything, running a periodic online check for nasty little viruses is wise. Try out HouseCall, a good online check that's free for home and individual users.

✔ www.tudogs.com: TuDogs gives you access to hundreds of top-quality, free software applications on the Web, as well as some useful free online services. Register for the free newsletter to get limited access or pay $12 a year for the whole shabang.

✔ www.freewarefiles.com: Freeware Files is another free software site like TuDogs. Find games, Internet tools, security utilities, multimedia, and Web development applications.

Narrowing your search

Most search engines make it easy to refine your search more exactly to target the pages you want to find. Here are some tips on how you may want to change your terms to narrow your search:

✔ Type most search words in lowercase. Type proper names with a single capital letter, such as **Elvis**. Don't type any words in all capital letters.

✔ If two or more words should appear together, put quotation marks around them, as in **"Elvis Presley"**. For another example, do the same with a pie search ("key lime pie") because, after all, that is what the pie

is called — although in this example, Google is clever enough to realize that it's a common phrase and pretends you typed the quotation marks anyway.

✔ Use + and - to indicate words that must either appear or not appear, such as **+Elvis +Costello -Presley** if you're looking for the modern Elvis, not the classic one.

✔ If you're like us, the number one reason your searches don't find anything is that one of the search words is spelled wrong. Check the spelling of your search word carefully as you type. If you spell it wrong, you may not find it.

Three things you have to know

Before you dive in and hit the Web (hmm, that metaphor needs work), you need to know the following:

✔ Every Web page has a name attached to it so that browsers, and you, can find it. Great figures in the world of software engineering named this name *URL,* or *Uniform Resource Locator.*

✔ A URL is a series of characters that begins with `http://` or `www`.

✔ To say "URL," pronounce each letter, *U-R-L* — no one says *earl*.

Now you know enough to go browsing.

Browsing off with three popular browsers

Now that you're savvy about the Web, you undoubtedly want to check it out for yourself. To do this, you need a *browser,* the software that gets Web pages and displays them on your screen. Fortunately, if you have Windows 95 or later (98, 2000, NT, Me, or XP), any recent Mac, or any computer with Internet access, you probably already have a browser. Also, one may have come from your Internet service provider (ISP) if you installed their Internet software.

Here are the two and a half most popular browsers:

- ✔ **Internet Explorer (IE)** is the browser that Microsoft builds into every version of Windows since Windows 98. In fact, Microsoft insists that it's an integral part of Windows itself. Microsoft now has versions for Windows, the Mac, and a few versions of UNIX. It frequently comes with Outlook Express, Microsoft's e-mail and newsgroup program, which we cover later in this chapter.

- ✔ **Netscape Navigator** comes in several varieties for Windows, Macs, and UNIX. Netscape also comes as part of a suite of programs called Netscape Communicator. Netscape includes a Web page editor, too, in case you want to create your own Web pages. Netscape Navigator and its cousin, Mozilla, are our hands-down favorite browsers.

- ✔ **Mozilla** is the open source browser on which Netscape is based. Mozilla and Netscape are nearly identical except that Netscape removes a few Mozilla features (pop-up blocking, most notably) and adds some AOL-specific stuff (AOL Instant Messenger and the ability to pick up mail from AOL accounts). Unless you need the AOL stuff, we suggest you use Mozilla.

Four easy ways to surf with your browser

When you start Internet Explorer, you see a screen similar to the one shown in Figure 22-2. Which page your browser displays depends on how it's set up. Many ISPs arrange for your browser to display their home page; otherwise, Internet Explorer tends to display a Microsoft page and Netscape usually shows a Netscape page, until you choose a home page of your own.

From the home page (or any page), you can "surf" the Net in any number of ways:

- ✔ **Jump directly to a page:** Type the URL for the Web page you want to view into the Address box in your browser.

- ✔ **Move from page to page:** Click any link that looks interesting. That's it. Underlined blue text and blue-bordered pictures are links. (Although links may be a color other than blue, depending on the look the Web page designer is going for, they're always underlined unless the page is the victim of a truly awful designer.) Anything that looks like a button is probably a link. You can tell when you're pointing to a link because the mouse pointer changes to a little hand. If you're not sure whether something is a link, click it anyway because if it's not, it doesn't hurt anything. Clicking outside a link selects the text you click, as in most other programs.

✔ **Move backward:** Web browsers remember the last few pages you visited, so if you click a link and decide that you're not so crazy about the new page, you can easily go back to the preceding one. To go back, click the Back button on the toolbar (its icon is an arrow pointing to the left, and it's the leftmost button on the toolbar) or press Alt+←.

If you move backward and decide you want to move forward again, simply click the Forward button. Refer to Figure 22-2 to see where these buttons are located.

✔ **Use image maps:** Some picture links are *image maps*. In a regular link, it doesn't matter where you click; on an image map, it does. The image map in this figure is typical and has a bunch of obvious places you click for various types of information. Some image maps are actual maps, whereas others are pictures that contain many different buttons to go different places.

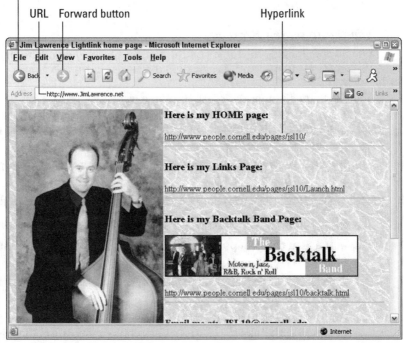

Figure 22-2:
Your typical
Web page,
viewed in
Internet
Explorer.

Finding stuff on the Net

The Internet has different types of indexes and directories for different types of material. Because the indexes tend to be organized, unfortunately, by the type of Internet service that they provide rather than by the nature of the material, you find Web resources in one place, e-mail resources in another place, and so on. You can search in dozens or hundreds of different ways, depending on what you're looking for and how you prefer to search.

To provide a smidgen of structure to this discussion, we describe several different sorts of searches:

- ✔ **Topics:** Places, things, ideas, companies — anything you want to find out more about
- ✔ **Built-in searches:** Topic searches that a browser does automatically, and why we're not always thrilled about that
- ✔ **People:** Actual human beings whom you want to contact or spy on
- ✔ **Goods and services:** Stuff to buy or find out about, from mortgages to mouthwash

Your basic search strategy

When we're looking for topics on the Net, we always begin with one of the Web guides (indexes and directories) discussed in this section.

You use them all in more or less the same way:

1. **Start your Web browser, such as Netscape, Internet Explorer, or Mozilla.**

2. **Pick a directory or index you like and tell your browser to go to the index or directory's home page.**

   We list the URLs (Web addresses) of the home pages later in this section.

   After you get there, you can choose between two approaches.

3. **a. If a Search box appears, type some likely keywords in the box and click Search.**

   This is the "index" approach: to look for topic areas that match your keywords.

   After perhaps a long delay (the Web is pretty big), an index page is returned with links to pages that match your keywords. The list of links may be way too long to deal with — like 300,000 of them.

or

b. If you see a list of links to topic areas, click a topic area of interest.

In this "directory" approach, you begin at a general topic and get more and more specific. Each page has links to pages that get more and more specific until they link to actual pages that are likely to be of interest.

4. **Adjust and repeat your search until you find something you like.**

After some clicking around to get the hang of it, you find all sorts of good stuff.

You hear a great deal of talk around the Web about search engines. *Search engines* is a fancy way to say *stuff-finding stuff.* All the directories and indexes we're about to describe are in the broad category called search engines, so don't get upset by some highfalutin' terms.

So much for the theory of searching for stuff on the Net. Now for some practice. (Theory and practice are much farther apart in practice than they are in theory.) We use our favorite search systems for examples: Google, which is mostly an index, and then Yahoo!, which is a directory.

Google-oogle, our favorite index

Our favorite Web index is Google. Google has little robots that spend their time merrily visiting Web pages all over the Net and reporting what they saw. It makes an humongous index of which words occurred in which pages; when you search for something, Google picks pages from the index that contain the words you asked for. Google uses a sophisticated ranking system based on how many *other* Web sites refer to each one in the index that more often than not puts the best pages first.

The best way to get a feel for the way Google works is to try some Google searches.

1. **Direct your browser to** www.google.com.

2. **Type some search terms, such as** key lime pie.

3. **Google finds the pages that best match your terms (see Figure 22-3).**

That's "best match," not "match" — if it can't match all the terms, it finds pages that match as well as possible. Also, your results may not look exactly like Figure 22-3 because Google will have updated its database since this book went to press.

Figure 22-3:
Plenty of
pages
of pie.

Google ignores words that occur too often to be usable as index terms, both the obvious ones such as `and`, `the`, and `of` and terms such as `internet` and `mail`. These rules can sound somewhat discouraging, but in fact it's still not hard to get useful results from Google. You just have to think up good search terms.

The "I'm Feeling Lucky" button searches and takes you directly to the first link, which works when, well, when you're lucky.

Yahoo!, ancient king of the directories

Yahoo! is one of the oldest directories and still a pretty good one. You can search for entries or click from category to category until you find something you like. We start our Yahoo! visit at its home page, at `www.yahoo.com`, as shown in Figure 22-4. (As with all Web pages, the exact design may have changed by the time you read this, but Yahoo's layout has remained pretty steady for years.) A whole bunch of categories and subcategories are listed. You can click any of them to see another page that has yet more subcategories and links to actual Web pages. You can click a link to a page if you see one you like or a sub-subcategory, and so on.

Do you Yahoo!?

Although Yahoo! was originally a directory of resources available on the Web, it's now a *portal,* which means that it has lots of other databases available to encourage you to stick around inside Yahoo!. Each has a link you can click just under the box in which you would enter search terms. They add new databases about once a week; some popular ones include

✔ **Yellow Pages:** A business directory.

✔ **People Search:** Finds addresses and phone numbers like a white pages directory.

✔ **Maps:** Gets a more or less accurate map of a street address you type.

✔ **Classifieds:** Lets you read and submit ads for automobiles, apartments, computers, and jobs.

✔ **Personals:** Lets you read and submit ads for dates in all (and we mean *all*) combinations.

✔ **Chat:** Gets you into online chat through the Web.

✔ **Email:** Free Web-based, e-mail service.

✔ **Auctions:** Web-based auctions, not unlike eBay.

✔ **TV:** Impressively complete TV and cable listings, by area.

✔ **Travel:** A link to the Travelocity reservation system, as well as a variety of other resources. (See `airline.iecc.com` for opinions and suggestions about online travel services.)

✔ **My Yahoo:** A customized starting page just for you with headlines, sports scores, and other news based on your preferences.

✔ **Today's News, Stock Quotes, and Sports Scores:** News from a variety of wire services, newspapers, and other media.

At the top of each Yahoo! directory page is the list of categories, subcategories, and so on, separated by colons, that lead to that page. If you want to back up a few levels and look at different subcategories, just click the place on that list to which you want to back up. After a little clicking up and down, it's second nature. Many pages appear in more than one place in the directory because they fall into more than one category. Web pages can have as many links referring to them as they want.

Microsoft's Autosearch

In Internet Explorer 4.0 or later, if you type keywords into the Address box, Internet Explorer sends them to MSN Search, which uses data from LookSmart, an adequate Web directory, along with a lot of links that look suspiciously like advertisements.

Internet Explorer (IE) also has the Search Bar. If you click the Search button on the toolbar, a Search Bar pane appears to the left of your Explorer window with a small search engine page.

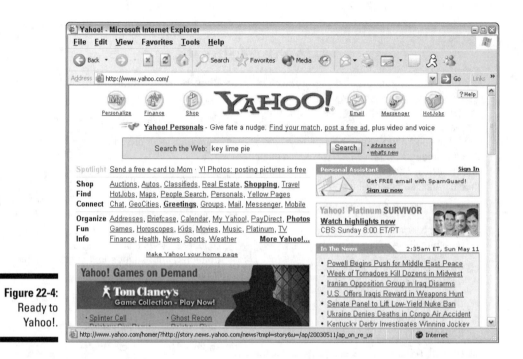

Figure 22-4:
Ready to
Yahoo!.

It's in the Mail

Electronic mail, or *e-mail,* is without a doubt the most popular Internet service, even though it's one of the oldest and least glitzy. Although e-mail doesn't get as much press as the World Wide Web, more people use it. Every system on the Net supports some sort of mail service, which means that no matter what kind of computer you're using, if it's on the Internet, you can send and receive mail.

Three popular e-mail programs

After you understand what an e-mail program is supposed to do, it's much easier to figure out how to make a specific e-mail program do what you want. We've picked the three most popular e-mail programs to show you the ropes:

✔ **Eudora:** This popular e-mail program runs under Windows (all versions) and on the Macintosh and communicates with your mail server. Eudora is popular for two reasons: It's easy to use, and it's cheap. Normally it's "sponsored," which means that it's free but shows ads when you use it. If you like it, you can register your copy for a modest fee; when you do, the ads disappear. Or you can drop back to "free" mode, which has no ads and fewer features.

- **Netscape:** The Netscape Web browser includes a pretty good e-mail program called Netscape Mail. If you use an AOL account, Netscape Mail is the only program (other than the AOL program itself and AOL's new AOL Communicator, which is similar to Netscape Mail) that can send and receive AOL e-mail.

- **Outlook Express:** Windows 98 and later come with versions of Outlook Express, Microsoft's free e-mail program. When you get a copy of the Microsoft Web browser, Internet Explorer, you get Outlook Express too. You can also download it from www.microsoft.com. *Note:* Despite the similar name, Outlook Express is unrelated to Outlook 97, 98, 2000, or XP, which come with various versions of Microsoft Office.

Can 20 million users really be wrong? Sure they can. But if you're brand new to the world of computers as well as to the world of the Internet, you may find using America Online easier than starting off with a traditional Internet service provider (ISP). Also, if you're interested in online chatting, AOL is the world capital of chat.

Five tips from the etiquette ladies

Sadly, the Great Ladies of Etiquette, such as Emily Post and Amy Vanderbilt, died before the invention of e-mail. Here's what they may have suggested about what to say and, more important, what *not* to say in electronic mail:

- When you send a message, watch the tone of your language.

- Don't use all capital letters — it looks like you're SHOUTING.

- If someone sends you an incredibly obnoxious and offensive message, as likely as not it's a mistake or a joke gone awry. In particular, be on the lookout for failed sarcasm.

- Pointless and excessive outrage in electronic mail is so common that it has a name of its own: *flaming.* Don't flame. It makes you look like a jerk.

- Sometimes it helps to put in a :-) (called a *smiley* or *emoticon*), which means, "This is a joke." (Try tilting your head to the left if you don't see why it's a smile.) In some communities, notably CompuServe, <g> or <grin> serves the same purpose. Here's a typical example:

People who don't believe that we are all part of a warm, caring community who love and support each other are no better than rabid dogs and should be hunted down and shot. :-)

What's my address?

Everyone with e-mail access to the Internet has at least one *e-mail address,* which is the cyberspace equivalent of a postal address or a phone number. When you send an e-mail message, you enter the address or addresses of the recipients so that the computer knows where to send it.

Internet mail addresses have two parts, separated by an @ (the *at* sign):

- ✔ The part before @ is the *mailbox,* which is (roughly speaking) your personal name.
- ✔ The part after @ is the *domain,* usually the name of your Internet service provider (ISP), such as `aol.com` or `fltg.net`.

So the whole thing looks like this: `username@domain.com`.

How private is e-mail?

E-mail is relatively private, but not totally. Here's why:

- ✔ Any recipient of your mail may forward it to other people.
- ✔ Some mail addresses are really mailing lists that redistribute messages to many other people.
- ✔ If you send mail from work or to someone at work, your mail is not private. When someone is accusing your company of leaking confidential information and the corporate lawyer says, "Examine the e-mail," even companies with the highest integrity will read all the e-mail.

If you really care about the content of your mail being read by anyone other than your intended recipient, you must encrypt it. The latest e-mail systems are beginning to include encryption features that make the privacy situation somewhat better so that anyone who doesn't know the keyword used to scramble a message can't decode it.

To whom do I write?

As you've probably figured out, one teensy detail is keeping you from sending e-mail to all your friends: You don't know their addresses. Here are two methods for finding out your friends' addresses:

✔ **Call them on the phone and ask them.** Pretty low-tech, huh? For some reason, this technique seems to be absolutely the last thing people want to do. Try it first. If you know or can find out their phone numbers, this method is much easier than any of the others.

✔ **Use an online directory.** Wouldn't it be cool if some online directory listed everybody's e-mail address? Maybe, but the Internet doesn't have one. For one thing, nothing says that somebody's e-mail address has any connection to her name. For another, not everybody wants everybody else to know his e-mail address.

Although lots of directories attempt to accumulate e-mail addresses, none of them is complete, most are somewhat out of date, and many work only if people voluntarily list themselves with the service.

This situation reiterates, of course, our point that the best way to find someone's e-mail address is to ask. When that method isn't an option, try one of these "white pages" directories:

✔ **SuperPages.com** at `wp.superpages.com`

✔ **BigFoot** at `www.bigfoot.com`

✔ **WhoWhere** at `whowhere.lycos.com`

✔ **Yahoo People Search** at `people.yahoo.com`

Another approach is to go to a search engine like Google (`google.com`) or AltaVista (`altavista.com`) and type the person's full name, enclosed in quotes. You'll see a list of pages that include the name — of course, there may be many people with the same name if your friend is called Allen Johnson or Bob Smith. Try searching for your own name and see what you find!

Ten most common Internet abbreviations (IMHO)

E-mail users are often lazy typists, and many abbreviations are common. Here are some of the most widely used:

Abbreviation	What It Means
AFAIK	As far as I know
BTW	By the way
IANAL	I am not a lawyer, (but...)
IMHO	In my humble opinion
ROTFL	Rolling on the floor laughing
RSN	Real soon now (vaporware)
RTFM	Read the manual — you could have and should have looked it up yourself
TIA	Thanks in advance
TLA	Three-letter acronym
YMMV	Your mileage may vary

Twelve fun things you can do on the Net

With so many options to choose from, how do you find the most fun things to do on the Internet? Here's a list of 12 to get you started . . .

Send greeting cards: The next time you remember someone's birthday at the last moment, send an online greeting card. Many online cards are free and sometimes arrive within minutes. The cards are just e-mail messages that include cute graphics or animation and a silly tune, with variations available for all occasions. You can even add your own personal greeting.

Share pictures with your friends and family: E-mail attachments are a great way to ship snapshots anywhere in the world for free. You don't even need a digital camera. Many film developing services will digitize your photos and deliver them to you online or on a CD.

Watch short movies and TV ads: The Internet has created a new way for makers of short and experimental movies to find an audience. Many sites feature miniflicks that you can watch for free. IFILM (ifilm.com) has a good selection. You can find a long list of movie sites at dmoz. org/Arts/Movies/Filmmaking/Online_ Venues. Be aware that the quality of these films varies from dreadful to inspired to the occasionally creepy.

Listen to current and classic NPR programs: Have you ever turned on your radio, found yourself in the middle of a fascinating story, and wished you could have heard the beginning? National Public Radio in the United States has many of its past programs available online. If you want to hear the whole program, visit www. npr.org. You can also use the site's search feature to browse for stories of interest that you missed completely. Many NPR affiliates and other radio stations have live streaming audio of their programs, so you can listen live to stations all over the country — go to Google and search for the station call letters or the program name.

Play a game of checkers: Or chess, hearts, bridge, backgammon, cribbage, or any other board game or card game. The classic games hold up well against the ever-more-bloody electronic games. You don't need to round up live friends to play with — you can find willing partners anytime, day or night, at sites like games. yahoo.com or www.zone.msn.com (Windows users only).

Watch the world go by: Webcams are live video cameras that you can access over the Internet. They let you see what is happening right now — wherever that camera is pointing. Watch wildlife, events of the day, a city street, a shopping mall, a highway interchange, Slovakia, or even someone's living room. The views are generally updated every few seconds. Go to www.dmoz. org/Computers/Internet/On_the_Web/ Webcams or just search on *webcams* at www. google.com or www.yahoo.com.

Share your diary: Posting your private diary on the Internet may seem as bizarre as having a webcam in your bedroom, but many people do it and enjoy getting feedback from other diarists. Check out DiaryLand (www.diaryland.com) to see what it's like. Most of those who post are young. For older folks, it's a window on what kids are thinking about (or not thinking about) these days.

Visit art museums around the world: Art museums are a great place to spend a rainy afternoon. Now you can visit museums and galleries all over the world via your browser. Not all museum Web sites have online art works, but many do. Our favorites include the Louvre in

Paris (www.louvre.fr), Boston's Museum of Fine Arts (www.mfa.org), The Metropolitan Museum of Art in New York (www.metmuseum.org), and the State Hermitage Museum in Russia (www.hermitagemuseum.org). You'll find a wide selection of others at dmoz.org/Reference/Museums.

Build your own world: Virtual worlds are electronic places you can visit on the Web, kind of like 3-D chat rooms. Instead of a screen name, you create a personal action figure, called an *avatar,* that walks, talks, and emotes (but doesn't make a mess on your floor). When you're in one of these worlds, your avatar interacts with the avatars of other people who are logged on in surroundings that range from quite realistic to truly fantastic. In some virtual worlds, you can even build your own places: a room, a house, a park, a city — whatever you can imagine.

Most virtual worlds require you to download a plug-in or special software. Here are some places where you can enter or create a virtual world: www.simcity.com, www.active worlds.com, www.digitalspace.com/avatars, and www.ccon.org/hotlinks/hotlinks.html.

Tour the solar system: The generation that will actually get to play tourist in the solar system remains to be seen, but virtual tours are available now at sites like www.solarviews.com, www.seds.org, and sse.jpl.nasa.gov. Be sure to bookmark the astronomy picture of the day at antwrp.gsfc.nasa.gov/apod/astropix.html. Above all, don't miss NASA's incredible montage of human civilization at antwrp.gsfc.nasa.gov/apod/image/0011/earthlights_dmsp_big.jpg.

Search for extraterrestrial life: SETI@home (setiathome.ssl.berkeley.edu) is a scientific experiment that uses Internet-connected home and office computers to search for extraterrestrial intelligence (SETI). The idea is to have thousands of otherwise idle PCs and Macs perform the massive calculations needed to extract the radio signals of other civilizations from intergalactic noise. You can participate by running a free program that downloads and analyzes data collected at the Arecibo radio telescope in Puerto Rico.

Adopt a kid: Do you surf the Web for hours each day? Maybe your life needs more meaning. Adopting a kid is more of a commitment than upgrading to the latest Microsoft operating system, but at least kids grow up eventually. Here are two excellent Web sites that list special children in need of homes: rainbowkids.com and www.capbook.org. It can't hurt to look.

Chapter 23

Chasing Down Internet Bargains

· ·

In This Chapter

▶ Why shop online: Benefits and drawbacks

▶ How to pay for stuff you buy online

▶ Internet shopping hot spots

▶ The excitement of Internet auctions

▶ Doing it eBay

▶ Travel planning on the cheap

· ·

*E*verybody's talking about shopping online. Whether you call it Web shopping, e-commerce, or going down to Ye Olde Cyberstore, buying online definitely is starting to catch on. But, like any new twist on a familiar experience, people have many questions and misconceptions about using the Internet as a shopping mall. From the most basic, "Is it safe?" to the more esoteric, "How do I know whom I can trust?" to the downright thrifty, "How much can I save?" many people have legitimate concerns about spending their hard-earned greenbacks on the Information Superhighway.

Not only can you get very tangible benefits (read as bargains, freebies, and what-a-deals) from this somewhat intangible entity, but you can also become more technologically savvy, culturally enriched, and broadly communicative in the process. Whether you're sending an electronic greeting card to a friend or planning your next European vacation, the Internet has what you need — all with just a few clicks of the mouse.

To Shop or Not? Pros and Cons of Shopping Online

Here are some reasons why we shop on the Net:

- ✔ Online stores are convenient, open all night, and don't mind if you aren't wearing shoes or if you window-shop for a week before you buy something.

- ✔ Prices are often lower online, and you can compare prices at several online establishments in a matter of minutes. Even if you eventually make your purchase in a brick and mortar store, what you find out online can save you money. Shipping and handling is similar to what you'd pay for mail order. You don't have to drive or park either.

- ✔ Online stores can sometimes offer a better selection. They usually ship from a central warehouse rather than having to keep stock on the shelf at dozens of branches. If you're looking for something hard to find — for example, a part for that vintage toaster oven you're repairing — the Web can save you weeks of searching.

- ✔ A lot of stuff just isn't available in small rural towns.

- ✔ Unlike malls, online stores don't have Muzak. (Occasionally Web sites play background music, but we move on to other sites quickly.)

Something for nothing: Six easy steps

If you know the right places to look, you can find a great number of free experiences and goods on the Net. For example, a nice little innovation emerged from the student laboratories at MIT: electronic greeting cards. The Web makes it possible for you to send your loved one, your boss, or even yourself a personalized, full-color greeting card, if they're online.

Here's a road map for "buying" a free electronic greeting card:

1. **Get online.**

2. **Search for a greeting card company.**

3. **Go to an online greeting card store, such as** www.hallmark.com or www.american greetings.com.

4. **Pick out a card.**

5. **Personalize it.**

6. **Send it!**

On the other hand, here are some reasons why we don't buy everything on the Net:

✔ You can't physically look at or try on stuff before you buy it, and in most cases, you have to wait for it to be shipped to you. We haven't had much luck buying shoes online, for instance.

✔ We like our local stores and prefer to support them when we can.

✔ You can't flirt with the staff at a Web store or find out about the latest town gossip.

How Do I Pay?

Stores on the Web work in two general ways: with and without virtual *shopping carts*. In stores without carts, you either order one item at a time or fill out a big order form with a check box for everything the store offers. In stores with shopping carts, you place items into a virtual shopping cart and then proceed to the checkout.

After you proceed to the checkout, your options for payment include entering your credit card information online or, if you're uncomfortable with that option, paying by phone or mail. The section "Should I use my credit card?" helps you decide which method is right for you.

Simple shopping

For an example of simple shopping, our randomly chosen site happens to sell books written by one of us.

1. **Follow the Autographed copies link from** net.gurus.com, **and in a few clicks, you'll arrive at the order page shown in Figure 23-1. This page shows the selected item and has an order form ready for your details.**

2. **In the form, enter the same stuff you'd put on a paper order form.**

   Most forms have a place for typing a credit card number; if you're not comfortable entering your card info here (see the section "Should I use my credit card?" later in this chapter), leave that blank — the store invariably has a way you can call the order in.

3. **Click the Prepare Order button.**

   You'll see an order review page (as shown in Figure 23-2) where you can check that the details are correct.

4. **Click Place Order, and your order is on its way.**

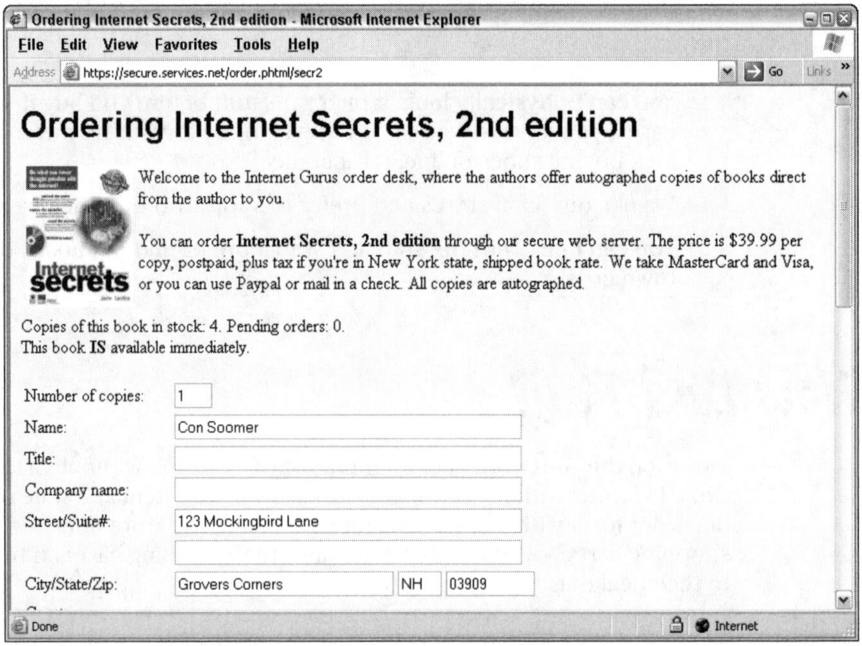

Figure 23-1:
Welcome
to a secure
online store.

You generally get an e-mail message confirming the details of your order and frequently get e-mail updates if any problems or delays occur.

Fancy shopping

Although a simple store works okay for stores that don't have many different items in their catalog or for businesses where you buy one thing at a time, this method is hopeless for stores with large catalogs. For these sites, a *shopping cart* is in order. Here's how it works:

1. **As you click your way around a site, you can toss items into your cart, adding and removing them as you want, by clicking a button labeled something like Add Item to Your Shopping Cart.**

2. **When you have the items you want, you visit the virtual checkout line and buy the items in your cart.**

   Until you visit the checkout, you can always take the items out of your cart if you decide that you don't want them, and at online stores, they don't get shopworn, no matter how often you do that.

Figure 23-3 shows a shopping cart for Great Tapes for Kids with two items in it. When you click the Proceed to Checkout button, the next page asks for the rest of your order details, much like the form in Figure 23-1.

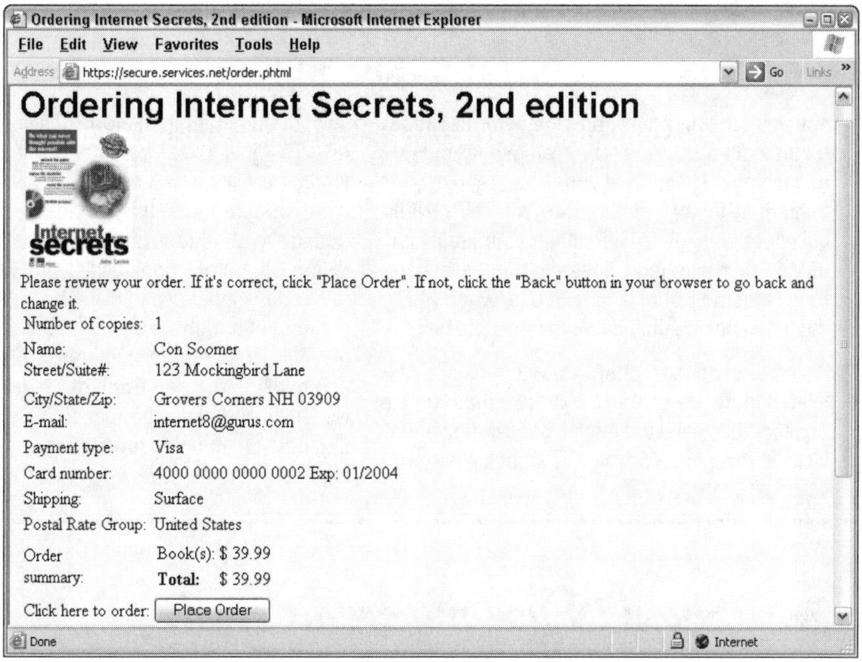

Figure 23-2: Ready to order some quality literature.

Figure 23-3: Have you finished your holiday shopping?

Cookie alert

You may have heard horrible stories about things called *cookies* that Web sites reputedly use to spy on you, steal your data, ravage your computer, inject cellulite into your hips while you sleep, and otherwise make your life miserable. After extensive investigation, we have found that most cookies aren't bad; when you're shopping online, they can even be quite helpful.

A *cookie* is no more than a little chunk of text a Web site sends to a PC with a request (not a command) to send the cookie back during future visits to the same Web site. The cookie is stored on your computer in the form of a tiny snippet of text. That's all it is. Mozilla and Netscape store all the cookies in a file called `cookies.txt`, whereas Internet Explorer uses a folder called Cookies with a separate file for each site. For online shopping, cookies let the Web server track your shopping cart of items you've selected but not yet bought, even if you log out and turn off your computer in the interim. Stores can also use cookies to keep track of the last time you visited and what you bought; they can also keep that data on their own computers, so what's the big deal?

Should I use my credit card?

How do you pay for stuff you buy online? Most often with a credit card, the same way you pay for anything else. Isn't it incredibly, awfully dangerous to give out your credit card number online, though? Well, no. Consider the following:

- ✔ Most online stores encrypt the message between your computer and the store's server. (An encrypted connection is indicated in your Web browser by a closed lock icon in the bottom-right corner of the window.)

- ✔ Plucking the occasional credit card number from the gigabytes of traffic that flows every minute on the Net would be close to impossible even without encryption.

- ✔ When you use plastic at a restaurant, you give your physical card with your physical signature to the wait staff who takes it to the back room, does who knows what with it, and then brings it back. Compared with that, the risk of sending your number to an online store is pretty small.

If, after this harangue, you still don't want to send your credit card number over the Net or you're one of the fiscally responsible holdouts who doesn't do plastic, most online stores are happy to have you call in your card number over the phone or send them a check or money order.

 Credit cards and debit cards look the same and spend the same, but credit cards bill you at the end of the month while debit cards take the money right out of your bank account. In the United States, consumer protection laws work differently for credit and debit cards, and they're much stronger for credit cards. We recommend that you use a credit card to get the better protection and then pay the bill at the end of the month so you don't owe interest.

Nine things that are easier to get online

Software: Distributing software over the Internet has become so accepted that only the rarest company doesn't have a download area on its Web site. Not only is online distribution a great way for companies to cut packaging costs, but it also gives customers a fast and easy way to get updates or to try out new software.

Information: The very core of the Internet is the data, documents, reports, and other words of wisdom that thousands of scientists, researchers, and other pundits enter. Best of all, however, is the inherent searchability of the Web.

Clip art: You can find a full range of photographs, illustrations, fonts, and even animations on the Web — at any number of prices. Everything from freeware to pay-per-use is available online. If you're searching for a particular topic, don't be surprised to find entire clip-art collections devoted to your subject.

Airline tickets: Every major airline has a Web site where you can check airfares, flight schedules, and ticket availability, and most sites enable you to purchase online through them directly or through an affiliated travel agent.

Credit cards: Looking for a lower APR with a longer grace period? How about anyone who's willing to touch you and your less-than-ideal credit rating? Try visiting the *Credit Card Advisor* (at www.gromco.com/cca). Not only can you get the lowdown on a variety of cards available across the country, but you can also send a preliminary application to as many as you want by filling out one form. Now you can preapply *before* you're preapproved. Excuse me while I *pre*pare my *pre*liminary *pre*dicament, *pre*cisely!

International items: If you don't have the money or the time to go globe-trotting, you can always scratch your wanderlust with a few odds and ends from an international online shopping spree.

Coupons: The Web offers a great variety of easy-to-find coupons. The *Internet Coupon Directory* (at www.coupondirectory.com) is a great place to start if you're looking for some coupons to whet your appetite. Not only does the site have a full listing of national name-brand coupons — for everything from dog food to toothpaste — but it also offers discounts for online stores.

Catalogs: What makes online catalog shopping easier than offline catalog shopping? One word: *backorder*. That's one word you never hear if you're shopping the online way because the Web-based catalogs are tied into the company's inventory. Whenever anyone orders an item, the item comes right from the available inventory. So if you go online and place an order, and a problem arises — for example, the product isn't available for two weeks — you know *before* you complete the transaction. And if you don't want to deal with it, you can cancel just that portion of the order.

Gifts: Maybe the extraordinary variety of merchandise available on the Web is what makes it so perfect for gift giving. Maybe it's the fact that you can shop for someone the way that you want to shop — either searching for something specific or browsing the virtual aisles. Maybe it's because online shopping always involves shipping, so sending the package to someone else's home instead of your billing address is no big deal. Moreover, most sites are happy to gift wrap or throw in a card with a message from you. But I think what really gives online gift giving the edge is that it can be so impulsive.

Computers

When you're shopping for computer hardware online, be sure that a vendor you're considering offers both a good return policy (in case the computer doesn't work when it arrives) and a long warranty.

✔ **Dell Computers** (www.dell.com): This site has an extensive catalog with online ordering and custom computer system configurations.

✔ **IBM** (www.ibm.com): The world's largest computer company has what feels like the world's largest Web site with a great deal of information about both IBM products and more general computing topics. The online store sells everything from home PCs to printed manuals to midrange business systems. We got as far as putting a $1.1 million AS/400 9406-650 in our cart, but then we chickened out. We did buy a nice manual for the 1965-era 360/67 for our historical collection. (At IBM, nothing seems to go out of print.)

✔ **Apple Computer** (store.apple.com): The Apple site has lots of information about Apple products, and now it has online purchasing of Macintosh systems, too.

✔ **PC Connection and Mac Connection** (www.pcconnection.com and www.macconnection.com): For computer hardware, software, and accessories, PC and Mac Connection is one of the oldest and most reliable online sources. And you can get overnight delivery within the continental United States even if you order as late as 2 a.m.!

Food

To show the range of edibles available online, here are our two favorite online dairies, a coffee roaster, a recipe site, and a grocery delivery service:

✔ **Cabot Creamery** (www.cabotcheese.com): This site sells the best cheese in Vermont. Good bovine sound effects on the Web site, too.

✔ **Bobolink Dairy** (www.cowsoutside.com): A recovering software nerd and his family in rural New Jersey make and sell cheese directly. Their own cheese, which they sell on the Web site, is fabulous — rich, gooey, French-style cheese. You can even order cheese made in Tibet from yak milk. The URL refers to cows out in the pasture rather than tied up in the barn.

✔ **Gimme Coffee** (www.gimmecoffee.com): Highly opinionated coffee from the wilds of upstate New York. Online orders handled through PayPal.

✔ **The Kitchen Link** (www.kitchenlink.com): Search their site for the perfect recipe and then shop for the ingredients.

✔ **Peapod** (www.peapod.com): Peapod lets you shop for groceries online and then delivers them to your home. You have to live in an area that their parent grocery chains serve. If you live somewhere else, Netgrocer (www.netgrocer.com) delivers nonperishables by rather pricey over-night express.

Going Once! Going Twice! Online Auctions

Traditional auctions are held periodically in locations around the world. Online auctions are the latest craze (by now you may have seen the eBay commercials on TV), and yet for some, their inner workings remain a mystery. The key to understanding how the online version works is to understand the differences between the two types of auctions:

✔ Traditional auctions are held periodically in locations around the world. The purchaser must either attend the auction or find someone to represent him on-site in order to make a bid. Bidders are given numbers to hold up when they want to bid. The auctioneer must be skilled in pacing bids and handling last-minute bidding, and he has the right to extend the auction when bids come in "as the hammer is coming down."

✔ Online auctions certainly have merchandise and bidders, and sometimes flurries of last-minute bids, but the timing and location of auctions are less relevant on the Internet. Items can be offered for sale at any time, and it matters not at all where buyer and seller are located as far as offering the item and bidding on it are concerned. When an auction takes place online, you can participate without leaving the comforts of home.

You can participate in online auctions of everything from computers and computer parts to antiques to vacation packages. And you can sell stuff as well as buy it — a slightly more subtle approach than hosting a neighborhood yard sale. Online auctions are like any other kind of auction in at least one respect: If you know what you're looking for and know what it's worth, you can get some great values; if you don't, you can easily overpay for junk.

The procedure for participating in online auctions differs depending on the type of auction you use. Each auction service has its own set of rules for bidding and selling. Read these guidelines carefully. They don't make for exciting reading, but they are important. Check out the bidding rules. Some auctions keep track of the time you first bid on an item, and subsequent bids can "bump" someone at the same price whose first bid was later than yours. Also, note the shipping charges, which can be excessive and can raise the actual value of your bid.

Bidding in five steps

The following numbered list explains the bidding process in a nutshell:

1. **Register.** Typically, you provide the auction service with a username and password that you then use to log in or place bids, as well as an e-mail address. You also provide the site with your real name and address in case it needs to contact you. Auction houses that function as the seller (many of which specialize in computer and other electronics equipment) usually require a credit card number when you register.

2. **Shop.** You search the selection of sale items in one of two ways: You can click links that denote categories of merchandise until you find the specific merchandise you're looking for, or you can search for particular brands or models by entering keywords in a search box.

3. **Place a bid.** You fill out a form on a Web page and submit your bid along with your registered username and password to the site. If you're the high bidder (or in the case of a Dutch auction, one of the low bidders) your bid is recorded on the Web page on which the auction item is displayed.

4. **Track your bid.** While the auction is going on, you can find out whether anyone has outbid you. Some sites automatically send you an e-mail message if this happens. Software programs, such as AuctionTicker, are available to help you track your auctions.

5. **If you're the winning bidder, make payment and shipping arrangements with the seller.** The seller tells you how much to pay (your winning bid plus shipping) and where to send payment.

Selling in six simple steps

The following steps explain the general process for selling items in an online auction:

1. **Register.** This is the same as registering as a bidder. However, depending on the site, you may have to submit credit card information to set up an account as a seller.

2. **Post an item.** "Posting" means that you place your description on the auction site's Web server by filling out a form in which you specify the length of the auction and describe what you're selling. You also make a link to an image of the item, if you have one.

3. **Watch the bids pour in.** Depending on your level of interest and available time, you can check in as often as you like by connecting to the auction

Web page on which your merchandise is displayed. If you reconnect often, click the Reload or Refresh button from your browser's button bar to see the changes since your last visit.

4. **End the auction.** Some sites let you end the auction before your ending time, but this can get you negative feedback from disgruntled buyers. Let the auction end at the time you originally chose. See if the high bid meets or exceeds your reserve price, if you specified one. Contact the high bidder with purchasing information.

5. **Get paid.** The most common forms of payment are cashier's checks or postal money orders. If you have a merchant account with a bank and can accept credit cards, so much the better. If you use an escrow service, the buyer can pay the escrow service with a credit card, and the service pays you after the shipment has been received and accepted.

6. **Deliver the goods.** It's important to pack your merchandise well and ship it in a way that lets you track its progress. You may also want to insure the item.

The four most popular auction sites

Here are the most popular auction sites on the Web:

✔ **eBay** (www.ebay.com): This is the most popular auction site on the Web and sells all sorts of stuff, which is why we cover it in detail in the next section. You can buy and sell stuff on eBay by simply registering on the site. eBay charges a small commission for auctions, which the seller pays. Searching the auctions at eBay is also a terrific way to find out what something is worth. If you were thinking of selling that rare Beanie Baby, search the completed auctions for the bad news that it's worth slightly less than it was when it was new.

✔ **Half.com** (www.half.com): This division of eBay is more like a consignment shop than an auction. You list used items you want to sell, such as books, CDs, movies, video games, electronic equipment, trading cards, and so on, and you name your price. When a buyer comes along, Half.com collects a 15 percent commission.

✔ **Yahoo! Auctions** (auctions.yahoo.com): eBay was such a big hit that Yahoo! decided to hold auctions, too. Yahoo! also has an online payment system called PayDirect, similar to PayPal.

✔ **priceline.com** (www.priceline.com): This site sells airline tickets, hotel rooms, new cars, prepaid long distance phone service, and a grab bag of other items. Not really an auction; you specify a price for what you want and they accept or reject it.

What Is eBay, and How Does It Work?

The Internet spawns all kinds of businesses (known as *e-commerce* to Wall Street types), and eBay is one of its few superstars. The reason is simple: It's the place where buyers and sellers can meet, do business, share stories and tips, and have fun. It's like one giant online potluck party — but instead of bringing a dish, you sell it!

How do I start?

When you go to the eBay site, you'll see one of two screens:

✔ The eBay home page shown in Figure 23-4 appears if you've logged into eBay in the past. From this screen, you can conduct searches, find out what's happening, and get an instant link to the My eBay page, which helps you keep track of every auction item you have up for sale or have a bid on.

✔ If you've never registered on eBay, your screen appears something like the one shown in Figure 23-5. From this screen, you can register for eBay, find, buy, and pay for items.

Figure 23-4:
The eBay home page, your starting point for bargains and for making some serious cash.

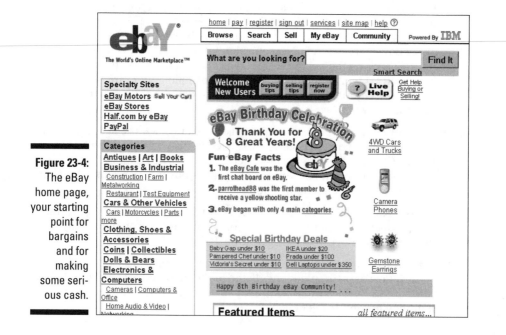

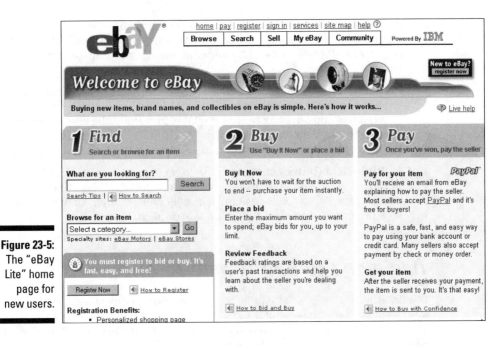

Figure 23-5:
The "eBay Lite" home page for new users.

Unlike "traditional" live auctions that end with the familiar phrase "Going once, going twice, sold!" eBay auctions are controlled by the clock. The seller pays a fee and lists the item on the site for a predetermined period of time; the highest bidder when the clock runs out takes home the prize.

Types of eBay auctions

eBay offers several types of auctions, including

- ✔ **Reserve-price auctions:** Unlike a minimum bid, which is required in any eBay auction, a *reserve price* protects sellers from having to sell an item for less than the minimum amount they want for it.

- ✔ **Live auctions:** In *eBay Live Auctions,* you can bid via eBay's Internet hook-up just as if you were sitting in a chair at the auction house. These auctions are usually for unique and interesting items that you're not likely to find in your locality.

- ✔ **Restricted-access auctions:** If you're over 18 years of age and interested in bidding on items of an adult nature, eBay has an adults only *(Mature Audiences)* category, which has restricted access.

If you aren't interested in seeing or bidding on items of an adult nature, or if you're worried that your children may be able to gain access to graphic adult material, worry not: eBay has solved that problem by excluding adult-content items from easily accessible areas like the Featured Items page. And children under the age of 18 aren't allowed to register at eBay and should be under an adult's supervision if they do wander onto the site.

✔ **Private (shhh-it's-a-secret) auctions:** Some sellers choose to hold private auctions because they know that some bidders may be embarrassed to be seen bidding on a box of racy neckties in front of the rest of the eBay community. Others may go the private route because they are selling big-ticket items and don't want to disclose their bidder's financial status.

✔ **Multiple item (Dutch) auctions:** A *Multiple Item auction* allows a seller to put multiple, identical items up for sale. Instead of holding 100 separate auctions for 100 items, for example, a seller can sell them all in one listing. As a buyer, you can elect to bid for 1, 3, or all 100 items.

Two ways to buy it now at eBay

You don't have to participate in an auction at eBay to buy something. If you want to make a purchase — if it's something you *must* have — you can usually find the item and buy it immediately. Of course, using Buy It Now (*BIN* in eBay speak) doesn't come with the thrill of an auction, but purchasing an item at a fraction of the retail price without leaving your chair or waiting for an auction to end has its own warm and fuzzy kind of excitement. If you seek this kind of instant gratification on eBay, try one of the following options:

✔ **eBay Stores:** Visiting eBay Stores is as easy as clicking the eBay Stores link from the home page. Thousands of eBay sellers have set up stores with merchandise meant for you to buy now. eBay Stores are classified just like eBay, and you can buy anything from socks to jewelry to appliances.

✔ **Buy It Now and fixed-price sales:** More and more sellers are selling items with a *Buy It Now* option or at a fixed price. This enables you to buy an item as soon as you see one at a price that suits you.

So you wanna sell stuff

If you're a seller, creating an auction page at eBay is as simple as filling out an online form.

1. **Type in the name of your item and a short description.**

2. **Add a crisp digital picture.**

3. **Set your price.**

   Voilà — it's auction time. (Okay, it's a tad more involved than that — but not much). eBay charges a small fee ($0.30 to $3.30) for the privilege.

When you list your item, millions of people (eBay has close to 80 million registered users) from all over the world can take a gander at it and place bids. With a little luck, a bidding war may break out and drive the bids up high enough for you to turn a nice profit. After the auction, you deal directly with the buyer, who sends you the payment either through a payment service or through the mail. Then you ship the item. Abracadabra — you just turned your item (everyday clutter, perhaps) into cash.

You can run as many auctions as you want, all at the same time.

Why Plan a Trip Online?

Why plan a trip online? The answer is easiest to sum up in an equation:

```
Many Sources + Good Information = Control Over Your Trip
```

There are so many travel choices that sorting through them all can be almost paralyzing. Every travel agent has his or her own preferred travel partners, and although a professional agent's advice is always valuable, knowing an agent's exact motivation for recommending one resort or a specific flight over another is sometimes hard to do.

By using online travel resources as a research tool, you can judge for yourself whether a destination fits your criteria. You can also examine as many fare, routing, and timetable permutations for transportation as you like. In essence, planning a trip online gives you as much or as little control as you want. Read on for more reasons to use the Internet when planning a trip.

- ✓ **Save time:** Planning a trip on the Net can save you loads of time. Most online travel agencies offer the following to anyone who has a modem connection to the Internet:

  - Fare-tracking services

  - Discount fare newsletters

  - Easy comparison shopping between airlines

  To get all this free help, all you need to do is sign up, sit back, and watch the travel info pour in. Use the stuff you want, discard the rest.

- ✓ **Save money:** Many people consistently save lots of money on flights, accommodations, and car rentals by using the Internet. Those who do so generally take the time to do the following:

  - Research the going rates.

  - Comparison shop.

- Try many permutations of dates, times, and destinations.

- Sign up for every discount e-mail available.

✔ **Get every type of travel info:** The travel industry has been forever transformed by the advent of the Internet. We're not just talking about airlines. Nearly every aspect of the travel experience, from guidebook information to accommodations to bag-packing advice is available on the Net — it's just a matter of finding it.

✔ **Tickets to ride:** As we're sure you know, buying airline tickets is the most common action for which travelers use the Web. Whether it's at an online agency or directly from an airline, travelers and the travel industry have been quick to embrace buying and selling airline tickets on the Net. You can also

- Book a hotel room

- Book cruise vacations and resort packages

- Reserve a rental car

✔ **Getting destination information:** Our favorite Net travel activity is searching for information on any destination in the world. Whether it's a short trip to the Upper West Side of Manhattan (often times a more foreboding trip than going out of the country) or a genuine vacation to Costa Rica, you can use the Internet to find current info about any destination.

All sorts of sites contain destination info. Use search engines to find

- State or government tourism sites

- Commercial destination sites

- Personal travelogues

- Travel guidebook sites

✔ **Talk to other people about travel:** As a traveler, you're likely to find yourself in good company on the Net. No longer are you reliant solely on professional guidebook writers for the inside scoop on a destination. The Internet isn't one community — it's millions of communities linked together. You can interact with world travelers on a level that was impossible just a decade ago. You have the entire online travel community to draw on when it's time to find out how firm the beds are at a specific hostel in Rome or when you need a second opinion about a restaurant in San Francisco.

✔ **Be a destination know-it-all:** Getting up-to-the-minute information about your destination can make the difference between a so-so vacation and an excellent adventure. Here's some of the information about a destination you can get online:

- Cartographic information

- Health, safety, and legal information

- Weather reports

Shopping for bargains online

You're guaranteed to find a bargain you can't pass up on one of the following sites. You just have to decide how many times you let yourself click that Buy button.

✔ www.overstock.com: Basically an online outlet store, Overstock has brand-name everything — clothing, housewares, books, DVDs, jewelry, electronics — at 40 to 80 percent off, every day of the week. And shipping is just $2.95 on any size order. If you pay the $29.95 to join Club O, you get 5 percent savings on all your Overstock.com purchases and $1 shipping on all your orders.

✔ www.smartbargain.com: Similar to Overstock.com, Smart Bargain offers all categories and price ranges of brand-name over-runs and cancelled items at up to 70 percent off retail value. You want to check out the special section on disappearing deals — the bargain of bargains. Shipping is a flat $4.95.

✔ http://froogle.google.com: Froogle uses Google's search technology to locate Internet sales across the Web and point you directly to the place where you can make a purchase. Search for just about anything you can imagine — art, clothing, gift baskets, or office supplies, to name a very few. You can also search by price range.

✔ www.abebooks.com: Abebooks searches over 12,000 independent booksellers from around the globe to give you a huge selection of new, used, rare, or out-of-print books. You can search by price range, edition, or condition.

✔ www.bargainandhaggle.com: Different from an auction site, BargainAndHaggle.com lets people with stuff to sell connect one-on-one with people who want to buy. Once the seller posts an item with an asking price, you can make an offer and negotiate. Both sides can ask questions, accept the sale terms, make a counter offer, or walk away. The great part is that you won't be outbid in the last minute like in an auction. Although the selection isn't quite as large as eBay, it's nothing to sneeze at — plenty of great deals.

✔ www.bestwebbuys.com: If you're not quite sure that the sale you've found is as good as it gets, go to Best Web Buys. It searches for your item and then lists all the prices found on the Web so that you can buy from the cheapest store.

Up, Up, and Away

We buy lots of airline tickets online. Although the online travel sites aren't as good as the best human travel agents, the sites are now better than so-so agents and vastly better than bad travel agents. Even if you have a good agent, online sites let you look around to see what your options are before you get on the phone. Often airlines themselves offer cheap fares online that aren't available any other way. They know that it costs them much less to let the Web do the work, and they'll pay you (in the form of a hefty discount) to use the Web.

Here's our distilled wisdom about buying tickets online:

- ✔ Check the online systems to see what flights are available and for an idea of the price ranges. Check sites that use different GDS. (Some sites are listed at the end of this section.)

- ✔ After you've found a likely airline, check that airline's site to see whether it has any special Web-only deals. If a low-fare airline flies the route, be sure to check that one, too.

- ✔ Check prices on flights serving all nearby airports. An extra 45 minutes of driving time can save you hundreds of dollars.

- ✔ Check with a travel agent (by phone, e-mail, or the agent's own Web site) to see whether he can beat the online price, and buy your tickets from the agent unless the online deal is better.

- ✔ For international tickets, do everything in this list, and check both online and with your agent for consolidator tickets, particularly if you don't qualify for the lowest published fare. For complex international trips such as around-the-world, agents can invariably find routes and prices that the automated systems can't.

- ✔ If you bid on airline tickets at a travel auction Web site, make sure that you already know the price at which you can buy the ticket, so you don't bid more.

If you hate flying or would rather take the train, Amtrak and Via Rail Canada offer online reservations (www.amtrak.com and www.viarail.ca). If you're visiting Europe, you can buy your Eurailpass online at www.raileurope.com.

Four best places to get cheap airline tickets

Major airline ticket sites, other than individual airlines, include

- ✔ **Expedia:** Microsoft's entry into the travel biz, now a part of the USA Interactive media empire (www.expedia.com).

- ✔ **Hotwire:** Multi-airline site offering discounted leftover tickets (www.hotwire.com).

- ✔ **Orbitz:** Five big airlines' entry into the travel biz, with most airlines' weekly Web specials (www.orbitz.com).

- ✔ **Travelocity:** Sabre's entry into the travel biz (www.travelocity.com). Yahoo Travel and AOL's travel section are both Travelocity underneath.

course, and their years of teaching experience. Check prospective schools' accreditation by various agencies.

- Ask questions to make sure that you're getting the equivalent course quality and content in the distance learning version of the actual course.

If you're really concerned about committing to a whole program before you try a real (as opposed to a demo) class, go ahead and take a low-cost, non-credit course from the school before going to the trouble and expense of committing yourself to a full degree program.

✔ **Do they have their distance-learning act together?** Distance learning is something everybody's doing because it's hot, but not everybody is doing it well. Some are just testing the waters, others have committed to it wholeheartedly. Finding a school that really understands what makes good distance learning tick is very important.

As you consider various schools, take a look at the following tip-offs:

- Their course development process

- The infrastructure they've created to support students

- The breadth of courses they offer via distance learning

Online training: Everybody's doing it

Many online training providers are focused on topics other than technical skills like computer programming. The following list shows a sample of other providers to give you an idea of the range of training courses available online:

✔ Dow Jones University (www.dju.com) offers courses in financial planning and investing.

✔ CECity.com (www.cecity.com) hosts courses for the medical profession, including courses for pharmacists.

✔ University.com (www.university.com) provides courses on real estate, law,

accounting, financial services, and healthcare.

✔ The American Institute for Paralegal Studies (www.aips.com) offers fully accredited online classes for becoming a paralegal.

✔ Digital University (www.digitaledu.com) specializes in courses on graphic design and multimedia.

✔ Emind.com (emind.com) specializes in training in accounting, IT, and securities.

Five great books for researching a program

Before you embark on a distance learning program, you're going to have to get out there and collect information about specific schools. Several good sources of information are out there just waiting for you.

If you want the nuts-and-bolts information about a particular school, including contact information, programs offered, tuition, and accreditation, consider turning to one of these books, all of which provide directories of colleges offering distance learning:

- *The Unofficial Guide to Distance Learning* by Shannon Turlington, published by Arco.
- *The Best Distance Learning Graduate Schools* by Vicky Phillips and Cindy Yager, published by The Princeton Review.
- *Barron's Guide to Distance Learning* by Pat Criscito, published by Barron's Educational Series, Inc.
- *College Degrees by Mail & Internet* by John Bear, Ph.D. and Mariah Bear, M.A., published by Ten Speed Press.
- *Peterson's Guide to Distance Learning Programs 2000,* compiled and published by Peterson's.

Eight great sites for finding the program that's right for you

A great many distance-learning sites are out there, offering information about various kinds of providers, search engines to find the school that offers courses in your field, and links to other useful sites. Some include links to articles about recent activities in the distance-learning arena at various schools. These articles can help you spot the schools that really seem to be at the forefront of distance learning.

Some helpful sites to visit include the following:

- **Peterson's,** the publisher of directories and guides for college-bound students, maintains a Web site at www.petersons.com/dlearn. Here, you can search for the right college in Peterson's extensive online directory of school information.
- **CollegeQuest** (www.collegequest.com) is another site run by Peterson's that helps you search for schools by various criteria.

✔ **geteducated.com** (`www.geteducated.com`) offers a free e-mail newsletter on distance learning, as well as listings of distance-learning providers. All listings have links to school sites, so this is a great one-stop place to get information and to get to the school itself, without having to search for their sites individually.

✔ **The Adult Distance Education Internet Surf Shack** (`www.edsurf.net/edshack`) is an oddly named but worthwhile place to visit to get the low-down on virtual universities, as well as online training providers.

✔ **The Digital Education Network** (`www.edunet.com`) is one place to visit if you're looking for an education from a provider in another country. You can search by dozens of types of providers, such as training organizations, technical schools, language schools, art and media schools, and so on in many countries around the world.

✔ **NewsDirectory.com's** section on college newspapers may be of help in understanding the student population and environment of the school you're considering. Go to `newsdirectory.com/college/press` to explore school newspapers from around the United States.

✔ `R1edu.org` is a site that acts as a portal to 28 institutions of higher education, all with appropriate accreditation, and described as the best in the United States. All schools are rated as Research Universities by the Carnegie Foundation for the Advancement of Teaching, creator of this well-recognized classification system for institutions of higher learning.

✔ If you go online through a service provider such as AOL or MSN, look for an area devoted to education. This section often presents an organized way to get information on many kinds of schools from one handy location.

Don't forget to look online for professional organizations that focus on the discipline you're interested in studying. You can narrow your search for such groups by entering the keywords "distance learning" (in quotation marks) in combination with a word like *psychology* into your search engine of choice (such as Yahoo!, Lycos, or AltaVista). An example of the results you may get is the Social Psychology Network page on Distance Learning in Psychology (`www.socialpsychology.org`).

Zeroing in on a school site

When you find the site for a school you're interested in (either by using one of the directories mentioned in the previous section or by simply entering the school name in a search engine), look for an area dedicated to distance-learning programs. This is where you can expect to find an explanation of delivery methods and approach — some schools even provide a demo of their distance-learning offerings on their Web sites. But don't limit your research to this area; look around the entire college or university Web site for these important features:

- ✔ An online catalog of courses
- ✔ An academic calendar with important dates for class registration and testing
- ✔ Information about student support services
- ✔ Information on the school application process, including any previous education or tests (such as the GRE) required to enter a degree program
- ✔ Information on the school's accreditation
- ✔ Details on degree and certificate programs available

Online training providers also offer a wealth of information about themselves on their own Web sites, including

- ✔ Course listings, often with a detailed course syllabus
- ✔ Demo courses so that you can see what their training looks like
- ✔ Self-administered pre-assessment tests that help you determine the appropriate level of class with which to start
- ✔ Information on pricing and the school's refund policy
- ✔ Information on faculty qualifications, course development partners, and any authorized training center status they might enjoy

College catalogs are jam-packed with all you ever wanted to know about a school and what it has to offer. And printed catalogs have the advantage over online catalogs in that you can browse through them while waiting at the dentist's office or sitting in front of the TV. You can order school catalogs by mail, by phone, or by sending a request via e-mail through the school's Web site. You can also find sites like CollegeSource Online (www.collegesource.org) that are clearinghouses for ordering multiple catalogs online.

Tools of the Trade: You Need a Computer

Computers seem to get smaller, faster, and better every other day or so. Given this frenzied pace of change, how can you be sure that your computer will make the grade in online learning? Your first step is to check your school's Web site for specific recommendations for hardware and software required to take its online courses. For example, you should check requirements for the following:

✔ Operating system

✔ Processor speed

✔ Memory

✔ Modem

✔ Browser

✔ Video cards

✔ CD/DVD-ROM drive

✔ Sound card

Three Internet options

When it comes to phones and your distance-learning experience, the two real questions are how many lines you should have, and what technology they should use.

✔ **Standard phone connection:** With a standard one-line phone connection, if you're online, your family can't use the phone. Period. If you think that you'll spend enough time online to send your family into telephone withdrawal while taking a degree program that could last for a few years, a second phone line may be a good idea.

✔ **DSL or cable modem:** With a DSL (digital subscriber line) or a cable modem connection, your Internet connection won't tie up your phone line. With these technologies, your family can watch TV, surf the Net, and even make an old-fashioned phone call all at the same time. And both of these technologies provide much speedier access to the Internet than your standard phone line, making surfing and downloading faster.

These technologies aren't available everywhere, but the phone and cable companies are working on it. If you can obtain this kind of connection, expect to pay anywhere from $30 to $60 a month, plus the cost of installation.

✔ **ISDN:** ISDN (Integrated Services Digital Network) is another common Internet-connection buzzword; however, ISDN is no longer cutting edge; it's being replaced by its successor, DSL. Unlike DSL or cable, if you experience a power outage with ISDN, your phone line won't work at all.

Concerning plug-ins, players, and other online utilities

Software plug-ins exist for many functions, but the ones you're most likely to use in your distance learning are those that enable you to read files or play multimedia. Two common uses for plug-ins in the online classroom include:

- ✔ During the course of a typical class, your instructor may ask you to visit Web sites that have audio, video, or animation files you can only play by using a plug-in.

- ✔ In addition to plug-ins, you may need to acquire freestanding players for multimedia files and software products, such as NetMeeting, for holding meetings online.

Your school may have licenses to some of these plug-ins, which allow students to download them from the school site. Check your school's computer-services department or ask your instructor about this possibility.

Which software applications will you need?

You've got your hardware, and you've got your Internet connection and your browser. But what about plain old-fashioned productivity software like word processors and spreadsheet programs? Nobody's going to give these to you for free, they aren't cheap, and you're likely to need at least a few of them ready and waiting on your computer the day your class starts.

If you think you'll need more than one of these programs, consider a full-blown office suite. A suite of productivity applications such as Microsoft Office or Lotus SmartSuite can run you several hundred dollars, but typically includes the following:

- ✔ Full-featured word processor
- ✔ Spreadsheet
- ✔ Database
- ✔ Presentation
- ✔ Desktop-design software
- ✔ Web-page-design software

Family Ties: Making Your Learning Fit Your Life

When you sign up for a typical online distance-learning program, you're investing in yourself in ways that can open doors in your career, or just plain give you the whack on the side of the head you've been craving to make your life more interesting. Making changes of this magnitude affects not only you, but the other people in your life — especially the people living with you.

The following sections offer some words of advice for adjusting your environment (and your attitude) to make your distance learning experience a positive one for you and your whole family.

Budgeting your time

A typical distance-learning program can take about 14 hours a week. If you take four or five classes that run about six weeks each, over the course of a year, that's about 450 hours of your time. When's the last time you found a spare 450 hours lying around under the Christmas tree? Don't kid yourself: Taking even a single course can have a significant impact on you and the people in your life.

Try making a time budget before you begin your studies to determine exactly how many courses you can handle at any one time. Here's how a time budget for a typical day might look:

Activity	Time Allotted
Sleep	8 hours
Work	8 hours
Family	2 hours
Chores (shopping, laundry, cooking)	1 hour
Meals	1 hour
Entertainment (TV, a movie, playing with the dog)	1 hour
Commuting	1 hour
Study	2 hours
Total	24 hours

Getting support from those you love

To paraphrase John Donne: No student is an island. To be successful in your distance learning, you need help from your friends and family. Beyond their tolerance of the hours you'll be spending away from them, you'll need their cooperation to help you focus when you're studying. Try creating an agreement that you and your family can live with, like the following one, and post it near your study station.

- ✔ I need you to respect my privacy while I'm studying. I appreciate your keeping voices, the TV, and other noise to a minimum.

- ✔ If I'm in the middle of studying, please don't interrupt me unless it's an emergency. If it is something you consider important, I promise to stop working and respect you by giving you my undivided attention until the situation is resolved.

- ✔ Please don't move my papers and books around. I'll try to keep clutter to a minimum around my workspace if you promise not to reorganize my stuff.

- ✔ If you need to use the same computer I use for class, please don't delete files or install software without asking me first. I'll respect your work on the computer with the same courtesy.

- ✔ If I'm ignoring you or being rude to you because of my studies, be honest and tell me so.

Coping with change

Realize that by studying new things, you're trying to change your life to some degree. Changes may include moving into a new career path, becoming more highly paid, or becoming involved with a new set of people with similar interests. If *you* change and your spouse or friends *don't* change, you have to appreciate the impact that discrepancy could have.

Keep these things in mind when making the commitment to a significant learning endeavor:

- ✔ Make sure that your family understands why you're studying, and confirm that they support the changes you're seeking.

- ✔ Be supportive of changes they may want to make in their lives at the same time, so that you're not monopolizing all the positive-change energy in the family.

- ✔ Be aware that your studies might change you, and address those changes honestly and sensitively.

✔ Keep lines of communication with your friends and family open. You're putting aside quiet time to study each week; put aside time to talk with your loved ones, as well. Then if a problem's arising, you can be aware of it early on.

✔ Find ways to involve your family in your studies. If you're taking courses in astronomy, make family outings to the planetarium. If you're studying marketing, create a family Web site and use it to create a family brand identity.

✔ Make sure that your significant other isn't threatened by relationships you're building online. Stories about Internet romances are frequent, and who could blame someone whose spouse is exchanging e-mails with members of the opposite sex for hours each night for being sensitive or even suspicious.

Free sources for distance learning info

Online and distance learning courses vary greatly in price, with the least expensive being continuing education classes like pottery and the most expensive being accredited courses for a B.A. or M.A. Check out these sites for free info on the options available to you. And remember to ask whether the program has a senior discount — many do, even if it's not listed.

✔ www.worldwidelearn.com: This Web page is a link-o-rama. When you click on a link — say, to cooking classes online — make sure that you scroll down to see all your options. You'll also find a great list of links to schools with long-distance programs — including such big name schools as Boston University and the University of Florida. And, you'll find lots of information on fun, not-for-credit distance learning.

✔ www.ed.psu.edu/acsde: Penn State's American Center for the Study of Distance Education has been around since 1986. Much of this page is oriented for academics, but a valuable group of links to programs and other info useful to you as a distance learner is also available. Click on Resources, then Useful Links.

✔ www.usdla.org: This slick Web page of the U.S. Distance Learning Association has a lot of great info under the Resources button. Check out the handy glossary, bone up on accreditation issues, and link to distance learning programs around the country.

✔ www.elearners.com: eLearners.com helps you research online degrees, certificates, and courses from online colleges, universities, and schools. The course selection is quite large, although a small number of schools actually provide them all. The site also gives advice for new online learners and resources about online learning!

✔ Okay, so this isn't a Web site, but your local writing center may offer online writing workshops. You can find out if you're the next Hemingway — without leaving your house! Search on any major search engine to find out whether a writers' group in your area has a Web-based class. Hey, this is distance learning — you can sign up for an online writers' workshop offered by the Writers Union of New York . . . even if you live in Boise.

Part VIII
The Part of Tens

"Oh, that there's just something I picked up as a grab bag special from the 'Curiosities' Web page."

In this part . . .

The Part of Tens is about the ten best of everything —
ten awesome online freebies, ten fabulous bargains for
those over 50, and the ten best things about being retired.
This part of the book is always fun, so sit back and enjoy!

Chapter 25

Ten or So Awesome
Online Freebies

· ·

*G*et ready: You're about to face more freebie offers than you ever knew existed.

The following Web sites are clearinghouses for both permanent and temporary freebies — everything from sample prescription meds to free coffee gift cards and software.

www.FreebieTools.com

Freebie Tools primarily offers Web-related freebies like software, domain names, e-commerce tools, graphics, scripts, search engines, Web hosting, and meta tag generators.

www.WeeklyFreebie.com

Each week's compilation includes ten new freebies, varying from free bottle openers to free recipes! You can check the archives by category: beauty, catalogs, computers, internet, coupons, food and health, and kids. The site also has a hot Internet bargains section for deals and discounts that aren't *quite* free. A good feature of this site is the new user guide that gives sage advice to the freebie novice. You can also sign up to get the WeeklyFreebie newsletter delivered to you every week.

www.TheFreeSite.com

One of the better organized, easier to navigate freebie sites out there, TheFreeSite lists freebies in these and many other categories: office supplies, household items, kids' freebies, entertainment, Web dial-up services, encryption, e-mail, Web privacy, job search, and mobile phones. Sign up for TheFreeSite.com's e-mail newsletter and get a weekly roundup of the Web's latest and greatest free stuff.

www.NoJunkFree.com

This site claims to filter out the junk stuff and seems to do a good job of it. The opening page is very well-organized into three main sections so that you aren't overwhelmed: Product samples are rated according to quality; Internet freebies like free essay/paper-writing help, good freebies that you have to work for (take surveys, give opinions), and free games; and Web master freebies such as e-mail service, Web site forms, graphics, mailing lists, and message boards.

The site also has a good tutorial on ordering freebies and a list of freebies that the site owner ordered and actually received.

www.CoolFreebieLinks.com

This really is the motherlode of freebie sites with more that 1,500 free sweepstakes, contests, coupons, and promotional giveaway sites. All the freebies are reviewed and rated. You also want to check out the section on scams and come-ons — places pretending to give away things but charging outrageous fees for shipping and handling or selling your information to bulk Internet advertisers.

Although the opening page is a little overwhelming, it's better organized than some. And the freebies in the Top Rated category really are great freebies.

www.PlanetFreebie.com

Check out the top-rated freebies first. The largest categories are Internet related, graphics and fonts, Web master freebies, and free samples. It also has links to some other good sites.

www.FreebieForest.com

You're entering a forest of freebies, but among the trees, you can find some good free baby stuff, coupons, clip art, and games.

www.Internet-Bargains.com

Although this isn't a freebie site, the deals offered are too good to pass up. Most listings are top-quality online merchants. The site owner claims to have either personally shopped at these merchants or received positive feedback about each one. The owner also claims that the merchants listed have clear return policies and reasonable shipping fees.

Many Internet deals require coupon codes that expire, but you don't need to worry about keeping track of them because they're incorporated into the site.

www.DealofDay.com

You can often get the best price of all on products listed here because the deals expire. This site also provides the deal/sale code. You can check out the lists of recent sales, popular deals of the week, and hot products or picks by category.

www.imegadeals.com

For the best deals at this great bargain site, click on "10 Deals under $10." Other bargains are often from big-name stores like Kohl's or Penney's.

Index

FOR DUMMIES®

The easy way to get more done and have more fun

PERSONAL FINANCE & BUSINESS

Investing FOR DUMMIES
0-7645-2431-3

Home Buying FOR DUMMIES
0-7645-5331-3

Grant Writing FOR DUMMIES
0-7645-5307-0

Also available:

Accounting For Dummies
(0-7645-5314-3)

Business Plans Kit For Dummies
(0-7645-5365-8)

Managing For Dummies
(1-5688-4858-7)

Mutual Funds For Dummies
(0-7645-5329-1)

QuickBooks All-in-One Desk Reference For Dummies
(0-7645-1963-8)

Resumes For Dummies
(0-7645-5471-9)

Small Business Kit For Dummies
(0-7645-5093-4)

Starting an eBay Business For Dummies
(0-7645-1547-0)

Taxes For Dummies 2003
(0-7645-5475-1)

HOME, GARDEN, FOOD & WINE

Feng Shui FOR DUMMIES
0-7645-5295-3

Gardening FOR DUMMIES
0-7645-5130-2

Cooking FOR DUMMIES
0-7645-5250-3

Also available:

Bartending For Dummies
(0-7645-5051-9)

Christmas Cooking For Dummies
(0-7645-5407-7)

Cookies For Dummies
(0-7645-5390-9)

Diabetes Cookbook For Dummies
(0-7645-5230-9)

Grilling For Dummies
(0-7645-5076-4)

Home Maintenance For Dummies
(0-7645-5215-5)

Slow Cookers For Dummies
(0-7645-5240-6)

Wine For Dummies
(0-7645-5114-0)

FITNESS, SPORTS, HOBBIES & PETS

Fitness FOR DUMMIES
0-7645-5167-1

Golf FOR DUMMIES
0-7645-5146-9

Guitar FOR DUMMIES
0-7645-5106-X

Also available:

Cats For Dummies
(0-7645-5275-9)

Chess For Dummies
(0-7645-5003-9)

Dog Training For Dummies
(0-7645-5286-4)

Labrador Retrievers For Dummies
(0-7645-5281-3)

Martial Arts For Dummies
(0-7645-5358-5)

Piano For Dummies
(0-7645-5105-1)

Pilates For Dummies
(0-7645-5397-6)

Power Yoga For Dummies
(0-7645-5342-9)

Puppies For Dummies
(0-7645-5255-4)

Quilting For Dummies
(0-7645-5118-3)

Rock Guitar For Dummies
(0-7645-5356-9)

Weight Training For Dummies
(0-7645-5168-X)

Available wherever books are sold.
Go to www.dummies.com or call 1-877-762-2974 to order direct

WILEY

FOR DUMMIES®

A world of resources to help you grow

TRAVEL

0-7645-5453-0

0-7645-5438-7

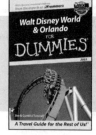

0-7645-5444-1

Also available:

America's National Parks For Dummies
(0-7645-6204-5)

Caribbean For Dummies
(0-7645-5445-X)

Cruise Vacations For Dummies 2003
(0-7645-5459-X)

Europe For Dummies
(0-7645-5456-5)

Ireland For Dummies
(0-7645-6199-5)

France For Dummies
(0-7645-6292-4)

Las Vegas For Dummies
(0-7645-5448-4)

London For Dummies
(0-7645-5416-6)

Mexico's Beach Resorts For Dummies
(0-7645-6262-2)

Paris For Dummies
(0-7645-5494-8)

RV Vacations For Dummies
(0-7645-5443-3)

EDUCATION & TEST PREPARATION

0-7645-5194-9

0-7645-5325-9

0-7645-5249-X

Also available:

The ACT For Dummies
(0-7645-5210-4)

Chemistry For Dummies
(0-7645-5430-1)

English Grammar For Dummies
(0-7645-5322-4)

French For Dummies
(0-7645-5193-0)

GMAT For Dummies
(0-7645-5251-1)

Inglés Para Dummies
(0-7645-5427-1)

Italian For Dummies
(0-7645-5196-5)

Research Papers For Dummies
(0-7645-5426-3)

SAT I For Dummies
(0-7645-5472-7)

U.S. History For Dummies
(0-7645-5249-X)

World History For Dummies
(0-7645-5242-2)

HEALTH, SELF-HELP & SPIRITUALITY

0-7645-5154-X

0-7645-5302-X

0-7645-5418-2

Also available:

The Bible For Dummies
(0-7645-5296-1)

Controlling Cholesterol For Dummies
(0-7645-5440-9)

Dating For Dummies
(0-7645-5072-1)

Dieting For Dummies
(0-7645-5126-4)

High Blood Pressure For Dummies
(0-7645-5424-7)

Judaism For Dummies
(0-7645-5299-6)

Menopause For Dummies
(0-7645-5458-1)

Nutrition For Dummies
(0-7645-5180-9)

Potty Training For Dummies
(0-7645-5417-4)

Pregnancy For Dummies
(0-7645-5074-8)

Rekindling Romance For Dummies
(0-7645-5303-8)

Religion For Dummies
(0-7645-5264-3)

Available wherever books are sold. Go to www.dummies.com or call 1-877-762-2974 to order direct

FOR DUMMIES®

Plain-English solutions for everyday challenges

HOME & BUSINESS COMPUTER BASICS

PCs For Dummies
0-7645-0838-5

The Flat-Screen iMac For Dummies
0-7645-1663-9

Windows XP All-in-One Desk Reference For Dummies
0-7645-1548-9

Also available:

Excel 2002 All-in-One Desk Reference For Dummies
(0-7645-1794-5)

Office XP 9-in-1 Desk Reference For Dummies
(0-7645-0819-9)

PCs All-in-One Desk Reference For Dummies
(0-7645-0791-5)

Troubleshooting Your PC For Dummies
(0-7645-1669-8)

Upgrading & Fixing PCs For Dummies
(0-7645-1665-5)

Windows XP For Dummies
(0-7645-0893-8)

Windows XP For Dummies Quick Reference
(0-7645-0897-0)

Word 2002 For Dummies
(0-7645-0839-3)

INTERNET & DIGITAL MEDIA

The Internet For Dummies
0-7645-0894-6

eBay For Dummies
0-7645-1642-6

Digital Photography For Dummies
0-7645-1664-7

Also available:

CD and DVD Recording For Dummies
(0-7645-1627-2)

Digital Photography All-in-One Desk Reference For Dummies
(0-7645-1800-3)

eBay For Dummies
(0-7645-1642-6)

Genealogy Online For Dummies
(0-7645-0807-5)

Internet All-in-One Desk Reference For Dummies
(0-7645-1659-0)

Internet For Dummies Quick Reference
(0-7645-1645-0)

Internet Privacy For Dummies
(0-7645-0846-6)

Paint Shop Pro For Dummies
(0-7645-2440-2)

Photo Retouching & Restoration For Dummies
(0-7645-1662-0)

Photoshop Elements For Dummies
(0-7645-1675-2)

Scanners For Dummies
(0-7645-0783-4)

Get smart! Visit www.dummies.com

- **Find listings of even more Dummies titles**
- **Browse online articles, excerpts, and how-to's**
- **Sign up for daily or weekly e-mail tips**
- **Check out Dummies fitness videos and other products**
- **Order from our online bookstore**

Available wherever books are sold. Go to www.dummies.com or call 1-877-762-2974 to order direct

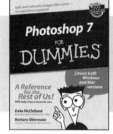